Reclaiming the Sociological Classics

Reclaiming the Sociological Classics:
The State of the Scholarship

Edited by Charles Camic

BLACKWELL
Publishers

Copyright © Blackwell Publishers Ltd 1997

First published 1997

Reprinted 1998

Blackwell Publishers Inc
350 Main Street
Malden, Massachusetts 02148, USA

Blackwell Publishers Ltd
108 Cowley Road
Oxford OX4 1JF, UK

Library of Congress Cataloging in Publication Data
Reclaiming the sociological classics: the state of the scholarship/edited by Charles Camic.
p. cm.
Includes bibliographical references and index.
ISBN 1–57718–030–5 — ISBN 1–57718–031–3 (pbk)
1. Sociology. 2. Sociologists. I. Camic, Charles.
HM51.R376   1998   97–20349
301—dc21   CIP

British Library Cataloguing in Publication Data
A CIP catalogue record for this book is available from the British Library

Typeset in 10.5 on 12pt Goudy
by GCS, Leighton Buzzard, Bedfordshire
Printed and bound in Great Britain
by MPG Books Ltd, Bodmin, Cornwall

This book is printed on acid-free paper

Contents

Contributors

Martin Bulmer is Foundation Fund Professor of Sociology at the University of Surrey and Academic Director of the Question Bank in the ESRC Centre for Applied Social Surveys in London. A historian of the social sciences, he is the author of *The Chicago School of Sociology* (1984) and other works on the history of empirical sociology. Among his most recent works is *Citizenship Today* (edited with A. Rees, 1996), a volume on T. H. Marshall.

Charles Camic is Professor of Sociology at the University of Wisconsin-Madison. He has written widely on the history of sociology, with special reference to developments in the United States between 1890 and 1940. Past Chair (1994–5) of the Theory Section of the American Sociological Association and editor of *Talcott Parsons: the early essays* (1991), he is completing a book on the formative years in Talcott Parsons's intellectual career.

Valerie A. Haines is Associate Professor of Sociology at the University of Calgary. Her research in the history of sociology has focused on Herbert Spencer. She has also conducted research that examines the production, reproduction, and transformation of social support networks using structuration theory and various strands of network analysis. Presently she is writing a book on the changing meaning of "evolution" in social theory.

Hans Joas is Professor of Sociology at the Free University of Berlin (John F. Kennedy Institute for North American Studies). His books include *George Herbert Mead: a contemporary reexamination of his thought* (1985), *Social Action and Human Nature* (with Axel Honneth, 1988), *Pragmatism and Social Theory* (1993), *The Creativity of Action* (1996), and *Die Entstehung der Werte* (*The Genesis of Values*, 1997).

Robert Alun Jones is Professor of Religious Studies, History, and Sociology at the University of Illinois in Urbana-Champaign. He is the author of *Emile Durkheim: an introduction to four major works* (1986) as well as numerous journal articles on Durkheim. Former editor of both *Knowledge and Society* and *Etudes durkheimiennes*, he is also responsible for the Durkheim site on the Internet (http://www.lang.uiue.edu/RelSt/Durkheim/DurkheimHome.html). Currently he is writing a book on Durkheim's social realism.

Stephen Kalberg teaches courses on sociological theory, comparative-historical sociology, and political sociology at Boston University, where he is Associate Professor of Sociology. He is the author of numerous works on Max Weber, including *Max Weber's Comparative-Historical Sociology* (1994). He has also published widely on German and American political and economic cultures.

Donald N. Levine is the Peter B. Ritzma Professor of Sociology and former Dean of the College at the University of Chicago. His publications include *Wax and Gold: tradition and innovation in Ethiopian culture* (1965), *Georg Simmel on Individuality and Social Forms* (1971), *Greater Ethiopia: the evolution of a multiethnic society* (1974), *The Flight from Ambiguity: essays in social and cultural theory* (1985), and *Visions of the Sociological Tradition* (1995). Since 1988 he has served as editor of The Heritage of Sociology series published by the University of Chicago Press. During 1996–7 he served as chair of the Theory Section of the American Sociological Association.

Lynn McDonald, a Professor of Sociology at the University of Guelph, Ontario, is currently preparing a collected works of Florence Nightingale. She is the author of *The Early Origins of the Social Sciences* (1993) and *Women Founders of the Social Sciences* (1994) and numerous papers and books in political sociology, criminology,

status of women, and environmental sociology. McDonald has also
pursued a political career. She was a Member of Parliament 1982–8
and is a former president of the National Action Committee on the
Status of Women, Canada's largest women's organization.

Mary Pickering is Associate Professor of History at San Jose State
University, where she teaches courses in French history, German
history, European women's history, and urban history. The first
volume of her work, *Auguste Comte: an intellectual biography*,
appeared in 1993. Currently, she is working on the second volume,
for which she received a Fellowship from the National Endowment of
the Humanities.

Moishe Postone is Associate Professor in the Department of History,
the Committee of Jewish Studies, and the College at the University of
Chicago. He has written *Time, Labor, and Social Domination: a
reinterpretation of Marx's critical theory* (1993), as well as numerous
articles on critical theory, anti-Semitism and National Socialism, and
postwar Germany.

Alan Sica is Professor of Sociology and Director of the Social
Thought Program at Pennsylvania State University. He was editor of
the American Sociological Association's journal, *Sociological
Theory*, publisher/editor of *History of Sociology*, and is the author of
Weber, Irrationality, and Social Order (1988). He has also edited and
introduced *Ideologies and the Corruption of Thought*, the selected
essays of Joseph Gabel (1997).

Introduction: Classical Sociological Theory as a Field of Research

Charles Camic

The studies making up this volume examine a number of classical sociological theorists in relation to various traditions of interpretation and research that have grown up around them. Taking different tacks, the studies are united in their interest to advance the collective intellectual project of understanding the "classics" of sociological analysis.

In pursuing this interest, the essays occupy the fertile but little-understood intellectual space that lies between two other fields, the history of sociology on the one side, and sociological theory on the other. The studies speak to both of these fields, while falling exclusively into neither. They do so because they adopt what Alan Sica (chapter 10) describes as a "heterodox approach to our knowledge of the past" – an approach that combines aspects of two orientations to the sociological classics that have ordinarily been counterposed: "presentism," which considers classical writings in light of their contribution and place in debates underway at the present time; and "historicism," which seeks to reconstruct past ideas in the terms in which they were originally written, generally by examining one or more of the contexts of their production (see below, and the discussions of presentism and historicism by Haines and Jones in chapters 3 and 5).

The contributors to this volume mix these orientations in different proportions, with the professional historians among them (Pickering, Jones) proceeding, as one would expect, in a more historicist manner than some of the sociologists. These revealing differences notwithstanding, however, in all the studies one sees the use of careful research on the history of sociology to address issues of contemporary theoretical consequence: the embrace, one might say, of historicist means to accomplish objectives whose points of departure and return lie in the present.

Visible throughout the essays, for instance, is what George Stocking has elsewhere referred to as "the role of present interest in the definition of a field for historical inquiry" (1992, p. 9). The effect of this interest factor is apparent in the very object of investigation that brings these essays together. For, by taking the theorists who wrote the sociological "classics" as their starting point, these studies are essentially endorsing present-day views of which past authors and texts now merit attention, thus accepting a conception of the sociological canon that itself emerged only in the course of the last half century or so (through processes that are still little understood: see Camic, 1992). This is true even in McDonald's study (chapter 4) which explicitly seeks to enlarge the canon, yet takes the present list of classical authors both as the comparison point for new additions to the canon and as the basic standard for what warrants inclusion among the classics. In this way, the following studies differ from scholarship on the history of sociology that is less tethered to the present period and to the current canon of theorists and, instead, more focused on thinkers, writings, and processes that were significant in their own time and place for the development of sociology as a cluster of ideas and practices – regardless of the status of these thinkers and writings in our own time (see, e.g., Bannister, 1987; Hinkle, 1994; Platt, 1996; *Sociological Theory* 1994–5, special issues on "Neglected theorists").

But not only do the studies in this collection take their object of investigation from the present, for the most part they are also strongly linked to the present by what Stocking calls a "commitment to defending or changing the [area] whose history [the studies] recount" (1992, p. 5) – in this case, the field of sociological theory itself. As their individual chapters will indicate, implicitly or explicitly the contributors to this volume stand in various forms of engagement – sometimes critical, sometimes constructive – with contemporary work in sociological theory. This applies even to the most historicist of these studies, which, as Jones has written elsewhere, still seeks to realize the "goal of a genuine dialogue between the history of theory and theory itself" (Jones and Kibbee, 1993, p. 153). Below I will propose a somewhat similar rationale for research into the history of classical theory, and it is a position to which not all of the contributors would necessarily subscribe.

Differences on this level to the contrary, however, there is a marked contrast between the essays that follow, with their critical and constructive stances toward contemporary theory, and studies of the history of sociology that are not anchored to the present by the "commitment" to which Stocking refers.

Yet, if the essays herein have current stakes in the theory area and the theory canon, in their *modes of analysis* they diverge significantly from the methods of study found in the presentist treatments of the classics which have been a staple of the scholarly literature for over fifty years. Presentist methods are extractive; typically, they involve lifting a given classic work from the immediacy of its time and place, and perhaps from the oeuvre of the thinker who wrote it, and interpreting its objectives, concepts, and arguments – anachronistically – as successful or failed contributions to particular intellectual debates underway at the point in the present where the textual interpretation itself is located. Historicist modes of analysis, in contrast, seek to embed: to interpret a classical text by situating it in relation to its author's work as a whole and the biographical, intellectual, and social contexts in which the text was produced. This is an open-ended project, aiming to reach not some complete and final statement about a classical theorist's ideas and circumstances, but to reclaim, through various contextualizing procedures, selected aspects of the theorist's work, many of them covered over, mis-remembered, or simply forgotten during the subsequent history of sociology and the other social sciences.

As shown by the following studies, not only can research along these lines be flexibly combined with other methods of analysis, but contextualizing procedures are themselves highly diverse. For Pickering (chapter 1), situating Comte in context involves examining his oeuvre, his biography, his immediate intellectual forerunners, and the political crisis of early nineteenth-century Europe. Levine's treatment of Simmel (chapter 6) likewise ranges broadly from formative intellectual experiences and biographical considerations to aspects of Simmel's oeuvre and of his later intellectual influence, while Joas's analysis of Mead (chapter 9) adopts a similarly expansive approach. Other contributors, however, choose more concentrated points of focus, with Haines (chapter 3) and Jones (chapter 5) investigating certain central arguments that Spencer and Durkheim put forth as their writings took shape amid specific intellectual (and also, for Durkheim, political) debates that were prominent in their own place and time; McDonald (chapter 4) and Bulmer (chapter 8) dealing with clusters of thinkers (the women founders; Park and Thomas) whose distinctive views about social science become evident when they are set against the views of their contemporaries and those who followed; Postone (chapter 2) and Kalberg (chapter 7) examining some of the foundational ideas of Marx and Weber that come to light when the effort is made to understand the work of these thinkers in the entirety of its development. The relative merits of these different modes of historical study might be fruitfully debated.

Differences of this sort notwithstanding, however, these studies all strongly attest to the value of approaching classical sociological theory *as a field of research*. This, after all, is exactly what the contributors are doing as they labor to come to terms with a given thinker's complete body of work, to uncover his or her fugitive manuscripts and letters, to clarify biographical circumstances, to determine the impact on the thinker of the ideas and attitudes of various predecessors and contemporaries, and to identify the relevant features of the political (or other social) contexts in which the thinker was located. Along the way, the contributors also systematically engage the existing secondary literature on the classical theorists, using the findings and interpretations of previous scholars, in some cases, as a basis upon which to build, in other cases (and more typically), as a counterpoint for the working out of a revisionist perspective. Since the secondary literature on each of the several theorists is presently in a somewhat different state of collective development, the uses to which this literature is put naturally vary from chapter to chapter, though all of the authors are careful to take account of the strengths and weaknesses of the available scholarly resources.

Why do these points deserve emphasis? Are these not practices to be expected in a scholarly field of this kind? One might reasonably suppose so, but in truth classical sociological theory has not generally been seen as a field of research. Indeed, outside the ranks of scholars such as those represented in this collection, widespread resistance to this conception of the field is still much in evidence – commonly in the form of two assumptions, sometimes stated openly, sometimes not. The first of these is the belief that the work of the classical theorists is *not* an appropriate subject of contemporary study; the second, the supposition that, to the extent that this work becomes the subject of investigation, analysis of it need *not* engage the existing secondary literature. It is useful briefly to consider these notions one by one.

The idea that classical works are inappropriate objects of investigation is itself a centuries-old point of view. As Merton (1967, pp. 31–2) has shown, Galileo's remark that "a man will never become

a philosopher by worrying forever about the writings of other men"
is an observation that has recurred in the reflections of scientists ever
since, with little deepening of the original insight. Among sociologists
today, the same thought returns: why dwell on Spencer, Weber, or
Mead when the task before us is to analyze contemporary migration
patterns, trends in labor force participation, health-care delivery
systems, dual-career households, transnational corporations, and so
on? But surely this question is too facile; it assumes that because there
are sound and compelling reasons to investigate these matters, such
topics alone merit study – by which standard, of course, research on
the classics is *ipso facto* misguided, useless for addressing
contemporary empirical issues. Reasoning of this sort is business-as-
usual in academic specialty areas, which often maintain their
identities and boundaries by denigrating the contributions of
specialty areas unlike their own. Work on classical theory is by no
means the only target of this attitude, which is of particular relevance
here only because it has recently become more and more common
within the theory area itself. This has occurred as the theory area has
progressively undergone a process of "identification with the
aggressor," seeking to elevate its professional standing by taking over
the very criticisms that outsiders have hurled upon it (for
elaboration, see Camic, 1993).

One thus finds prominent voices in the theory area increasingly
disdainful of "studies of deceased social theorists" unless the primary
goal of these studies is to demonstrate "how the revered ancestor's
work would advance contemporary analytic projects" (Calhoun,
1996, p. 1), the general assumption being that the "discipline's long
dead forebears [provide sociologists of today] little of use . . . to help
them understand whatever it is they are examining" (Chafetz, 1993, p.
61). It is this outlook that fuels much of the resistance to regarding
classical theory as a field of research. To the extent that it does not
simply dry up scholarly interest in the sociological classics, this
viewpoint demands the most thorough- going presentism, expecting
studies of the classics not only to have their general points of
departure and return in the present, but also to use presentist
methods of analysis: to lift classic works out of their own contexts
and "to 'mine' them for usable bits of lore which happen to suit
contemporary projects" (to quote Sica's formulation, p. 296 in this
volume). Such an expectation is fundamentally at variance with
efforts to make the classics the subject of the type of historical
research described above and exhibited in this volume.

It is telling, however, that advocates of this "anti-classics" position
have nearly always overlooked arguments on the other side. Indeed,

in again and again announcing their objection to the study of "dead theorists," they have scarcely noticed that a diversity of serious answers to this objection has been furnished over the years by commentators ranging from Shils (1961), Merton (1967), and Coser (1971), to Jones (1977), Alexander (1989), Lemert (1993), Levine (1995), and Joas (1996), among others. My own view, as I have indicated elsewhere, is that research on classical sociological theory offers indispensable benefits to the present at the very point where presentists fail to look: that the principal contribution to the present of reclaiming the classics lies not in turning up "usable bits of lore" that may fit with our particular projects of the moment, but in providing a larger critical distance which frees us from the immediate present, exposes us to voices that do more than duplicate our own, and enlarges the horizon of theoretical alternatives beyond the finite bounds of current possibilities.

Not only this, but by contextualizing classical theories, research in the field also brings to light some of the historical contingencies that led particular theories to be established at the expense of others; and recognition of these contingencies problematizes various "choices" that came to be institutionalized as sociology developed, thus calling into question what the discipline excluded as well as what it included (see Camic, 1986, 1989, 1992). Foucault once put the matter as follows: the value of the study of past ideas lies in demonstrating "how that-which-is has not always been: i.e., that the things which seem most evident to us are always formed . . . during a precarious and fragile history . . .; and that since these things have been made, they can be unmade, as long as we know how it was that they were made" (1988, p. 39; see also the argument of the "rhetoric of inquiry" movement, in Nelson et al., 1987). This, as the following chapters will indicate, is by no means the only reason for carrying out historical research on the sociological classics. Nor do all the reasons combined mean that it is now incumbent upon every sociological theorist to undertake this type of research. Quite obviously, there are many ways of advancing the theory area – and no warrant for privileging the study of the classics over other profitable approaches. By the same token, however, the time has long since arrived for proponents of these other approaches to cease their railings against "deceased social theorists" and to consider what solid historical research on the subject can actually offer.

But railings of this sort have not been the only impediment to efforts to make classical sociological theory a field of research. A second consequential force has been the massive disregard, even by those sociologists who remain interested in classical sociological theory, of the findings and interpretations contained in the existing scholarly literature on the classical thinkers and their works. The result has been an academic area largely bereft of cumulative development: an area where one sees, in paper after paper, article after article, book after book, a repetition of the same misleading stereotypes and distorting cliches about the classical theorists that serious scholarship on the subject dissolved long ago, though to very little avail. Outside small pockets of researchers, Comte's views on positivism, Spencer's on evolution, Durkheim's on social facts, Simmel's on exchange – all these and more continue to be retailed in much the way they were a quarter century ago, as if the historical scholarship from the intervening years had simply not happened, let alone furnished major revisionist assessments.

In this respect, the study of the classics currently compares unfavorably with research in other areas of sociology. In any area, it is true, a researcher may fail to take proper account of a relevant previous contribution to the literature of his or her field. One of the functions of pre-publication peer review in scientific communities is to detect omissions of this sort and to direct researchers to findings and interpretations they may have overlooked. No doubt the review process to which studies in the theory area are subject serves something of the same purpose, though the situation in this case still diverges significantly from what is typical in other academic fields. Where research on the classics is concerned, it is not only certain recent or out-of the-way publications, but even well-respected major works that frequently remain unknown to considerable numbers of sociologists writing and teaching in the area. It appears, moreover, that even when those in the area *are* cognizant of relevant scholarship on the classics, they often are reluctant to engage this research when it proves convenient to do otherwise. Under these conditions, there naturally occurs a proliferation of studies that either simply replay discredited stereotypes, belabor interpretations already available, or easily dodge existing findings that run counter to their own arguments.

Why this situation prevails is a complex issue, which cannot be fully addressed at the present juncture. To some extent, neglect of the relevant secondary literature derives from a kind of hubris sometimes evident among those drawn to the classics, particularly in the face of widespread opposition to the study of dead forebears. This is the feeling that any classical scholar worthy of the name – and willing to stand up defiantly against the anti-classics position – is one able and entitled to carry on his or her own direct encounter with the classical theorists, unencumbered by the intrusive presence of the

available secondary sources. The best that can be said for this
attitude is that it is probably preferable to the opposite belief which
occasionally surfaces among sociologists outside the theory area: viz.,
the notion that an understanding of the classical thinkers can be
attained by consulting a few secondary synopses and bypassing the
classics altogether. Nevertheless, it is simply presumptuous to
imagine that any scholar will be especially successful at coming to
terms with works that are as sprawling, complex, and removed in
time and place as the classics of sociology if he or she ignores
previous scholarly contributions in the area. If any proof be needed
for so basic a principle of academic life, it will suffice to refer back to
the papers, articles, and books that, because they violate this
principle, vacillate between rehashing old cliches and reinventing the
wheel.

But in addition to an attitude of hubris, there is a more concrete
obstacle to cumulative research on the sociological classics. This is
the intellectual and social organization of the theory area itself. Some
years ago, Whitley (1984) initiated a line of investigation focusing on
the relation between the organizational conditions in academic fields
and their resulting intellectual patterns, including the degree to which
members of a particular field know of and make use of one another's
ideas, methods, and data (see also Collins, 1975). The upshot of this
research has been the finding that in "loosely coupled and
decentralized [fields, which] have minimal hardware and social
solidarity . . . there is little pressure or potential for [the] integration
and coordination" of the existing scholarly literature (Fuchs and
Ward, 1994, pp. 481, 495). A moment's reflection will indicate,
however, that this is precisely the present structure of the theory area,
which – even by the standard of other subfields in sociology – is
highly dispersed across countries, languages, audiences, publication
outlets, professional meetings and associations, institutions for
graduate training, and more. Conspicuously absent under these
circumstances is, in Bazerman's terms, a "collective literature" that
serves to codify the "framework of claims representing the [field's]
shared knowledge" (1988, pp. 77–9). And the inevitable consequence
of this organizational situation is the frequent disregard of important
prior research contributions that vitiates many current studies in the
classical theory area.

The essays in this collection originated from a concern to direct
attention to this situation and begin the task of addressing it.
Approaching classical sociological theory as a field of research that
has also been the site of previous scholarly work, the majority of the
chapters provide a systematic overview of the current state of the

scholarship on the theorists under examination. These chapters identify the major contributions to the existing literature, the lines of past interpretation that have proven to be untenable, the recent findings that have been uncovered, and the new perspectives that are currently taking shape. In so doing, they inaugurate the kind of systematic intellectual stocktaking that is essential if a collective literature about the sociological classics is to emerge – and in due course to call forth the additional changes in organization and attitude needed for cumulative work in the area. Of course, as indicated above, the existing literatures on the different classical thinkers are by no means at the same stage of development; presently, some of these literatures are broader and deeper than others in what they cover, thus providing firmer foundations for revisionist work. As all the chapters make clear, however, reclaiming sociology's intellectual heritage is an important challenge that remains very much underway, with a vast field for historical research still ahead. This volume is an invitation to this collective project of understanding the sociological classics.

REFERENCES

Alexander, Jeffrey C. 1989: Sociology and discourse: on the centrality of the classics. In Jeffrey C. Alexander, *Structure and Meaning*, New York: Columbia University Press, 8–67.

Bannister, Robert C. 1987: *Sociology and Scientism.* Chapel Hill, NC: University of North Carolina Press.

Bazerman, Charles 1988: *Shaping Written Knowledge.* Madison, Wis.: University of Wisconsin Press.

Calhoun, Craig 1996: Editor's Comment. *Sociological Theory,* 14, 1–2.

Camic, Charles 1986: The matter of habit. *American Journal of Sociology,* 91, 1,039–87.

—— 1989: *Structure* after 50 years. *American Journal of Sociology,* 95, 38–107.

—— 1992: Reputation and predecessor-selection. *American Sociological Review,* 57, 421–45.

—— 1993: Talmudic exegesis or identification with the aggressor? *The American Sociologist,* 24, 63–5.

Chafetz, Janet Saltzman 1993: Sociological theory: a case of multiple personality disorder. *The American Sociologist,* 24, 60 2.

Collins, Randall 1975: *Conflict Sociology.* New York: Academic Press.

Coser, Lewis A. [1971], 1977: *Masters of Sociological Thought,* 2nd edn. New York: Harcourt Brace Jovanovich.

Foucault, Michel 1988: *Politics, Philosophy, Culture.* New York: Routledge.

Fuchs, Stephan, and Ward, Steven 1994: What is deconstruction, and where and when does it take place? *American Sociological Review,* 59, 481–500.

Hinkle, Roscoe C. 1994: *Developments in American Sociological Theory, 1915–1950.* Albany, NY: State University of New York Press.

Joas, Hans 1996: *The Creativity of Action.* Cambridge: Polity Press.

Jones, Robert Alun 1977: On understanding a sociological classic. *American Journal of Sociology,* 83, 279–321.

Jones, Robert Alun and Kibbee, Douglas A. 1993: Durkheim, language, and history. *Sociological Theory,* 11, 152–70.

Lemert, Charles (ed.) 1993: *Social Theory: the multicultural and classical readings.* Boulder, Co.: Westview Press.

Levine, Donald N. 1995: *Visions of the Sociological Tradition.* Chicago: University of Chicago Press.

Merton, Robert K. 1967: On the history and systematics of sociological theory. In Robert K. Merton, *On Theoretical Sociology,* New York: Free Press, 1–37.

Nelson, John S., Megill, Allen and McClosky, Donald N. (eds) 1987: *The Rhetoric of the Human Sciences.* Madison, Wis.: University of Wisconsin Press.

Platt, Jennifer 1996: *A History of Sociological Research Methods in America, 1920–1960.* Cambridge: Cambridge University Press.

Shils, Edward 1961: The calling of sociology. In Talcott Parsons, Edward Shils, Kaspar D. Naegele, and Jesse R. Pitts (eds), *Theories of Society.* New York: Free Press, 1,405–48.

Sociological Theory 1994–5: Special issues on "Neglected theorists." 12 (3) and 13 (1).

Stocking, George W., Jr 1992: *The Ethnographer's Magic and Other Essays in the History of Anthropology.* Madison, Wis.: University of Wisconsin Press.

Whitley, Richard 1984: *The Intellectual and Social Organization of the Sciences.* Oxford: Clarendon.

1

A New Look at Auguste Comte

Mary Pickering

Meanwhile, have you read a book termed Cours de Philosophie
Positive *by Auguste Comte . . .? This said book is, I think, one of the
most profound books ever written on the philosophy of the sciences;
and that of the higher branches it appears to me to have created . . . I
shall be much astonished if this book of Comte's does not strike you
more than any logical speculations of our time.*
John Stuart Mill to John Nichol, December 21, 1837

INTRODUCTION

Although Auguste Comte is often called the founder of sociology
and positivism, few scholars have studied in depth his life, work, or
impact. Called a "demented fool" in a leading textbook, Comte
seems to be an embarrassment to the sociology profession (Turner,
Beeghley, and Powers, 1995, p. 16). In their respective surveys of the
development of sociology, Don Martindale and Richard Münch
cover Comte in a mere two or three pages (Martindale, 1981, pp. 77–
80; Münch, 1994, pp. 122–4). Such neglect has been typical.
Historians of philosophy and of nineteenth-century France also
gloss over him in their works (Rorty, 1984, p. 65; Pilbeam, 1995,
p. 100). Indeed, positivist history and positivist philosophy have
been as unfashionable as positivist sociology.

Yet partly inspired by the bicentennial of Comte's birth, which
demands a rethinking of his work, Comtean studies are experiencing

a long-overdue revival. During the past few years, many important
books have appeared. Juliette Grange and Jacques Muglioni have
written new introductions to his philosophy, while André Sernin
has produced a popular biography (Grange, 1996; Muglioni, 1995;
Sernin, 1993). Oscar Haac has annotated and translated Comte's
important correspondence with John Stuart Mill (Haac, 1995). Gillis
Harp has analyzed Comte's influence on American liberalism (Harp,
1995). Robert Scharff has demonstrated Comte's relevance to
contemporary post-positivist debates (Scharff, 1995). Whereas
many of these books are by philosophers, my intellectual biography
is written from a historian's point of view (Pickering, 1989, 1993a,
1993b). Firmly placing his development in the context of post-
revolutionary France, it challenges traditional assumptions about
Comte's life and his work. This chapter will examine five areas of
controversy in order to reveal the rich nuances of his thought.

The first problem in Comtean studies has to do with determining
Comte's intellectual debt to the radical social reformer Claude-Henri
de Saint-Simon, with whom he worked closely for seven years, from
1817 to 1824. The source of this dilemma is Comte himself. In 1818,
Comte wrote that he found Saint-Simon to be "an original being in
all respects," one who had taught him "a mass of things" that he
"would have vainly searched for in books" (Comte [1814–57], 1973–
90, vol. 1, p. 28). But in 1853, he insisted, "I owed nothing to this
personage, not even the slightest instruction" (Comte [1851–4],
1929, vol. 3, p. xvi). In his three-volume survey of Comte's youth,
Henri Gouhier took him at his word and minimized Saint-Simon's
influence on his development. In this fashion, Gouhier ensured that
Comte was not contaminated by the socialist tradition, to which
Saint-Simon belonged (Gouhier, 1933–41). Ted Benton basically
repeated Gouhier's view when he wrote that "in all essentials the
thought of Comte is determined, whether mediately or immediately,
by the same influences as that of St. Simon" (1994, p. 61). Both
Comte and Saint-Simon seized ideas from the surrounding
intellectual environment and went their separate ways. Countering
the view that Comte and Saint-Simon had no impact on each other,
other scholars have gone to the opposite extreme. Comte's disciple
Pierre Laffitte maintained that Comte owed "absolutely nothing" to
Saint-Simon and suggests that it was the former who influenced the
latter (Laffitte, 1895, p. 7). Emile Durkheim overemphasized Saint-
Simon's impact, thus leaving Comte without any creative
contribution whatsoever (Durkheim, 1925, pp. 338–41).

The second problem in Comtean scholarship is the common
assumption that positivism is equivalent to scientism, that is, a naive

faith in science's ability to solve all problems through the use of empirical, experimental, and quantitative methods of research. Jürgen Habermas maintains that "positivism stands and falls with the principle of scientism" (Habermas, 1971, p. 67). A leading dictionary defines positivism as "a philosophical doctrine contending that sense perceptions are the only admissible basis of human knowledge and precise thought" (Morris, 1981, p. 1,023). This equation of positivism with empiricism appears frequently in the works of such scholars as Alan Swingewood, Irving Zeitlin, and Craig Dilworth (Swingewood, 1991, p. 51; Zeitlin, 1990, pp. 82–3; Dilworth, 1990, p. 435). Irving Louis Horowitz provides an example of how this interpretation has infiltrated sociology: "By positivism is meant the development of a total portrait of man derived from the combination of discrete questionnaires, surveys, and other atomic facts" (Horowitz, 1968, p. 200). According to the Comtean critic Gertrud Lenzer, the positivist approach leads inevitably to a kind of reductionism: "The triumph of the positive spirit consists in the reduction of quality to quantity in all realms of existence – in the realm of society and man as well as in the realm of nature" (Lenzer, 1975, p. xxi). Another major difficulty with Comte's empirical approach, in the eyes of Anthony Giddens and other scholars, is that its stress on observation compels it to reject the validity of introspection and thus psychology (Giddens, 1995, p. 150; Collins and Makowsky, 1989, p. 27; Ashley and Orenstein, 1995, p. 76). In sum, positivism is considered a materialistic and antisubjective doctrine, one that deliberately eschews the problem of values, prefers raw data to theories, and offers no advice about "large-scale considerations" of the social system (Horowitz, 1993, p. 141). It is morally inadequate, if not dangerous (Brown and Lyman, 1978, p. 13).

The third problem concerns Comte's alleged desire to control society in a "totalitarian" manner (Zeitlin, 1990, p. 82). According to Zeitlin, Swingewood, Jonathan Turner, Leonard Beeghley, Charles Powers, and most commentators, Comte wanted an elite of scientists to run the positive regime (Zeitlin, 1990, p. 82; Swingewood, 1991 p. 48; Turner et al., 1995, p. 41) The historian Jack Hayward argues that it was Comte who took the "ultimately retrograde step of turning scientists into dogmatic, secular priests of positivism" (Hayward, 1991, p. 81). The kind of system these positivist priests supported, according to Herbert Marcuse, Lenzer, and Zeitlin, was a bourgeois regime that sanctioned capitalism (Marcuse, 1960, p. 342; Lenzer, 1975, p. xliii; Zeitlin, 1990, pp. 80–81, 85). Comte was, in short, an apologist for the status quo.

The fourth controversy relates to the supposed rupture in Comte's intellectual development. His life is usually broken into two parts. His so-called first career was devoted to creating the scientistic doctrine of positivism. In his "second career," he repudiated this important scientific program in an "ironic turn of events" and became a mad religious reformer. The cause of this sudden transformation was his unfulfilled love affair with the young Clotilde de Vaux, who died in 1846, a year after they met (Zeitlin, 1990, p. 84). One of Comte's earliest admirers, John Stuart Mill was partly responsible for this view of the discontinuity in his development. In *Auguste Comte and Positivism* (1865), Mill lamented that Comte's relationship with Clotilde de Vaux caused a marked "deterioration in his speculations," causing him to erect "his philosophy into a religion" (Mill [1865], p. 132). Even Jonathan Turner, who has done much to counter erroneous views of Comte, asserts along with the co-authors of his textbook that in Comte's later work, science took a "back seat to his advocacy" as the philosopher became increasingly despondent and marginalized (Turner et al., 1995, p. 15). Raymond Aron suggests that the Religion of Humanity erected by Comte after Vaux's death was a "biographical accident," which would never have emerged without her influence (1968, p. 124).

The fifth area of debate among Comtean scholars centers on his attitude toward women. It is generally assumed that Comte was a rank misogynist, indeed a "phallocrat" (Kofman, 1978 p. 233). According to the celebrated feminist scholar Geneviève Fraisse, Comte regarded feminism as "inane" and believed "the real problems" of the world "lay elsewhere" (Fraisse, 1993, p. 56). Most surveys of his thought repeat his infamous theory that women were infants – a theory that led to his well-publicized argument with John Stuart Mill (Zeitlin, 1990, p. 84).

In sum, scholars usually depict positivism as a scientistic doctrine arising from the "pre-positivist" atmosphere of early nineteenth-century France in order to support the male bourgeoisie's control over a technocratic society (Gouhier, 1933–41, vol. 3, p. 387). According to their accounts, Comte's turn to religion resulted from a midlife crisis caused by his unfulfilled relationship with a younger woman. Yet if Comte's doctrine is properly analyzed in the context of early nineteenth-century France and as an outgrowth of crises within his own life, it is clear that his intellectual development was marked by originality and continuity, that from the start he distrusted the very type of morally neutral, "positivist" or "scientistic" thinking now associated with his name, and that he appropriated different aspects of feminist discourse to appeal to women.

THE PROBLEM OF COMTE AND SAINT-SIMON

Saint-Simon's and Comte's systems cannot be understood without a grasp of the historical context, for both doctrines were created while the thinkers were experiencing the aftershocks of the French Revolution of 1789. During their lives, France was racked by political divisions stemming from the disappearance of a universally recognized principle of legitimacy necessary for the exercise of power. The majority of French people, from traditionalists on the right to republicans on the left, yearned for moral unanimity and social harmony. With constitutions and governments changing at a rapid rate, they displayed little faith in the liberal attempt to limit political authority through abstract language and representative institutions, which seemed only to increase fragmentation. In their ideal society, politics would play a minor role; individuals would be like-minded and thus able to celebrate "community," a word that appeared frequently in the discourse of the times (Sa'adah, 1990, p. 14, 18).

Comte was thoroughly familiar with this desire for social cohesion long before meeting his mentor, who was likewise affected by it. Born in 1798, four years after the end of the Terror, Comte was raised in a royalist, Catholic family in Montpellier, which had been a center of the counterrevolution. His loyalties were challenged by his republican teachers at the local high school and at the Ecole Polytechnique, an engineering school in Paris and one of the foremost institutions of science in the world. At age fourteen, he had already gone "through all the essential stages of the revolutionary spirit" and felt "the fundamental need for a universal regeneration" that would be both "political and philosophic" (Comte [1830–42], 1975, vol. 2, p. 466). By this point an atheist and republican, the young Comte had absorbed the language of global renewal established by the Revolution. His adoption of such a language is evident in an early essay of 1816, where he condemned the tyranny of the new Bourbon monarchy and urged "enlightened men," especially scientists and philosophers, to create a new regime based on popular consent; it would ensure justice and liberty and do away with the "appalling league of Kings and Priests" (Comte [1816–35], 1970, p. 431). Thanks to his natural rebelliousness, his personal experience of the divisions caused by the Revolution in his family and town, and the influence of his teachers, he thus committed himself at an early age to completing the work of the radical revolutionaries, that of setting up a secular republic. Yet there already emerged a significant tension within his thought between his commitment to a form of government based on the will of the people and his elitism. This tension would become more acute as his thought matured.

After his dismissal in 1816 from the Ecole Polytechnique for insubordination and defiance of the new royalist regime, Comte expanded his already considerable knowledge of the sciences, political economy, and history. He read the works of Condorcet and Montesquieu, who introduced him to the idea that society could be examined in a scientific manner. Condorcet's concept of history as a secular narrative of continuous progress had a particularly strong impact on him. He was thus already an idealist devoted to the progressive regeneration of France when he took a job as secretary to Saint-Simon in 1817.

Plying him with various schemes for social reform and showing him how to combine his disparate interests in society and the sciences, Saint-Simon gave his thought a more definite direction. During the Napoleonic Empire, Saint-Simon had written a number of important works: *Lettres d'un habitant de Genève à ses contemporains* (1802), *Introduction aux travaux scientifiques du XIXᵉ siècle* (1807), *Lettres au Bureau des Longitudes* (1808), *Projet d'Encyclopédie* (1809), *Esquisse d'une nouvelle Encyclopédie* (1810), *Mémoire sur la science de l'homme* (1813), and *Travail sur la gravitation universelle* (1813). In these books, he argued that the nineteenth century had to be devoted to constructing a new society founded on industry as well as a new "positive philosophy" based on the sciences. Sharing the period's enthusiasm for the sciences, he believed they held the key to progress. To him, it was possible to use Newton's physical law of gravity to unite the two parts of "positive philosophy," the "physics" of inorganic matter and that of organic matter. The law of gravity, formulated in mathematic terms, would replace God as "the sole cause of all physical and moral phenomena" (Saint-Simon [1802–25], 1966, vol. 6, pp. 121 n. 1, 154). This new unified system of scientific knowledge would be completed once the study of man and society, which was crucial to rational social reorganization, became an exact or "positive science," based on "observed facts" (Saint-Simon [1802–25], 1975, 84–5; Saint-Simon [1802–25], 1966, vol. 5, part 2, p. 17). Saint-Simon wrote, "We are at the point that the first good summary of the particular sciences will constitute positive philosophy" (Saint-Simon [1802–25], 1966, vol. 1, part 1, p. 109). Once unified in this fashion, the "positive system" would help usher in a new era, where producers would replace the military leaders as the temporal power and the scientists would take over from the clergy as the spiritual power (Saint-Simon [1802–25], 1966, vol. 6, p. 259). In this meritocracy, the directing elite would place supreme value on work, especially activity benefiting humanity. To add weight to this industrial ethos, the scientists, who were the most enlightened members of society, would create a new church and a religion that would reflect the reigning positive philosophy. Such ideas were dispersed throughout Saint-Simon's muddled, poorly written works. For example; in the *Introduction aux travaux scientifiques du XIXᵉ siècle*, he produced a mishmash of insights that were lost in his stream-of-consciousness style:

> I am writing because I have new things to say; I will present my ideas as they have been forged by my mind; I am leaving to the professional writers the trouble of polishing them; I am writing as a nobleman, as a descendant of the counts of Vermandois, as an inheritor of the pen of the Duke of Saint-Simon. Whatever has been the greatest thing to do, the greatest thing to say, has been done, has been said by noblemen. (Saint-Simon [1802–25], 1966, vol. 6, p. 16)

Even his famous disciple Prosper Enfantin complained that Saint-Simon's principles were often "confused" and that his presentation was so "bizarre" that it could only "disgust" his readers.[1]

An extravagant autodidact who called for intellectual coherence as the key to social and political reconstruction, Saint-Simon knew that he himself lacked this quality of clarity and hired Comte to bring order to his ideas. Yet when Comte started working for him, Saint-Simon had grown less interested in establishing the theoretical basis of social reconstruction and had begun tackling the industrial and political reorganization of society. Comte later acknowledged that Saint-Simon taught him to pay more attention to economic factors in modern civilization and the social ramifications of industrial development. Comte's materialism is evident in his view that civilization consisted to a large degree of the "development of the action of man on nature." (Comte [1851–4], 1929, vol. 4, "Appendice," p. 86). Yet he was most absorbed by Saint-Simon's trenchant philosophical and historical critique of the crisis wreaking havoc in Europe. Saint-Simon had shown him that each social system was an application of a system of ideas, especially moral precepts, because people were linked by a common way of thinking.

[1] Enfantin to Pichard, August 23, 1825, Fonds Enfantin 7643, fol. 10v, Bibliothèque de l'Arsenal.

As the reigning philosophical system changed, so did morality and politics, which reflected it. Although Saint-Simon's historical outlook was confused because he constantly changed his periodization both in the number of eras and their dates, he put the degeneration of the moral and political structure into historical perspective, showing the relationship of this decline to the fall of the whole intellectual system. Comte decided that Saint-Simon's change of direction was hasty, for he had not finished defining the new intellectual system, which was the basis of the material structure of society. Consequently, Comte took up Saint-Simon's original unrealized plan of first founding the scientific system, that is, the positive philosophy, together with its keystone, the science of society. Understanding the significance of Saint-Simon's system better than Saint-Simon did, Comte sought to bring his seminal ideas to fruition, especially by using his own talents for synthesis and system-building.

In 1824 he took the first major step in this direction when he completed the *Plan des travaux scientifiques nécessaires pour réorganiser la société*. In this essay, he adopted Saint-Simon's basic schema of social reconstruction but made crucial changes – changes that were so significant that he immediately broke with Saint-Simon after accusing him of trying to steal his ideas. Comte dropped Saint-Simon's notion that the sciences could be unified and society reconstructed by a single natural law, such as the law of gravity. Instead, he proposed to resolve the post-revolutionary crisis by means of a new science of society based on the historical law of three stages. Although he claimed to have discovered the law in 1822, it owed much to Saint-Simon's view that each science passed through three stages – a conjectural stage, a half-conjectural and half-positive stage, and a positive stage – according to its degree of complexity. Yet Comte gave this law a new central role in his system, making it the key to social science and to his understanding of humanity's evolution in the past, present, and future.

In Comte's global version of his law, which he further developed in subsequent writings, each branch of knowledge as well as every social and political structure passed through three stages of history – the theological, metaphysical, and positive. The theological stage was one in which supernatural ideas, such as God, were used to link observations, and society was run by priests and military men. The metaphysical stage was a transitional stage, where personified abstractions, such as nature, replaced God; metaphysicians and lawyers ruled over a society which directed its activities toward production, not simply conquest. In the positive stage, scientists of society and industrialists would organize a society devoted entirely to production. Descriptive laws would be substituted for supernatural and abstract forces. Instead of seeking first or final causes, which these forces represented, the scientific laws would express the "relations of resemblance and succession that facts have among themselves" (Comte [1851–4], 1929, vol. 4, "Appendice," p. 144).

Comte denied that this last, positive era could be established by practical, institutional reforms, which struck him as ineffective and premature. He used his law of three stages to prove that the coming of this era was a certainty. Because all aspects of knowledge were interrelated and the mind was naturally compelled to make all ideas homogeneous, the scientific, or "positive," method would be inevitably extended to the study of society, the last stronghold of theology and metaphysics. Once all ideas became scientific in this fashion, the positive philosophy, comprising the major sciences, would be completed and unified and would bring about the intellectual consensus required to build the stable industrial society of the future. Whereas Saint-Simon increasingly praised the role of the *industriels* (people involved in productive work) in bringing about the new order, Comte focused on the intellectual work the scientists of society had to do to prepare the way. Faithful to Saint-Simon's original idea that theory had to precede practice, he tried to develop concepts that his erratic mentor had left by the wayside. Although Comte later denied Saint-Simon's influence, he was more candid right after their break-up in explaining his debt to him in 1824: "I certainly owe a great deal intellectually to Saint-Simon, that is to say, he has powerfully contributed to launching me in the philosophical direction that I have clearly created for myself today and that I will follow without hesitation all my life" (Comte [1814–57], 1973–90, vol. 1, p. 90). Saint-Simon increased Comte's awareness that they lived in a time of transition requiring a radical new approach to reconstruction. More upheaval would result if people continued to rely solely on the critical skepticism and the conventional abstractions, such as the "rights of man" and "popular sovereignty," which they had inherited from the Enlightenment philosophes and revolutionaries. Saint-Simon gave Comte the mission of completing the transition to a new era by creating a new positive system of knowledge that would include the study of man and society and would lead to political and moral changes. Despite the fact that Saint-Simon thought of the essence of positivism and sociology, he did not establish them. It was Comte who focused his energies on systematically developing sociology as a means of unifying society and creating the positivist system, the general outlines of which Saint-Simon had vaguely alluded to but never methodically described. With a disciplined mind vastly different from that of the capricious Saint-Simon, Comte would acquire an originality of his own.

THE PROBLEM OF POSITIVISM AND SCIENTISM

Comte's ability to make a far more systematic exposition of history and the scientific spirit was evident in his major work, the six-volume *Cours de philosophie positive*, published between 1830 and 1842. In this introductory course on positive philosophy, he sought to unify knowledge through the "positive," or scientific, method and more boldly condemned philosophers, such as Saint-Simon, who tried to achieve a "vague and absurd unity" on the basis of one explanatory physical law (Comte [1830–42], 1975, vol. 1, p. 874). Exhibiting the development of the positive method, much of the work covered the history of the sciences, "the most important" and "neglected" part of the development of humanity (Comte [1830–42], 1975, vol. 1, p. 53). One of the founders of the history of science, Comte demonstrated that the development of each science was closely related to the growth of other sciences. He also showed the interrelationships between the sciences and society as a whole. His very influential epistemology thus rejected the traditional approach of grounding the sciences on universal logical principles; to him, scientific knowledge itself had to be considered a historical process (Heilbron, 1990, pp. 155, 161). Emphasizing Comte's statement that "no conception can be fully understood without its history" (Comte [1830–42], 1975, vol. 1, p. 21), Robert Scharff has argued that Comte promoted a "historico-critical reflectiveness" among philosophers that is highly relevant today (Scharff, 1995, p. 16). The main point of Comte's strategy was to use history to prove the inevitability of the triumph of the positive method in the study of society, especially the area of morality and politics.

To this end, Comte invented a new classification of the sciences, which demonstrated the order in which the sciences were established. According to this schema, each science went through the theological and metaphysical stages and then became positive according to the simplicity of its phenomena and the distance of these phenomena from man. The positive method was established first in astronomy, which studied the simplest phenomena, those farthest from man. Then physics, chemistry, and biology became sciences in that order. These more complex sciences took longer to reach the positive stage, for they depended on the knowledge of the simpler sciences and could not advance until the preceding sciences did. Comte argued that because the positive method was firmly established in the natural sciences, it now was possible to extend it to the study of society, which involved the most complex phenomena, those closest to man. To mark the launching of this last science, which would have the certainty and authority of the natural sciences, Comte in 1839 coined a new term for it – "sociology" (Comte [1830–42], 1975, vol. 2, p. 88).

As shown in his criticism of Montesquieu and political economists, Comte asserted that objectivity was an inappropriate goal in studying society; every social theory had to depict a better society. In fact, positivism was never meant to be a "value-free" scientific doctrine. He embraced the need to make value judgments because his central concerns were political activism and social reform. He wanted to shape the world of action indirectly by molding people's ideas and opinions. Stressing the unifying power of ideas, Comte was an idealist, not simply a materialist, as Hayek and other critics believe (Hayek, 1952, p. 139). In an important passage, Comte pointed out "that ideas govern and overturn the world, or in other words, that the entire social mechanism rests ultimately on opinions" ([1830–42], 1975, vol. 1, p. 38). By disseminating a system of ideas that were scientific, irrefutable, and universally acceptable and by creating sociology, which would make scholars and all other people focus on fulfilling the needs of society as a whole, positivism would inaugurate an intellectual revolution. Because Comte believed that intellectual well-roundedness was linked to altruism, a word he also coined, he declared that this change in mental outlook would lead first to a new moral order marked by the bonding together of individuals through sympathy and then a political transformation that would usher in a new positivist era of consensus and social stability. By presenting humanity with the rational social theory which the revolutionaries had lacked and which gave people power over the social world, positivism would end the destructive phase of the Revolution and preside over the second, constructive phase. No longer would people be subject to painfully futile political experimentations. His mission, that of overcoming the intellectual, social, and political tensions stemming from the French Revolution, would be realized.

Comte thus never glorified the sciences for their own sakes but considered them tools for improving the welfare of the entire society. Unlike many scientistic thinkers, he did not believe the sciences were all-powerful. Since his youth, he had been wary of those who sought to use science to exert unlimited power over nature and social and political structures, none of which could be modified to the extent that modern man imagined. Moreover, the sciences could not overcome the limited range of the human mind. Even in the narrow realm of what was understandable, our knowledge was deficient. Throughout the *Cours*, Comte insisted that:

> it was necessary to recognize that by an indisputable law of human nature, our means for conceiving new questions . . . [is] much more powerful than our resources for solving them, or in other words the human mind . . . [is] far more capable of imagining than of reasoning. ([1830–42], 1975, vol. 1, p. 99)

In fact, Comte did not believe in absolute truth. Advising political moderation, he announced his relativism in an early essay:

> It is no longer a question of expounding interminably in order to know what is the best government; speaking in an absolute sense, there is nothing good, there is nothing bad; the only absolute is that everything is relative; everything is relative especially when social institutions are concerned. ([1816–35], 1970, p. 71)

His relativism was connected to his conviction that "exact reality can never, in any way, be perfectly unveiled" to our weak mind ([1830–42], 1975, vol. 2, pp. 103–4).

Because of his skepticism, Comte recognized the limits of pure objectivity and the shortcomings of empiricism. He did not believe there was an outer reality that could be rigorously and objectively described by the human mind. Objectivity, he argued, was particularly unattainable in the science of society, whose phenomena were so close to us. Pseudo-impartiality, along with modern egoism and specialization, led people to focus excessively on facts. Although observed facts were crucial to the establishment and verification of scientific laws, the accumulation of discrete facts struck him as unsystematic and unproductive. They were not even scientific. Because Comte outlawed appeals to a non-existent absolute truth, he came to the new, very influential, conclusion that knowledge was scientific if it displayed predictive power, that is, the capability to go from the present to the future and from the known to the unknown (Laudan, 1971, pp. 37–40). He wrote, *"from science comes prediction; from prediction comes action"* (Comte [1830–42], 1975, vol. 1, p. 45). Facts in themselves had no predictive capability and therefore no scientific status. By neglecting to formulate general laws, empiricists failed, in· other words, to provide useful knowledge. In the *Discours sur l'esprit positif* of 1844, Comte stated that "the positive" designated not only the real, the certain, the precise, the constructive, and the relative, but the useful ([1844], 1963, pp. 126–30). Pure empiricism was not positivism because it served no purpose.

He was, moreover, convinced that observation itself required more than experiencing sense impressions; facts could not be perceived or remembered without the guidance of an a priori theory. Social facts were among the hardest to perceive. Because scientists of society lived in society, it was impossible for them to notice what was ordinary; however, familiar social phenomena were the most important facts. Revealing again his awareness of the mind's limitations and his own inclination toward Cartesian rationalism, Comte wrote:

> Man is incapable by his nature not only of combining facts and deducing from them several consequences, but of even simply observing them with attention and retaining them with certainty if he does not attach them immediately to some explanation. He cannot have connected observations without some theory any more than [he can have] a positive theory without regular observations. ([1851–4], 1929, vol. 4, "Appendice," p. 144)

Thus the mind was always torn between "the necessity of observing to form real theories and the necessity, not any less imperious, of creating some theories in order to devote oneself to coherent observations" (Comte [1830–42], 1975, vol. 1, p. 23).

Comte insisted on the necessity of coordinating observed facts by forming provisional hypotheses or theories. Indispensable to the discovery of natural laws, these hypotheses were convenient devices for approximating reality and fulfilling our needs. Although geometers had devised the artifice of a theory, Comte was the first to explore the fundamental condition that legitimized its usage:

> This condition . . . consists of imagining only hypotheses [that are] susceptible . . . of a positive verification, more or less distant, but always clearly inevitable, and whose degree of precision is exactly in harmony with that which the study of the corresponding phenomena comprises. In other words, truly philosophical hypotheses must constantly present the character of simple anticipations of that which experiment and reason would have revealed immediately, if the circumstances of the problem had been more favorable. (Comte [1830–42], 1975, vol. 1, p. 457)

Once a hypothesis that accorded with previously determined data

was conceived, the science could freely develop, exploring new consequences that would confirm or negate the conjecture. Hypotheses
could not be considered scientific theories until they were verified
by induction and deduction. An unverifiable hypothesis would be,
for example, a theory about God because it could never be affirmed
or refuted. Comte's representation of hypotheses as useful, convenient, and respectable devices that serve a crucial function in
scientific discovery was a novel idea, one that became very
influential. He even anticipated the work of Thomas Kuhn because
he appreciated the large role that aesthetic considerations played
in scientists' construction of hypotheses (Comte [1830–42], 1975,
vol. 2, pp. 735–6).

Besides his approach to provisional hypotheses, Comte's "art" of
"scientific fiction" demonstrates that he was not a slave to his belief
in the importance of observation. These fictions derived from the
"poetic imagination." Whereas the art of hypothesis created fictions
to solve a problem, this other art applied them to elucidate the
problem itself by inventing a series of purely hypothetical cases. One
example of this new method in biology involved inserting "purely
fictive organisms," which one hoped to discover later, between
already known organisms in order to make the biological series
more homogeneous, continuous, and regular (Comte [1830–42],
1975, vol. 2, p. 728). Comte's approach to hypotheses and scientific
fictions demonstrates that he intended to offer imagination the
"most vast and fertile" field for discovering and coordinating facts
(Comte [1830–42], 1975, vol. 2, pp. 102, 179). In sum, each positivist
scientist would use a variety of resources to construct laws and
theories that would eliminate the tedious task of observing facts and
enable him to go beyond direct evidence.

Though loyal to Descartes and deduction, Comte recognized that
rationalism, like empiricism, had potential problems. To avoid
giving reason excessive importance in scientific research, Comte
deliberately refused to offer elaborate, universal, ahistorical rules of
scientific procedure; he never produced an organon of proof. To
him, such exercises in pure abstract reasoning not only limited
flexibility in scientific research but dangerously skirted metaphysical
practices (Scharff, 1995, pp. 7, 65). Even the most rational science
had to remember its roots in experience and observation, for there
was no a priori knowledge. Thus every positive theory had to refer
ultimately to real, concrete phenomena. In 1852, Comte clearly
stated his position that scientific investigation rested on the use of
both induction and deduction:

I consider Descartes and even Leibniz infinitely superior to Bacon. The latter, who wrote so much on induction, never made a single inductive discovery of any value, ... while Descartes, who ... philosophically appreciated only deduction, made important advances in mathematics and elsewhere by means of induction. (Comte [1814–57], 1973–90, vol. 6, p. 433)

His warning that both observation and reasoning had to be employed in the discovery of natural laws demonstrates that he did not reduce science to the purely experiential as Don Martindale and others have asserted (Martindale, 1981, p. 56).

Comte's animus against setting down formal detailed rules of scientific activity was part of his campaign to ensure recognition of the principle that every science had to be based on the "observation of facts that are proper to it" (Comte, [1816–35], 1970, p. 481). He warned that no science should ever be reduced to another. Especially because of its consideration of historical facts, sociology could not be reduced to a natural science. It could certainly not be reduced to mathematics, as many scholars, such as Condorcet, believed.

Comte repeatedly denounced the statistical approach to scientific research that scholars today tend to equate with positivism. He opposed the modern positivists' quantification of human experience, for although a gifted mathematician himself, he did not believe that mathematics offered the only certain knowledge. Comte rejected Descartes's attempt to make mathematics the universal science by reducing every problem in natural philosophy to a question of numbers. Comte maintained that the human mind could represent mathematically only the least complicated and most general inorganic phenomena, those with fixed properties. Complex inorganic phenomena and all organic phenomena would forever remain closed to mathematical analysis because they exhibited much numerical variability and were affected by so many factors that no two cases were alike. Because of their variability, diversity, interconnectedness, and complexity, social phenomena in particular could never be expressed by mathematical equations. Comte's criticism of the abuse of statistics, particularly in biology and sociology, formed part of his campaign to preserve the autonomy and individuality of each science.

Because of his interest in giving sociology a distinctive character, one freed from all remnants of theological and metaphysical thinking, he did not favor extending the boundaries of his new science to include psychology. In a famous passage, he stated in 1818:

The human mind . . . cannot be a subject of observation because
someone obviously cannot observe the mind of others; and on the
other hand, he cannot observe his own mind. In effect, we observe
phenomena with our mind; but with what do we observe the mind
itself, its operations, its way of proceeding? We cannot divide our
mind, that is to say, our brain, into two parts, one which acts, while the
other watches it to see the way it goes to work (Comte [1814–57],
1973–90, vol. 1, p. 58)

Many scholars have criticized Comte's opposition to psychology,
but they have not understood the context of his remarks. Scharff
has shown that Comte's critique of interior observation derived
from his crusade against the prescientific, "old-fashioned rational
psychology," which was originally inspired by Descartes's method of
meditation and was espoused in Comte's day by Victor Cousin
(1995, p. 35). This brand of psychology had produced many
conflicting doctrines of the soul, mind, and self, which Comte
condemned as theological and metaphysical; to him, the
introspective study of purely intellectual processes was too
speculative to be the basis of a science. Thus Comte was not
necessarily opposed to all types of psychology; he rejected only the
kind of psychology that was promoted in his day.

THE PROBLEM OF POSITIVISM AND POLITICS

Comte was also not an advocate of the status quo, who supported
the capitalist system. He was highly critical of the existing social and
political situation in early nineteenth-century France and argued that
the existing political parties were unqualified to head the government. Influenced by the organicism of the counter-revolutionaries
and the image of a moral community espoused by many working-
class leaders and bourgeois intellectuals, Comte found the emphasis
on self-interest and individualism that was inherent in liberalism to
be morally inadequate. In his eyes, the revolutionaries were too
critical and incapable of devising a constructive solution to the
problem of government. Yet he did not engage in nostalgia for the
old regime. To him, the reactionaries were absurd, for they opposed
progress and continued to espouse decrepit principles. Combining
the vices of the other political positions, the center party had no
principles whatsoever.

Comte believed that positivism's all-encompassing, synthetic
character would enable it to appeal to all parties. His science of

society had roots in the liberal tradition of Condorcet and the Idéologues and embraced the liberal concept that political authority must derive from the people's "explicit or implicit" consent (Comte [1830–42], 1975, vol. 2, p. 115). The left, he believed, would therefore be attracted by his anticlericalism and hostility toward established religions; his republicanism; his espousal of relativism and progress; his vision of a new industrial and secular order; his devotion to the working class; and his loyal commitment to the revolutionaries' "cause of reason and Humanity," which he had advocated since 1815 (Comte [1814–57], 1973–90, vol. 1, p. 8). He maintained that the right would approve of his insistence on traditional values; his stress on a strong spiritual power, duties, hierarchy, order, and stability; and his rejection of equality and individualism. Positivism, in Comte's eyes, would thus triumph because it alone could satisfy contemporary needs for both order and progress and transcend the divisions caused by the French Revolution.

Comte also criticized the government for becoming too cen-tralized and powerful as a reaction to the social dissolution caused by a lack of moral authority. Condemning autocracy, especially the emergence of a new kind of corrupt "administrative despotism," he advocated the establishment of a spiritual power to advise and check the material power. Whereas the material or temporal part of the government controlled human actions, the moral or spiritual power would regulate opinions, inclinations, and ideas. It would provide moral guidelines to counter antisocial and pleasure-seeking tendencies, which were the "most energetic impulses of human nature" (Comte [1851–4], 1929, vol. 4; "Appendice," pp. 154, 187).

Foreshadowing Emile Durkheim's concern with *anomie*, Comte maintained that with the development of the division of labor and increased specialization, people were becoming more self-interested, alienated, and out of touch with others; their communities were dissolving. The solution lay in the establishment of a spiritual power, which would encourage individuals to develop their inherent sociability, work for a common goal, and contribute to the general good of society. Only in this coercive way, could the division of labor lead to greater social cooperation.

The spiritual power was also necessary because it alone could solve the "social question." Comte's analysis of the alienating and exploitative aspects of the industrial revolution and the rise of class conflict was remarkably similar to Marx's but did not lead him to the same radical conclusions. Contrary to current assumptions, Comte condemned those who sought to substitute the "despotism founded on the right of the most wealthy for the despotism founded on the right of the strongest" (Comte [1851–4], 1929, vol. 4, "Appendice," p. 210). Like Marx, and in contrast to Saint-Simon, Comte despised the industrialists for their egoism, social apathy, and political ineptitude. Like Marx, he envisioned some sort of alliance between a special category of intellectuals and the proletariat, both of whom were marginalized in the new industrial society. However, in contrast to Marx's intellectuals, who would work to eliminate the class structure altogether, Comte maintained that his "independent" intellectuals – the spiritual power – could intervene in the class struggle to make each class fulfill its duties to the other and thereby resolve their conflicts. Marx would label this approach "utopian."

The people who would compose Comte's spiritual power would not be an elite of scientists in control of society, as is commonly believed. He was extremely critical of the coming reign of both industrialists and scientists, whose autonomy, he believed, should be limited. Comte distrusted scientific specialization, for he was convinced that the division of labor, though necessary for progress, led to narrow views, the fragmentation of knowledge, and social and political indifference. In an early essay of 1818, he criticized scientists in much the same terms that he did the industrialists: they were mediocre, egoistic, and uncaring ([1816–35], 1970, p. 440). Comte's dislike of scientists grew after he failed to achieve his goal of becoming a member of the Academy of Sciences and a professor at the Ecole Polytechnique. In the *Cours*, he embarked upon a public tirade against the scientists, who, he said, feared positivism because it would rob them of prestigious posts.

In reacting against them, he argued that the people who would represent the spiritual power should be the positive philosophers. They possessed the most general knowledge because they understood the applications of the positive method in all the major sciences, including sociology, which covered history, political economy, and morality. These intellectuals would know how to apply the positive method to social phenomena and how to relate society to natural phenomena. Comte assumed that because of the breadth of their knowledge, they had the widest views and sympathies, which legitimized their authority to speak for the entire community. Replacing the traditional clergy, they would guide the new positivist society toward a common goal, the improvement of humanity. They would make not only industrialists but scientists accountable to the public.

Yet even these generalists should never be given full authority. Borrowing a term from Mill, Comte declared that a government of philosophers or intellectuals was a dangerous "pedantocracy";

they would seek complete domination of society and prevent the very progress that they were there to ensure (Comte [1830–42], 1975, p. 656). Comte argued that the separation of powers would eliminate this peril in the positivist society. Because he limited the spiritual power's hegemony to education and counselling and forbade it to exercise practical or political power, the usual accusation that he actively sought to erect a technocratic or theocratic society is unfounded.

Comte was keenly aware that he was in a paradoxical situation. He was erecting a social philosophy based upon the sciences, but he did not trust the purely scientific spirit to regenerate the political and social world. Contrary to Friedrick Hayek's assertion, he had not passively absorbed the technological mentality of the Ecole Polytechnique (Hayek, 1952, p. 16). Comte's disillusionment with this mindset surfaced in the closing sentence of the *Cours*, which castigated "the prejudices and passions of our deplorable scientific regime." Instead of representing a scientistic tract, the *Cours* was meant to contain the scientific spirit, especially the narrow, specialized "positivity" of the modern age (Comte [1830–42], 1975, vol. 2, p. 701). The science of society, which cultivated feelings of solidarity with other members of society and a sense of connection with past and future generations of the human species, was to be an antidote to the egoism and indifference of the scientific spirit and of modern life in general.

The Problem of Comte's Intellectual Evolution

Comte's system arose from a paradox deep within him. Disturbed by the growing skepticism of the post-revolutionary period, he experienced a religious calling but suffered from an inability to believe in God. This ordeal gave him a multi-dimensional picture of human nature, which was reinforced by the romanticism of the period. Comte knew that reason could not satisfy all human needs. In fact, in the *Cours*, he stated that philosophers erred when they portrayed man "against all evidence as an essentially reasoning being, executing continually, without his knowledge, a multitude of imperceptible calculations with almost no spontaneity of action, even from the most tender age of childhood" (Comte [1830–42], 1975, vol. 1, p. 856). Years before meeting Vaux, Comte denounced the exclusive attention given to the mind and discussed the power of the emotions. As early as 1818, he wrote to a friend, "The gentle and tender affections are the happiest, the source of the only true happiness that one can get hold of on this miserable planet, and one could never have enough of them" (Comte [1814–57], 1973–90, vol. 1, p. 46). Reason could not possibly satisfy all human needs. "Daily experience" demonstrated that it was the "passions" that stimulated the intellectual faculties and constituted the "principal motives of human action" (Comte [1830–42], 1975, vol. 1, p. 856).

Thus, early on, Comte recognized that the needs of society were not only intellectual but emotional and that its spiritual reorganization had to involve the heart at least as much as the mind. Even if a general doctrine were established, a solid social consensus could not exist without the growth of the sympathies; it was wrong to assume that "it is above all by intelligence that man can be changed and improved" (Comte [1830–42], 1975, vol. 1, p. 856). As he endeavored to respond to the demands of the heart and mind, Comte sought to create an intellectual system based on science that would appeal to all classes by satisfying the human need for faith. Dogmatism, in his eyes, was the natural mental state of humanity – the state that ensured the sanity of the individual and the community and allowed for the possibility of action. By creating a new set of respectable beliefs that would extend to all people and transform their feelings and values, positivism would establish the kind of intellectual, emotional, and moral consensus that was the salient characteristic of a religious system and a smoothly operating society. The creation of this belief system and a clergy to implement it remained Comte's spiritual mission throughout his life. He always considered his goal to be "spiritual" because his project involved the organization of people's ideas, sentiments, and values.

The first volumes of the *Cours* appeared scientistic, for he discussed exclusively the natural sciences in a style that he made deliberately dry and passionless. He avoided literary devices that would have made reading his works more pleasant in order to differentiate himself from other social thinkers, whom he considered dangerous rhetoricians. His difficult style made his study of society seem scientific and objective and thus more worthy of respect.

Comte also initially focused on the sciences alone, for in his mind social regeneration would fall into a "vague mysticism" if it treated the feelings without first systematizing ideas. He explained to Mill in 1845:

This is why my fundamental work [the *Cours*] had to address itself almost exclusively to the intellect: this had to be a work of research, and even incidentally, of discussion, destined to discover and constitute true universal principles by climbing by hierarchical degrees from the most simple scientific questions to the highest social speculations. (Comte [1814–57], 1973–90, vol. 3, p. 61)

Only when social issues came up at the end of the *Cours* did Comte believe that he could logically develop his concepts of a spiritual power and a spiritual doctrine touching on the emotions. Broaching these subjects at the beginning would have ruined the anti-theological and scientific impressions of his enterprise, which were initially most important to impart to his readers because they distinguished his philosophy from that of other social reformers.

At the end of the *Cours*, Comte therefore launched into the spiritual aspects of social reorganization. In one of the closing volumes, written years before he met Vaux, he wrote that:

universal love ... is certainly far more important than the intellect itself in ... our existence ... because love spontaneously uses even the lowest mental faculties for everyone's profit, while egoism distorts or paralyzes the most eminent dispositions, which consequently are often far more disturbing than efficacious in regard to ... happiness. ([1830–42], 1975, vol. 2, p. 362)

Moreover, he suggested that the belief system of positivism was religious because it would replace Catholicism and have its own "Positive Church" ([1830–42], 1975, vol. 2, p. 696). Armed with the rational, coherent system of positive philosophy, the positivist clergy would "finally seize the spiritual government of humanity" and ensure the triumph of a new, more effective morality, which in the closing pages of the *Cours* was already attracting Comte's attention more than sociology ([1830–42], 1975, vol. 2, p. 15).

Comte would further develop his ideas on these issues in the 1850s, when he established the Religion of Humanity in the *Système de politique positive* (1851–4), which focused on the moral and emotional aspects of social regeneration. Because he had already established a system of "fundamental ideas," he now had to describe their operation in society. This "social application" would consist of the "systematization of human sentiments, which is the necessary consequence of that of ideas and the indispensable basis of that of institutions" (Comte [1814–57], 1973–90, vol. 3, p. 61 [letter dated 1845]). In the *Système*, he made morality a seventh science and explored ways of ensuring social consensus. Here he anticipated the work of the sociologist Maurice Halbwachs in emphasizing the importance of collective memory from a social point of view. Private and public acts of commemoration in the form of worshipping important figures from one's own past and that of Western civilization would provide a sense of continuity between past and present generations and help to unite society. Seeds of this concept can be found in the *Cours*, where he stated that individuals could best satisfy their natural "need for eternity" by contributing daily to the progress of humanity, especially through "benevolent actions" and "sympathetic emotions" ([1830–42], 1975, vol. 2, p. 778). In the *Système*, he described the rituals and positivist culture that would rejuvenate people's emotional life, bring them back into contact with the concrete, and stimulate the arts. The *Système* was not entirely "outrageous" as George Ritzer implies (Ritzer, 1996, p. 106). It represented the logical result of Comte's fervent desire to effect a return to fetishism, the most emotionally intense form of early theology, in a way suitable to modern society.

In conclusion, there was no sudden change of direction from Comte's "first" career to his "second," as most scholars have argued. The second part of his life, which involved setting up his religious and political system, flowed logically from the first part of his career, which established the intellectual basis of that system. There was no break in Comte's development because from the start his solution to the malaise of his era was a new belief system that functioned as a religion. If anything, Comte's approach was indebted to Saint-Simon's conviction that the "positive doctrine" was a religion because all religions consisted of the reigning intellectual system, that is, the ideas and moral precepts held in common by the members of society (Saint-Simon [1802–25], 1966, vol. 6, p. 297). Comte's interest in religion was a natural outgrowth of his concern with moral regeneration, an interest he had had since his earliest writings for Saint-Simon. In 1817, while working for Saint-Simon, he had proclaimed the need to organize "a system of terrestrial morality" that would replace Christianity ([1816–35], 1970, p. 40). Later, he decided that the word "system" was too restrictive and intellectual. The Revolution of 1848 made him particularly eager to experience what he assumed would be the final, decisive clash between positivism and its main rival, Catholicism. To encourage this last battle, he began to call his system the "Religion of Humanity," a term he borrowed from the Saint-Simonians, who had invented it in the early 1830s (*Religion Saint-Simonienne*, 1832, vol., 2, p. 64). Defending his terminology, he explained in 1849 that he had "dared to join . . . the name [religion] to the thing [positivism], in order to institute directly an open competition with all the other systems (Comte [1814–57], 1973–90, vol. 4, p. 22).

Although logical, this decision caused a rift among Comte's followers, even during his lifetime. Those disciples who believed his scientific program was of key importance fought against those who asserted that his religious ideas were most significant. A fruitful area of research would involve analyzing the struggle between these two groups; especially during the Third Republic, when the influence of positivism reached its peak.

THE PROBLEM OF COMTE'S ATTITUDE TOWARD WOMEN

Comte's views on women were not static or entirely misogynist as is usually assumed but went through several transformations, reflecting events in his own life and in the social and political realms. In his youth, he tended towards feminism, for he was influenced by the eighteenth-century campaign to transform the relations between the sexes. He was familiar with the writings of Condorcet, who advocated women's equality. Mary Wollstonecraft's *Vindication of the Rights of Woman* (1792) also had a particularly "strong impact" on him (Comte [1814–57], 1973–90, vol. 2, p. 198 [letter dated 1843]). In 1818 Comte strongly criticized men who manipulated "the horrible law of the strongest" to lord it over women, whom they regarded as a kind of "domestic animal" or "toy destined for all eternity for the good pleasure and usage of his Majesty *Man*" (Comte [1814–57], 1973–90, vol. 1, p. 56). To him, progress included women's freedom from male domination and improvements in their economic condition.

Yet after his marriage to Caroline Massin in 1825, he adopted an anti-feminist position, partly in response to her attempt to dominate him and partly in reaction against the renewal of the concept of women's rights inherent in the schemes of the Saint-Simonians and Charles Fourier and in the example of George Sand. In the *Cours* and in his famous debate with John Stuart Mill in 1843, Comte maintained that domestic life was necessarily founded on sexual inequality. He used the authority of science to prove his point, insisting that biology confirmed that the female was physiologically and anatomically in a "state of extreme infancy" which made her inferior to the male, who was, in Comte's eyes, the standard (Comte [1814–57], 1973–90, vol. 2, p. 179 [letter dated 1843]). The "fact" that a woman's skull was smaller than a man's was proof of her inferior intellectual capacities. Scientific arguments demonstrating woman's weak reason, imperfect character, and excessive emotions disqualified her from having a directing role in the public sphere.

Yet in the late 1840s, Comte once again modified his attitude toward women, going back to some extent to the position he held in his youth. In 1845, three years after separating from his wife, he had fallen in love with the aspiring novelist and journalist, Clotilde de Vaux, who was 17 years younger than he and represented to him, the perfect woman, the model for all others. Even after her death from tuberculosis in 1846, she remained his muse and collaborator. Impressed by Vaux's forceful, thoughtful persona, stirred by the activities of the women's movement in the 1840s and 1850s, and disillusioned with male political regimes, Comte became convinced that the participation of women in the positivist republic was the key to its success. To him, the problem of anarchy could not be resolved "as long as the revolution does not become feminine." The "disorders of male reason" were too painful to bear. Only women, with their nurturing qualities, could create a unified, compassionate society. Seeking to take advantage of the "feminine revolution" that he believed was about to occur, Comte waited "with anxiety" for women's judgment of his own "feminine theory," which he now called "the principal basis" of his system (Comte [1814–57], 1973–90, vol. 5, p. 25; vol. 6, p. 108, 183 [letters dated 1849, 1851]). Rebuffed by scientists and other scholars, who did not take him seriously, he manipulated the feminist discourse to rally women to his side.

To strengthen his appeal to them, he reshaped his doctrine, emphasizing religious, emotional, and moral issues, which he assumed were more to their taste. He wrote, "Better judges than we in moral understanding, women will feel in several regards that the affective superiority of positivism . . . is even more pronounced than its speculative preeminence . . . They will soon come to this conclusion when they have stopped confusing the new philosophy with its scientific preamble ([1851–4] 1929, vol. 1, p. 224). Agents of morality and social unity and experts in the emotions, women were crucial for combating the egoism, shallowness, and narrow-mindedness of men and for saving the increasingly fragmented West from complete dissolution.

Comte did not support the idea of equality or sexual liberation for either sex. Nevertheless, he believed strongly in the coming reign of women, who would be allies of the positivist clergy. Women, he said, should be given the same education as men. Switching the position that he had taken previously, he asserted that "feminine imperfections" in both character and intellect "have less to do with nature than with regime," that is, nurture ([1851–4] 1929, vol. 4, p. 70). To increase women's influence in the public sphere, he favored reviving the pre-revolutionary salons, where women were significant power-brokers who shaped public opinion. In 1853, Comte also argued that political life should strengthen domestic life in order to make nurturing the goal of public life. Women would then be "in first place" in the positivist society (Comte [1814–57], 1973–90, vol. 7, p. 160). As moral beings endowed with the best trait of the human species, that of sociability, women would represent Humanity itself. In the positivist temples, Humanity would be depicted as a woman of about thirty with a son. When he called for a "feminine revolution," revolted against a male God, and sought to create ways for women to intermingle with men so as not to remain entirely silent, Comte was using woman as a sign of change and revealing cracks in the traditional patriarchal system.

Comte was caught in one of the central paradoxes of the period. He wanted women to fortify the male republic by acting as agents of cohesion. But he also wanted them to correct the injustices of this same system by effecting social change (Dijkstra, 1992, p. 1). Ultimately, his version of the "feminism of difference" was one stripped of the key ingredients of individualism, rights, and equality and inspired instead by the values of interdependence, community, and cooperation (Le Doeuff, 1987, p. 182). As such, it proved compatible with his vision of an illiberal, organic republic.

CONCLUSION

Today Comte would deny that he was a positivist, for he would not recognize the contemporary version of positivism as his own creation. Even at the end of his life, he was already countering disciples, such as Emile Littré and John Stuart Mill, who sought to transform positivism into a manifesto for the scientific age by removing many of the nuances of his thought. It was against his intentions that positivism became a convenient, simplistic term for the reductive, quantifiable approach to human knowledge.

A complex thinker, Comte was not a naive advocate of scientism, the politics of the right, or misogyny. Comte's system was chiefly characterized by the search for a synthesis (Skarga, 1974, pp. 385–9). He always pursued the middle way between the extremes in all realms. He sought to balance the needs of the heart and those of the mind, order and progress, rationalism and empiricism, materialism and idealism, the spiritual power and the temporal power, religion and science, objectivity and subjectivity, liberalism and conservatism, feminism and patriarchalism. In imitation of his beloved

Convention, Comte set the people and their welfare at the center of his positivist republic, but at the same time, he wanted them to take heed of the counsels of a superior intellectual authority. The individualism at the heart of capitalism had to be offset by the sociability of the Religion of Humanity. Scholars who neglect Comte's balancing act in all these realms and present him as an extremist are glossing over the intricacies of his thought.

Comte was the ultimate synthesizer because unity and coherence were, to him, the signs of mental health and normality (Kofman, 1978, p. 206). His ideas emerged from the interaction between the tense state of the post-revolutionary world around him and crises within his own inner world caused by his struggle against mental illness. The French term for madness, *"aliénation,"* reveals that the madman was considered a stranger to society. Comte's attacks of madness signified his rupture with the entity that was his object of study – society. In truth, he alienated almost everyone around him, his mentor Saint-Simon, his disciples John Stuart Mill and Emile Littré, his family, his friends, his colleagues, and his wife. (See Appendix.) It is indeed paradoxical that the founder of sociology – the science that specializes in the study of social relations – was a man who felt so uncomfortable in the most basic human associations. In his philosophical system and social theory, he thus privileged the values of integration, harmony, and unity – qualities that were missing in society at large, in his own life, and in his own psyche.

Ultimately, Comte urged a balanced search for solutions to the uncertainty of post-revolutionary France because he sought to appeal to all social groups. To advocate one position at the expense of others risked reviving the narrowness, selfishness, and meanness at the heart of party politics, which had repeatedly proved its ineffectiveness. If everyone could be persuaded to work together for the common good, they would revive the unanimity and community that Comte and his contemporaries assumed had existed before the Revolution. His effort to create a new community that would avoid political factionalism and rest on a citizenry educated to be virtuous and like-minded owed much to Rousseau and the revolutionary tradition. It was not a liberal political vision, but a communitarian one, one very much in keeping with the political culture of early nineteenth-century France (Hunt, 1984, pp. 44–5, 219, 229).

Comte's effort to cure society of its ills has remained a principal objective of sociology. His warnings against allowing sociology to succumb to the "positivity" and specialization of the scientific age are still germane today, when the model of the physical sciences continues to have much appeal and some sociologists and other scholars remain attracted to an excessively empirical, jargon-laden discourse, one fearful of generalization. The bitter debates among the various schools of sociology reveal that the certitude and consensus that Comte assumed would exist at least in his new discipline remain elusive. Moreover, his conviction that reality itself may never be fully comprehended, especially in the most complex science, that of society, seems highly relevant in our postmodern era. Even to Comte, the study of society was often closer to being an art form than a science. In one of his first essays for Saint-Simon, Comte revealed his awareness that to a certain extent social scientists were merely novelists constructing narratives that perhaps divulged more about themselves and their own condition than the real world: "Each [political writer] gives himself his own theme; each takes off from his own ideas, his own system, and his own theory, and often his ideas are prejudices, his system is a novel, and his theory a chimera" ([1816–35], 1970, p. 64).

APPENDIX

The preceding analysis passes over one further controversy surrounding Comte. This problem is of a more biographical nature than the controversies covered in the body of this chapter, which are more intellectual and historical. It concerns the women in Comte's life, who have never been the subject of any extensive analysis. Clotilde de Vaux is widely regarded as the woman who had the most influence on Comte, but her character and aspirations remain unexplored. Moreover, it is widely assumed that Comte's first wife, Caroline Massin, was a prostitute. He announced in the "Secret Addition" to his *Testament* that he married her to save her from going to prison (Comte [1884], 1896, 36a–36g). Even recent accounts, which should be more sensitive to gender issues, repeat Comte's assertion that she was a prostitute (Ritzer, 1996, p. 92). Yet there is much evidence that casts doubt on this allegation.

Comte married Massin in 1825. She was the illegitimate daughter of two provincial actors. Raised by her grandmother, the wife of a tailor, she worked for a while as a seamstress or laundress. Thanks to the help of a lover, she then came to manage one of the many reading rooms that arose in Paris during the Bourbon Restoration. Although positivists, who believed she had mistreated their master, destroyed many of her letters, her remaining correspondence shows her to have been highly literate, self-confident, and witty.

Comte gave her lessons in mathematics and soon became attracted
to her partly because he was impressed by her "exceptional mind"
(Comte [1814–57], 1973–90, vol. 1, p. 152 [letter dated 1824]). He
compared her favorably to the brilliant intellectual Madame de Staël.
Even in 1843, a year after they separated, he told John Stuart Mill
that Massin possessed "more mental force, depth, and . . .
soundness than the majority of the most justly vaunted personages
of her sex" (Comte [1814–57], 1973–90, vol. 2, p. 200).

Yet their marriage was a "civil war," as Comte put it in 1842
(Comte [1814–57], 1973–90, vol. 2, p. 76). Both Comte and Massin
sought the dominant role in their relationship and proved incapable
of compromise on this issue. She was irked by his "puerile and
meticulous attention to prove and impose [on her] the power of he
who earns the money." He always wanted to show that he was
"incontestably the strongest."[2] Years later she analyzed the cause of
their problems and concluded that it had to do with her refusal to
allow Comte to be master.

> I have always been devoted to you, but I was not at all submissive. If
> there had been less real devotion and more submission, things would
> have been better between us. How many times you were basically
> right, but you asked me to yield in the name of your authority, and I
> stood up to you when I should have submitted. Really, I did not know
> how to be submissive, but even so, I did love you.[3]

She showed her love for him during their years together in constantly supporting his philosophical work and his academic career.
She tried especially to counter the effects of his paranoia and manic
depression, which caused him to experience several breakdowns. His
most dangerous attack was in April 1826, when he was admitted to
an insane asylum where he languished in a semi-vegetative state until
he was released as incurable in December. After a year, he recovered
his sanity, thanks largely to the devoted care of his wife, which he
himself acknowledged. However, although Comte was no longer
strictly insane after 1826, he never completely surmounted his illness, and he struggled to avoid intense intellectual effort and
emotional conflicts, which threatened his mental well-being.
Experiencing a particularly severe attack of madness in 1838, he
began to adhere to a regime of "cerebral hygiene," whereby he

[2]Caroline Massin to Blainville, December 20, 1839, Archives of the Maison
d'Auguste Comte (hereafter, MAC); Caroline Massin to Comte, October 25,
1842, MAC.
[3]Caroline Massin to Comte, January 17, 1850, MAC.

stopped reading anything at all to preserve his fragile ego from attacks by critics. Any kind of disagreement or controversy was unbearable to him. Because of his illness, he also could not tolerate relationships based upon equality. As he retreated more and more from the world, he made a conscious decision to have very little to do with his wife, who exasperated him. She suffered enormously, especially because every time he had an attack, he accused her of having affairs behind his back.

His contemporaries rightly pointed out that Comte was annoyingly stubborn, self-assured, and arrogant. His colleagues at the Ecole Polytechnique were so offended by his antagonistic behavior that they would not promote him to professor. In the preface to the last volume of the *Cours*, Comte decided to seek revenge by publicly lambasting the faculty. Massin tried to dissuade him but in the end gave up, saying "Go ahead, dear friend, because all that I could tell you would do nothing. I will wait unhappily, very certain that you have not known how to make yourself strong enough to be feared."[4] She was right; his preface caused his eventual dismissal from his posts of tutor and admissions examiner. His academic career was in ruins. In despair at her husband's self-preoccupation and belligerence, Massin left Comte soon after he completed the preface in the summer of 1842. He accused her of abandoning him.

Later worried that after his death she would take control of his manuscripts and obliterate his Religion of Humanity, which she disliked, Comte sought to punish her in a "Secret Addition" to his *Testament* by calling her a prostitute (Comte [1884], 1896, p. 36a). Although cited in every account of Comte's life, this allegation is highly questionable. Massin's letters reveal that she had an aversion to going out alone in public – scarcely a characteristic of a prostitute. Moreover, it is important to remember Comte's mental condition. He did not trust her close relationship with her former lover, who was kind enough to loan them over a thousand francs at the time of Comte's bout of insanity in 1826 and was only repaid in 1840. Comte also did not appreciate Massin's friendship with his disciple, Emile Littré. His extreme paranoia, coupled with his jealousy, may have led him to manipulate the familiar image of the evil woman, the prostitute, to discredit her. Her lawyer stated:

> We have to believe that he [Comte] brought against his wife an accusation that he knew was false [and] that he succeeded in believing in the existence of an imaginary fact . . . One must not doubt, then, that Auguste Comte was ill. He invented the fatal secret . . . His hatred

[4]Caroline Massin to Comte, September 20, 1841, MAC.

for his wife grew with his love for Clotilde de Vaulx [sic]; he pictured his wife capable of everything. From this to believing that she had committed everything that he imagined, there was only one step.[5]

Comte's accusation reflects the culture of the times, when women were regarded as sexless angels in the household or fatal demonic temptresses (Auerbach, 1982, p. 9). These two images were at war in Comte's imagination. Because of her independent spirit, Massin did not fit into the first category. Following the binary logic of the period, Comte placed her in the second. In discussing in 1852 the struggle between the two factions of positivists (the scientistic ones and the religious ones), he wrote that "this struggle will be carried out under two feminine banners... between the angel who will never cease to be thirty, and the demon who just commenced her 51st year" (Comte [1814–57], 1973–90, vol. 6, pp. 334–5). Because Massin did not live up to his ideal of the selfless, submissive woman, she represented the "anti-feminine type" – a "social monstrosity" (Comte [1814–57], 1973–90, vol. 6, p. 63 [letter dated 1851]; [1851–4], 1929, vol. 1, p. 227). The typical monstrous female in the mid-nineteenth-century imagination was the prostitute.

In Comte's mind, the opposite of this demon was the angel Clotilde de Vaux, who symbolized virtue and redemption. She is generally considered to have been responsible for his turn to religion. Yet in a way she simply enabled Comte to fill in the details of his image of the ideal woman. Already in the *Cours*, Comte had mentioned that the spiritual power needed women assistants to help develop social harmony by cultivating the feelings ([1830–42], 1975, vol. 2, p. 286). He was also searching for someone to love in order to experience "affectionate sentiments," for he believed that his unhappy family life had repressed his emotional development (Comte [1814–57], 1973–90, vol. 2, p. 287 [letter dated 1844]). In the *Cours*, he had asserted that "no great intellect" could develop "in a suitable manner without a certain amount of universal benevolence," which alone set honorable goals. Convinced that he was an intellectually superior being, Comte sought to demonstrate that he was a paragon of morality, a man with strong "social affections" ([1830–42], 1975, p. 181). His attachment to Vaux became part of his campaign to prove he was lovable and capable of loving others. This proof was essential in order to show that positivist moral principles could exist solely on human grounds and were even more effective than Christian precepts because they eliminated the egotistical search for salvation.

Although Comte and positivists presented a one-dimensional

---

[5]Griolet's statement, quoted in "Tribunal Civil de la Seine," *Gazette des Tribunaux*, March 2, 1870, p. 208.

image of Vaux as sweet and docile, she was actually strong and intelligent like Massin. Abandoned soon after her marriage by her profligate husband, she resembled other indigent bourgeois women in seeking to escape absolute dependence on her relatives' financial support by devoting herself to her writing, which she hoped would earn her some money. She contributed to the prestigious newspaper *Le National* and was working on a novel at the time of her death. She was pleased to meet Comte, who gave her the intellectual companionship and moral support she needed. Yet she had to remind him constantly of her desire to confine their discussions to matters pertaining to their "heads," not their hearts (Clotilde de Vaux [1845], in Comte [1814–57], 1973–90, vol. 3, p. 23). Although positivists celebrated their love for each other, Vaux kept Comte at a distance as a friend, repeatedly frustrating his sexual advances, which he continued to make even while she was dying. She insisted on her need for independence and resisted Comte's attempt to worship her as much as Massin fought against his effort to dominate her. However, her sudden death prevented her from achieving the success she desired. Unable to recover from this blow, Comte began to idolize her and refashioned her into the perfectly pure and submissive woman, the opposite of his wife. Worship of Vaux even became a component of Comte's Religion of Humanity.

Both women in Comte's life played a role in his development. Vaux, who was uninterested in philosophy and felt intimidated by positivism, did not intentionally steer Comte toward religion. Nevertheless, the fact that she did not feel comfortable with his system led him to conclude that some people, especially women and workers, whom he wished to attract as supporters, could be initiated into positivism through the heart and without any scientific preparation. She helped to confirm the direction toward religion that he was already beginning to take.

Massin, who was not as well educated as Vaux, appeared, nevertheless, more devoted to Comte's scientific doctrine. She was able to persuade Emile Littré to take a large role in eliminating the religious accretions to positivism and making the original scientific strand triumphant. She also induced him to write a biography of Comte, which highlighted his "first" career and denigrated Vaux and the Religion of Humanity. Finally, she helped establish the positivist periodical, the *Revue de la Philosophe positive.* Thus although Clotilde de Vaux is the woman most usually associated with Auguste Comte, her influence was really inadvertent. In the end, it was Massin who did the most to solidify Comte's reputation. Yet positivists neglected her role in the hope of ensuring that the new scientistic discourse of positivism remained firmly masculinist.

References

Aron, Raymond 1968: *Main Currents in Sociological Thought*, tr. Richard Howard and Helen Weaver, Vol. 1. Garden City, New York: Doubleday, Anchor Books.

Ashley, David and Orenstein, David Michael 1995: *Sociological Theory: classical statements*, 3rd edn. Boston: Allyn and Bacon.

Auerbach, Nina 1982: *Woman and the Demon: the life of a Victorian myth*. Cambridge, Mass.: Harvard University Press.

Benton, Ted 1994: Auguste Comte and positivist sociology. In Peter Halfpenny and Peter McMylor (eds), *Positivist Sociology and its Critics*, Vol. 1. Brookfield, Vermont: Edward Elgar Publishing Company, 18–45.

Brown, Richard Harvey and Lyman, Stanford (eds) 1978: *Structure, Consciousness, and History*. Cambridge: Cambridge University Press.

Collins, Randall and Makowsky, Michael 1989: *The Discovery of Society*, 4th edn. New York: Random House.

Comte, Auguste [1884], 1896: *Testament d'Auguste Comte avec les documents qui s'y rapportent: Pièces justificatives, prières quotidiennes, confessions annuelles, correspondance avec Mme de Vaux*, 2nd edn. Paris.

—— [1851–4], 1929 (reprint of first edition): *Système de politique positive ou Traité du sociologie instituant la religion de l'Humanité*, 4 vols. Paris: Au Siège de la Société positiviste.

—— [1844], 1963: *Discours sur l'esprit positif*. Paris: Union générale d'editions.

—— [1852], 1966: *Catéchisme positiviste, ou Sommaire exposition de la religion universelle en treize entretiens systématiques entre une femme et un prêtre de l'humanité*. Paris: Garnier-Flammarion.

—— [1816–35], 1970: *Ecrits de jeunesse 1816–1828: Suivis du Mémoire sur la Cosmogonie de Laplace 1835*, ed. Paulo E. de Berrêdo Carneiro and Pierre Arnaud. Paris: Ecole Pratique des Hautes Etudes.

—— [1814–57], 1973–1990: *Correspondance générale et confessions*, ed. Paulo E. de Berrêdo Carneiro, Pierre Arnaud, Paul Arbousse-Bastide, and Angèle Kremer-Marietti, 8 vols. Paris: Ecole des Hautes Etudes en Sciences Sociales.

—— [1830–42], 1975: *Cours de philosophie positive*, ed. Michel Serres, François Dagognet, Allal Sinaceur, and Jean-Paul Enthoven, 2 vols. Paris: Hermann.

—— [1844], 1985: *Traité philosophique d'astronomie populaire*. Paris: Fayard.

Dijkstra, Sandra 1992: *Flora Tristan: feminism in the age of George Sand*. London: Pluto Press.

Dilworth, Craig, 1990: Empiricism vs. realism: high points in the debate during the past 150 years. *Studies in History and Philosophy of Science*, 21, 431–62.

Durkheim, Emile 1925: Saint-Simon, fondateur du positivisme et de la sociologie: Extrait d'un cours d'histoire du socialism. *Revue philosophique*, 99, 321–41.

Fraisse, Geneviève 1993: A philosophical history of sexual difference. In Geneviève Fraisse and Michelle Perrot (eds), *Emerging Feminism from Revolution to World War*, Vol. 4 of Georges Duby and Michelle Perrot (eds), *A History of Women in the West*, Cambridge, Mass.: Harvard University Press, 48–79.

Giddens, Anthony 1995: *Politics, Sociology and Social Theory: encounters with classical and contemporary social thought.* Stanford: Stanford University Press.

Gouhier, Henri 1933–41: *La Jeunesse d'Auguste Comte et la formation du positivisme*, 3 vols. Paris: J. Vrin.

Grange, Juliette 1996: *La Philosophie d'Auguste Comte: science, politique, religion.* Paris: Presses Universitaires de France.

Haac, Oscar (ed. and tr.) 1995: *The Correspondence of John Stuart Mill and Auguste Comte.* New Brunswick, New Jersey: Transaction Publishers.

Habermas, Jürgen 1971: *Knowledge and Human Interests*, tr. Jeremy J. Shapiro. Boston: Beacon Press.

Harp, Gillis J. 1995: *Positivist Republic: Auguste Comte and the reconstruction of American liberalism, 1865–1920.* University Park, Pa: Penn State University Press.

Hayek, F. A. 1952: *The Counter-Revolution of Science: studies on the abuse of reason.* Glencoe, Ill.: The Free Press.

Hayward, Jack 1991: *After the French Revolution: six critics of democracy and nationalism.* New York: New York University Press.

Heilbron, Johan 1990: Auguste Comte and modern epistemology. *Sociological Theory*, 8, 153–62.

Holmes, Stephen 1984: *Benjamin Constant and the Making of Modern Liberalism.* New Haven: Yale University Press.

Horowitz, Irving Louis 1968: *Professing Sociology: studies in the life cycle of social science.* Chicago: Aldine Publishing Company.

—— 1993: *The Decomposition of Sociology.* Oxford: Oxford University Press.

Hunt, Lynn 1984: *Politics, Culture, and Class in the French Revolution.* Berkeley: University of California Press.

Kofman, Sarah 1978: *Aberrations: Le Devenir-Femme d'Auguste Comte.* Paris: Aubier Flammarion.

Laffitte, Pierre 1895: Opuscule fondamental d'Auguste Comte, publié en Mai, 1822. *Revue Occidentale*, 2nd ser., 10, 1–10.

Laudan, Larry 1971: Towards a reassessment of Comte's "Méthode positive." *Philosophy of Science*, 38, 35–53.

Le Doeuff, Michèle 1987: Women and philosophy. In Toril Moi (ed.), *French Feminist Thought: a reader.* London: Basil Blackwell, 181–209.

Lenzer, Gertrud (ed.) 1975: *Auguste Comte and Positivism: the essential writings.* New York: Harper & Row, Harper Torchbooks.

Manuel, Frank E. 1962: *The Prophets of Paris.* Cambridge, Mass: Harvard University Press.

Marcuse, Herbert 1960: *Reason and Revolution: Hegel and the rise of social theory.* Boston: Beacon Press.

Martindale, Don 1981: *The Nature and Types of Sociological Theory*, 2nd edn. Boston: Houghton Mifflin.

Mill, John Stuart [1865], 1961: *Auguste Comte and Positivism.* Ann Arbor: The University of Michigan Press, Ann Arbor Paperbacks.

Morris, William (ed.) 1981: *The American Heritage Dictionary of the English Language.* Boston: Houghton Mifflin.

Muglioni, Jacques 1995: *Auguste Comte: Un Philosophe pour Notre Temps.* Paris: Kimé.

Münch, Richard 1994: *Sociological Theory*, Vol. 1. Chicago: Nelson-Hall.

Pickering, Mary 1989: New evidence of the link between Comte and German philosophy. *Journal of the History of Ideas*, 50, 443–63.

—— 1993a: *Auguste Comte: an intellectual biography*. Cambridge: Cambridge University Press.

—— 1993b: Comte and the Saint-Simonians. *French Historical Studies*, 18, 211–36.

—— 1996: Angels and demons in the moral vision of Auguste Comte. *Journal of Women's History*, 8, 10–40.

Pilbeam, Pamela M. 1995: *Republicanism in Nineteenth-Century France, 1814– 1871*. New York: St Martin's Press.

Religion Saint-Simonienne. Receuil de prédications 1832, 2 vols. Paris.

Ritzer, George 1996: *Classical Sociological Theory*. New York: McGraw-Hill.

Rorty, Richard 1984: The historiography of philosophy: four genres. In Richard Rorty, J. B. Schneewind, and Quentin Skinner (eds), *Philosophy in History: essays on the historiography of philosophy*, New York: Cambridge University Press, 49–75.

Sa'adah, Anne 1990: *The Shaping of Liberal Politics in Revolutionary France: a comparative perspective*. Princeton: Princeton University Press.

Saint-Simon, Claude-Henri de [1802–25], 1966: *Oeuvres de Claude-Henri de Saint-Simon*, 6 vols. Paris: Anthropos.

—— [1802–25], 1975: *Henri Saint-Simon (1760–1825) : selected writings on science, industry and social organization*, ed. and tr. Keith Taylor. London: Croom Helm.

Scharff, Robert C. 1995: *Comte after Positivism*. Cambridge: Cambridge University Press.

Sernin, André, 1993: *Auguste Comte: Prophète du XIXe siècle*. Paris: Albatros.

Skarga, Barbara 1974: Le Coeur et la raison ou les antinomies du système de Comte. *Les Etudes philosophiques*, no. 3, 383–90.

Swingewood, Alan 1991: *A Short History of Sociological Thought*, 2nd edn. New York: St Martin's Press.

"Tribunal Civil de la Seine." *Gazette des Tribunaux*, March 2, 1870, p. 208.

Turner, Jonathan, Beeghley, Leonard, and Powers, Charles H. 1995: *The Emergence of Sociological Theory*, 3rd edn. New York: Wadsworth Publishing Company.

Zeitlin, Irving M. 1990: *Ideology and the Development of Sociological Theory*, 4th edn. Englewood Cliffs, New Jersey: Prentice Hall.

2

Rethinking Marx
(in a Post-Marxist World)

Moishe Postone

I

Sociology arose as the theory of modern, capitalist society and has been the one discipline in the social sciences that retains its relation to the problem of society as a whole.[1] It does so, one could add, to the degree it maintains an ongoing dialogue with and appropriation of classic social theories.

If social theory's task is to elucidate the basic nature of our society and the character of its historical development, classic social theory can be characterized as theory that still has something to say to us (Habermas, [1981], 1984, p. xl) – theory sufficiently rich and complex that rereading and reworking it can help illuminate the general features of our social universe. Such theory, which becomes particularly important during periods of fundamental structural change, is central to our ongoing attempts to formulate an adequate understanding of our world; it should not be relegated to the prehistory of sociology. Although the question of the possible relevance of such theory for contemporary issues can certainly be posed, it must be posed on an analytic level different from that of much current research agendas, for classic theory interrogates the basic social framework that the latter tend to presuppose.

I would like to thank Nicole Jarnagin Deqtvaal for her invaluable critical feedback.
[1]This formulation is Jürgen Habermas's. See Habermas, [1981], 1984, p. 5.

Such a fundamental interrogation of our social and historical context is especially important today. The epochal transformations of advanced industrialized societies and of the global order in the past two decades have significantly changed the nature of our world. This period has been characterized by the rollback of welfare states in the capitalist West and the collapse or fundamental metamorphosis of bureaucratic party-states in the communist East – more generally, by the weakening of national states as economically sovereign entities – and the apparently triumphant reemergence of unregulated market capitalism. It has also seen changes in the structure of social labor domestically and internationally, the decline of classical labor movements, the rise of new social movements, the resurgence of democratic as well as nationalist movements, and the growing importance of global means of communications and international financial networks.

Because these changes have included the dramatic collapse and final dissolution of the Soviet Union and of European communism, they have been interpreted as marking the historical end of Marxism and, more generally, of the theoretical relevance of Marx's social theory. Nevertheless, precisely because recent historical trans-formations have reasserted the central importance for social theory of the problematics of historical dynamics and large-scale structural changes, a renewed encounter with Marx's critical theory of modernity could, in my view, contribute importantly to the process of coming to terms theoretically with our social universe. This is not only because, as Daniel Bell has pointed out, any serious consideration of social transformation must come to terms with Marx's powerful theory of historical development (Bell, 1973, pp. 55–6), but also because the past two decades can be viewed as marking the end of a period of the state-centered organization of social and economic life whose beginnings can be located in World War I and the Russian Revolution – a period characterized by the effective primacy of the political over the economic – and the manifest reemergence of the social centrality of quasi-automatic economic processes. That is, recent historical transformations suggest the importance of a renewed theoretical concern with capitalism.

They also, however, suggest that if a critical theory of capitalism is to be adequate to the contemporary world, it must differ in important and basic ways from traditional Marxist critiques of capitalism. And I would argue that Marx's mature social theory provides the point of departure for precisely such a reconceptualized critical theory of capitalism. I shall outline aspects of a reinterpretation of Marx's mature social theory that reconceptualizes his analysis of the basic nature of capitalism – its social relations, forms of domination, and historical dynamic – in ways that break fundamentally with traditional Marxist approaches. This reinterpretation could help illuminate the essential structuring elements and overarching historical dynamic of contemporary advanced industrial society while providing a basic critique of traditional Marxism and recasting the relation of Marxian theory to other major currents of social theory.

II

The interpretation I shall outline grows out of recent scholarship on Marx, but also tries to shift fundamentally the terms with which capitalism is conceptualized. Following a thirty-year period in which readings of Marx and Marxian theory were regimented by Stalinist orthodoxy, on the one hand, and reductionistically understood and rejected as "communist ideology" in western capitalist countries, on the other, the process of de-Stalinization, the ebbing of the first wave of the Cold War, and the reemergence of radical movements in the 1960s led to renewed interest in Marx's works – especially in manuscripts that were unknown to classical Marxism – such as the *Economic and Philosophic Manuscripts of 1844* and the *Grundrisse* (Bottomore, 1983, pp. 103–41). This helped generate a great deal of new scholarship on Marx and promoted the theoretical appropriation of western Marxist thinkers – many of whom had been marginalized in both East and West – such as Georg Lukács, Karl Korsch, Antonio Gramsci, Max Horkheimer, and Theodor Adorno.[2] At the same time, major new works were being written by theorists such as Jean-Paul Sartre, Henri Lefebvre, Louis Althusser, Adorno, Herbert Marcuse, Jürgen Habermas, and Alfred Schmidt.[3]

This intense revival of Marxian theory and scholarship took a variety of theoretical paths, some overlapping, others strongly divergent – including "humanistic" readings of Marx that focused on his theory of alienation and emphasized human practice and

[2]See Lukács, [1923], 1971; Korsch, [1923], 1971; Gramsci, [1929–35], 1972; Adorno and Horkheimer, [1944], 1972.
[3]See, for example, Sartre, [1960–85], 1982–91; Lefebvre, [1939], 1968; Althusser, [1965], 1970; Althusser and Balibar, [1968], 1970; Adorno, [1966], 1973; Marcuse, 1964a; Habermas, [1963], 1973a; Habermas, [1968], 1971; Schmidt, [1962], 1971.

subjectivity,[4] works emphasizing the Hegelian dimensions of Marx's thought,[5] the Frankfurt School's explorations of the historical relation of psyche and society and the transformations of culture in twentieth-century capitalism,[6] and structuralism's critique of the concept of the subject.[7] (For many commentators, such as Tom Bottomore and Alvin Gouldner, the revival and further development of Marxian thought in the 1960s and 1970s can best be described in terms of an underlying opposition between Critical Theory and structuralist Marxism.[8])

Yet, in spite of this efflorescence of Marxian theory, the understanding of Marx that continued to predominate in American sociology did not, for the most part, fully appropriate this new work and its implications and, instead, tended to assimilate concepts discussed in that work (such as "alienation") to older interpretive frameworks.[9]

[4]See, for example, Mészáros, 1970; Ollman, 1976.
[5]See, for example, Hyppolite, [1965], 1969; Avineri, 1968.
[6]See, for example, Marcuse, 1955; Adorno and Horkheimer, [1944], 1972.
[7]See Althusser, [1965], 1970.
[8]Their treatments of the opposition between these two theoretical approaches, however, are not fully adequate. Bottomore's characterization of it as one between Critical Theory's emphasis on cultural forms of domination and structuralism's attempt to establish the scientificity of Marx neither does justice to Critical Theory's notion of totality nor to Althusser's emphasis on ideology (Bottomore, 1983, pp. 126-9). On the other hand, Gouldner describes the opposition as one between objectivistic and subjectivistic approaches, identifies the Hegelian–Marxist tradition with the latter, and roots the opposition in an internal tension in Marx's work (Gouldner, 1980). This, however, overlooks that the members of the Frankfurt School attempted to theoretically overcome the dichotomy between objectivism and subjectivism. They did so on the basis of a position similar to that expressed by Shlomo Avineri who strongly rejects the dichotomy Gouldner, among others, makes between a young "humanistic" and "idealist" Marx and an older "determinist" and "materialist" Marx, and points out that, for Marx, objective circumstances themselves are an outcome of human agency (Avineri, 1968, pp. 63-4).
[9]See, for example, Collins, 1994. It is telling that, whereas theorists like Lukács and Avineri distinguish between Marx and Engels in order to highlight the differences between Marx's sophisticated analysis of capitalism and orthodox mainstream Marxism, Collins proceeds from the same distinction in order to affirm Engels's more "orthodox" positions (as contributing productively to the so-called conflict tradition), and dismisses the *Grundrisse* and *Capital* as works of technical economics rooted in Hegelian "mystification" (Collins, 1994, p. 118, n.1). For an approach that does seek to appropriate more current work on Marx see Alexander, 1982, pp. 11-74, 163-210, 328-70.

Moreover, although several important attempts have been undertaken in the recent past to rethink Marx's social theory in fundamental ways,[10] much of the new discourse on Marx, in spite of its remarkable sophistication, ultimately also has remained bound within the limits of traditional Marxism's understanding of capitalism. These limits have weakened and undermined the theoretical power of the recent turn to Marx.

By "traditional Marxism" I do not mean a specific historical tendency in Marxism, such as orthodox Second International Marxism, for example, but, more generally, all analyses that understand capitalism – its basic social relations – essentially in terms of class relations structured by a market economy and private ownership and control of the means of production, and grasps its relations of domination primarily in terms of class domination and exploitation. Within this general interpretive framework, capitalism is characterized by a historical dynamic (driven by class conflict, capitalist competition, or technological development)[11] which gives rise to a growing structural contradiction between that society's basic social relations (interpreted as private property and the market) and the forces of production (interpreted as the industrial mode of producing).[12] When capitalism's contradiction is grasped in such

[10]See, for example, Harvey, 1982; Murray, 1988; Sayer, 1979; Sayer, 1987.

[11]G.A. Cohen, whose approach remains very much within the bounds of traditional Marxism, has cogently argued that, although class struggles and exploitation are important aspects of historical change, they themselves cannot explain an ongoing trajectory of historical development. Cohen's conception of an intrinsic historical dynamic, however, is transhistorical (whereas, as I shall argue, such a dynamic must be understood as a historically specific aspect of capitalism itself). He is unable to ground that dynamic in historically specific and, therefore, social terms and, instead, conceptualizes history in terms of the evolutionary development of technology (Cohen, 1986a, pp. 12–22). The problem with most criticisms of such technological determinism, however, is that they usually seek to recover the theoretical possibility of social action with reference to class struggles or within the framework of methodological individualism, neither of which can explain what Cohen was seeking to elucidate, namely, a directional historical dynamic. (See, for example, Jon Elster's criticism of Cohen in Elster, 1986, pp. 202–20.) I shall argue that the historically specific dynamic of capitalism can be explained with reference to the peculiar forms of social mediation expressed by categories such as "commodity" and "capital" which cannot be reduced to class terms.

[12]This understanding of the forces and relations of production is central to the traditional reading of Marx's analysis of capitalism. It is one that is shared by theorists as disparate as Richard Flacks, Anthony Giddens, Ernest Mandel, and Neil Smelser. See Flacks, 1982, pp. 9–52; Giddens, 1995, pp. xii–xv; Mandel, 1978, pp. 14–15; Smelser, 1973, pp. vii–xxxviii.

terms, its possible historical overcoming is understood – implicitly or explicitly – in terms of collective ownership of the means of production and economic planning in an industrialized context – that is, in terms of a just and consciously regulated mode of distribution that is adequate to industrial production. The latter, in turn, is not the object of critical analysis; it is viewed as a technical process, which is used by capitalists for their particularistic ends, but is intrinsically independent of capitalism and could be used for the benefit of all members of society.[13]

This structural contradiction of capitalism is expressed, on another level, as a class opposition between the capitalist class, which owns and controls production, and the proletariat, which creates the wealth of society with its labor.[14] This opposition is one between particular and universal interests, and is historical: whereas the capitalist class is the dominant class of the present order, the working class is rooted in industrial production and, hence, in the historical foundations of a new, socialist order.

This understanding is tied to a determinate reading of the basic categories of Marx's critique of political economy. His category of value, for example, has generally been interpreted as an attempt to show that social wealth is always and everywhere created by human labor and that, in capitalism, labor underlies the quasi-automatic, market-mediated mode of distribution. His theory of surplus-value,

[13]Harry Braverman broke decisively with positions affirming the process of production when he analyzed the labor process itself as structured by capitalism. Such an analysis implies that the traditional understanding of capitalism must be rethought, but Braverman did not pursue those implications further. See Braverman, 1974. I shall try to show that a very different reading of the nature of capitalism could provide the theoretical basis for Braverman's analysis of the labor process.

[14]It is the case that some analysts, such as Herb Gintis, have broadened the focus of the traditional critique of capitalism by emphasizing control over the producers rather than private property in describing capitalism (which would allow for a critique of what had been termed "actually existing socialist" societies). However, this approach is ultimately a variation of the traditional analysis. Its focus is on unequal distribution (of wealth and power) but not on the organization of labor and nature of production, and the ways they are structured and restructured (i.e. "controlled") by the historical dynamic of capitalism. A similar point could be made with regard to the attempts by Richard Wolff and Stephen Resnick to focus on the issue of the appropriation of surplus labor in order to analyze the Soviet Union as a state-capitalist state structure. See Gintis, 1982, pp. 58–60; Resnick and Wolff, 1995, pp. 323–33.

according to such views, seeks to demonstrate the existence of exploitation by showing that the surplus product is created by labor alone and, in capitalism, is appropriated by the capitalist class. Within this general framework, then, Marx's labor theory of value is first and foremost a theory of prices and profits; his categories are categories of the market and class exploitation.[15]

At the heart of this theory is a transhistorical – and common-sensical – understanding of labor as an activity mediating humans and nature that transforms matter in a goal-directed manner and is a condition of social life. Labor, so understood, is posited as the source of wealth in all societies and as that which underlies processes of social constitution; it constitutes what is universal and truly social (Mészáros, 1970, pp. 79–90; Avineri, 1968, pp. 76–7). In capitalism, however, labor is hindered by particularistic and fragmenting relations from becoming fully realized. Emancipation, then, is realized in a social form where transhistorical "labor," freed from the fetters of the market and private property, has openly emerged as the regulating principle of society. (This notion, of course, is bound to that of socialist revolution as the "self-realization" of the proletariat.)

Within the basic framework of what I have termed "traditional Marxism," there has been a broad range of very different theoretical, methodological, and political approaches. Nevertheless, to the extent they all rest on the basic assumptions regarding labor and the essential characteristics of capitalism and of socialism outlined above, they remain bound within the framework of traditional Marxism. This has also been the case with both dominant strands of recent Marx interpretations – structuralism and Critical Theory. Althusser, for example, formulated an epistemologically sophisticated and trenchant critique of the "idealism of labor" – the traditional notion that labor is the source of all wealth – and the related conception of people as subjects. Instead he introduced the notion of social relations as structures that are irreducible to anthropological intersubjectivity. Nevertheless, his focus on the question of the surplus in terms of exploitation, as well as on the physical "material" dimension of production, is related to what

[15]See, for example, Dobb, 1940, pp. 70–1; Cohen, 1988, pp. 209–38; Elster, 1985, p. 127; Gintis, 1982; Roemer, 1981, pp. 158–9; Steedman, 1981, pp. 11–19; Meek, 1956; Sweezy, 1968, pp. 52–3. Elster, Gintis, Roemer, and Steedman are critical of Marx's value theory because, they claim, equilibrium prices and profits can be explained without reference to such a theory. I will argue that the object of Marx's analysis was different from that assumed by such interpretations.

ultimately is a traditional understanding of capitalism (Althusser and Balibar, [1968], 1970, pp. 145–54, 165–82).

And although various economic, political, social, historical, and cultural analyses which have been generated within the traditional framework have been very powerful and insightful, the limitations of the framework itself have long been discernible in the face of historical developments such as the rise of state-interventionist capitalism and "actually existing socialism." They have become increasingly evident with the growing importance of scientific knowledge and advanced technology in the process of production, growing criticisms of technological progress and growth, and the increased importance of non-class-based social identities. Indeed classic social theorists such as Weber and Durkheim had already argued at the turn of the century that a critical theory of capitalism – understood in terms of property relations – is too narrow to grasp fundamental features of modern society.

It is against this historical background that one can best understand the trajectory of the other major recent strand of Marxian analysis, Critical Theory. Although that cluster of approaches has frequently been interpreted as being concerned with the so-called "superstructure" (state and culture) in order to explain why workers had not made the revolution (Wiley, 1987, pp. 8–11), I shall briefly consider that theoretical strand in other terms – as an attempt to reconceptualize a critical theory of capitalism adequate to the twentieth century that sought to get beyond traditional Marxism's limitations, but retained some of its basic pre-suppositions.

Responding to large-scale historical changes in the twentieth century as well as to critiques like those of Weber and Durkheim, a number of theorists within the broader Marxist tradition – notably Georg Lukács as well as members of the Frankfurt School of critical theory – attempted to develop a critical social theory that would overcome the limitations of the traditional paradigm and be more adequate to those historical developments. These theorists proceeded on the basis of a sophisticated understanding of Marx's theory, which they did not take to be one of production and class structure alone, much less an economics. Instead they treated it as a critical analysis of the cultural forms as well as the social structures of capitalist society, one that also sought to grasp the relationship of theory to society in a self-reflexive manner. That is, they viewed that theory as one that attempts to analyze its own social context – capitalist society – in a way that reflexively accounts for the possibility of its own standpoint. (This reflexive attempt to ground socially the possibility of theoretical critique is, at the same time, an attempt to ground the possibility of oppositional and transformative social action.)

On the basis of their complex understandings of Marx's theory, these thinkers sought to respond to the historical transformation of capitalism from a market-centered form to a bureaucratic, state-centered form by reconceptualizing capitalism. Yet, as a result of some of their theoretical assumptions, Lukács as well as members of the Frankfurt School were not able to fully realize their theoretical aims of developing an analysis of capitalism adequate to the twentieth century. On the one hand, they recognized the inadequacies of a critical theory of modernity that defined capitalism solely in nineteenth-century terms – that is, in terms of the market and private ownership of the means of production. On the other hand, they remained bound to some of the assumptions of that very sort of theory.

This can be seen clearly in the case of Lukács's *History and Class Consciousness*, written in the early 1920s, in which he sought to reconceptualize capitalism by synthesizing Marx and Weber (Lukács, [1923], 1971, pp. 83–222). He adopted Weber's characterization of modern society in terms of a historical process of rationalization, and attempted to embed that analysis within the framework of Marx's analysis of the commodity form as the basic structuring principle of capitalist society. By grounding the process of rationalization in this manner, Lukács sought to show that what Weber described as the "iron cage" of modern life is not a necessary concomitant of any form of modern society, but a function of capitalism – and, hence, could be transformed. At the same time, the conception of capitalism implied by his analysis is much broader than that of a system of exploitation based on private property and the market; it implies that the latter are not ultimately the central features of capitalism.

Yet Lukács's attempt to conceptualize post-liberal capitalism was deeply inconsistent. When he addressed the question of the possible overcoming of capitalism, he had recourse to the notion of the proletariat as the revolutionary Subject of history. This idea, however, only makes sense if capitalism is defined essentially in terms of private ownership of the means of production, and if labor is considered to be the standpoint of the critique. Although, then, Lukács recognized that capitalism could not be defined in traditional terms if its critique were to remain adequate as a critique of modernity, he undermined his own historical insight by continuing to regard the standpoint of the critique in precisely those traditional terms, that is, in terms of the proletariat and, relatedly, a social totality constituted by labor.

The approaches developed by members of the Frankfurt School can also be understood in terms of a tension between the recognition that traditional Marxism is inadequate as a theory of twentieth-century capitalism, and the retention of some of its basic presuppositions regarding labor. For example, in the face of historical developments such as the triumph of National Socialism, the victory of Stalinism, and the general increase of state control in the West, Max Horkheimer came to the conclusion in the 1930s that what earlier had characterized capitalism – the market and private property – no longer were its essential organizing principles (Horkheimer, [1940], 1978, pp. 95–117). Yet he did not, on the basis of this insight, proceed to reconceptualize the social relations that fundamentally characterize capitalism. Instead, retaining the traditional conception of those relations and of the contradiction of capitalism (as one between labor, on the one hand, and the market and private property, on the other), Horkheimer argued that the structural contradiction of capitalism had been overcome; society was now directly constituted by labor. Far from signifying emancipation, however, this development had led to an even greater degree of unfreedom in the form of a new technocratic form of domination.

This, however, indicated, according to Horkheimer, that labor (which he continued to conceptualize in traditional, transhistorical terms) could not be considered the basis of emancipation but, rather, should be grasped as the source of technocratic domination. Capitalist society, in his analysis, no longer possessed a structural contradiction; it had become one-dimensional – a society governed by instrumental rationality without any possibility of fundamental critique and transformation.

Because Horkheimer retained some of traditional Marxism's basic presuppositions, such as its understanding of labor and of capitalism's basic contradiction, his attempt to overcome its limits was problematic. Not having elaborated an alternative conception of capitalism's basic social relations, he could not really justify his continued characterization of modern society as capitalist, given his claim that the market and private property had been effectively abolished. Moreover, the thesis of the one-dimensional character of post-liberal capitalism posed additional theoretical problems. The notion of social contradiction had been central to the idea of a self-reflexive critique. It allowed the theory to ground itself in its context and yet take critical distance from that context.

Having claimed that capitalism's contradiction had been overcome, Horkheimer's analysis could no longer give an account of its own standpoint and, hence, lost its reflexive character (Postone, 1993, pp. 84–120).

The best-known recent attempt to get beyond the problems encountered by Lukács and the Frankfurt School in grappling with post-liberal capitalism is that of Jürgen Habermas (Habermas, [1968], 1970, [1968], 1971, [1981], 1984, [1981], 1987). Responding to the dilemmas entailed by Horkheimer's analysis, Habermas has attempted to reformulate the basis of Critical Theory, arguing that modern society is not constituted by labor alone, but by communicative action as well, that each of these constituting principles has its own independent logic, and that it is the social sphere constituted by communicative action that allows for the possibility of social critique.

Habermas's approach succeeds in recovering Critical Theory's reflexive dimension, but it does so in a manner that is based on the same traditional understanding of labor and, as a result, gives rise to a new set of theoretical difficulties. Although I cannot elaborate here, let me simply state that Habermas's analysis of modern economic, social, and cultural forms is fundamentally underspecified, and lacks a great deal of the power of earlier Frankfurt School approaches to grasp twentieth-century culture and society. Moreover, (and this is crucial for our considerations) Habermas's approach no longer adequately grounds and delineates the historical dynamic of capitalist society – one of the central objects of Marx's analysis. Instead, Habermas develops a transhistorical evolutionary theory of human development (Postone, 1990, pp. 170–6).

The issue of the historical dynamic of capitalist society and large-scale structural change has also posed problems for other recent attempts to formulate an overarching social theory of twentieth-century society. For example, whereas members of the Frankfurt School responded to the transformations of the first half of the twentieth century by attempting to formulate a theory of post-liberal capitalism, Daniel Bell extended the arguments of Weber, Durkheim, and, later, Raymond Aron, in the early 1970s, arguing that the concept of "capitalism" (which Bell understood in traditional Marxist terms) no longer grasped important aspects of modern society. He claimed that the historical experience of the twentieth century had shown that "capitalism" and "socialism" do not refer to fundamentally different forms of social life and, hence, to different historical epochs, but to different forms of organization of the same underlying mode of social life, namely, industrial society (which, according to Bell, was in the process of developing in the direction of a "post-industrial" society) (Bell, 1973).

However well taken Bell's critique of a theory of modernity centered on the market and private property may be, his own approach also is problematic. It is bound implicitly to a conception of historical development as technologically driven, and does not provide a social explanation for the historically dynamic character of modern society. Bell's conception of historical development is essentially linear and presupposes effective state control of the economy. It, therefore, cannot address the non-linear character of important recent social and economic developments in advanced industrialized countries – such as the decline of the interventionist state's power to control the economy, the tendency for increasing income differentiation, the stagnation in real income for large portions of the working population and/or the growth in structural unemployment.

These developments call into question important aspects of Bell's theory of post-industrial society. More generally, they have rendered anachronistic the idea, widespread in the postwar era, that the rise of the interventionist state had signified the end of any quasi-autonomous dynamic of capitalist society.

The overt reemergence of such a dynamic suggests the continued need for a theory of capitalism. Nevertheless, such a theory must be able to respond to the insights of the Frankfurt School theorists, as well as Aron and Bell, that the market and private ownership cannot be regarded as the centrally defining features of modern society. Such a theory, in other words, must be based on a conception of capitalism that does not grasp that society's most fundamental social relations in terms of class relations structured by private ownership of the means of production and the market.

I would like to outline a reinterpretation of Marx's mature works – especially *Capital* – that provides the basis for such a reconceptualized theory of capitalism (Postone, 1993). I chose Marx's mature theory as my point of departure because, in my view, it provides the best foundation for a rigorous analysis of the dynamic processes that underlie the overarching historical development of the modern world. At the same time, my intention was to develop analytic categories expressing an understanding of the basic structuring principles of capitalist society essentially different from that of traditional Marxism, while also overcoming the familiar theoretical dichotomies of structure and action, meaning and material life. I tried to show that these categories could serve as the foundation for a rigorous and self-reflexive critical theory of capitalism as a theory of modernity, encompassing both contemporary advanced western industrial societies as well as what had been called "actually existing socialism." Such a theory could prove to be a fruitful point of departure for an analysis of the large-scale transformations of the past two decades.

III

Let me begin by describing a major shift that occurred in Marx's thought in the course of writing the *Grundrisse* (Marx, [1857–8], 1973), a preparatory manuscript for *Capital*. Marx began the *Grundrisse* with a consideration of transhistorical, indeterminate categories such as "production" and "consumption" (Marx, [1857–8], 1973, pp. 83ff). However, he was not satisfied with this point of departure. Towards the very end of the manuscript, Marx proposed a new beginning, which he then retained for his subsequent texts.[16] That new beginning was the category of the commodity.[17] In his later works, Marx's analysis is not of commodities as they may exist in many societies, nor is it of a hypothetical pre-capitalist stage of "simple commodity production." Rather, his analysis is of the commodity as it exists in capitalist society. Marx now analyzed the commodity not merely as an object, but as the historically specific, most fundamental form of social relations that characterize that society (Marx, [1863–6], 1976d, pp. 949–51).

This move from a transhistorical to a historically specific point of departure indicated a significant shift in Marx's thinking. It implied that the categories of the theory are historically specific. Moreover, given Marx's assumption that thought is socially embedded, his turn to a notion of the historical specificity of the categories of capitalist society, that is, of his own historical context, implicitly entailed a turn to a notion of the historical specificity of his own theory.

This implied the necessity for a different sort of social critique. Its standpoint could not be located transhistorically or transcendentally, but had to be located as an immanent dimension of the social object of the investigation. No theory – including that of Marx – has, within this conceptual framework, absolute, transhistorical validity. An important task of the theory now was reflexive: it had to render plausible its own standpoint by means

---

[16]Martin Nicolaus drew attention to this shift. See Nicolaus, 1973, pp. 35–7.
[17]Marx, [1857–8], 1973, p. 881; Marx, [1859], 1970, p. 27; Marx, [1867], 1976a, p. 125.

of the same categories with which it analyzed its historical context.

A second major implication of Marx's turn to the historical specificity of his categories was that transhistorical notions, such as that of a dialectical logic underlying human history, now became historically relativized. In disputing their transhistorical validity, however, Marx did not claim that such notions were never valid. Instead, he restricted their validity to the capitalist social formation, while showing how that which is historically specific to capitalism could be taken to be transhistorical. On this basis, Marx proceeded to critically analyze theories that project onto history or society in general categories that, according to him, are valid only for the capitalist epoch. This critique also holds implicitly for Marx's own earlier writings with their transhistorical projections, such as the notion that class struggle has been at the heart of all of history, for example, or the notion of an intrinsic logic to all of history or, of course, the notion that labor is the major constituting element of social life.

If, however, many of Marx's earlier notions regarding history, society, and labor had been projections, and actually were valid only for capitalist society, he now had to uncover the grounds for their validity in the specific characteristics of that society. Marx sought to do so by locating what he regarded as the most fundamental form of social relations that characterizes capitalist society and, on that basis, carefully constructing a series of integrated categories with which he sought to explain the underlying workings of that society. That fundamental form, as I already have mentioned, is the commodity. Marx took the term "commodity" and used it to designate a historically specific form of social relations, one constituted as a structured form of social practice that, at the same time, is a structuring principle of the actions, world views, and dispositions of people. As a category of practice, it is a form both of social subjectivity and objectivity. In some respects, it occupies a similar place in Marx's analysis of modernity that kinship might in an anthropologist's analysis of another form of society.

What characterizes the commodity form of social relations, as analyzed by Marx, is that it is constituted by labor, it exists in objectified form, and it has a dualistic character.

In order to elucidate this description, Marx's conception of the historical specificity of labor in capitalism must be clarified. According to his analysis of the commodity, labor does indeed constitute the fundamental social relations of capitalism. Yet, being historically specific, that constituting function cannot be understood to be an attribute of labor per se, as it exists in all societies. Indeed, one of Marx's major criticisms of Ricardo was that he had not grasped the historical specificity of value and of the labor that constitutes it (Marx, [1861–3], 1968, p. 164; [1859], 1970, p. 60).

What, then, is the historical specificity of labor in capitalism? Marx maintains that labor in capitalism has a "double character:" it is both "concrete labor" and "abstract labor" (Marx, [1867], 1976a, pp. 131–9). "Concrete labor" refers to the fact that some form of what we consider laboring activity mediates the interactions of humans with nature in all societies. "Abstract labor," I argue, signifies that, in capitalism, labor also has a unique social function: it mediates a new form of social interdependence.

Let me elaborate: In a society in which the commodity is the basic structuring category of the whole, labor and its products are not socially distributed by traditional ties, norms, or overt relations of power and domination – that is, by manifest social relations – as is the case in other societies. Instead, labor itself replaces those relations by serving as a kind of quasi-objective means by which the products of others are acquired. That is to say, a new form of interdependence comes into being where no one consumes what they produce, but where, nevertheless, one's own labor or labor-products function as the necessary means of obtaining the products of others. In serving as such a means, labor and its products in effect preempt that function on the part of manifest social relations. Instead of being defined, distributed, and accorded significance by manifest social relations, as is the case in other societies, labor in capitalism is defined, distributed, and accorded significance by structures (commodity, capital) that are constituted by labor itself. That is, labor in capitalism constitutes a form of social relations which has an impersonal, apparently non-social, quasi-objective character and which embeds, transforms, and, to some degree, undermines and supersedes traditional social ties and relations of power.

In Marx's mature works, then, the notion of the centrality of labor to social life is not a transhistorical proposition. It does not refer to the fact that material production is always a precondition of social life. Nor should it be taken as meaning that material production is the most essential dimension of social life in general, or even of capitalism in particular. Rather, it refers to the historically specific constitution by labor in capitalism of the social relations that fundamentally characterize that society. In other words, Marx analyzes labor in capitalism as constituting a historically determinate form of social mediation which is the ultimate social ground of the basic features of modernity – in particular, its overarching historical dynamic. Rather than positing the social primacy of material production, Marx's mature theory seeks to show the primacy in capitalism of a form of social mediation (constituted by "abstract labor") that molds both the process of material production ("concrete labor") and consumption.

Labor in capitalism, then, is not only labor as we transhistorically and commonsensically understand it, according to Marx, but is a historically specific socially mediating activity. Hence its products – commodity, capital – are both concrete labor products and objectified forms of social mediation. According to this analysis, the social relations that most basically characterize capitalist society are very different from the qualitatively specific, overt social relations – such as kinship relations or relations of personal or direct domination – which characterize non-capitalist societies. Although the latter kind of social relations continue to exist in capitalism, what ultimately structures that society is a new, underlying level of social relations that is constituted by labor. Those relations have a peculiar quasi-objective, formal character and are dualistic – they are characterized by the opposition of an abstract, general, homogeneous dimension and a concrete, particular, material dimension, both of which appear to be "natural," rather than social, and condition social conceptions of natural reality.

The abstract character of the social mediation underlying capitalism is also expressed in the form of wealth dominant in that society. As we have seen, Marx's "labor theory of value" frequently has been misunderstood as a labor theory of wealth, that is, as a theory that seeks to explain the workings of the market and prove the existence of exploitation by arguing that labor, at all times and in all places, is the only social source of wealth. Marx's analysis, however, is not one of wealth in general, any more than it is one of labor in general. He analyzed value as a historically specific form of wealth which is bound to the historically unique role of labor in capitalism; as a form of wealth, it is also a form of social mediation. Marx explicitly distinguished value from material wealth and related these two distinct forms of wealth to the duality of labor in capitalism. Material wealth is measured by the quantity of products produced and is a function of a number of factors such as knowledge, social organization, and natural conditions, in addition to labor. Value is constituted by human labor-time expenditure alone, according to Marx, and is the dominant form of wealth in capitalism (Marx, [1867], 1976a, pp. 136–7; [1857–8], 1973, pp. 704–5). Whereas material wealth, when it is the dominant form of wealth, is mediated by overt social relations, value is a self-mediating form of wealth.

Far from arguing that value is a transhistorical form of wealth, Marx sought to explain central features of capitalism by arguing that it is uniquely based on value. His categories are intended to grasp a historically specific form of social domination and a unique immanent dynamic – not simply to ground equilibrium prices and demonstrate the structural centrality of exploitation.[18] According to Marx's analysis, the ultimate goal of production in capitalism is not the goods produced but value, or, more precisely, surplus value. As a form of wealth, however, value – the objectification of labor functioning as a quasi-objective means of acquiring goods it has not produced – is independent of the physical characteristics of the commodities in which it is embodied. Hence, it is a purely quantitative form of wealth. Within this framework, production in capitalism necessarily is quantitatively oriented – toward ever-increasing amounts of (surplus) value. As production for (surplus) value, production in capitalism is no longer a means to a substantive end, but a moment in a never-ending chain. It is production for the sake of production (Marx, [1867], 1976a, p. 742).

Marx's theory of value provides the basis for an analysis of capital as a socially constituted form of mediation and wealth whose primary characteristic is a tendency toward its limitless expansion. A crucially important aspect of this attempt to specify and ground the dynamic of modern society is its emphasis on temporality. Just as value, within this framework, is not related to the physical characteristics of the products, its measure is not immediately identical with the mass of goods produced ("material wealth"). Rather, as an abstract form of wealth, value is based on an abstract measure – socially average, or necessary, labor-time expenditure.

The category of socially necessary labor-time is not merely descriptive, but expresses a general temporal norm, resulting from the actions of the producers, to which they must conform. Such temporal norms exert an abstract form of compulsion which is intrinsic to capitalism's form of mediation and wealth. In other words, the goal of production in capitalism confronts the producers as an external necessity. It is not given by social tradition or by overt social coercion, nor is it decided upon consciously. Rather, the goal

---

[18]In this general sense Althusser was right when he claimed that Marx took the categories of political economy and changed the terms of the problem; he used them to answer questions political economy never posed (Althusser and Balibar, [1968], 1970, pp. 21–5). Most discussions of Marx's theory of value, however, remain within the bounds of the question posed by political economy.

presents itself as beyond human control. The sort of abstract domination constituted by labor in capitalism is the domination of time.

The form of mediation constitutive of capitalism, then, gives rise to a new form of social domination – one that subjects people to impersonal, increasingly rationalized structural imperatives and constraints (Marx, [1857–8], 1973, p. 164). This form of self-generated structural domination is the social and historical elaboration in Marx's mature works of the concept of alienation developed in his early works. It applies to capitalists as well as workers, in spite of their great differences in power and wealth.

The abstract form of domination analyzed by Marx in *Capital* cannot, then, be grasped adequately in terms of class domination or, more generally, in terms of the concrete domination of social groupings or of institutional agencies of the state and/or the economy. It has no determinate locus[19] and, although constituted by specific forms of social practice, appears not to be social at all. The structure is such that one's own needs, rather than the threat of force or of other social sanctions, appear to be the source of such "necessity."

In Marx's terms, out of a pre-capitalist context characterized by relations of personal dependence, a new one emerged characterized by individual personal freedom within a social framework of "objective dependence" (Marx, [1857–8], 1973, p. 158). Both terms of the classical modern antinomic opposition – the freely self-determining individual and society as an extrinsic sphere of objective necessity –are, according to Marx's analysis, historically constituted with the rise and spread of the commodity-determined form of social relations.

Within the framework of this interpretation, then, the most basic social relations of capitalism are not relations of class exploitation and domination alone. The Marxian analysis includes this dimension, of course, but goes beyond it. It is not only concerned with how the distribution of goods and, ultimately, of power is effected, but also seeks to grasp the very nature of the social mediation that structures modernity. Marx sought to show in *Capital* that the forms of social mediation expressed by categories such as the commodity and capital develop into a sort of objective system, which

[19]This analysis of the form of domination associated with the commodity form provides a powerful point of departure for analyzing the pervasive and immanent form of power Michel Foucault described as characteristic of modern Western societies (Foucault, [1975], 1977).

increasingly determines the goals and means of much human activity. That is to say, Marx attempted to analyze capitalism as a quasi-objective social system and, at the same time, to ground that system in structured forms of social practice.[20]

The form of domination I have begun describing is not static; as we have seen, it generates an intrinsic dynamic underlying modern society. Further determinations of that dynamic can be outlined by considering some implications of the temporal determination of value.

Value's temporal dimension implies a determinate relationship between productivity and value, which can only be briefly mentioned here. Because value is a function of socially necessary labor-time alone, increased productivity results only in short-term increases in value. Once increases in productivity become socially general, however, they redetermine socially average (or necessary) labor-time; the amount of value produced per unit time then falls back to its original "base level" (Marx, [1867], 1976a, p. 129). This means that higher levels of productivity, once they become socially general, are structurally reconstituted as the new "base level" of productivity. They generate greater amounts of material wealth, but not higher levels of value per unit time. By the same token – and this is crucial – higher socially general levels of productivity do not diminish the socially general necessity for labor-time expenditure (which would be the case if material wealth were the dominant form of wealth); instead that necessity is constantly reconstituted. In a system based on value, there is a drive for ever-increasing levels of productivity, yet direct human labor-time expenditure remains necessary to the system as a whole. This pattern promotes still further increases in productivity.

This results in a very complex, non-linear historical dynamic. On the one hand, this dynamic is characterized by ongoing transformations of the technical processes of labor, of the social and detail division of labor and, more generally, of social life – of the nature,

[20]The interpretation of the Marxian theory which I have outlined can also be read as a sophisticated theory of the sort proposed by Pierre Bourdieu, as a theory of the mutually constituting relationship of social structure and everyday action and thought (Bourdieu, [1972], 1977, pp. 1-30, 87-95). What frequently has been interpreted only as an economic problem in Marx's work, namely the question of the relation of value to price, should, in my opinion, be considered as part of an attempt to formulate a theory of the relationship between deep social structure and the everyday actions of social actors who constitute that structure, although they may be unaware of its existence.

structure, and interrelations of social classes and other groupings, the
nature of production, transportation, circulation, patterns of living,
the form of the family, and so on. On the other hand, this historical
dynamic entails the ongoing reconstitution of its own fundamental
condition as an unchanging feature of social life – namely that social
mediation ultimately is effected by labor and, hence, that living labor
remains integral to the process of production (considered in terms of
society as a whole), regardless of the level of productivity.

This analysis provides a point of departure for understanding why
the course of capitalist development has not been linear, why the
enormous increases in productivity generated by capitalism have led
neither to ever-higher general levels of affluence, nor to a fundamental restructuring of social labor entailing significant general
reductions in working time. History in capitalism, within this
framework, is neither a simple story of progress (technical or
otherwise) nor one of regression and decline. Rather, capitalism is a
society that is in constant flux and, yet, constantly reconstitutes its
underlying identity (whereby that identity, it should be noted, is
grasped in terms of the quasi-objective and dynamic social form
constituted by labor as a historically specific mediating activity,
rather than in terms of private property or the market). This dynamic
both generates the possibility of another organization of social life
and, yet, hinders that possibility from being realized.

Such an understanding of capitalism's complex dynamic allows
for a critical, social (rather than technological) analysis of the
trajectory of growth and the structure of production in modern
society. We have seen that a system based on value gives rise to an
ongoing drive towards increased productivity. Marx's analysis of the
category of surplus-value specifies this further. What is important
about Marx's key concept of surplus-value is not only, as traditional
interpretations would have it, that it purportedly shows that the
surplus is produced by the working class – but that it shows that the
relevant surplus in capitalist society is one of value, rather than of
material wealth. Marx's analysis of this form of the surplus indicates
that, the higher the socially general level of productivity already is,
the more productivity must be still further increased in order to
generate a determinate increase in surplus-value (Marx, [1867], 1976a,
pp. 657–8). In other words, the expansion of surplus-value required
by capital tends to generate accelerating rates of increase in
productivity and, hence, in the masses of goods produced and raw
materials consumed. Yet, the ever-increasing amounts of material
wealth produced do not represent correspondingly high levels of
social wealth in the form of value. This analysis suggests that a

perplexing feature of modern capitalism – the absence of general prosperity in the midst of material plenty – is not only a matter of unequal distribution, but is a function of the value form of wealth at the heart of capitalism.

Another consequence implied by this dynamic pattern, which generates increases in material wealth greater than those in surplus-value, is the accelerating destruction of the natural environment. The problem of economic growth in capitalism, within this framework, is not only that it is crisis-ridden, as has frequently been emphasized by traditional Marxist approaches; the form of growth itself is problematic. The trajectory of growth would be different, according to this approach, if the ultimate goal of production were increased quantities of goods rather than of surplus-value. The trajectory of expansion in capitalism, in other words, should not be equated with "economic growth" per se. It is a determinate trajectory, one that generates an increasing tension between ecological considerations and the imperatives of value as a form of wealth and social mediation.

The distinction between material wealth and value, then, allows for an approach that can address the negative ecological consequences of modern industrial production within the framework of a critical theory of capitalism. Moreover, it is able to point beyond the opposition between runaway growth as a condition of social wealth, and austerity as a condition of an ecologically sound organization of social life, by grounding this opposition in a historically specific form of mediation and wealth.

The relationship between value and productivity I have begun to outline also provides the basis for a critical analysis of the structure of social labor and the nature of production in capitalism. Marx, in his mature works, did not treat the industrial process of production as a technical process that, although increasingly socialized, is used by private capitalists for their own ends. Rather, he analyzed that process as molded by capital and, hence, as intrinsically capitalist (Marx, [1867], 1976a, pp. 492ff). According to his analysis, the value form of wealth induces both ever-increasing levels of productivity and the structural retention of direct human labor in production, despite the great increases in productivity. The result is increasingly large-scale, technologically advanced production, coupled with the increasing fragmentation of much individual labor.

This analysis provides the beginnings of a structural explanation for a central paradox of production in capitalism. On the one hand, capital's drive for ongoing increases in productivity gives rise to a productive apparatus of considerable technological sophistication that renders the production of material wealth essentially independent of direct human labor-time expenditure. This, in turn, opens the possibility of large-scale socially general reductions in labor-time and fundamental changes in the nature and social organization of labor. Yet these possibilities are not realized in capitalism (Marx, [1857–8], 1973, pp. 704ff). Although there is a growing shift away from manual labor, the development of technologically sophisticated production does not liberate most people from fragmented and repetitive labor. Similarly, labor-time is not reduced on a socially general level, but is distributed unequally, even increasing for many. The actual structure of labor and organization of production, then, cannot be understood adequately in technological terms alone; the development of production in capitalism must be understood in social terms as well. It, like consumption, is molded by the social mediations expressed by the categories of commodity and capital.

Considered in terms of the structure of wage-labor, another dimension of this paradox of production is that a growing gap arises between labor-time inputs and material outputs. Hence, wages and salaries increasingly become a form of socially general distribution that retains the form of appearance of remuneration for labor-time expenditure. Yet, according to Marx's analysis of capitalism's dynamic (as entailing the ongoing structural reconstitution of the necessity of the value-form), labor-time inputs remain structurally essential to capitalism.

Marx's analysis of the dialectic of value and material wealth, then, implicitly argues that both a runaway form of economic growth as well as the proletarian-based form of industrial production are molded by the commodity form, and suggests that both the form of growth and of production could be different in a society in which material wealth had replaced value as the dominant form of wealth. Capitalism itself gives rise to the possibility of such a society, of a different structuring of work, a different form of growth, and a different form of complex global interdependence; at the same time, however, it structurally undermines the realization of those possibilities.

According to this interpretation, then, Marx's theory does not posit a linear developmental schema which points beyond the existing structure and organization of labor (as do theories of postindustrial society); nor, however, does it treat industrial production and the proletariat as the bases for a future society (as do many traditional Marxist approaches). Rather, it allows for an attempt that does justice to the increasing importance of science and technology and elucidates the historical possibility of a new postindustrial and post-proletarian organization of labor while, at the same time, analyzing the discrepancies between the actual form of capitalist development and the possibilities it generates.

The structural contradiction of capitalism, according to this interpretation, is not one, then, between distribution (the market, private property) and production, but one that emerges as a contradiction between existing forms of growth and production, and what could be the case if social relations no longer were mediated in a quasi-objective fashion by labor and if people, therefore, had a greater degree of control over the organization and direction of social life.

Marx's mature theory of history, according to this interpretation, cannot be read out of his earlier works, such as *The German Ideology* or *The Communist Manifesto*, but is an implicit dimension of his exposition in *Capital*. We have seen that, according to the approach I have begun to outline, the dialectical interactions of the two dimensions of labor and of wealth in capitalism give rise to a complex directional dynamic which, although constituted socially, is quasi-independent of its constituting individuals. It has the properties of an intrinsic historical logic. In other words, Marx's mature theory did not hypostatize history as a sort of force moving all human societies; it no longer presupposed that a directional dynamic of history in general exists. It did, however, characterize modern society in terms of an ongoing directional dynamic and sought to explain that historical dynamic with reference to the dual character of the social forms expressed by the categories of the commodity and capital.

By grounding the contradictory character of the social formation in those dualistic forms, Marx implied that structurally based social contradiction is specific to capitalism. The notion that reality or social relations in general are essentially contradictory and dialectical appears, in light of this analysis, to be one that can only be assumed metaphysically, not explained. Marx's analysis now implicitly dispensed with evolutionary conceptions of history,[21] suggesting that any theory that posits an intrinsic developmental logic to history as such, whether dialectical or evolutionary, projects what is the case for capitalism onto history in general.

[21]It also dispensed with the (ultimately Hegelian) idea that human social life is based on an essential principle that comes into its own in the course of historical development (for example, transhistorical "labor" in traditional Marxism, or communicative action in Habermas's recent work).

IV

Having outlined some aspects of my reinterpretation of Marx's analysis of capitalism, I would like to turn briefly to a preliminary consideration of its implications for the question of the relationship between social labor and social meaning in Marx's theory. Most discussions of this issue conceptualize the problem as one of the relation between labor, understood transhistorically, and forms of thought. This is the assumption underlying the common idea that, for Marx, material production constitutes the fundamental "base" of society, whereas ideas are part of the more epiphenomenal "super-structure,"[22] or, relatedly, that beliefs, for Marx, are determined by material interests (Collins, 1994, pp. 65–70). This was also Habermas's assumption when he argued in *Knowledge and Human Interests* that an analysis based upon labor (which he, like the later Horkheimer, related, as an epistemological category, to instrumental knowledge) must be supplemented by one based on a theory of interaction, in order to recover the notion of a social grounding for non-instrumental forms of meaning and, hence, for the possibility of critical consciousness (Habermas, [1968], 1971, pp. 25–63).

However, as I have been arguing, Marx's mature theory of social constitution is not one of labor per se, but of labor acting as a socially mediating activity in capitalism. This interpretation transforms the terms of the problem of the relationship between labor and thought. The relationship he delineated is not one between concrete labor and thought, but one between labor-mediated social relations and thought. Marx's analysis suggests that what in other societies may very well be structured differently – production and interaction, to use Habermas's earlier terminology – are, on a deep level, conflated in capitalism; they are similarly mediated by labor. At the same time, he maintained that the specificity of the forms of thought (or, more broadly, of subjectivity) characteristic of modern society can be understood with reference to those forms of mediation. That is, inasmuch as Marx analyzed social life and production with reference to a structured form of everyday mediation, and did not define production in concrete "material" terms alone, his approach did not dichotomize subject and object, culture and social life. The categories of his mature critique, in other words, were intended to be determinations of social subjectivity and objectivity at once. They represent an attempt to get beyond a subject–object dualism, an

---

[22]For a critique of this orthodox conception, see Williams, 1977, pp. 75–82.

attempt to grasp socially aspects of modern views of nature, society, and history, with reference to historically specific forms of social mediation constituted by determinate forms of social practice.

This approach entails a very different theory of knowledge than that implied by the well-known base-superstructure model, where thought is a mere reflection of a material base. It also is not a functionalist approach – either in the sense of explaining ideas because they are functional for capitalist society or for the capitalist class. What is noteworthy about Marx's, frequently implicit, attempts at a social-historical theory of knowledge in *Capital* is that he did not deal with modes of thought essentially and ultimately in terms of social position and social interest, including class position and class interest. Instead he attempted first to ground categorially the overarching, historically specific modes of thought within which differentiation according to classes then takes place. Those modes of thought may benefit a class; they are not, however, necessarily the expressions of that class.

One of the more explicit indications in *Capital* of this approach to a social-historical theory of knowledge is in the famous section on the so-called fetish of commodities, where Marx speaks of the object-like relations among people in capitalism (Marx, [1867], 1976a, pp. 163–77). Unfortunately those passages frequently have been taken to be no more than a criticism of the creeping commercialism of all aspects of social life. Marx's notion of the fetish, however, is an aspect of his theory of knowledge that seeks to make plausible aspects of modern thought – for example, the rise of the concept of Reason as a category of totality, or the view of nature as objective, homogeneous, and rational – with reference to the peculiar objective character of the underlying forms of social mediation that constitute capitalist society. This approach – given the complexity of Marx's categories and the fact that they are historically dynamic and contradictory – allows for a historical theory of forms of subjectivity, one very different from approaches that leave the nature of thought indeterminate while examining its social function.[23] It differs both

---

[23]I have found this general approach to a non-functionalist social and historical theory of knowledge to be very helpful in attempting to understand the centrality of modern anti-Semitism to National Socialism in a manner that, in my view, makes better sense of those forms of thought than do theories of National Socialism as an ideology reflecting the interests of big capital, or even as a revolt against modernity. By making use of Marx's analysis of the fundamental social forms of capitalism and his concept of the fetish, I was able to describe a form of thought that was anti-capitalist in its impulse and yet affirmative with regard to industrial

from Bourdieu's theory of social misrecognition, which ultimately is functionalist, and which cannot intrinsically relate that which is purportedly misrecognized and the form of misrecognition itself (Bourdieu, [1972], 1977, pp. 159–97), and from Althusser's conception of ideology, which is transhistorical, predicated on Engels's base-superstructure model, and which does not allow the critical theorist to reflexively ground the possibility of the critique of ideology.[24]

The "material" of Marx's mature materialist theory, then, is social. Meaning is not analyzed as an epiphenomenal reflex of a physical, material base. Neither, of course, is it idealistically treated as a completely self-grounded, autonomous sphere. Rather, the structure of meaning is treated as an immanent aspect of the structure of social mediation. It is because labor in capitalism is not only a productive activity, according to Marx, but is also socially mediating, that it is indeed constitutive of meaning. In general, within the framework of my proposed reinterpretation, the Marxian theory is not one of the material conditions of life alone but is, rather, a self-reflexive critical social theory of a historically specific, constituted intersection of culture and society, meaning and material life.

V

The reinterpretation of Marx's theory I have outlined constitutes a basic break with, and critique of, more traditional interpretations. As we have seen, such interpretations grasp capitalism in terms of class relations structured by the market and private property, its form of domination primarily in terms of class domination and exploitation, and the critique of capitalism as a normative and historical critique from the standpoint of labor and production (understood transhistorically in terms of the interactions of humans with material nature). I have argued that such a common, transhistorical under-

---

capital. On that basis, I then sought to elucidate in social and historical terms the core of Nazi anti-Semitism, the conception of a tremendously powerful, mysterious source of evil, and the identification of this evil with the Jews. In this way I attempted to provide a social explanation of the logic underlying a program of complete extermination (as opposed to mass murder). See Postone, 1986.

[24]Althusser, [1970], 1971, pp. 127–88. Dichotomizing social being and social consciousness, as Althusser does, reintroduces the problem of causal direction.

standing of labor does not underlie Marx's critique, that his theory is not concerned with the production of social wealth in general, and that his understanding of the essential social relations and form of domination characteristic of capitalism must be rethought. That is to say, I have sought to show that, whereas most traditional interpretations remain within the bounds of the problems posed by classical political economy, Marx changed the terms of those problems.

According to the reinterpretation I have outlined, Marx's analysis of labor in capitalism is historically specific; it seeks to elucidate a peculiar quasi-objective form of social mediation and wealth (value) that, as a form of domination, structures the process of production in capitalism and generates a historically unique dynamic. Hence, labor and the process of production are not separable from, and opposed to, the social relations of capitalism, but constitute their very core. Marx's theory, then, extends far beyond the traditional critique of the bourgeois relations of distribution (the market and private property); it is not simply a critique of exploitation and the unequal distribution of wealth and power. Rather, it grasps modern industrial society itself as capitalist, and critically analyzes capitalism primarily in terms of abstract structures of domination, increasing fragmentation of individual labor and individual existence, and a blind runaway developmental logic. It treats the working class as the basic element of capitalism rather than as the embodiment of its negation, and implicitly conceptualizes socialism in terms not of the realization of labor and of industrial production, but of the possible abolition of the proletariat and of the organization of production based on proletarian labor, as well as of the dynamic system of abstract compulsions constituted by labor as a socially mediating activity.

This reinterpretation of Marx's theory thus implies a fundamental rethinking of the nature of capitalism and of its possible historical transformation. By shifting the focus of the critique away from an exclusive concern with the market and private property, it provides the basis for a critical theory of post-liberal society as capitalist and also could provide the basis for a critical theory of the so-called "actually-existing socialist" countries as alternative (and failed) forms of capital accumulation, rather than as social modes that represented the historical negation of capital, in however imperfect a form.

Although the logically abstract level of analysis outlined here does not immediately address the issue of the specific factors underlying the structural transformations since the 1970s, it can provide a framework within which those transformations can be grounded socially and understood historically. It provides the basis for an understanding of the non-linear developmental dynamic of modern society that could incorporate many important insights of postindustrial theory while also elucidating the constraints intrinsic to that dynamic and, hence, the gap between the actual organization of social life and the way it could be organized – especially given the increasing importance of science and technology.

By developing a non-linear account of capitalism's pattern of historical development, this reconceptualization allows for a systematic elucidation of features of modern society that can seem anomalous within the framework of linear development theories: notable are the continued production of poverty in the midst of plenty, the apparently paradoxical effects of labor-saving and time-saving technology on the organization of social labor and social time, and the degree to which important aspects of modern life are shaped by abstract and impersonal forces despite the growing ability of people to control their social and natural environments.

Inasmuch as it seeks to ground socially, and is critical of, the abstract, quasi-objective social relations, and the nature of production, work, and the imperatives of growth in capitalism, this interpretation could also begin to address a range of contemporary concerns, dissatisfactions, and aspirations in a way that could provide a fruitful point of departure for a consideration of the new social movements of recent decades and the sorts of historically constituted world views they embody and express.

Finally, this approach also has implications for the question of the social preconditions of democracy, inasmuch as it analyzes not only the inequalities of real social power that are inimical to democratic politics, but also reveals as socially constituted – and hence as legitimate objects of political debates – the systemic constraints imposed by capital's global dynamic on democratic self-determination.

By fundamentally rethinking the significance of value theory and reconceptualizing the nature of capitalism, this interpretation changes the terms of discourse between critical theories of capitalism and other sorts of social theory. It implicitly suggests that an adequate theory of modernity should be a self-reflexive theory capable of overcoming the theoretical dichotomies of culture and material life, structure and action, while grounding socially the overarching non-linear directional dynamic of the modern world, its form of economic growth, and the nature and trajectory of its production process. That is, such a theory must be capable of providing a social account of the paradoxical features of modernity outlined above.

In addressing these issues, the interpretation I have presented seeks to contribute to the discourse of contemporary social theory and, relatedly, to our understanding of the far-reaching trans-formations of our social universe.

REFERENCES

Adorno, T. W. [1966], 1973: *Negative Dialectics*, tr. E. B. Ashton. New York: Seabury Press.
—— [1969], 1976: On the logic of the social sciences. In *The Positivist Dispute in German Sociology*, tr. Glyn Adey and David Frisbey. London: Heinemann.
Adorno, T. W. and Horkheimer, Max [1944], 1972: *Dialectic of Enlightenment*, tr. John Cummings. New York: Seabury Press.
Alexander, Jeffrey 1982: *Theoretical Logic in Sociology*, Vol. 2: *The Antinomies of Classical Thought: Marx and Durkheim*. Berkeley and Los Angeles: University of California Press.
Althusser, Louis [1965], 1970: *For Marx*, tr. Ben Brewster. New York: Pantheon Books.
—— [1970], 1971: Ideology and ideological state apparatuses (notes towards an investigation). In *Lenin and Philosophy and Other Essays*, tr. Ben Brewster. New York and London: Monthly Review Press, 127–88.
Althusser, Louis, and Balibar, Etienne [1968], 1970: *Reading Capital*, tr. Ben Brewster. London: NLB.
Anderson, Perry 1976: *Considerations on Western Marxism*. London: NLB.
—— 1983: *In the Tracks of Historical Materialism*. Chicago and London: University of Chicago Press.
Arato, Andrew 1978: Introduction. In Andrew Arato and Eike Gebhardt (eds), *The Essential Frankfurt School Reader*. New York: Urizen Books.
Arato, Andrew, and Breines, Paul 1979: *The Young Lukács and the Origins of Western Marxism*. New York: Seabury Press.
Archibald, W. Peter 1978: Using Marx's theory of alienation empirically. *Theory and Society*, 6 (1), 119–32.
Aron, Raymond [1962–3], 1965: *Main Currents in Social Thought*, Vol. 1. tr. Richard Howard and Helen Weaver. London: Anchor Books.
—— [1963], 1967: *The Industrial Society: three essays on ideology and development*. New York: Simon & Schuster.
Aronowitz, Stanley 1981: *The Crisis in Historical Materialism: class, culture, and politics in Marxist theory*. New York: Praeger.
Avineri, Shlomo 1968: *The Social and Political Thought of Karl Marx*. London: Cambridge University Press.
Becker, James F. 1977: *Marxian Political Economy: an outline*. Cambridge: Cambridge University Press.
Bell, Daniel 1973: *The Coming of Post-Industrial Society*. New York: Basic Books.
Benhabib, Seyla 1986: *Critique, Norm, and Utopia: on the foundations of critical social theory*. New York: Columbia University Press.
Bologh, Roslyn Wallach 1979: *Dialectical Phenomenology: Marx's method*. Boston, London, and Henley: Routledge & Kegan Paul.

Bottomore, Tom 1973: Introduction. In *Karl Marx*. Oxford: Basil Blackwell.

—— 1983: Sociology. In David McLennan (ed.) *Marx: the first hundred years*. New York: Pinter in association with Fontana Books.

Bourdieu, Pierre [1972], 1977: *Outline of a Theory of Practice*, tr. Richard Nice. Cambridge: Cambridge University Press.

Braverman, Harry 1974: *Labor and Monopoly Capital: the degradation of work in the twentieth century*. New York and London: Monthly Review Press.

Brown, Michael 1986: *The Production of Society*. Totowa, NJ: Rowman and Littlefield.

Burawoy, Michael 1982: Introduction: the resurgence of Marxism in American Sociology. In Michael Burawoy and Theda Skocpol (eds), *Marxist Inquiries: studies of labor, class, and states. American Journal of Sociology*, 88 (supplement), 1–30.

—— 1985: *The Politics of Production*. London: Verso.

Castoriadis, Cornelius 1978: From Marx to Aristotle, from Aristotle to Marx. *Social Research*, 45 (4), 667–738.

Cohen, G. A. 1978: *Karl Marx's Theory of History: a defence*. Oxford: Oxford University Press.

—— 1986a: Forces and relations of production. In J. Roemer (ed.), *Analytical Marxism*. Cambridge: Cambridge University Press.

—— 1986b: Marxism and functional explanation. In J. Roemer (ed.), *Analytical Marxism*. Cambridge: Cambridge University Press.

—— 1988: *History, Labour and Freedom: themes from Marx*. Oxford: Clarendon Press.

Cohen, Jean 1982: *Class and Civil Society: the limits of Marxian critical theory*. Amherst, Mass.: University of Massachusetts Press.

Colletti, Lucio [1970], 1972: Bernstein and the Marxism of the Second International. In *From Rousseau to Lenin*, tr. John Merrington and Judith White. London: NLB.

—— [1969], 1973: *Marxism and Hegel*. London: NLB.

Collins, Randall 1994: *Four Sociological Traditions*. New York and Oxford: Oxford University Press.

Dobb, Maurice 1940: *Political Economy and Capitalism*. London: Routledge and Sons.

Dubiel, Helmut [1978], 1985. *Theory and Politics: studies in the development of critical theory*, tr. Benjamin Gregg. Cambridge, Mass. and London: MIT Press.

Elson, Diane 1979: The value theory of labour. In D. Elson (ed.), *Value: the representation of labour in capitalism*. London: CSE Books.

Elster, Jon 1985: *Making Sense of Marx*. Cambridge: Cambridge University Press.

—— 1986: Further thoughts on Marxism, functionalism and game theory. In J. Roemer (ed.), *Analytical Marxism*. Cambridge: Cambridge University Press.

Fetscher, Iring [1967], 1971: *Marx and Marxism*. tr. John Hargreaves. New York: Herder and Herder.

Flacks, Richard 1982: Marxism and sociology. In Bertell Ollman and Edward Vernoff (eds), *The Left Academy: Marxist scholarship on American campuses*. New York: McGraw-Hill, 9–52.

Foucault, Michel [1975], 1977: *Discipline and Punish: the birth of the prison*, tr. Alan Sheridan. New York: Vintage Books.

Friedman, George 1986: Eschatology vs. aesthetics: the Marxist critique of Weberian rationality. *Sociological Theory*, 4 (2), 186–93.

Giddens, Anthony 1979: *Central Problems in Social Theory: action, structure, and contradiction in social analysis.* Berkeley and Los Angeles: University of California Press.

—— 1995: *A Contemporary Critique of Historical Materialism*, 2nd ed. Stanford: Stanford University Press.

Gintis, Herb 1982: The reemergence of Marxian economics in America. In Ollman and Vernoff (eds), *The Left Academy*. New York: McGraw Hill, 53–81.

Gorz, André [1988], 1989: *Critique of Economic Reason*, tr. Gillian Handyside and Chris Turner. London and New York: Verso.

Gouldner, Alvin 1974: Marxism and social theory. *Theory and Society*, 1, 17–35.

—— 1980: *The Two Marxisms: contradictions and anomalies in the development of theory*. New York: Seabury Press.

Gramsci, Antonio [1929–35], 1972: *Selections from the Prison Notebooks*, ed. and tr. Quintin Hoare and Geoffrey Nowell Smith. New York: International Publishers.

Habermas, Jürgen [1968], 1970: Technology and science as "ideology." In *Towards a Rational Society*, tr. Jeremy J. Shapiro. Boston: Beacon Press.

—— [1968], 1971: *Knowledge and Human Interests*, tr. Jeremy Shapiro. Boston: Beacon Press.

—— [1963], 1973a: Between philosophy and science: Marxism as critique. In *Theory and Practice*, tr. John Viertel. Boston: Beacon Press.

—— [1968], 1973b: Labor and interaction: remarks on Hegel's Jena *Phenomenology of Mind*. In *Theory and Practice*, tr. John Viertel. Boston: Beacon Press.

—— [1981], 1984: *The Theory of Communicative Action*, Vol. 1: *Reason and the Rationalization of Society*, tr. Thomas McCarthy. Boston: Beacon Press.

—— [1981], 1987: *The Theory of Communicative Action*, Vol. 2: *Lifeworld and System: a Critique of Functionalist Reason*, tr. Thomas McCarthy. Boston: Beacon Press.

—— [1976], 1989: Toward a reconstruction of historical materialism. In Steven Seidman (ed.), *Jürgen Habermas on Society and Politics.* Boston: Beacon Press.

Hall, Stuart 1983: The problem of ideology – Marxism without guarantees. In Betty Matthews (ed.), *Marx: a hundred years on*. London: Lawrence & Wishart and New Jersey: Humanities Press, 60–84.

Harvey, David 1982: *The Limits to Capital*. Chicago: University of Chicago Press.

—— 1989: *The Condition of Postmodernity: an enquiry into the origins of cultural change*. Oxford and Cambridge, Mass.: Blackwell.

Hawley, Amos 1984: Human ecology and Marxian theories. *American Journal of Sociology*, 89 (4), 904–17.

Heilbroner, Robert L. 1980: *The Worldly Philosophers: the lives, times, and ideas of the great economic thinkers*, 5th edn. New York: Simon & Schuster.

76   Moishe Postone

Held, David 1980: *Introduction to Critical Theory*. Berkeley: University of California Press.
Heller, Agnes [1974], 1976: *The Theory of Need in Marx*. London: Allison & Busby.
Horkheimer, Max [1937], 1972: Traditional and critical theory. In *Critical Theory*, tr. Matthew J. O'Connell et al. New York: Herder and Herder.
—— [1947], 1974: *The Eclipse of Reason*. New York: Continuum.
—— [1940], 1978: The authoritarian state. In Andrew Arato and Eike Gebhardt (eds), *The Essential Frankfurt School Reader*. New York: Urizen Books.
Horkheimer, Max, and Adorno, Theodor W. [1944], 1972: *Dialectic of Enlightenment*, tr. John Cumming. New York: Seabury Press.
Howard, Dick 1977: *The Marxian Legacy*. New York: Urizen Books.
Hyppolite, Jean [1965], 1969: *Studies on Marx and Hegel*, tr. John O'Neill. New York: Basic Books.
Jay, Martin 1973: *The Dialectical Imagination: a history of the Frankfurt School and the Institute for Social Research, 1923–1950*. Boston and Toronto: Little, Brown.
—— 1984: *Marxism and Totality: the adventures of a concept from Lukács to Habermas*. Berkeley and Los Angeles: University of California Press.
Kellner, Douglas 1989: *Critical Theory, Marxism, and Modernity*. Baltimore: Johns Hopkins University Press.
Kolakowski, Leszek [1966], 1968: *Toward a Marxist Humanism*, tr. Jane Zielonko Peel. New York: Grove Press.
—— [1976], 1978: *Main Currents of Marxism: its rise, growth, and dissolution*, 3 vols, tr. P. S. Falla. Oxford: Clarendon Press.
Korsch, Karl [1923], 1971: *Marxism and Philosophy*, tr. Fred Halliday. London: NLB.
Lefebvre, Henri [1939], 1968: *Dialectical Materialism*, tr. John Sturrock. London: Jonathan Cape.
—— [1966], 1969: *The Sociology of Marx*, tr. Norbert Guterman. New York: Columbia University Press.
Levine, Rhonda and Lembcke, Jerry 1987: Introduction: Marxism, neo-Marxism and US sociology. In Rhonda Levine and Jerry Lembcke (eds), *Recapturing Marxism: an appraisal of recent trends in sociological theory*. New York: Praeger, 1–12.
Lichtheim, George 1965: *Marxism: an historical and critical study*. New York: Praeger.
—— 1971: *From Marx to Hegel*. London: Seabury Press.
Löwith, Karl [1941], 1964: *From Hegel to Nietzsche: the revolution in nineteenth-century thought*, tr. David E. Green. New York: Holt, Rinehart and Winston.
Lukács, Georg [1923], 1971: *History and Class Consciousness*, tr. Rodney Livingstone. Cambridge, Mass.: MIT Press.
—— [1962], 1978: *The Ontology of Social Being*, tr. David Fernbach. London: Merlin.
McCarthy, Thomas 1978: *The Critical Theory of Jürgen Habermas*. Cambridge, Mass. and London: MIT Press.
McLellan, David 1980: *The Thought of Karl Marx: an introduction*. London and Basingstoke.

—— 1983: Politics. In David McLellan (ed.), *Marx: the first hundred years.* New York: F. Pinter in association with Fontana Books.

Macy, Michael W. 1988: Value theory and the "golden eggs": appropriating the magic of accumulation. *Sociological Theory*, 6 (2), 131–52.

Mandel, Ernest [1962], 1970: *Marxist Economic Theory*, tr. Brian Pearce. New York: Monthly Review Press.

—— [1967], 1971: *The Formation of the Economic Thought of Karl Marx.* New York and London: NLB.

—— [1972], 1975: *Late Capitalism*, tr. Joris De Bres. London: NLB.

—— 1978: Introduction. In Karl Marx, *Capital*, Vol. 2, tr. D. Fernbach. London: Penguin Books in association with New Left Review.

—— 1983: Economics. In David McLellan (ed.), *Marx: the first hundred years.* New York: F. Pinter in association with Fontana Books.

Marcuse, Herbert 1955: *Eros and Civilization.* Boston: Beacon Press.

—— 1964a: *One-dimensional Man: studies in the ideology of advanced industrial society.* Boston: Beacon Press.

—— 1964b: *Reason and Revolution: Hegel and the rise of social theory.* Boston: Beacon Press.

—— [1932], 1972: The foundation of historical materialism. In Joris de Bres (ed. and tr.), *From Luther to Popper.* London: NLB.

Marx, Karl [1861–3], 1963: *Theories of Surplus Value*, Part 1, tr. Emile Burns. Moscow: Progress Publishers.

—— [1861–3], 1968: *Theories of Surplus Value*, Part 2, tr. Renate Simpson. Moscow: Progress Publishers.

—— [1859], 1970: *A Contribution to the Critique of Political Economy*, tr. S. W. Ryazanskaya. Moscow: Progress Publishers.

—— [1861–3], 1971: *Theories of Surplus Value*, Part 3, tr. Jack Cohen and S. W. Ryazanskaya. Moscow: Progress Publishers.

—— [1857–8], 1973: *Grundrisse: foundations of the critique of political economy*, tr. Martin Nicolaus. London, New York: Penguin Books in association with New Left Review.

—— [1844], 1975a: Contribution to the critique of Hegel's philosophy of law: introduction. In Karl Marx and Frederick Engels, *Collected Works*, Vol. 3: *Marx and Engels: 1843–1844.* New York: International Publishers.

—— [1844], 1975b: Contribution to the critique of Hegel's philosophy of law. In Karl Marx and Frederick Engels, *Collected Works*, Vol. 3: *Marx and Engels: 1843–1844.* New York: International Publishers.

—— [1875], 1975c: Critique of the Gotha program. In Karl Marx and Frederick Engels, *Collected Works*, Vol. 24: *Marx and Engels: 1874–1883.* New York: International Publishers.

—— [1844], 1975d: *Economic and Philosophic Manuscripts of 1844.* In Karl Marx and Frederick Engels, *Collected Works*, Vol. 3: *Marx and Engels: 1843–1844.* New York: International Publishers.

—— [1879–80], 1975e: Marginal Notes on Adolf Wagner's *Lehrbuch der politischen Ökonomie.* In Karl Marx and Frederick Engels, *Collected Works*, Vol. 24: *Marx and Engels: 1874–1883.* New York: International Publishers.

—— [1867], 1976a: *Capital*, Vol. 1, tr. Ben Fowkes. London: Penguin Books in association with New Left Review.

—— [1843], 1976b: On the Jewish question. In Karl Marx and Frederick Engels, *Collected Works*, Vol. 3: *Marx and Engels, 1843–1844.* New York: International Publishers.

—— [1847], 1976c: *The Poverty of Philosophy.* In Karl Marx and Frederick Engels, *Collected Works*, Vol. 6: *Marx and Engels: 1845–1848.* New York: International Publishers.

—— [1863–6], 1976d: *Results of the Immediate Process of Production,* tr. Rodney Livingstone. In *Capital*, Vol. 1, tr. Ben Fowkes. London: Penguin Books in association with New Left Review.

—— [1845], 1976e: Theses on Feuerbach. In Karl Marx and Frederick Engels, *Collected Works*, Vol. 5: *Marx and Engels: 1845–1847.* New York: International Publishers.

—— [1849], 1977: *Wage Labor and Capital.* In Karl Marx and Frederick Engels, *Collected Works*, Vol. 9: *Marx and Engels: 1849.* New York: International Publishers.

—— [1885], 1978a: *Capital*, Vol. 2, tr. David Fernbach. London: Penguin Books in association with New Left Review.

—— [1856], 1978b: Speech at the anniversary of the *People's Paper*, April 14, 1856. In *The Marx–Engels Reader*, 2nd edn, ed. Robert C. Tucker. New York: Norton.

—— [1852], 1979: *The Eighteenth Brumaire of Louis Bonaparte.* In Karl Marx and Frederick Engels, *Collected Works*, Vol. 11: *Marx and Engels: 1851–1853.* New York: International Publishers.

—— [1894], 1981: *Capital*, Vol. 3, tr. David Fernbach. Harmondsworth, England: Penguin Books in association with New Left Review.

—— [1865], 1985: *Value, Price, and Profit.* In Karl Marx and Frederick Engels, *Collected Works*, Vol. 20: *Marx and Engels: 1864–1868.* New York: International Publishers.

Marx, Karl, and Engels, Frederick [1845], 1967: The Holy Family. In *Writings of the Young Marx on Philosophy and Society,* ed. Lloyd D. Easton and Kurt H. Guddat. Garden City, NY: Doubleday.

—— [1845–6], 1976a: *The German Ideology.* In Karl Marx and Frederick Engels, *Collected Works*, Vol. 5: *Marx and Engels: 1845–1847.* New York: International Publishers.

—— [1848], 1976b: *Manifesto of the Communist Party.* In Karl Marx and Frederick Engels, *Collected Works*, Vol. 6: *Marx and Engels: 1845–1848.* New York: International Publishers.

Mattick, Paul 1969: *Marx and Keynes: the limits of the mixed economy.* Boston: P. Sargent.

Meek, Ronald 1956: *Studies in the Labour Theory of Value.* New York and London: Lawrence and Wishart.

Mészáros, István 1970: *Marx's Theory of Alienation.* London: Harper & Row.

Murray, John Patrick 1988: *Marx's Theory of Scientific Knowledge.* Atlantic Highlands, NJ: Humanities Press International.

Negri, Antonio [1979], 1984: *Marx beyond Marx: lessons on the "Grundrisse,"* ed. Jim Fleming, tr. Harry Cleaver, Michael Ryan, and Maurizio Viano. South Hadley, Mass.: Bergin & Garvey.

Nell, E. 1981: Value and capital in Marxian economics. In *The Crisis in Economic Theory*, ed. D. Bell and I. Kristol. New York: Basic Books.

Nicolaus, Martin 1968: The unknown Marx. *New Left Review*, 48 (March–April), 41–61.

—— 1973: Introduction. In Karl Marx, *Grundrisse*, tr. Martin Nicolaus. London: Penguin Books in association with New Left Review.

Ollman, Bertell 1976: *Alienation: Marx's conception of man in capitalist society*, 2nd edn. Cambridge: Cambridge University Press.

Pollock, Friedrich 1941: State capitalism. *Studies in Philosophy and Social Studies*, 9, 200–25.

Postone, Moishe 1986: Anti-Semitism and National Socialism. In Anson Rabinbach and Jack Zipes (eds), *Germans and Jews Since the Holocaust*, New York: Holmes & Meier.

—— 1990: History and critical social theory. *Contemporary Sociology*, 19 (2), 170–6.

—— 1993: *Time, Labor, and Social Domination: a reinterpretation of Marx's critical theory*. New York and Cambridge: Cambridge University Press.

Resnick, Stephen and Wolff, Richard 1995: The end of the USSR: a Marxian class analysis. In Antonio Callari, Stephen Cullenberg, and Carole Biewener (eds), *Marxism in the Postmodern Age*. New York and London: Guilford Press.

Robinson, Joan 1967: *An Essay on Marxian Economics*, 2nd edn. London, Melbourne, Toronto: Macmillan.

Roemer, John 1981: *Analytic Foundations of Marxian Economic Theory*. Cambridge: Cambridge University Press.

—— (ed.) 1986: *Analytical Marxism*. Cambridge: Cambridge University Press.

Rosdolsky, Roman [1968], 1977: *The Making of Marx's "Capital,"* tr. Pete Burgess. London: Pluto Press.

Rubin, Isaak Illich [1928], 1972: *Essays on Marx's Theory of Value*, tr. Milos Samardzija and Fredy Perlman. Detroit, Mich.: Black & Red.

Sartre, Jean-Paul [1960–85], 1982–91: *Critique of Dialectical Reason*, tr. Jonathan Rée et al. London and New York: Verso.

Sayer, Derek 1979: *Marx's Method: ideology, science, and critique in "Capital."* Atlantic Highlands, NJ: Humanities Press.

—— 1987: *The Violence of Abstraction: the analytic foundations of historical materialism*. Oxford and New York: Basil Blackwell.

Schmidt, Alfred [1962], 1971: *The Concept of Nature in Marx*, tr. Ben Fowkes. London: NLB.

—— [1971], 1981: *History and Structure: an essay on Hegelian-Marxist and structuralist theories of history*, tr. Jeffrey Herf. Cambridge, Mass.: MIT Press.

Sciulli, David 1984: Talcott Parsons' analytical critique of Marxism's concept of alienation. *American Journal of Sociology*, 90 (3), 514–40.

Shaikh, Anwar 1981: The poverty of algebra. In I. Steedman, P. Sweezy et al. (eds), *The Value Controversy*, London: NLB.

Smelser, Neil J. 1973: Introduction. In Neil J. Smelser (ed.), *Karl Marx on Society and Social Change*. Chicago: University of Chicago Press.

Sohn-Rethel, Alfred [1970], 1978: *Intellectual and Manual Labour: a critique of epistemology*, tr. Martin Sohn-Rethel. Atlantic Highlands, NJ: Humanities Press.

Steedman, Ian 1981: Ricardo, Marx, Sraffa. In Ian Steedman (ed.), *The Value*

Controversy. London: NLB.

Sweezy, Paul M. 1968: *The Theory of Capitalist Development.* New York: Monthly Review Press.

Tiryakian, Edward 1975: Neither Marx nor Durkheim . . . perhaps Weber. *American Journal of Sociology,* 81 (1), 1–33.

Tucker, Robert C. 1969: *The Marxian Revolutionary Idea.* New York: Norton Library.

Uchida, Hiroshi 1988: *Marx's "Grundrisse" and Hegel's "Logic,"* ed. Terrell Carver. London and Boston.

Walton, Paul, and Gamble, Andrew 1972: *From Alienation to Surplus Value.* London: Sheed and Ward.

Wellmer, Albrecht [1969], 1971: *Critical Theory of Society,* tr. John Cummings. New York: Herder and Herder.

Wiggershaus, Rolf [1986], 1994: *The Frankfurt School,* tr. Michael Robertson. Cambridge, Mass.: MIT Press.

Wiley, Norbert 1987: Introduction. In Norbert Wiley (ed.), *The Marx-Weber Debate.* Newbury Park, Calif.: Sage Publications.

Williams, Raymond 1977: *Marxism and Literature.* Oxford and New York: Oxford University Press.

—— 1983: Culture. In David McLellan (ed.), *Marx: the first hundred years.* New York: F. Pinter in association with Fontana Books.

Winfield, Richard 1976: The Logic of Marx's *Capital. Telos,* 27 (Spring), 111–39.

Wolff, Robert Paul 1984: *Understanding Marx: a reconstruction and critique of "Capital."* Princeton: Princeton University Press.

Wright, Erik O. 1978: *Class, Crisis and the State.* London and New York: NLB.

—— 1985: *Classes.* London: Verso.

—— 1993: Explanation and emancipation in Marxism and feminism. *Sociological Theory,* 11 (1), 39–54.

Wright, Erik O., and Perrone, Luca 1977: Marxist class categories and income inequality. *American Sociological Review,* 42 (February), 32–55.

3

Spencer and His Critics

Valerie A. Haines

"Who now reads Spencer? It is difficult for us to realize how great a stir he made in the world . . . We must agree with the verdict. Spencer is dead. But who killed him and how? This is the problem" (Parsons, [1937], 1968, p. 3). This quotation from *The Structure of Social Action* has become the standard opening for modern critics of Herbert Spencer's theory of social evolution.[1] According to them, this theory is a form of developmentalism, a teleological approach "endowing" the historical process with "internal logic, sense and direction" (Sztompka, 1993, p. 181). Because it has been demonstrated conclusively that developmentalism cannot account adequately for social change, for Spencer's modern critics, the solution to the problem posed by Parsons is obvious: "We have evolved beyond Spencer" to the post-developmentalist view of social change with its focus on agency and contingency. Parsons's verdict holds for Spencer's causal explanation of social change, then, only if the developmental reconstruction is valid.[2]

---

[1]Parsons's ([1937], 1968, p. 3) target, of course, was not Spencer the evolutionary theorist but Spencer the "typical representative of the later stages of development of a system of thought about man and society which has played a very great part in the intellectual history of the English-speaking peoples, the positivistic-utilitarian tradition."

[2]When used without further qualification, the terms "evolutionary theory," "evolutionary theorizing," "theory of social evolution," and "theory of organic evolution" should be taken to mean a theory to explain the mechanism of organic/social change.

My goal is to demonstrate that Spencer's theory of social evolution is not a form of developmentalism. Like the causal explanation of organic evolution it reproduces, Spencer's causal explanation of social change is evolutionary in the modern biological sense of the term "evolution." If Spencer is dead, then, he is dead because the developmental reconstruction misrepresents his assumptions about the nature of social change. To defend this solution to the problem of who killed Spencer and how, I begin by exploring the arguments, evidence and historiographic assumptions of the modern critics who are largely responsible for the received view. Here I show that whether their focus is organic evolution or social evolution and whether their controlling assumptions are presentist or historicist, these critics converge on the developmental reconstruction of Spencer's evolutionary theorizing. Then, after setting out as clearly as possible what Spencer actually said about the mechanisms of organic and social evolution in his published works and letters, I establish that the consensus on developmentalism breaks down when Spencer's most influential nineteenth-century critics are considered. Their critiques corroborate the evolutionary reconstruction that my reading of Spencer suggests. I conclude by investigating the implications of the evolutionary reconstruction for the contemporary debate about the nature of social change.

THE DEVELOPMENTAL RECONSTRUCTION OF SPENCER'S EVOLUTIONARY THEORIZING: FROM BIOLOGY TO SOCIOLOGY AND BACK

My exploration of the arguments, evidence and historiographic assumptions that sustain the developmental reconstruction centers on the works of five of Spencer's most prominent and influential modern critics. Spencer believed that the mechanism of organic evolution set out in his biological writings also explained social evolution. Therefore, the content and tenacity of the developmental reconstruction can be understood only by considering his causal explanations of organic evolution and social evolution. Derek Freeman, Robert Nisbet, and Jonathan Turner illustrate the presentist approach to their study; Peter J. Bowler and J. D. Y. Peel, the historicist alternative.

Sociologists routinely use development and evolution as synonyms to denote endogenous or unfolding models of change. In biology today, development and evolution are universally recognized as fundamentally different processes. To avoid confusion when moving back and forth between biological and sociological critiques, I use the modern biological definitions of development and evolution. Development is an unfolding of pre-existing potentials inherent in an individual organism at the time it begins life. Because this is a process of immanent change, environmental factors can only accelerate, retard or prevent the unfolding of pre-existing potentials; they cannot create new potentials. Evolution is not controlled by a preset, internal program (Gould, 1977; Mayr, 1991a). Because it depends upon organism–environment interactions, environmental contingency, historical specificity, and probabilism are hallmarks of evolutionary theories.

Two evolutionary explanations of organic change co-existed in the nineteenth century: use inheritance and natural selection. Use inheritance or the Lamarckian mechanism of organic change (named for the French biologist Jean-Baptiste Lamarck (1744–1829)) turns on the argument that structures which organisms acquire during their lives through use or disuse in response to environmental influences (e.g., the stronger legs (use) and weaker wings (disuse) of domestic fowl) can be passed to their offspring. Charles Darwin's (1809–82) alternative to this inheritance of acquired characters explains organic change through the environmental selection of random variation. Evolutionary change "is due to the production of variation in a population and the survival and reproductive success ('selection') of some of these variants" (Mayr, 1991a, p. 109) – those that are best adapted to local environmental conditions. The Lamarckian and Darwinian mechanisms are both nontelelogical. Where they differ is in their explanations of the origins of variation. Lamarck argued that the environment caused variation but for Darwin "random variation was present first, and the ordering activity of the environment ('natural selection') followed afterwards" (Mayr, 1982, p. 354).[3]

Most nineteenth-century evolutionists who accepted natural selection (including Darwin) also accepted the inheritance of acquired characters. It was not until the 1880s that the reality of the Lamarckian mechanism became an issue. One of its most influential critics was the German embryologist August Weismann (1834–1914). His case against use inheritance helped to prepare the way for

[3]Ruse (1988) and Richards (1988, p. 138; 1992) have argued that Darwin accepted the idea that evolution was generally progressive. Their arguments do not contest the evolutionary status of natural selection, however, because, if correct, their interpretation still accords causal primacy to the environment. Under it, progress is "the result, not of an internal drive pushing organisms to perfection, but of an external dynamic pulling them to perfection."

the modern (neo-Darwinian) view of natural selection as the sole mechanism of organic evolution.[4] Because Spencer (1820–1903) was an active participant in the controversy over the mechanism of evolution, it is not surprising that developmental reconstructions focus on his links with Lamarck, Darwin and Weismann and, through them, on the question of whether his explanations of organic evolution and social evolution are developmental (teleological) or evolutionary (nonteleological).

Presentist Reconstructions

The presentist or Whig model of historiography makes the present the sole judge of past controversies. Presentist histories of evolutionary biology evaluate competing explanations of organic evolution against three points of general agreement among modern evolutionary biologists. First, species evolution cannot be modeled on individual development. Second, use inheritance and natural selection are both nonteleological explanations of organic change (Mayr, 1972; Burkhardt, 1977). Third, because acquired characters cannot be inherited, only natural selection is a valid explanation of organic evolution. Not surprisingly, then, when the history of causal explanations of organic evolution is approached from this post-Darwinian vantage point, it becomes the history of Darwin's theory of natural selection (Bowler, 1988).

This one-sided approach to studying Darwin's contemporaries is obvious in Derek Freeman's (1974) widely cited comparison of the evolutionary theories of Darwin and Spencer. Spencer, Darwin, and their contemporaries used the similarities between these theories to defend the evolutionary explanation of organic change. Freeman, in contrast, focuses on four "crucial differences" which clarify "those concepts of Charles Darwin on which the modern biological theory

[4]Since Weismann developed his case against use inheritance biologists have established that the inheritance of acquired characters ("characteristics of an organism's appearance (phenotype) that result from environmental influences rather than inheritance" (Mayr, 1991a, p. 177)) cannot occur. The twentieth-century "recognition that DNA does not directly participate in the making of the phenotype and that the phenotype, in turn, does not control the composition of the DNA represents the ultimate invalidation of all theories involving the inheritance of acquired characters" (Mayr, 1976, p. 222). Darwin did believe that the inheritance of acquired characters was an important source of variation. But because natural selection depends only on the fact that variation exists in all generations, the discovery that acquired characters cannot be inherited did not undermine the Darwinian mechanism of organic change.

of evolution is founded," concepts which "should not be confused with the obsolete Lamarckian evolutionism of Herbert Spencer" (p. 221). First, Darwin used the modern methodology of hypothetico-deduction – "the testing of an hypothesis developed on the basis of prior observations" (p. 213). Spencer's theory, "not having resulted from any kind of sustained empirical inquiry, was explicitly deductive in character" (p. 215). Second, Spencer accepted Lamarck's argument for "an inherent progressive tendency" in nature; Darwin did not, telling Hooker: "Heaven forfend me from Lamarck nonsense of a 'tendency to progression' " (p. 218). Third, where Darwin was concerned only with organic evolution, Spencer attempted to explain evolution at large by introducing "a meta-physical entity," the persistence of force, which in his view "made evolutionary change inevitable" (p. 230). Fourth, although both Spencer and Darwin incorporated use inheritance and natural selection in their theories, they disagreed about their relative importance. Spencer believed that use inheritance was the chief factor of organic evolution; therefore, Weismann's discovery that acquired characters cannot be inherited "was fatal to [his] theory of evolution." Darwin's insistence on the overwhelming importance of natural selection allowed the neo-Darwinians simply to eliminate "that small amount of doctrine" (Lankester, 1890, p. 415) (Freeman, 1974, p. 234) that this discovery had rendered obsolete.

For Freeman these differences explain the different fates of Darwin's and Spencer's theories of organic evolution. An "authentically-scientific", "non-teleological" explanation (p. 215), "Darwinian natural selection has survived as the *fons et origo* of the modern biological theory of evolution" (p. 217). The teleological alternative of Spencer, in contrast, "is now, looked at in strictly scientific terms, little more than an historical curiosity. And those who would sit at the feet of its architect, whether they realise it or not, are in rubble" (p. 230) – a "deductive manner of treating every subject" (C. Darwin, [1887], 1958, p. 109), the developmental as-sumption that nature has an inherent progressive tendency and its corollary, the assumption that the operation of a metaphysical entity, the persistence of force, makes progress inevitable and the belief that acquired characters are heritable. And, continues Freeman, because Spencer did not make the modern distinction between organic evolution and cultural evolution, this mutually reinforcing set of ideas also underpinned his theory of social evolution. When Spencer's causal explanation of organic evolution collapsed into rubble, then, so did his causal explanation of social evolution. As a form of developmentalism, it too is "little more than an historical curiosity."

Robert Nisbet (1969) agrees with Freeman's conclusion that only Darwin's causal explanation was evolutionary but his reading of Spencer suggests that Spencer's theory was developmental for a different reason: It was built upon the conception of organismic growth that formed the core of "the" theory of social evolution in the nineteenth century. "No one stated this fact more explicitly than Herbert Spencer when he declared, in his essay 'Progress: Its Law and Cause' written in 1857, that 'the series of changes gone through during the development of the seed into a tree, or an ovum into an animal, constitute an advance from homogeneity of structure to heterogeneity of structure' and that 'this law or organic process is the law of all progress'" (Nisbet, 1969, p. 164). And, because Nisbet believes that Spencer's mechanism of social evolution also followed logically from this analogy to ontogeny, three corollaries follow: (1) for Spencer, social change is immanent (in the social organism), (2) "given the principle of development, of potentiality in unceasing drive toward actuality" (p. 115), Spencer can draw only one conclusion – progress is "not an accident but a beneficent necessity" (*Social Statics*) and, therefore, as a form of developmentalism, (3) Spencer's theory of social evolution is "without merit when it comes to our understanding of the nature of change" (p. 270).

In Freeman's (1974) and Nisbet's (1969) hands, the presentist model of historiography shores up arguments for ignoring Spencer in histories of evolutionary biology and in contemporary debates on the basic nature of social change. Jonathan Turner (1985, 1993, p. 58), in contrast, used an "admittedly presentist" approach to highlight Spencer's relevance for contemporary sociology. Turner's rationale for excluding some works (e.g., *Social Statics*) and including others (e.g., *First Principles*), his strategy of translating Spencer's ideas into terms which were not available to Spencer and his preoccupation with places where Spencer either contributed to or anticipated key concepts of modern sociology all follow logically from the controlling assumptions of Whig historiography.

Turner's study is not focused on Spencer's causal explanation of social evolution. But because Spencer's evolutionary ideas permeate all of his works, Turner covers this aspect of Spencer's sociology indirectly in his analysis of "the general systems theory" set out in *First Principles* and, more directly, in his discussion of the two systems for classifying societies which inform the institutional analysis which makes up the bulk of *The Principles of Sociology.*

Beginning with *First Principles*, Turner claims that its arguments clarify Spencer's assumptions about the nature of social change in three ways. First, by establishing that "Spencer drew his basic principles from the physics of his time" (Turner, 1985, p. 35), they contest the view (e.g., by Freeman and Peel) that the persistence of force is a metaphysical entity. Second, by conceptualizing the processes of "evolution *and* dissolution" (p. 35) or "in more modern terms, structuring and destructuring of elements" (p. 33), they develop a cosmic theory of cyclical change. Third, by establishing Spencer as the first general systems theorist, they clarify the role of Spencer's first principles in his sociology: "The vocabulary of *First Principles* is still prominent, but the major thrust of his analysis is to explore actual dynamics of the super-organic realm rather than to view this realm as an illustration of his first principles of the universe" (p. 43).

As Turner's exegesis of *The Principles of Sociology* demonstrates, this exploration of the superorganic realm is framed by two systems for classifying societies. Where the classificatory criterion is the degree of compounding, societies form an "evolutionary sequence" (p. 22) from simple to complex. But, continues Turner, this descriptive model of evolution is far less important than the explanatory model framed by "the elements of the 'militant–industrial' dichotomy". As Turner understands it, this dichotomy measures variation in the degree of political centralization or decentralization in a society. "The critical point in Spencer's model is that centralized power sets into motion forces that bring about decentralization. Conversely, decentralized power generates conditions that cause the centralization of power. There is an inherent dialectic in political regulation. Politically centralized systems create pressures for their decentralization and vice versa" (pp. 79–80). For Turner, then, Spencer's sociology of change anticipates Pareto's cyclical mode of analysis rather than the optimistic evolutionism of Marx, Durkheim, and others in the late nineteenth century (p. 34). Like them, however, it is a form of developmentalism.

Historicist Alternatives

Critics of the presentist model of historiography do not deny that "scientists have a legitimate right to focus on certain lines of theoretical development which hindsight tells us are important" (Bowler, 1987, p. 598). But, as they point out, this strategy for reconstructing the past breaks down when presentist histories focus on past developments which anticipated the present, regardless of their importance in their own time, or when they neglect earlier thinkers who "got it wrong" even if their ideas were of considerable importance in their own time. Because these uses of knowledge of the present distort our knowledge of the past, critics from Butterfield (1931) on (e.g., Skinner, 1968; Jones, 1974, 1977, 1983) have called for a historicist approach which interprets the past on its own terms.

Peter J. Bowler's (1988) reappraisal of the impact of natural selection on nineteenth-century thought is one of the most influential critiques of Whig histories of evolutionary biology. Centered on the now familiar distinction between evolutionary (Darwinian) and developmental (non-Darwinian) explanations of organic and social change, it shifts the focus from the former to the latter.

> My suggestion is that Darwin's theory should be seen not as the central theme in nineteenth-century evolutionism but as a catalyst that helped to bring about the transition to an evolutionary viewpoint within an essentially non-Darwinian conceptual framework. This was the "Non-Darwinian Revolution"; it was a revolution because it required the rejection of certain key aspects of creationism, but it was non-Darwinian because it succeeded in preserving and modernizing the old teleological view of things.
>
> Interpreted in this way, the story of nineteenth-century evolutionism centers not on Darwinism (as it is recognized today) but on the emergence of what might be called the "developmental" model of evolution ... stressing the orderly, goal-directed, and usually progressive character of evolution, often through a comparison with individual growth. (p. 5)

In this alternative history of evolutionism, Spencer's use of von Baerian epigenesis (a model of development) as the source analogy for his theory of organic evolution, his image of cosmological evolution as a "process grinding inexorably on toward a predictable goal, with no room for haphazard divergence in response to changing conditions" (p. 132) and his "conviction that European society was progressing steadily from militarism to laissez-faire individualism, and that the latter would inevitably dominate the world" (p. 138) all contribute to the "developmentalism which unifies so large a part of nineteenth-century thought" (p. 19).

Bowler's (1988) historicist study suggests that Spencer played a more important role in the development of nineteenth-century evolutionism than presentist histories suggest. But the way in which he develops this argument reinforces the presentist claim that Spencer can be ignored in contemporary debates. Spencer's most influential critic, J. D. Y. Peel, also agrees with this presentist claim but for a different reason. Using the historicist assumption of discontinuity in theoretical conventions between the past and present as a jumping off point, Peel (1971, pp. 264, vii) makes two arguments. First, "[v]ery often the theories of the classical sociologists are neither true nor false in the light of the purposes which have led us to theorize; because they are in large measure the attempts to grapple with a different reality, the answers to different problems, the upshot of different purposes" and, therefore, second, "sociology, more than any other kind of thought, makes sense only when it is set in the social context which produced it and provided its chief subject-matter."

Under the historicist model of historiography, the "problem of interpretation is always the problem of closing the context" (Dunn, 1968, p. 98). But because context "is not something obvious and given", it "has to be constructed, indeed created by the commentator" (Parekh and Berki, 1973, p. 182). The key to understanding Peel's interpretation, then, is his solution to the problem of closing the context.

In the course of constructing the context, Peel identified a wide-ranging set of factors which influenced the development of Spencer's thought, including the philosophies of science of Whewell, Herschel, and Mill, the content and reception of Chambers's *Vestiges of Creation*, Lyell's refutation of Lamarck's evolutionary ideas in *Principles of Geology*, Carpenter's discussion of von Baer's law of individual development in *Principles of Physiology*, Darwin's discovery of natural selection and Weismann's claim that natural selection was the sole cause of organic evolution. But Peel believes that "Spencer's assumptions and outlook belonged to provincial Dissent whose traditions, albeit in a rather secular form, had shaped him" (1971, p. viii). Using these social forces to explain the content, rise and fall of Spencer's theory of social evolution, he begins and ends with the arguments set out in *Social Statics* (1850), the work where the Nonconformist influence is clearest.

Peel presents *Social Statics* as an attempt to demonstrate the perfect condition of morality toward which mankind was tending. To be successful, Spencer had to specify the "details of this morality" which he did as "the policies of the extreme *laissez-faire* radicals of the late 1840s" (p. 92) and he had to convince his contemporaries that the human race was actually moving in this direction. According to Peel, it was to this end that Spencer introduced the developmental model of change which was to inform all of his subsequent works, including his sociology.

To support this developmental reconstruction of Spencer's causal explanation of social change, Peel (1971, pp. 100–1) first establishes that the theory of social change set out in *Social Statics* is teleological by using what have become the most widely cited passages from Spencer's works:

> All evil results from the non-adaptation of constitution to conditions. This is true of everything that lives . . . No matter what the special nature of the evil, it is invariably referable to the one generic cause – want of congruity between the faculties and their spheres of action . . . Equally true is it that evil perpetually tends to disappear. In virtue of an essential principle of life, this non-adaptation of an organism to its conditions is ever being rectified: and modification of one or both, continues until the adaptation is complete. . . .
>
> Progress . . . is not an accident, but a necessity. Instead of civilization being artificial, it is a part of nature; all of a piece with the development of the embryo or the unfolding of a flower. The modifications mankind have undergone, and are still undergoing, result from a law underlying the whole organic creation; and provided the human race continues, and the constitution of things remains the same, those modifications must end in completeness. As surely as the tree becomes bulky when it stands alone, and slender if one of a group . . . as surely as a blacksmith's arm grows large, and the skin of a labourer's hand thick . . . so surely must the human faculties be moulded into complete fitness for the social state; so surely must the things we call evil and [immorality] disappear; so surely must man become perfect.

Then, describing the "effective tone" of *Social Statics* as one of "necessitarian optimism" (p. 100), Peel draws two conclusions: (1) "all the essential elements of social evolution are present here – progress, necessity, adaptation, continual modification until perfection is reached" (p. 101) and, therefore, (2) when the full range of Spencer's works is considered,

> Little of what had gone before was abandoned, and thereafter there was (indeed there could be) little development. Apparent shifts of emphasis are due less to any change in Spencer's general conception of evolution than to the exigencies of convincing explanation in one or another of its parts. A theory as ambitious and all-embracing as Spencer's is sure to result in persistent tension between the part and the whole. But he still wanted to preserve the whole. The only major exception (which, significantly, did not affect the general theory) was that he became more pessimistic about man's imminent attainment of the social state, and so shifted to regarding present character-change as a very slow process. (p. 31)

Despite this claim for continuity across Spencer's works, Peel acknowledges that Spencer was ambivalent about teleology: "He expels it from the front door of the evolutionary palace, because otherwise he cannot claim the legitimacy of science: Erasmus Darwin, the author of *Vestiges*, and even Lamarck are reprimanded because 'they imply the belief that organic progress is a result of some indwelling tendency to develop, supernaturally impressed on living matter at the outset – some ever-acting constructive force, which, independently of other forces, moulds organisms into higher and higher forms' " (p. 135). And, continues Peel, even though use inheritance offered the possibility of a non-teleological mechanism of progress, Spencer does not, and indeed cannot, exploit this possibility. He is "still obliged to smuggle teleology in by back ways since, because he wants to demonstrate history's inevitable path to perfection, he needs a guarantee of direction in evolution. This cannot be provided by adaptation, since that provides no account of how the environment may change" (p. 135). A guarantee of direction in evolution can be provided by the metaphysical principle of the persistence of force set out in *First Principles*, however. For Peel, then, "adaptation to the social state [to use the terms of *Social Statics*] is essentially a secular process which is immanent in society itself, and like all such processes conceals teleology – the psychological telos of a human nature with a potential, and the sociological telos of an unrealized perfect society which seems to be drawing the human race towards itself through history" (p. 155).

The persistence of force holds throughout Evolution's inorganic, organic and superorganic divisions. To characterize a second aspect of evolution which is "peculiar to social evolution," Peel argues that Spencer transformed "what had become a commonplace in societal contrasts since the mid-eighteenth century, the distinction between military (or 'militant' as Spencer actually said) and industrial societies" (p. 192) into a pattern for general social evolution" (p. 198). Because this framework for the "analysis of real social change" embodies the "necessitarian optimism" of *Social Statics*, the transition from militancy to industrialism is inevitable – a conclusion that the transitions from savagery, through feudal aristocracy into the early stages of industrialization seemed to support. But, Peel continues, the "unprecedented shift to militancy" and the trend toward increased governmental interference which occurred in Britain toward the end of the nineteenth century undermined this fit between theory and reality. It is in this mismatch between the predictions of Spencer's theory of social evolution and the reality of late nineteenth-century England that Peel finds his explanation of why Spencer's ideas were obsolete by the end of the nineteenth century. "At the end of the century evolutionary theories, Spencer's above all, lost their power to convince very suddenly because history played them false: their predictions, stages and continua just did not fit events any more" (p. 245).

Peel's conclusion that Spencer is superseded "not primarily because his theories are wrong about Society" but because "they refer to a very different social reality from that which confronts us" (p. x) follows logically from the controlling assumptions of historicism. So does his refusal to consider Spencer's contemporary relevance. For Peel, "[w]e can learn the most profound lessons from the history of sociology when we use it to point up the particular features of our own society and the requirements of our purposes in theorizing, both so different from Spencer's" (p. x).

RECONTEXTUALIZING SPENCER'S CAUSAL EXPLANATION OF ORGANIC AND SOCIAL CHANGE: SPENCER, DARWIN, AND WEISMANN ON ORGANIC EVOLUTION

Two things are clear from this overview of modern critiques of Spencer's evolutionary theorizing. First, there is considerable disagreement among Spencer's modern critics about his mechanism of organic and social evolution. Second, when we move from the mechanism to the assumptions about the nature of change which it entails, we find agreement rather than disagreement. At this level of abstraction these interpretations are all forms of developmentalism. Because each interpretation validates the others, it is not surprising that the developmental reconstruction is the received view in histories of evolutionary theory in biology and sociology. But are these modern critics right? Did Spencer explain organic and social evolution as an unfolding of immanent qualities? or did he develop a genuine evolutionary theory as critics of the developmental reconstruction (e.g., Carneiro, 1967, 1973, 1974; Gould, 1977; Haines, 1988, 1991, 1992) argue?

To answer these questions I attempt to disprove the developmental reconstruction and flesh out the evolutionary alternative by combining two strategies that have been used in anti-Whig histories of evolutionary biology (e.g., by Mayr, 1982, 1985, 1990, 1991b; Richards, 1987; Bowler, 1988). First, I present an overview of the development of Spencer's evolutionary theorizing that attempts to bring out as clearly as possible what Spencer actually said about Lamarck's assumption of an inherent drive toward perfection, von Baerian epigenesis, the persistence of force and the militant–industrial classification on the one hand (the ideas which supposedly render Spencer's explanatory model developmental) and use inheritance and natural selection on the other (the evolutionary alternatives that were available to Spencer). Second, I explore Spencer's relationships with the two most influential nineteenth-century evolutionists – Charles Darwin and August Weismann – to see if what they said about Spencer's causal explanation of organic evolution supports the developmental reconstruction or the evolutionary alternative.

Using these strategies to close the context does not discount the influence of Nonconformity on the development of Spencer's evolutionary ideas. But, as Richards (1987, p. 557) points out, "there is no justification to assume a priori that only social forces (e.g., political and ideological interests) fully determine ideas. Historians must rather empirically analyze both the conceptual system in question and its intellectual environment to discriminate the several kinds of force that are operative and to estimate their relative strengths." In Spencer's case this involves moving the other factors that Peel identified in his construction of the context of Spencer's sociology of change from the background to the foreground – a move which is consistent with the importance Spencer (1904a, 1904b; Duncan, 1908a, 1908b) himself accorded these factors in the development of his evolutionary theorizing.[5]

Spencer developed his theories of organic and social evolution by participating in the nineteenth-century debates about the fact and mechanism of organic evolution. To establish the fact of evolution, the first evolutionists had to dislodge the special creation solution to the organic origins problem. In his biological works (e g., "The Development Hypothesis" ([1852], 1966) and The Principles of Biology (1864, [1898], 1966), Spencer used standard nineteenth-century arguments from classification, embryology, morphology, and distribution to challenge the hypothesis of special creation. By demonstrating that the hypothesis of evolution can explain facts which anti-evolutionists claimed could be explained only by special creation and facts which special creation cannot explain, these works helped to establish the fact of organic evolution. Thus, by 1895

[5]It is not without interest to note that Peel (1971, p. viii) concludes that "in his autobiographical essay, 'The Filiation of Ideas' [Spencer] neglected the deepest roots of his thought (which he only may have been dimly aware of, like most of us) for a number of late and specific borrowings of ideas from scientific sources."

Weismann (1895, p. 456) could write: "*As to the fact* that evolution has taken place there can no longer be any doubt nowadays; and, accordingly, Huxley was able to affirm recently that 'if the Darwinian hypothesis [natural selection] were swept away, evolution would still stand where it is.' Certainly, evolution has the value of a fact; it is only as regards the tracing of it back to its natural causes that there is any diversity of opinion among us."

Some of Spencer's contemporaries (e.g., Robert Chambers, Richard Owen, Lord Salisbury) simply incorporated the fact of evolution into natural theology and argued that organic evolution was proof of the existence of God. Others (e.g., Karl Ernst von Baer, Theodor Eimer) replaced the hand of God with an inherent drive toward ever-greater perfection in organisms and the world. Spencer's rejection of these teleological explanations of organic evolution was explicit: In

> whatever way it is formulated, or by whatever language it is obscured, this ascription of organic evolution to some aptitude naturally possessed by organisms, or miraculously imposed on them, is unphilosophical . . . this assumption of a persistent formative power, inherent in organisms, and making them unfold into higher forms, is an assumption no more tenable than the assumption of special creations: of which, indeed, it is but a modification; differing only by the fusion of separate unknown processes into a continuous unknown process. (Spencer, [1898], 1966, p. 404)

The correct explanation of organic evolution can be obtained by obversion from teleology, however. For,

> though on the hypothesis of Evolution, it is clear that things are not arranged thus or thus for securing special ends, it is also clear, that arrangements which *do* secure these special ends, tend continually to establish themselves – are established by their fulfilment of these ends. Besides insuring a structural fitness between each kind of organism and its circumstances, the working of "natural selection" also insures a fitness between the mode and rate of multiplication of each kind of organism and its circumstances. We may, therefore, without any teleological implication, consider the fitness of homogenesis and heterogenesis to the needs of the different classes of organisms which exhibit them. (Spencer, [1898], 1966, pp. 234–5)

In his early biological works Spencer's anti-teleological alternative was use inheritance. Borrowed from Lamarck's *Zoological Philosophy* (1809), it explained "the process of descent with modification" (Spencer, [1898], 1966, p. 559) through the joint operation of two laws. According to the first law of differential use and disuse of organs in response to environmental contingencies, high levels of use strengthen and develop organs, while low levels of use lead to their deterioration and eventual disappearance. The second law states that these environmentally induced modifications are "preserved by reproduction" (Lamarck, [1809], 1984, p. 113). Lamarck believed that the environment had a direct effect on the hereditary material in the plant series and in the simplest animals. In more complex animals (i.e., animals with nervous systems), however, habits define a key intervening variable between environmental circumstances and organic change. Here, environmental changes create new needs, new needs require new habits, which, in turn, exercise organs differentially to produce changes in organic structures which can be inherited.

Spencer discovered the Lamarckian formulation of use inheritance in 1840 when he read the geologist Charles Lyell's *Principles of Geology* (1831–3). Lyell's refutation of Lamarck's evolutionary ideas convinced most of the scientific community to reject this explanation of organic evolution as unscientific (Young, 1971; Hull, 1973, 1985; Richards, 1987). Spencer was unconvinced. "But my reading of Lyell, one of whose chapters was devoted to a refutation of Lamarck's views concerning the origin of species, had the effect of giving me a decided leaning to them" (1904a, p. 201).

From this point on, use inheritance remained one of the cornerstones of Spencer's theory of organic evolution. The subsequent introduction of its other cornerstone, von Baer's law of individual development, in "Progress: Its Law and Cause" ([1857a], 1966), left the Lamarckian foundation of his theory unchanged. Von Baer's specification of the course of change did, however, lead Spencer to abandon the teleological conception of progress he had adopted in *Social Statics* ([1850], 1966). If, as Spencer now believed, the nature of progress "in itself" had been discovered by the German embryologists von Baer and Wolff, then the "current conception" that contemplated phenomena "solely as bearing on human happiness" must be discarded because "it is in great measure erroneous" ([1857a], 1966, pp. 8–9).

Spencer replaced this teleological conception of progress (which informed *Social Statics*) with a more explicitly biological one. In his view, von Baer and Wolff had "settled beyond dispute" (Spencer, [1857a], 1966, p. 10) that organic progress was an advance from homogeneity of structure to heterogeneity of structure through a process of successive differentiations. Six months later, in "Transcendental Physiology" ([1857b], 1966), Spencer introduced an important corrective to this conception of the course of organic evolution. Differentiation is necessary but not sufficient for evolution. Evolution also presupposes integration, by which Spencer meant the coalescence of parts performing similar functions.

Spencer's goal was to show that this law of organic progress was the law of all progress, including social progress. He did not call this universal law "progress" because the process it describes is nonteleological. Explained by use inheritance, the transition from homogeneity to heterogeneity is contingent upon favorable environmental conditions. A more heterogeneous or "advanced" structure will develop only if the environment demands more complex habits. Otherwise, there will be stasis or retrogression.

In these versions of his theorizing on evolution, Spencer used evolution and use inheritance as synonyms. Then in 1859 Darwin presented his alternative explanation of organic evolution in *The Origin of Species*. Evolution by natural selection is a two-step process (Mayr, 1982, p. 57; 1988, pp. 97–100). Step 1 is the production of variation. Step 2 is selection through survival of the fittest, where "the fittest" are the individuals whose hereditary constitutions are best adapted to the current environment. Differential survival and/or differential reproduction produce the variation for the next cycle of selection. Over the generations, this "preservation of favourable variations and the rejection of injurious variations" (Darwin, [1859], 1964, p. 81) leads to gradual continuous change of populations.

Like use inheritance, this explanatory model is nonteleological; therefore, Spencer was forced to address the challenge it presented for his own causal explanation of organic evolution. Unlike most of Darwin's contemporaries (Bowler, 1983; 1988; Mayr, 1985, 1991b), Spencer immediately adopted natural selection as a cause of evolutionary change. In a letter to Darwin on February 22, 1860, he wrote:

> You have wrought a considerable modification in the views I held – while having the same general conception of the relation of species, genera, orders &C as gradually arising by differentiation and divergence like the branches of a tree & while regarding these cumulative modifications as wholly due to the influence of surrounding circumstances I was under the erroneous impression that the sole-cause was adaptation to changing conditions brought about by habit, using the phrase conditions of existence in its widest sense as including climate, food, & contact with other organisms . . . But you

have convinced me that throughout a great proportion of cases, direct adaptation does not explain the facts, but that they are explained only by adaptation through natural selection. (Burkhardt et al., 1993, p 98)

In *The Principles of Biology*, in his other post-Darwinian works, and in post-Darwinian editions of earlier works, Spencer followed Darwin and argued that neither use inheritance nor natural selection was a sufficient cause of organic evolution. Each accounted for some, but not all, of the facts of nature.

Use inheritance and natural selection are both "true causes" (Spencer, [1898], 1966, p. 446). But, as proximate causes, neither satisfied the criteria for complete explanation set out in *First Principles*. "Only when the process of evolution of organisms is affiliated on the process of evolution in general, can it be truly said to be explained. The thing required is to show that its various results are corollaries of first principles. We have to reconcile the facts with the universal laws of the re-distribution of matter and motion" ([1898], 1966, pp. 497–8).

To understand why this reconciliation was required, *First Principles* must be read against the backdrop of the philosophies of science set out by John F. W. Herschel ([1830], 1987), William Whewell ([1837, 1967, [1840], 1967), and John Stuart Mill (1843). Reading it in this way establishes that Spencer's general philosophy is a philosophy of science organized around the distinction between phenomenal laws and fundamental laws – the two kinds of laws that Herschel, Whewell, and Mill argued were necessary for good science (Haines, 1992). Exemplified by Kepler's laws of planetary motion, phenomenal laws describe empirical regularities in the succession and coexistence of phenomena (e.g., the planets move in ellipses around the sun). Fundamental laws – like gravitation, "the most universal truth at which human has yet arrived" – explain why observed regularities occur (Herschel, [1830], 1987, p. 123).

In Spencer's philosophy of science, the law of evolution has the same logical status as Kepler's laws of planetary motion. As a phenomenal law, it identified a phenomenon that must be explained. This led Spencer to ask: "Must we rest satisfied with the conclusion that throughout all classes of concrete phenomena such is the course of transformation. Or is it possible for us to ascertain *why* such is the course of transformation" ([1862], 1911, p. 322). The way in which this question is framed illustrates the influence of the Whewell–Herschel–Mill canons of good science on Spencer's philosophy of science. So does the way in which Spencer chose to answer this question: "Just as it was possible to interpret the empirical generalizations called Kepler's laws, as necessary consequences of the law of gravitation; so it may be possible to interpret the foregoing empirical generalizations as necessary consequences of some deeper law" (p. 322). This "deeper law" is the persistence of force, a fundamental law that – together with its corollaries, the other first principles – explains why this is the course of transformation. As the most general and most simple proposition of Spencer's philosophy of science, the principle that "force can neither come into existence or cease to exist" (p. 180) cannot be merged into nor derived from any other truth: it is "the truth by derivation from which all other truths are to be proved" (p. 433). In the same way in which gravitation is the cause of each of the groups of phenomena that Kepler's laws generalized, the persistence of force is the cause of the groups of phenomena generalized by the law of evolution.

Spencer's distinction between proximate-causal and ultimate-causal explanations also reflects the influence of the Whewell–Herschel–Mill canons of good science on his thinking. Produced by inductive inference and the testing of hypotheses against empirical observations, proximate-causal explanations are science specific. They explain organic evolution in biological terms. But, like other scientists of his day who accepted the Whewell–Herschel–Mill view of how science ought to be done (e.g., Darwin (Ruse, 1975) and Weismann (Mayr, 1982)), Spencer felt compelled to interpret his findings in terms of matter, motion and force. Because only ultimate-causal explanations can do this, where ultimate is used in the Herschellian sense of incapable of further analysis, for Spencer, a complete explanation of organic evolution must include the proximate- and ultimate-causal explanatory levels. This combination is practicable only because the persistence of force and the law of evolution satisfy the Whewell–Herschel–Mill canons of good science. If they were metaphysical principles, then ultimate-causal explanations would have no place in a science of biology.[6]

Darwin's critique of Spencer's ultimate-causal explanation of organic evolution must also be read against the backdrop of nineteenth-century philosophy of science. At issue was the criticism (e.g., by Louis Agassiz, Richard Owen, and Adam Sedgwick) that Darwin's own theory of evolution by natural selection was not properly scientific, where the standard of comparison was Baconian

[6] *First Principles* did include a discussion of theologico-metaphysical beliefs in part 1, "The unknowable" but, as Spencer himself stressed, these beliefs stand outside of the philosophy of science which was set out in part 2, "The knowable."

induction. To counter this criticism, Darwin used two interrelated, yet distinct, strategies. First, he emphasized, whenever possible, his reliance on the inductive method. Thus, in his autobiography, he claimed that on the *Beagle* he had "worked on true Baconian principles, and without any theory collected facts on a wholesale scale" (Howard, 1982, p. 93).[7] Second, he used his writings and correspondence to distance himself from evolutionary theorists who had been criticized for relying largely on speculation and deduction, where deduction referred to "an irresponsible leap to a conclusion of high generality and the subsequent deduction of consequences of these generalizations regardless of the observed facts" (Hull, 1973, p. 4).

Darwin's letter to Spencer on November 25, 1858 acknowledging the "very kind present" of a copy of *Essays: Scientific, Political and Speculative* illustrates his concern for the scientific status of the theory of natural selection: "Your remarks on the general argument of the so-called development theory seem to me admirable. I am at present preparing an Abstract of a larger work on the changes of species; but I treat the subject simply as a naturalist, and not from a general point of view; otherwise, in my opinion, your argument could not have been improved on, and might have been quoted by me with great advantage" (Duncan, 1908a, p. 113). The "general point of view" which prevented Darwin from quoting it "with great advantage" was Spencer's ultimate-causal framing of essentially biological arguments. The evaluation of the fourth installment of *The Principles of Biology* in a letter from Darwin to J. D. Hooker on June 30, 1866, draws the same distinction between Darwin's scientific approach and Spencer's philosophical alternative. "I have almost finished the last number of H. Spencer, and am astonished at its prodigality of original thought. But the reflection constantly recurred to me that each suggestion, to be of real value to science, would require years of work" (F. Darwin, 1903, p. 235). So does the assessment of Spencer in Darwin's autobiography:

> After reading any of his books I generally feel enthusiastic admiration for his transcendent talents, and have often wondered whether in the distant future he would rank with such great men as Descartes, Leibnitz, etc., about whom, however, I know very little. Nevertheless I am not conscious of having profited in my own work by Spencer's writings. His deductive manner of treating any subject is wholly opposed to my frame of mind. His conclusions never convince me: and over and over again I have said to myself, after reading one of his

[7]In using this strategy, Darwin misrepresented his (and Spencer's) methodology.

discussions – "Here would be a fine subject for half-a-dozen years'
work." His fundamental generalisations (which have been compared
in importance by some persons with Newton's Laws!) – which I
daresay may be very valuable under a philosophical point of view, are
of such a nature that they do not seem to me to be of any strictly
scientific use. They partake more of the nature of definitions than of
laws of nature. They do not aid one in predicting what will happen in
any particular case. Anyhow they have not been of any use to me.
(C. Darwin, [1887], 1958, pp. 108–9)

Darwin, the scientist, attributes his success to his "love of science –
unbounded patience in long reflecting over any subject – industry in
observing and collecting facts – and a fair share of invention as well
as common sense" (Schweber, 1978, p. 321). Spencer, the
philosopher, should have "trained himself to observe more" and to
use his "transcendent talents" less.

By stressing his aversion to Spencer's deductive, speculative, a
priori approach to the development of evolutionary theory, Darwin
attempted to undermine the charge that his own work was not
properly scientific. He was careful, however, not to challenge those
aspects of Spencer's work which supported his own theory –
Spencer's defence of the fact of evolution and his use of natural
selection and use inheritance to explain this fact. This agreement
notwithstanding, neither Darwin nor Spencer denied that they
disagreed about the relative importance of these mechanisms of
organic change. For Darwin, natural selection was the most
important factor of organic evolution at all times and in all places.
Spencer, in contrast, believed that natural selection was the principal
cause of organic evolution only for the early evolutionary stages and
for plants and inferior animals. In other species, evolution was a
product of use inheritance. And, even though their positions had
begun to converge as Darwin came to assign more importance to use
inheritance in his later works (Spencer, [1898], 1966, p. 630), Spencer
openly admitted "I hold that the inheritance of functionally-caused
alterations played a larger part than [Darwin] admitted even at the
close of his life; and that, coming more to the front as evolution has
advanced, it has played the chief part in producing the highest types"
(p. 560).

Until Darwin's death in 1882 this disagreement about the relative
importance of use inheritance and natural selection remained
relatively unimportant to Spencer and his contemporaries. It
became important when Spencer was forced to confront the most
serious challenge to his causal explanation of organic and social
evolution: the claim by the "neo-Darwinians" that natural selection

was the sole cause of organic change (Lankester, 1890; Wallace, 1893; Weismann, 1893, 1894, 1895) and social change (Ball, 1890, 1893; Kidd, 1894; C. L. Morgan, 1898; T. H. Morgan, 1903). Centered on the question "Can the effects of use and disuse be transmitted?" (Weismann, 1895, p. 421), the controversy over use inheritance intensified during the last decades of Spencer's life, with Spencer and Weismann taking the leading roles.

Like Spencer and Darwin, Weismann believed in use inheritance until at least 1881 (Mayr, 1985). His subsequent rejection of it followed logically from the two arguments which formed the core of his theory of heredity. If the germ-plasm (the material of heredity) and the soma (body) are separate from the beginning and if only the soma is environmentally malleable, then acquired characters cannot be inherited. To support this argument for the all-sufficiency of natural selection, Weismann adopted the same strategy that Spencer (and Darwin) had used to refute the hypothesis of special creation. He identified biological facts that he claimed could not be explained by use inheritance (e.g., special adaptations of worker and soldier castes of insects) and he argued that facts that were used by Spencer and others to shore up the case for use inheritance were actually explicable by natural selection (e.g., degeneration of structure during evolution).

Spencer (1893a, 1893b, 1893c, 1894, 1895, [1898], 1966) attacked on all three fronts. Dismissing the distinction between the germ-plasm and the soma as "speculation," he then attempted to establish the insufficiency of natural selection by using the principle of elimination. After introducing a series of biological facts that he claimed cannot be explained by natural selection (e.g., the co-adaptation of multiple parts, the distribution of tactual discrimina-tiveness in humans, the small jaws of humans who eat prepared food and domesticate dogs living peaceful and protected lives and the existence of rudimentary structures), Spencer simply concluded these facts must be explained by use inheritance – the only other vera causa. Not all of the participants in the controversy over use inheritance found this logic convincing. "Mr. Spencer appears to think that if he disposes of Weismann's explanation of blindness of cave-animals according to 'Panmyxia' – there remains only the explanation by transmission of acquired characters in the field" – an assumption which renders the empirical demonstration unnecessary. Without such evidence, the "important question is still as it was five years ago, *'Does* it take place?'" (Lankester, 1893, p. 389). Because "Weismann, no less than Spencer, had to rely on an argument by elimination to dispose of his opponent's theory"

(Churchill, 1977, p. 458), it is not surprising that the Spencer–Weismann controversy ended with Spencer (1895) and Weismann (1895) agreeing to disagree

When the Spencer–Weismann debate ended, the verdict was still not in on use inheritance. Not surprisingly, their contemporaries offered different assessments of the status of use inheritance. Some sided with Weismann: "Suffice it to say that no evidence has yet been produced in proof of that belief, which now is entertained only by a negligible minority of biologists" (Elliot, 1917, p. 257) and "Though this was considered by Darwin to be one among other modes in which evolution proceeds, yet it is manifestly inadequate to account for evolution when taken by itself, and, the great majority of modern biologists consider that 'use-inheritance' is altogether a fiction" (Anonymous, 1908, p. 115). Others drew the opposite conclusion: "How, then, does the matter stand when we pass from these merely antecedent grounds of logic, to the real battlefield of facts? Here the questions are three in number. (1) Do we meet with facts in organic nature which cannot be explained by the theory of Natural Selection? (2) Are any of these facts capable of being explained by the theory of Use-inheritance? (3) Is there any further evidence in favour of this theory? The answers to all these questions must be provisionally in the affirmative, at all events, until the neo-Darwinians have more effectually disposed of the evidence" (Romanes, 1893, p. 516). As recent histories of evolutionary biology confirm, use inheritance was not refuted during Spencer's lifetime (Ruse, 1979; Mayr, 1985; Bowler, 1988). The majority of biologists did not accept natural selection as the sole mechanism of organic evolution until the development of the modern synthesis in the 1940s (Mayr, 1991a). Until then, use inheritance and natural selection were both accepted as evolutionary explanations of organic and social change.

Most of Spencer's contemporaries in the scientific community used the controversy over use inheritance to clarify their explanations of organic evolution. Spencer, in contrast, used it to defend his explanations of organic and social evolution and it was his concern for the latter that explains the otherwise surprising extent of his participation in this controversy. By this time in his life (his seventies) Spencer was no stranger to controversy. But persistent health problems had long before forced him to ignore most attacks on his ideas. What was it about the controversy over use inheritance, then, which led him to abandon this strategy? Simply this: Spencer believed that the inheritance of acquired characters was the primary mechanism of organic evolution and social evolution.

Because he did not make the modern distinction between organic evolution and cultural evolution, for him this was not a controversy by biologists, for biologists. Organic and social evolution were explained by the same mechanisms – use inheritance and natural selection. Therefore, as the following quotation from the last chapter of Spencer's *The Principles of Sociology* makes clear, causal explanations of organic evolution and social evolution were part of the same debate.

> Evolution does not imply a latent tendency to improve, everywhere in operation. There is no uniform ascent from lower to higher, but only an occasional production of a form which, in virtue of greater fitness for more complex conditions, becomes capable of a longer life of a more varied kind. And while such higher type begins to dominate over lower types and to spread at their expense, the lower types survive in habitats or modes of life that are not usurped, or are thrust into inferior habitats or modes of life in which they retrogress.
>
> What thus holds with organic types must also hold with types of societies. (1897, p. 609)

For Spencer, then, "considering the width and depth of the effects which our acceptance of one or other of these hypotheses [namely, that acquired characters are inherited, or that they are not] must have upon our views of Life, Mind, Morals, and Politics, the question – Which of them is true? demands beyond all other questions whatever the attention of scientific men." Because his contemporaries agreed (cf. Romanes, 1887, 1890; Ball, 1890, 1893; Kidd, 1894; C. L. Morgan, 1898; T. H. Morgan, 1903; Bourne, 1909; Elliot, 1917), nineteenth-century responses to Spencer's theory of organic evolution were, in effect, responses to his theory of social evolution. Read in this way, the Spencer–Darwin and Spencer–Weismann exchanges corroborate the evolutionary reconstruction that my reading of Spencer's books, articles, reviews, and letters suggests.

This way of contextualizing Spencer's evolutionary theorizing also highlights where modern critics went wrong in constructing their developmental alternative. According to them, Spencer's explanatory model is developmental for one of four reasons: (1) it confounds the evolutionary and developmental models of change; (2) its mechanism is the Lamarckian law of progressive development; (3) its mechanism is the metaphysical principle of the persistence of force; or (4) its mechanism is the immanent dialectic set out in the militant–industrial dichotomy. The first argument acknowledges Spencer's debt to von Baer but misrepresents his law of individual development as a source analogy for Spencer's specification of the mechanism of organic and social evolution. In Spencer's theories von Baerian epigenesis specifies the course of change. The second argument assigns Lamarckism its proper role but is marred by a fundamental misunderstanding of what Lamarckism meant to Spencer. Spencer did identify the argument for an inherent tendency toward progress or perfection as a core component of Lamarck's evolutionary theory. But he rejected it on the grounds that the "single *vera causa*" which Lamarck had discovered was the inheritance of acquired characters ([1886], 1966, p. 390). Lamarckism, for Spencer, meant use inheritance.

The third argument misconstrues the logical status of the persistence of force and its role in Spencer's biology and sociology. Restating the law of conservation of energy, the persistence of force is not a metaphysical principle.[8] It is a fundamental law which together with the law of evolution generates the kind of causal explanation that Spencer called ultimate-causal explanation. Ultimate-causal explanations verify proximate causal explanations (e.g., use inheritance and natural selection) by deducing them from simpler and more general laws. Because the principles of biology and principles of sociology are the most general laws of the sciences of biology and sociology, they can be deductively interpreted only by documenting their affiliation on the law of evolution. By tying together facts from biology and sociology, the persistence of force pointed to a fundamental unity that underlies their apparent diversity – exactly what the Whewell–Herschel–Mill canons of good science prescribed.

The fourth argument misses Spencer's Lamarckian argument for the superorganic environment as the major source of adaptational variation. Whether the organization for offence and defense or the sustaining organization is more "largely developed" depends upon the nature of the interactions that occur between a society and its neighboring societies in the struggle for existence. If these interactions are hostile, then militancy evolves; if peaceful, then industrialism is adaptive. Because the shift from militant to

---

[8]Spencer ([1862], 1911, p. 146) preferred "persistence" to "conservation" because he believed that the word conservation incorrectly implies: (1) "a conserver and an act of conserving"; (2) "without some act of conservation, force would disappear"; and (3) force does not exist "before the particular manifestation of it which is contemplated." "Force" was preferable to "energy" because it covers the force possessed by matter in action (energy) and the force that allows matter to maintain its shape and occupy space, "a force which physicists appear to think needs no name."

industrial organization occurs only in response to changes in the superorganic environment, societies do not cycle between militancy and industrialism regardless of their superorganic environments as Turner's immanent dialectic suggests. Like its organic counterpart, Spencer's explanation of social change is evolutionary, not developmental.

SPENCER AND THE POST-DEVELOPMENTALIST VIEW OF SOCIAL CHANGE

By demonstrating how and why the developmental reconstruction misrepresents Spencer's assumptions about the nature of social change, this analysis of Spencer's evolutionary theorizing on its own terms established two things. First, the developmental reconstruction was created largely by Spencer's modern critics using presentist and historicist models of historiography. Darwin ([1859], 1964, p. 154) and Weismann (1895, p. 456) both attacked developmental explanations of organic change but neither extended this line of attack to Spencer. They accepted that, like them, Spencer had rejected the assumption of immanent or intrinsic causation that modern critics claim is the core of Spencer's evolutionary theorizing. When Spencer's nineteenth-century critics are considered, the consensus on developmentalism breaks down. Second, Spencer played a more important role in the development of evolutionary theory than standard histories suggest, but not for the reason Bowler (1988) gives. The developmental model of evolution may belong to the nineteenth century but it does not belong to Spencer. If it did, then it would be "difficult for us to realize how great a stir he made in the world" (Parsons, [1937], 1968, p. 3) and we would have to agree with Parsons's verdict on Spencer's contemporary significance.

Because the conclusions we draw about the contemporary significance of past sociologies depend upon the historiographic model we adopt, Spencer's relevance for modern sociology can be reassessed only by abandoning the historicist assumption of discontinuity between the theoretical conventions of past and present sociologies (Jones, 1974, 1983, 1985a, 1985b; Seidman, 1985a, 1985b). If "classic texts cannot be concerned with our questions and answers, but only with their own;" as Skinner (1968, p. 50) argued in his defense of historicism, then "there are simply no perennial problems in philosophy [or sociology]: there are only individual answers to individual questions." But, as critics of historicism argue, "[a]lthough Plato dealt with political problems in a different context and a different idiom, he was still concerned to find answers to questions which are still with us today" (Parekh and Berki, 1973, p. 179). This argument for continuity restates a caveat that Skinner (1968, p. 52) attached to his own claim that problems and answers arise from and remain embedded in particular contexts. "The claim that there are no perennial problems in philosophy [or sociology] is not a denial of the possibility that they may be perennial *questions*, if these are sufficiently abstractly framed."

Recent participants in the historiographic debate continue to find Skinner's caveat more convincing than the claim it qualifies. They argue that at some level of abstraction, past texts have some autonomy from their originating context (Seidman, 1983) and, therefore, that the presentist assumption of continuity between past and present is valid when framed at this level (e.g., the central problems in social theory). For them, extreme anti-Whiggery becomes, priggery (to borrow Harrison's (1987) term). Stocking's (1965) enlightened presentism, Hull's (1979) defense of presentism in the history of science, Seidman's (1983, 1985a, 1985b) revised presentism, Alexander's (1987) case for the centrality of the classics, Mayr's (1982, 1990) developmental historiography and Richards's (1987) natural selection model of historiography all call for a model of historiography that is presentist but not Whiggish, and historicist but not priggish. Following its controlling assumptions means judging past sociologies against standards actually employed by contemporaries in the scientific community of the time (Richards, 1987, p. 244) while recognizing that properly con-textualized reconstructions can be deployed in contemporary debates (Fisch and Schaffer, 1991). In Spencer's case, the contemporary debate is about the nature of social change and the properly contextualized reconstruction is the evolutionary reconstruction.

In the sociology of social change today, "evolution" and "development" are used routinely as synonyms. If the developmental reconstruction of Spencer's theory of social evolution was valid, then this convention would not be problematic – at least in Spencer's case. But the developmental reconstruction is not valid. Through its combination of use inheritance and natural selection Spencer's causal explanation of social change embodies the hallmarks of the evolutionary model of change: environmental contingency, historical specificity and probabilism. The modern case against developmentalism in sociology (e.g., by Popper, 1957, 1968; Nisbet, 1969, 1970; Smith, 1973; Peel, 1971; Giddens, 1979, 1984;

Tilly, 1984; Wallerstein, 1991) may have cleared the way for the post-developmentalist alternative that is "now coming to the fore of sociological imagination" (Sztompka, 1993, p. 190). But by confounding developmentalism and evolutionism in a way Spencer did not, it has left unexplored the potential contribution of Spencer's evolutionary theory to this post-developmentalist movement. Because, in an important sense, the post-developmentalist view of social change is becoming evolutionary, now may be the time to begin this exploration.

REFERENCES

Alexander, Jeffrey C. 1987: The centrality of the classics. In Anthony Giddens and Jonathan H. Turner (eds), *Social Theory Today*, Stanford: Stanford University Press, 11–57.

Anonymous 1908: Herbert Spencer. *Edinburgh Review*, 208, 105–35.

Ball, William Platt 1890: *Are the Effects of Use and Disuse Inherited? An examination of the view held by Spencer and Darwin*. London: Macmillan and Co.

—— 1893: Natural selection and Lamarckism. *Natural Science*, 2, 337–49.

Bourne, Gilbert Charles 1909: *Herbert Spencer and Animal Evolution*. Oxford: Clarendon Press.

Bowler, Peter J. 1983: *The Eclipse of Darwinism: anti-Darwinian evolution theories in the decades around 1900*. Baltimore: The Johns Hopkins University Press.

—— 1987: Historians, Whigs and progress. *Nature*, 330, 598.

—— 1988: *The Non-Darwinian Revolution: reinterpreting a historical myth*. Baltimore: The Johns Hopkins University Press.

Burkhardt, Richard 1977: *The Spirit of System: Lamarck and evolutionary biology*. Cambridge, Mass.: Harvard University Press.

Burkhardt, Frederick, Porter, Duncan M., Browne, Janet and Richmond, Marsha 1993: *The Correspondence of Charles Darwin*, Vol. 8: *1860*. Cambridge: Cambridge University Press.

Butterfield, H. 1931: *The Whig Interpretation of History*. London: Bell & Sons.

Carneiro, Robert L. 1967: *The Evolution of Society: selections from Herbert Spencer's Principles of Sociology*. Chicago: University of Chicago Press.

—— 1973: Structure, function and equilibrium in the evolutionism of Herbert Spencer. *Journal of Anthropological Research*, 29, 77–95.

—— 1974: Comments. *Current Anthropology*, 15, 222–3.

Churchill, Frederick B. 1977: The Weismann–Spencer controversy over the inheritance of acquired characters. In E. G. Forbes (ed.), *Human Implications of Scientific Advance*, Edinburgh: Edinburgh University Press, 451–68.

Darwin, Charles [1859], 1964: *On the Origin of Species. A facsimile of the first edition*. Cambridge, Mass.: Harvard University Press.

—— [1872], 1958: *The Origin of Species*. New York: Mentor Books.

—— [1887], 1958: *The Autobiography of Charles Darwin*, ed. Nora Barlow. London: Collins.

Darwin, Francis (ed.) 1903: *More Letters of Charles Darwin.* London: John Murray.

Duncan, David (ed.) 1908a: *Life and Letters of Herbert Spencer,* Vol. 1. New York: D. Appleton and Company.

—— (ed.) 1908b: *Life and Letters of Herbert Spencer,* Vol 2. New York: D. Appleton and Company.

Dunn, John 1968: The identity of the history of ideas. *Journal of the Royal Institute of Philosophy,* 42, 85–104.

Elliot, Hugh 1917: *Herbert Spencer.* London: Constable and Company Ltd.

Fisch, Menachem and Schaffer, Simon (eds) 1991: *William Whewell: a composite portrait.* Oxford: Oxford University Press.

Freeman, Derek 1974: The evolutionary theories of Charles Darwin and Herbert Spencer. *Current Anthropology,* 15, 211–37.

Giddens, Anthony 1979: *Central Problems in Social Theory.* Berkeley: University of California Press.

—— 1984: *The Constitution of Society.* Cambridge: Polity Press.

Gould, Stephen J. 1977: *Ontogeny and Phylogeny.* Cambridge, Mass.: Harvard University Press.

Haines, Valerie A. 1988: Is Spencer's theory an evolutionary theory? *American Journal of Sociology,* 93, 1,200–23.

—— 1991: Spencer, Darwin, and the question of reciprocal influence. *Journal of the History of Biology,* 24, 409–31.

—— 1992: Spencer's philosophy of science. *British Journal of Sociology,* 43, 155–72.

Harrison, Edward 1987: Whigs, prigs and historians of science. *Nature,* 329, 213–14.

Herschel, John F. W. [1830], 1987: *Preliminary Discourse on the Study of Natural Philosophy.* Chicago: University of Chicago Press.

Howard, J. 1982: *Darwin.* Oxford: Oxford University Press.

Hull, David L. 1973: *Darwin and His Critics: the reception of Darwin's theory of evolution by the scientific community.* Cambridge, Mass.: Harvard University Press.

—— 1979: In defense of presentism. *History and Theory,* 18, 1–15.

—— 1985: Darwinism as a historical entity: a historiographic proposal. In David Kohn (ed.), *The Darwinian Heritage,* Princeton: Princeton University Press, 773–812.

Jones, Robert Alun 1974: Durkheim's response to Spencer: an essay toward historicism in the historiography of sociology. *The Sociological Quarterly,* 15, 341–58.

—— 1977: On understanding a sociological classic. *American Journal of Sociology,* 84, 175–81.

—— 1983: The new history of sociology. *Annual Review of Sociology,* 9, 447–69.

—— 1985a: Presentism, anachronism, and continuity in the history of sociology: a reply to Seidman. *History of Sociology,* 6, 153–60.

—— 1985b: Second thoughts on privileged access. *Sociological Theory,* 3, 16–19.

Kidd, Benjamin 1894: *Social Evolution.* London: Macmillan and Co.

Lamarck, Jean Baptiste [1809], 1984: *Zoological Philosophy: an exposition with regard to the natural history of animals.* Chicago: University of Chicago Press.

Lankester, E. Ray 1890: The transmission of acquired characters and panmixia. *Nature,* 41, 486–8.

—— 1893: Blind animals in caves. *Nature*, 47, 389.

Mayr, Ernst 1972: Lamarck revisited. *Journal of the History of Biology*, 5, 55–94.

—— 1976: Lamarck revisited. In Ernst Mayr, *Evolution and the Diversity of Life: selected essays*. Cambridge , Mass.: Harvard University Press, 222–50.

—— 1982: *The Growth of Biological Thought*. Cambridge, Mass.: Harvard University Press.

—— 1985: Weismann and evolution. *Journal of the History of Biology*, 18, 295–329.

—— 1988: *Toward a New Philosophy of Biology*. Cambridge, Mass.: Harvard University Press.

—— 1990: When is historiography Whiggish? *Journal of the History of Ideas*, 51, 301–9.

—— 1991a: *One Long Argument: Charles Darwin and the genesis of modern evolutionary thought*. Cambridge, Mass.: Harvard University Press.

—— 1991b: The ideological resistance to Darwin's theory of natural selection. *Proceedings of the American Philosophical Society*, 135, 123–39.

Mill, John Stuart 1843: *A System of Logic, Ratiocinative and Inductive*. London: J. W. Parker.

Morgan, C. Lloyd 1898: Mr. Herbert Spencer's biology. *Natural Science*, 13, 377–83.

Morgan, Thomas Hunt 1903: *Evolution and Adaptation*. New York: The Macmillan Company.

Nisbet, Robert A. 1969: *Social Change and History*. London: Oxford University Press.

—— 1970. Developmentalism: a critical analysis. In J. C. McKinney and E. A. Tiryakian (eds), *Theoretical Sociology*, New York: Appleton–Century–Crofts, 167–204.

Parekh, Bhikhu and Berki, R. N. 1973: The history of political ideas: a critique of Q. Skinner's methodology. *Journal of the History of Ideas*, 34, 163–84.

Parsons, Talcott [1937], 1968: *The Structure of Social Action*. New York: The Free Press.

Peel, J. D. Y. 1971: *Herbert Spencer: the evolution of a sociologist*. New York: Basic Books.

Popper, Karl R. 1957: *The Poverty of Historicism*. New York: Harper & Row.

—— 1968: *Logic of Scientific Discovery*. New York: Harper & Row.

Richards, Robert J. 1987: *Darwin and the Emergence of Evolutionary Theories of Mind and Behavior*. Chicago: University of Chicago Press.

—— 1988: The moral foundations of evolutionary progress: Darwin, Spencer, and the neo-Darwinians. In M. H. Nitecki (ed.), *Evolutionary Progress*, Chicago: University of Chicago Press, 129–48.

—— 1992: *The Meaning of Evolution*. Chicago: University of Chicago Press.

Romanes, George J. 1887: The factors of organic evolution. *Nature*, August 25, 401–7.

—— 1890: Weismann's theory of heredity. *Contemporary Review*, 57, 686–99.

—— 1893: Mr. Herbert Spencer on "natural selection." *Contemporary Review*, 63, 499–517.

Ruse, Michael 1975: Darwin's debt to philosophy: an examination of the influence of John F. W. Herschel and William Whewell on the development of Charles Darwin's theory of evolution. *Studies in History and Philosophy of Science*, 6, 159–81.

—— 1979: *The Darwinian Revolution.* Chicago: University of Chicago Press.

—— 1988: Molecules to men: evolutionary biology and thoughts on progress. In M. H. Nitecki (ed.), *Evolutionary Progress,* Chicago: University of Chicago Press, 97–126.

Schweber, S. S. 1978: The genesis of natural selection – 1938: some further insights. *BioScience,* 28, 321–6.

Seidman, Steven 1983: Beyond presentism and historicism: understanding the history of social science. *Sociological Inquiry,* 53, 79–94.

—— 1985a: Classics and contemporaries: the history and systematics of sociology revisited. *History of Sociology,* 6, 121–35.

—— 1985b: The historicist controversy: a critical review with a defense of a revised presentism. *Sociological Theory,* 3, 13–16.

Skinner, Quentin 1968: Meaning and understanding in the history of ideas. *History and Theory,* 8, 3–53.

Smith, Anthony D. 1973: *The Concept of Social Change.* London: Routledge & Kegan Paul.

Spencer, Herbert [1850], 1966: *Social Statics, abridged and revised, together with The Man Versus the State.* Osnabruck: Otto Zeller.

—— [1852], 1966: The development hypothesis. In Herbert Spencer, *Essays: scientific, political and speculative,* Osnabruck: Otto Zeller, 1–12.

—— [1857a], 1966: Progress: its law and cause. In H. Spencer, *Essays: scientific, political and speculative,* Osnabruck: Otto Zeller, 8–62.

—— [1857b], 1966: Transcendental physiology. In H. Spencer, *Essays: scientific, political and speculative,* Osnabruck: Otto Zeller, 63–107.

—— [1862], 1911: *First Principles.* London: Williams and Norgate.

—— 1864: *The Principles of Biology,* Vol. 1. New York: D. Appleton and Company.

—— [1886], 1966: The factors of organic evolution. In H. Spencer, *Essays: scientific, political and speculative,* Osnabruck: Otto Zeller, 389–466.

—— 1893a: The inadequacy of natural selection. *Contemporary Review,* 63, 153–66, 439–56.

—— 1893b: Professor Weismann's theories. *Contemporary Review,* 63, 743–60.

—— 1893c: A rejoinder to Professor Weismann. *Contemporary Review,* 64, 893–912.

—— 1894: Weismannism once more. *Contemporary Review,* 66, 592–608.

—— 1895: Heredity once more. *Contemporary Review,* 68, 608.

—— 1897: *The Principles of Sociology,* Vol. 3. New York: D. Appleton and Company.

—— [1898], 1966: *The Principles of Biology,* Vol. 1. Osnabruck: Otto Zeller.

—— 1904a: *An Autobiography,* Vol. 1. London: Williams and Norgate.

—— 1904b: *An Autobiography,* Vol. 2. London: Williams and Norgate.

Stocking, George W. Jr 1965: On the limits of "presentism" and "historicism" in the historiography of the behavioral sciences. *Journal of the History of the Behavioral Sciences,* 1, 211–18.

Sztompka, Piotr 1993: *The Sociology of Social Change.* Oxford: Blackwell.

Tilly, Charles 1984: *Big Structures, Large Processes, Huge Comparisons.* New York: Russell Sage Foundation.

Turner, Jonathan H. 1985: *Herbert Spencer: a renewed appreciation.* Beverley Hills: Sage.

—— 1993: *Classical Sociological Theory: a positivist's perspective.* Chicago: Nelson-Hall Publishers.

Wallace, Alfred R. 1893: Are individually acquired characters inherited? *Fortnightly Review,* 53, 490–8, 655–68.

Wallerstein, Immanuel 1991: *Unthinking Social Science: the limits of nineteenth-century paradigms.* Cambridge: Polity Press.

Weismann, August 1893: The all-sufficiency of natural selection: a reply to Herbert Spencer. *Contemporary Review,* 64, 309–38, 596–610.

—— 1894: *The Effect of External Influences upon Development.* London: The Romanes Lecture.

—— 1895: Heredity once more. *Contemporary Review,* 68, 420–56.

Whewell, William [1837], 1967: *History of the Inductive Sciences,* Vols 1, 2, and 3. London: Frank Cass & Co.

—— [1840], 1967: *The Philosophy of the Inductive Sciences,* Vols. 1 and 2. New York: Johnson Reprint Corporation.

Young, Robert M. 1971: Darwin's metaphor: does nature select? *Monist,* 55, 442–503.

4

Classical Social Theory with the Women Founders Included

Lynn McDonald

A number of women over the past several centuries have made significant contributions to the founding of the social sciences, in the development of methodological assumptions and research techniques, by providing concrete examples of research, and the formulation of basic theory and concepts. That they do not appear in standard texts, histories of the discipline, and course syllabuses on classical theory are problems the profession has yet to address seriously. In doing the research for my *Early Origins of the Social Sciences* (1993) I set out to find the women founders and did. They are reported there as a minority along with many more men. In my *Women Founders of the Social Sciences* (1994) more detail is provided, including biographical notes, overviews of key contributions and references both to their works and the growing secondary literature on them. Thus I claim a place for such British theorists as Mary Astell, Mary Wortley Montagu, Catharine Macaulay, Mary Wollstonecraft, Mary Hays, Harriet Martineau, Harriet Taylor, Florence Nightingale, and Beatrice Webb; the French Marie de Gournay, Emilie du Châtelet, Marie-Jeanne Roland, Germaine de Staël and Flora Tristan; and the American Jane Addams.

Good critical editions and collected works for these women are, alas, still rare – something I hope to remedy, at least for the more

Excerpts cited have been edited to modernize spelling and punctuation. Works cited in French are my translation.

important of them – but there is no excuse now not to admit a number of these women to the histories of our discipline and the courses that pass on this culture to new generations of scholars. Token gestures by some recent writers on theory to admit *recent* feminist theorists do not make up for the continued exclusion of women as *founders* of or important contributors to the discipline.

The fact of these contributions is the starting point for this paper. The task here is to examine *how* the social sciences might be different today if these women had been given the serious attention their writing deserves. After outlining the most important differences in both theory and methodology that appeared I will go on to relate the work of five of the most notable: Germaine de Staël, Catharine Macaulay, Florence Nightingale, Beatrice Webb, and Jane Addams.

THE DISTINCTIVE CONTRIBUTION OF WOMEN TO THEORY

1   Theoretical reconstructions of early society would be different, emphasizing the *positive* bonds between mother and children, points to be shown with reference to Emilie du Châtelet as well as Macaulay and de Staël. Conversely there would be less fascination with Thomas Hobbes's portrayal of life as "solitary, poor, nasty, brutish and short" ([1651], 1968, p. 186). A more benign portrayal of the state of nature, as preferred by the women theorists, would have profoundly affected social contract theory in political science.

2   In political and social theory there would be more interest in the middle ground, less on the extremes. Notions of social obligation would have moderated the political theory of possessive individualism, beginning with work by Astell ([1700], 1730, 1986). Martineau's early, hardline *Illustrations of Political Economy* ([1832], 1834), with its strictures against government intervention evolved into a considerable role for government in her later journalism. Utility theory would have become kinder and gentler if Catharine Macaulay's version, in *Letters on Education* ([1790], 1974), had been adopted instead of Jeremy Bentham's *Introduction to the Principles of Morals and Legislation* ([1780–1820], 1962, vol. 1).

3   Theorists would early have begun to consider stratification by gender as well as by class if the work of Astell ([1700], 1730), Macaulay ([1790], 1974) and Wollstonecraft ([1787–97], 1989, vol. 5) had been taken seriously. All of these writers gave extensive attention to gender issues. So also would there have been an earlier start on analysis of gender roles. Anyone who believes that interest in a

distinct contribution by women is recent would do well to examine the work of Nightingale, Webb, and Addams, for whom examples will be given below.

4   The literature would be marked with greater interest in issues of peace and non-violent conflict resolution, greater skepticism as to military institutions and hierarchy and less glorification of war and military values had the writing of Wollstonecraft ([1787–97], 1989, vol. 5, pp. 86–93), de Staël, and Addams been given greater weight.

5   More attention would have been paid to the biophysical environment and continuities between human beings and other species, so that environmentalists would have less reason to condemn us for our neglect of the environment and speciesism. Examples will be given for Macaulay and Nightingale; others are available for Wollstonecraft ([1787–97], 1989, vol. 4, pp. 367–73) and Martineau (in much of her journalism).

6   The literature on major male founders would be different; notably there would be less esteem for Herbert Spencer if Beatrice Webb's devastating critique were heeded ([1926], 1938); the empirical, practical and more applied sides of Max Weber would be more prominent if Marianne Weber's interpretation of her husband's work had not been rejected by later scholars ([1926], 1975); Thomas Hobbes, as noted before, would have a lower place in the political pantheon if Macaulay's critique (1767) were accepted.

THE DISTINCTIVE CONTRIBUTION OF WOMEN TO METHODOLOGY

1   Methodologically, the integration of quantitative and qualitative would have become routine. Instead of feminists rejecting empiricism as "malestream methodology," they would be active promoters of empirical techniques, following Nightingale, Webb, and Addams, as useful means to advance their causes. Examples will be given shortly for each of these three women. Martineau, as well, was expert in using both quantitative and qualitative data ([1838], 1989).

2   There would be a greater interest in applied work, especially in the field of health promotion and public health. Nightingale and Martineau are the important examples here. There is also an interesting early example of Mary Wortley Montagu promoting the practice of inoculation against smallpox, and her friend Mary Astell writing in support, citing the best available statistics.

3   Statistical evaluation on the introduction of new social

programs and major governmental expenditures would have become routine, points to be discussed especially for Nightingale and Webb. De Staël's contribution on public administration as well has been sadly neglected.

4   Care would have been taken to make data accessible to the community concerned and the public at large. One of Martineau's first works on methodology showed how ordinary people in their occupations or running a household could apply the best knowledge available (1836). Nightingale got her applied work out in cheap, popular editions to make it widely available ([1860–75], 1992). Macaulay published her most polemical work in pamphlet form to make it available. Addams and her colleagues at Hull House posted the results of their research so that the people who used it, their subjects, could read them ([1895], 1970).

GERMAINE DE STAËL – FOUNDATIONS, THEORY, INTERNATIONAL RELATIONS

Germaine de Staël (1766–1817) is known now, as before, as a literary figure. Her novels, many again in print, attract the attention previously devoted to her notorious love life. Yet she was an astute political theorist and an advocate of quantitative social and political science à la Condorcet (who was a better feminist than she and far more expert on probability theory). But de Staël holds her own against any as an analyst of the French Revolution, government, and social institutions. Her observations on the relationship between public opinion and government are still of interest. So are her prescient remarks in *Literature and Social Institutions* on the relationship between technological change and the social and political institutions needed to manage it (1871, p. 199). Here also de Staël used Condorcet's language on the need for a social *science* to ground the social *art*, or knowledge, for application in our terms. Her *On Germany*, 1813, explicates social institutions in a comparative manner, including a significant discussion of the status and role of women.

De Staël's *Influence of the Passions* ([1796], 1798) used Adam Smith's notion of sympathy. Pity was a bond in the human community. She described the positive bonds between mother and children as fundamental in the constitution of human society. Morality was driven by passions/emotions, not mere rational calculation. Those for whom Carol Gilligan's *In a Different Voice* (1982) resonates will find de Staël struck just the same chord, nearly two centuries earlier.

The Influence of the Passions plainly states de Staël's association of passion and virtue. While her contemporary, Immanuel Kant, and a host of male philosophers, denigrated passion and related morality to reason, de Staël believed that:

> In whatever situation we may be placed by a deep-rooted passion, I can never believe that it misleads us from the path of virtue. Everything is sacrifice, everything is indifference to our own gratifications in the exalted attachment of love; selfishness alone degrades. Everything is goodness, everything is pity in the heart that truly loves. Inhumanity alone banishes all morality from the heart of man. (p. 133)

The Renaissance writer Christine de Pisan had similarly focused on pity and love in her social and political writing. In her "Lament on the Evils of Civil War," 1410, she made the plea: "Whoever has pity, let him put it to use. The time which requires it has come" (1984, p. 85). Emilie du Châtelet in her translation and commentary on Mandeville's *Fable of the Bees*, written ca. 1735–7, held that "love seems to have been the beginning of society" ([1735–7], 1947, p. 142). Love resulted in procreation and the mutual needs of young families gave birth to society. This emphasis on sympathy/feeling as the basis of morality is highlighted also in Sophie Grouchy de Condorcet's *Letters on Sympathy*, a book-length commentary published initially in 1798, along with her translation of Smith's *Theory of Moral Sentiments*; the letters have again become available ([1798], 1994).

De Staël declared no less that: "The only sentiment that can serve as a guide to us in all situations and that may be applicable to all circumstances is pity" ([1796], 1798, p. 330). " Here also is de Staël's unambiguous statement about the primordial tie between parents and their children:

> The most sacred of the moral elements of the world are the ties that bind together parents and their children. On this holy duty is equally poised the basis of nature and society and nothing short of extreme depravity can make us spurn at this involuntary instinct which, in these relations, prompts us to everything which virtue can impose. (p. 233)

De Staël was critical of Adam Smith's *Theory of Moral Sentiments* for being *too* utilitarian. That we are able to feel like another person in distress (Smith's opening example was "our brother on the rack") was *one* cause of pity, but not the only one. His definition of sympathy was too narrow:

Smith, in his excellent work, *The Theory of Moral Sentiments*, makes pity consist in that sympathy which places us in the situation of another and renders us sensible to all the feelings which such a situation may impress. That most undoubtedly is one of the causes of pity, but there is this inconvenience in that definition . . . it narrows the thought to which the word to be defined gives rise. (p. 331)

De Staël noted that a sentiment combined sensations and thoughts, using both judgment and emotion: "In a word, the spectacle of misfortune must move and melt mankind by means of commotion or, as it were, by a talisman, and not by examination or combination" (p. 331). It was almost always wise policy to listen to the voice of pity.

> In fine, in whatever point of view we contemplate the sentiment of pity, it will be found wonderfully fertile in the production of beneficial consequences both to individuals and to nations. Nor shall we feel reluctant to persuade ourselves that it is the only primitive idea that is implanted in the nature of man, for it is the only one that is necessary to the culture of every virtue and to the enjoyment of every blessing. (p. 335)

In *Circonstances actuelles* de Staël came out expressly against the harsh view of human nature that led to the tyrannical social contract. She had little to say about the original state of nature, even denigrating the endeavor to describe it. "Society is formed in thousands of different ways," she insisted. Our knowledge must depend on facts, which could only be relied on after the invention of printing, which permitted their preservation and use in prediction:

> If history, before the discovery of printing, cannot serve to make known the progress the human mind is capable of, there is even more reason to consider research on the origin of society useless. These sorts of metaphysical novels have neither the interest of invention nor the precision of truth. One stumbles about by chance, as the imagination, but one loses oneself in a desert and chimerical abstraction is as much arid and futile. Society is formed in a thousand different ways. We know nothing except what we have gained from facts, and that only after printing, so that achievements already made can be used to predict subsequent ones. ([1798], 1979, p. 280)

The crack about "metaphysical novels" is presumably directed to Rousseau's *Social Contract*, if not also Hobbes's *Leviathan*. Rousseau was the subject of de Staël's first published essay [1798], 1979), when she was aged twenty-two.

De Staël wrote two books on the French Revolution, both of

which abound with good sense and moderation. The first, more descriptive *Principal Events of the French Revolution*, was published posthumously in 1818. The second, and in my view better, book, *Des circonstances actuelles*, was published for the first time only in 1906, in French; there is a good critical edition ([1798], 1979), but as yet no translation. Both books offer extensive causal analysis of what went wrong: why the French were so cruel. She explained the barbarity in terms of the abuses of the old regime, providing a sophisticated account of the institutions of class, property, privilege and education. *Circonstances actuelles* is devoted to elucidating the means required to end the civil war unleashed by the revolution. De Staël's proposal was to establish a *republic*, specifically to end aristocratic privilege in favour of representation of the whole (male) nation and a merit system. There is some astute analysis of the trade-offs between liberty and equality.

The proposals of *Circonstances actuelles* are eminently moderate and practical, so much so that they would have offended virtually everybody in some respect or other. De Staël riled royalists by accepting the principles of the revolution, while she angered revolutionaries by condemning the excesses and assisting aristocratic refugees to escape. In a pamphlet she argued that Marie Antoinette should not be held responsible with the King for his decisions! (1820–1, vol. 2, pp. 1–33). De Staël's prescriptions for institutional reform in *Circonstances actuelles* include extensive de-centralization, even to the point of federalism, in the notoriously centralized French system.

De Staël's observations on international relations in the Napoleonic era still bear reading. Napoleon, who hated her, had her exiled and prohibited publication of her work in France. Her correspondence with Thomas Jefferson shows her commending Britain, then at war with the United States, for defending liberty against Napoleon's tyranny. An ardent opponent of slavery, de Staël dared to tell Jefferson, a slave owner: "If you should succeed in destroying slavery in the South there would be at least one government in the world as perfect as the human mind can achieve" (1918, p. 70).

The need to defeat Napoleon apart, de Staël disdained military values for their anti-democratic tendencies. "Nothing is more contrary to liberty than the military spirit. A long and violent war is scarcely compatible with the maintenance of any constitution and everything that assures triumph is subversive of the rule of law" ([1798], 1979, p. 289). While the military spirit sacrifices people, liberty increases the ties among them. "The military mind hates reason as the beginning of indiscipline; liberty bases its authority on conviction" (p. 290). She compared military institutions with those of learning, and her defence of Enlightenment values could still cheer the faint hearted. Consistent with this she postulated the impossibility of exporting revolution by force (Napoleon's game). Soldiers might triumph militarily, but could never be liberators of another country (p. 6).

> Nothing is more worthy of admiration than success in arms, the invincible valour of generals and soldiers, but nothing is more contrary to liberty than the military mind. A long and violent war is scarcely compatible with the maintenance of any constitution and everything that assures triumph is subversive of the reign of law. Revolutionary enthusiasm without doubt adds greatly to soldierly gallantry. Liberty succeeds the war sustained for it but never accompanies it. ([1798], 1979, p. 289)

De Staël pointed out that even armies comprised of citizens took on the same corporate spirit of all the armies of the world. While the military mind was for conquest, liberty sought conservation, and its authority was based on conviction. "The military mind explains everything, functions in everything by force" (p. 289). Soldiers might tell you that they had opinions as individuals, "but as a soldier I must obey." France needed people to contribute their ideas/learning, without being so bound. The military also fostered the wrong attitudes:

> Anger is often a heroic principle in a warrior; in government anger produces nothing but injustice and tyranny, and all governments which win by arms end up by being resentful. ([1798], 1979, p. 290)

Mary Wollstonecraft's *Vindication of the Rights of Woman*, 1792, similarly reveals both a contempt for military virtues and an incipient understanding that military institutions are antithetical to a free society.[1] Like many other women theorists she argued that women *could* be soldiers, but they chose not to. "I think it would puzzle a keen casuist to prove the reasonableness of the greater number of

---

[1] The gallantry and polished manners of officers were positively dangerous in a country town because they concealed "vice and folly." Soldiers were like uneducated women: both had the misfortune to acquire "manners" before "morals" – the external behavior before the inward conviction ([1787–97], 1989 pp. 5, 92). Wollstonecraft criticized Rousseau for his derision of women because they were unsuited to being soldiers.

wars that have dubbed heroes" ([1787–97], 1989, vol. 5, p. 216). We will see Florence Nightingale, in the nineteenth century, making points similar to those of Wollstonecraft and de Staël on the incompatibility of military and democratic institutions.

CATHARINE MACAULAY – KINDER, GENTLER UTILITY THEORY

Catharine Macaulay (1731–91) denounced Hobbes's portrayal of the state of nature and the social contract in an essay, *Loose Remarks on Hobbes's Philosophical Rudiments* (1767) and in her superb full-length book, *Letters on Education* ([1790], 1974) which defends women's rights to and need of education – the book that made a feminist of Mary Wollstonecraft.

> Mr. Hobbes, in his *Philosophical Elements of a True Citizen*, sets out with an intention to confute this received opinion, that man is a creature born fit for society. To do this he enumerates the vicious affections inherent in human nature, which affections are confined to the innate quality of selfishness. From these premises he draws this inference, that man cannot desire society from love, but through hope of gain. Therefore, says he, the origin of all great and lasting societies consisted not in the mutual good-will men had toward each other, but in the mutual fear they had of each other. (1767, p. 1)

The essay is a point-by-point trouncing of Hobbes's analysis, insisting that a contract is binding on the sovereign as well as the people. The people are accorded considerable rights, the sovereign serious and precise responsibilities. Instead of the state of equality in the original, brutish state of nature, Macaulay held that political equality and the laws of good government were mutually compatible and indeed complementary. Instead of justifying the ongoing rights of oppressive sovereigns Macaulay argued that there had to be means to put the most capable people into government, and remove them when they governed badly.

For Macaulay, in *Letters on Education*, sympathy was the core human affection from which all other virtues arose. Without sympathy, moreover, we probably would not have attained any ideas of equity. It was sympathy, moving us emotionally, "that first inclined man to a forbearance of his own gratifications" to consider the feelings of "fellow creatures." Those "fellow creatures" would even include species other than the human. For Macaulay the source of the principle of equity was the feeling of sympathy; reason followed feeling: "All human virtue must derive its source from this useful affection," sympathy ([1790], 1974, p. 275).

The passions were latent in every mind and had to be put into motion to grow and prevail – hence the importance of education and good laws. Instead of a contract among terrified people, there was the positive communication, by parents, of right and wrong to their children:

> Men as they gained ideas of good and evil, by experience, communicated their observations to their offspring. Domestic education, therefore, must have begun with the beginning of the life of man, and, when the species formed themselves into societies, their ideas were necessarily extended from the variety of impressions and instructions which they received in such associations.
>
> With the increase of the stock of his ideas, man increased his power of making comparisons, and consequently enlarged his knowledge of the relation of things. Some modes of conduct generally adopted, some rules and exercises fitted to a state of offence and defence, necessarily belong to all associations. Education then, in a state of the rudest society, must necessarily be more complex and more methodical than education in the natural or more solitary state of man. ([1790], 1974, pp. 237–8)

Macaulay described a gradual process of socialization in even the most rude state of society, ending in complex motives and enlarged duties and obligations, and critical observation of and punishment for offenses.

Sympathy, according to Macaulay, lay dormant in every mind and had to be prompted to become active. Governments had considerable power to affect its development through enacting or promoting laws, precepts, and customs. Macaulay was influenced here by Beccaria's *Treatise of Crimes and Punishments*, which she cited with approval and which gave detailed arguments for the formulation of laws that would deter bad behavior and elicit good behavior by the penalties and rewards attached to them. The entire account is a thorough repudiation of the illiberal social contract and its replacement with a naturalistic, sympathy-based theory. Yet Macaulay is scarcely even mentioned in the development of utility theory.

Macaulay did not believe that the calculation of pleasures and pains of utility theory should be confined to the human species. Utility had to be a *general* principle, involving consideration of the feelings of *all* creatures of sense. The fact that humans abuse their powers over animals bore a "melancholy testimony" to the " low and barbarous" state of human sentiments. Macaulay's prescription featured giving children animals to look after, which was expected to cure their prejudices of "human conceit" by the "practice of benevolence."

> It raises in me a mixed sentiment of contempt and anger to hear the vain and contradictory creature, man, addressing the deity as the god of all perfection, yet dealing out a severe and short mortality to the various tribes of his fellow animals, and assigning to himself an eternity of happiness beyond even the reach of his imagination. What was man before he was called into existence but the dust of the earth? Can the meanest insect be less; and if man and brute were upon an equal footing before the almighty *fiat* went forth, what motive, worthy of divine wisdom, could influence the deity to draw the line of separation thus wide between his creatures? ([1790], 1974, p. 2)

> We cannot help feeling a little angry with systems which confine rectitude to that mode of conduct which is the best adapted to support the happiness of man. Thus, when God subjected the far greater number of his creatures to this lord of the creation, he subjected them to a being, not bound by any tie in nature, or the reason of things, to use equity and mercy in the exercise of his power. ([1790], 1974, p. 192)

Macaulay expressly repudiated the views of the Scottish moral philosopher David Hume for being too anthropocentric. She held instead that the utility principle, the calculation of pleasures and pains, had to be taken "in a general sense," that people should not confine utility "to the benefit of their own species" (p. 192). Ecologists continue to credit Bentham for his application of utility theory to "the whole sensitive creation" ([1780–1820], 1962, pp. 1, 25) and for his very brief mention of species other than human. Yet Macaulay's much more comprehensive treatment and deeper concern goes unmentioned. Hume tends to get at least an honorable mention for his espousal of "gentle usage" for non-human creatures, short of justice ([1751], 1920, p. 190). Macaulay's far more demanding ethics, less anthropocentric discussion, and critique of Hume, are ignored. Her extensive and extremely interesting political theory is similarly ignored, although there is now excellent secondary material on it (Hill, 1992).

John Rawls in his influential *Theory of Justice* similarly went no further than Hume in conceding "duties of compassion," but not "strict justice," to non-human animals. He considered the subject "outside the scope of the theory of justice" (1971, p. 512). Two centuries earlier Macaulay found ways to integrate animals in her ethical theory, but Rawls apparently never read her.

FLORENCE NIGHTINGALE – GRAND THEORY AND APPLIED STATISTICS

The contributions of Florence Nightingale (1820–1910) to social theory range from the enunciation of grand theory – a religious-philosophical understanding of law ([1860], 1991 and [1860], 1994) – through the early use of evaluative statistics and the development of ingenious methods for portraying data graphically (Cohen, 1984), recommendations for the Census, pioneering work on mortality in childbirth (1871) and even some early sociology of religion and comparative sociology (1987; [1860], 1991; [1860], 1994). In the Enlightenment tradition, and with a religious faith leading her in the same direction, Nightingale sought to understand the laws that run the world, physical and social, so that people could intervene for good. Nightingale's world view was of law-like regulation, for the social world as much as the physical. This did not lead her into acceptance of existing conditions but provided the intellectual framework within which she would seek change. Nightingale's statement of philosophical assumptions was influenced by Quetelet, especially his *Physique sociale*, which she annotated extensively. He was the author of "the most important science in the world," social physics, for, as she stated to the great epidemiologist William Farr, on it depended all the others (February 23, 1874, Wellcome Institute for the History of Medicine).

Yet Nightingale went much further than Quetelet in practising what both preached. While his empirical work was confined to the analysis of already collected government statistics, Nightingale conducted her own surveys. She was, as well, more emphatic than Quetelet on the possibility of practical application of the laws of social science and worked on a greater range of social problems. While Quetelet's research was overwhelmingly on demography and criminology, Nightingale covered public health and preventive medicine, the prevention of famine and such social problems as the regulation of prostitution. Nightingale's research ranged into India, New Zealand, Australia, and China while Quetelet remained tied to European material.

Because of the scale of the problems she sought to remedy (for example, famine and disease in India and unnecessary mortality in war) Nightingale used royal commissions and official inquiries as the means of data collection and analysis. For decades of her life as well she sent out her own questionnaires and memoranda to hospitals, maternity institutions, Army stations, viceroys, municipal governments in Britain, India and the British colonies, on public health, mortality, irrigation, agricultural practices, finance and taxation. The following excerpts will give an example of Nightingale's very practical approach to social science and her justification for it (the unpublished sources are all from the Nightingale Collection, British Library).

> Moral laws of God can be found by induction as by physical laws. Indeed God's moral, social and physical laws act and react on one another. By Quetelet's method moral laws can be stated in numerical results. If anything can be called a law, is not that the effects of which can be prophesied like an eclipse? (Additional Manuscripts (AM) 45842, f. 51)

> A law does not "govern" or "subordinate," does not compel people to commit crime or suicide. On the contrary, it puts means into our hands to prevent them, if we did but observe and use these means. It simply reduces to calculation observed facts, this is all that a law means. These laws or results change of course with the causes which give them birth; for example, civilization, sanitary and moral, changes the law on mortality by diminishing the death rate. So it is with the law of morality. The causes influencing the social system are to be recognized and modified. From the past we may predict the future. (AM 45842 ff. 157–8 and Diamond and Stone, 1981, p. 338)

> The influence of civilization, of political and religious institutions, on the moral and physical nature of man is at present little known as an exact science, still less as an art by which to do perfectly that which we now do gropingly and in the dark ...
> Above all it is governments which dispose of life. Is it not then the first, the most essential step to have a political science – to raise it, if it is a science at all, into an exact science – to determine the actual results of legislative measures, and political institutions in figures, not to go in this blind way, changing laws almost at random, at the caprice of party, but to make that an art which is the most essential of all arts? (AM 45842, ff. 349–50)

Committed reformer and rationalist that she was, Nightingale gave great scope to the possibilities for *unintended* consequences of social intervention. She advocated careful evaluation of *every* new program. She had a strong sense of the similarities between the social and natural worlds; both were regulated by law.

Supposing us to study the laws under which the political and moral world is governed as we study those under which the solar system, the material world, is governed – could we arrive at something of the same certainty in predicting the future condition of human society? How it will be with Europe? How will it be with England? (1873, p. 25)

Nightingale as well deserves better recognition for her role in the development of public health care and the welfare state. She not only established nursing as a respectable profession, but considered the systems needed to fund and staff both hospitals and nursing care at home. Long before social democrats and socialists began to advocate public health insurance, Nightingale articulated the founding principles of public health care, as early as 1864. The harsh rules that applied to "paupers" in workhouses did not hold "when the poor pauper becomes sick. From that moment he ceases to be a pauper and becomes brother to the best of us and as a brother he should be cared for" (AM 47753, f. 54). A more comprehensive memorandum from 1865 to the president of the Poor Law Board, stated:

Sick infirm, idiots and mad persons require special construction arrangements, special medical care and nursing and special dieting. Of all these they have little or none that is worthy the name in the present London workhouses. They are not "paupers." They are "poor and in affliction." Society certainly owes them, if it owes anything, every necessary care for recovery. In practice, there should be consolidated and uniform administrative arrangements. Sickness is not parochial; it is general and human and its cost should be borne by all.

N.B. Those who come from the worst dwellings are always the most sickly. For sick you want hospitals as good as the best civil hospitals. You want the best nurses you can find. You want efficient and sufficient medical attendance. You want an energetic and wise administration. (AM 47753, ff. 614–5)

To her colleague, the eminent Victorian sanitarian Edwin Chadwick, Nightingale observed that improved morals required better living standards.

Nightingale's criticism of the paltry provisions for social assistance for the destitute was thorough and vigorous. She called the "workhouse test," the requirement that people go into workhouses (and perhaps work on a treadmill) to obtain food, a "torture test." She centered in on the loss to productivity by this use of human energy. She rejected the complaints of members of her own class on taxes to pay for relief as the "least" of the concerns (AM 47753, ff.

50–3).[2] Yet Nightingale is not mentioned in the development of Christian socialism and only rarely (as in Abel-Smith, 1964, ch. 5; Baly, [1854–70], 1991, pp. 37–8) even in the establishment of public health care in Britain. Abel-Smith further highlighted the "remarkable similarities" with the proposals of the Webbs in the Minority Report on the Poor Law, 1909, some forty years later (Baly, [1854–70], 1991, xii). The measures the Nightingale team did effect, modest as they were relative to her aspirations, formed the basis of the health care system in Britain as it developed in the late nineteenth century.

Environmentalists today would be pleased at how easily she went back and forth between the social and natural spheres. As a public health expert she understood the connection between social institutions (such as local government, land ownership and taxation) and disease and environmental damage (including cholera and typhoid, de-forestation, and desertification). In the course of arguing for a publicly funded health care system Nightingale stressed the links between the biophysical environment (especially clean water and air) and good health:

> The state of the dwellings of the poor, the sanitary or rather un-sanitary state of London in general is not often taken into account in the ill heath it produces, for example consumption, weakness of intellect, rheumatism. We only think of the "violent" and "sudden" deaths of typhus and cholera. Yet the poor cannot drain their own streets, nor reform their own dwellings. Is it not hard to visit our shortcomings (in making London unhealthy) upon the disease they engender by calling it pauperism . . . ? (AM 47753, f. 57)

Her understanding of system went from the biophysical environment, through the built environment of streets, houses, sewage, and water systems, the location of factories and their pollutants, and on to mechanisms for the treatment of diseases that could not be prevented, the care of people with permanent disabilities (mental or physical), to care for the aged and children.

Nightingale recruited another eminent woman to work with her on her various reform causes, although one also typically a "missing person" in the histories of the discipline. Harriet Martineau (1802–76) analyzed the data Nightingale sent her and wrote it up for publication in the popular press. The two worked together on preventive medicine/health promotion in the Army, the application of the

---

[2]More on Nightingale's social policy advocacy can be seen in McDonald, 1996, chapter 3.

Nightingale method in the American Civil War (at least by the North), public health, irrigation and transportation in India, and opposition to the Contagious Diseases Acts – legislation that attempted to reduce the incidence of syphilis by targeting women prostitutes for compulsory examination and treatment, while ignoring the role of men in spreading the disease (McDonald, 1994, pp. 206–11).

Nightingale's analysis of gender issues remains largely unpublished or available only in obscure places. Her (initial) refusal to sign a suffrage petition, and occasional nasty remarks about feminist activists, have been emphasized to the neglect of her path-breaking work on the Contagious Diseases Acts and the regulation of prostitution. It was the campaign led by Josephine Butler that eventually led to the repeal of these discriminatory laws, but it was Nightingale who led the struggle for the first years and whose analytic position was largely adopted by later campaigners. Nightingale's objection was to the double standard. She utterly rejected the conventional wisdom of her day of a radical disjunction in nature between men and women such that justified the provision of prostitutes for men in the Army and Navy who could not marry or whose wives could not be with them. Her analysis focused instead on the social factors that prompted recourse to prostitutes: alcohol, the wrong diet, inadequate work and leisure facilities in garrisons (especially in India where servants did the practical work). She, with Martineau and the next generation of opponents to the Contagious Diseases Acts, argued for changes in *social* conditions. (Nightingale especially would have brought in tough measures to go after the pimps.) Moreover women should not be regarded as *means*. Quite apart from the contention that the proposed control measures would not work (Nightingale used comparative statistics from jurisdictions with and without them), women's best interests as moral beings themselves had to be considered.

As to the etiology of prostitution itself Nightingale repudiated the standard explanation of "depravity" in favor of economic factors (especially for part-time and occasional prostitutes) and abusive home conditions. She cited data showing increased numbers of prostitutes with increasing recession, as unemployed or underemployed women workers temporarily turned to prostitution. A letter to Henry (later Cardinal) Manning described prostitution as "the most lucrative profession in England, except the stage, for a woman. Those who do not follow it as a trade help themselves out with it, as the miserable earnings of needlework are nothing like enough to satisfy a woman's wants" (Emory University/BL AM 45796, ff. 1–8).

It is perhaps even more remarkable that Nightingale is not routinely cited in the theoretical literature on peace, war, and militarism. She not only was the heroine of the Crimean War but she gave advice to the War Office, including specific plans for the nursing/medical care of armies in succeeding decades. She was decorated by both sides in the Franco-Prussian War. Henri Dunant, founder of the Red Cross, gave her the credit for the fundamental principle of the "neutralization" of war sick and wounded, that is, their treatment without respect to nationality.

Like Macaulay, Wollstonecraft and de Staël before her, Nightingale saw the threat of militarism to democratic institutions.[3] She cited with approval a French article on the defeat of Italy at the battles of Custoza [in the Italian Wars of Independence] and Lipa: "how happy to have won her independence and not been victorious. Had she won those battles she would have fallen under military dictatorship; now she can turn her attention to internal reform and improvement." Germany was never farther "from free representative institutions than at this moment" in the Franco-Prussian War (AM 45845, f. 32). The annexation of Alsace and Lorraine by Germany was a mistake which would weaken Germany. Nevertheless she doubted whether "any statesman, whether even the emperor, is strong enough to march the German Army out of Strasburg" without risk to the throne (AM 45845, f. 89). The contrast in philosophy with Bismarck, who dominated European politics 1860–90, is stark. Bismarck considered that war was the "natural condition of mankind," specifically using the language of social Darwinism on struggle and survival to justify war. Nightingale's conceptualization of human nature was much more benign and she utterly rejected social Darwinism as unscientific. As an unpublished paper from 1870 has it:

> The danger of German militarism is not so much the danger of war, though that is not small, as that danger to its own institutions, to its own national progress. All representative rights and liberties, all freedom of the press, such as they were, are not only declining but absolutely annihilating, if not annihilated, under the present régime. A military dictatorship seems all that is before them – absorbing all the better tendencies not only of Prussia but the tenderer far noble, and better than Prussian of all that is not Prussian into Prussian. (AM 45845, f. 34)

[3]For more material on this point on all four of these theorists see McDonald, 1996.

BEATRICE WEBB – QUANTITATIVE AND QUALITATIVE METHODS

Beatrice Webb, (1858 –1943) is occasionally recognized as a founder of the social sciences with her husband Sidney Webb. The two are listed, with twenty-three other men, in Timothy Raison's *Founding Fathers of Social Science* (1969); in the 1979 edition six more men were added but no more women. But Beatrice Webb was the better methodologist of the two, and her pioneering work in participant observation predates their partnership. The amalgamation of quantitative and qualitative methods of analysis, so much a feature of the Webbs' joint work, figured in the great pioneer study, *Life and Labour of the Poor in London*, led by Charles Booth (1902), assisted by Mary Booth, and on which the then Beatrice Potter was an early collaborator. Webb's *My Apprenticeship* is both an excellent source on her own early development of research methods and Booth's methods for *Life and Labour.*

Her statement of the connection between the quantitative and qualitative aspects of research still makes sense:

> Statistical enquiry without personal observation lacks all sure foundation, while personal observation unless followed by statistical enquiry leads to no verified conclusion. The two methods are in reality two equally essential acts in all scientific investigation of the structure and growth of existing societies. ([1926], 1938, p. 466)

This essay was written in 1887, *before* the methodological work of Max Weber and Emile Durkheim, the founding of the Chicago School and any sociological journal. Similarly in a lecture at the London School of Economics she observed:

> It is the qualitative methods of observation – experiment and the use of documents and literature – which enables one to discover the processes of society, and it is the statistical method which enables one to check these observations, to see that they apply to a large number of instances instead of to one only. (1906, p. 350)

At the time she gave this lecture Webb was herself a member of the Royal Commission on the Poor Law. A week later she sent the chair a memorandum, "Methods of inquiry."[4] Clearly it is vital for purposes of changing social policy to have credible data on the extent

---

[4]Passfield Papers, Feb. 5, 1906, p. 2385.

of the problem. Webb was also concerned that her colleagues on the commission know the scientific basis for her claims.

One of Webb's chief objections to Herbert Spencer as a sociologist was methodological: he did not seek data to verify or disconfirm hypotheses but gathered material as a lawyer would to build a case. Webb was embarrassed at having worked for a time as his "apprentice, or was it his accomplice?" ([1926], 1938, p. 44). She also disagreed with his organic formulation of society and insistence that state institutions were artificial, while market institutions were natural ([1926], 1938, p. 221). He incorrectly crossed the boundaries between biological and social science: "his social theories are biological laws illustrated by social facts" (p. 218). Even more strongly, "one might as well attempt to describe the nature of organic life to the laws which govern inorganic existence" (p. 219). Spencer, incidentally, then considered "England's greatest philosopher" (p. 210), attended the first lecture Webb ever gave, in 1891.[5]

Beatrice Webb herself, for all her insistence on statistical verification, was a skilled interviewer with much to say on the *process* of observation and data collection, including some odd remarks about women's peculiar aptitude for obtaining information from unwary officials. Here Webb made the obvious point that men's tendency not to notice women worked to women's advantage: males threatened officials so that women made better social investigators.

She was also much more skeptical about official sources of data than most social scientists have been. Webb had herself been a member of a major royal commission and early in her career worked behind the scenes as a social investigator for a House of Lords' inquiry. Hence she had personal knowledge of the obstacles to accurate data collection. Official sources she saw as being valuable in the suggestion of hypotheses, but independent corroboration was required.

Webb stressed the need for multiple hypotheses to guide the collection of data and keep investigators' minds open:

> What is dangerous is to have only a single hypothesis, for this inevitably biasses the selection of facts, or nothing but far-reaching theories as to ultimate causes and general results, for these cannot be tested by any fact that a single student can unravel. (Webb and Webb, 1902, p. x)

[5]In her diary (March 28, 1891) she described the lecture as "a deplorable failure," although just, barely, not a fiasco. Passfield Papers v. 14 (1), p. 79.

The student should "cherish all the hypotheses he can lay his hands on, however far-fetched they may seem" (p. x). Again, this is deceptively simple, but one suspects that many researchers would benefit from such clarity.

Webb is also eminently sound on the issue of ethical neutrality, so much associated with Max Weber. Science cannot give us *ends*, but only *process*, she held. An economist can tell if a desired result can be achieved by a certain measure, but not whether or not that result *is* desirable. In a speech to the London Sociological Society she stated:

> Medical science could perhaps tell you how to kill or cure a man, but it could not tell you whether you want to kill or cure him. The matter of ends or aims has nothing to do with science, but generally falls within the field of religion. (1906, p. 351)

Weber's famous essay on ethical neutrality (1949) dates from 1917, his speech "Science as a vocation" (1974) from 1918, although his "Objectivity in social science and social policy" appeared in the *Archiv für Sozialwissenschaft und Sozialpolitik* when Weber became a co-editor in 1904. Webb's statements on the subject are at least as lucid and have the merit also of having been better respected in her own practice. Weber was notorious for letting his values and political agenda influence his scientific work. The Webbs' assiduous efforts to keep these matters separate were more successful.

For example, in their preface to *Industrial Democracy* the Webbs acknowledged that there were elements of "fact, generalization into theory and moral judgments," which would be used differently by different readers. Their description of structure and function they hoped would have "its own permanent value in sociology" as an analytic record. Their economic generalizations, if proved sound on verification by other investigators, would yet be only stepping stones for "reasoners who will begin where we have left off." Yet even those who regarded their facts as accurate, and accepted their economic theory as scientific, would only agree in their judgment of the desirability of trade unionism as a permanent, if limited, part of industrial democracy only "in so far as they happen to be one with us in the view of what state is desirable" (1902, p. lx).

The two Webbs were just as careful in the establishment of the London School of Economics to make scientific knowledge, not ideological correctness or the advocacy of their own "pet ideas," the object ([1926], 1938, p. 93). However much the creation of a "science of society" was their goal, Webb recognized the difficulties and obstacles. In her diary she wondered if their work would result in "genuine science" as opposed to "mere culture or shallow technical instruction." Would she and Sidney Webb "have the intellectual grasp to rise superior to our material – or shall we be simply compilers and chroniclers?" (p. 168). On making an early appointment to the staff of the London School of Economics, for example, she commented on the irony of hiring a political scientist "to teach a science which does not yet exist" (p. 94).

The preface to *Industrial Democracy* links theory and application, data collection and generalization:

> Perfect wisdom we can never attain, in sociology or in any other science but this does not absolve us from using, in our action, the most authoritative exposition, for the time being, of what is known. ([1897], 1902, p. xvii)

> Whether . . . [we] will discover any new scientific law will depend on the possession of a somewhat rare combination of insight and inventiveness, with the capacity for prolonged and intense reasoning. When such a generalization is arrived at, it provides a new field of work for the ensuing generation, whose task it is, by an incessant testing of this "order of thought" by comparison with the "order of things," to extend, limit and qualify the first imperfect statement of the law. By these means alone, whether in sociology or any other sphere of human inquiry, does mankind enter into possession of that body of organized knowledge which is termed science. (pp. xv–xvi)

Their methodology required subtlety and imagination as well as factual compilation and number crunching.

For Webb sociological explanation posed greater difficulties than historical with its recourse to chronological order. While working on their trade union history she recorded in her diary:

> With history, the threads are supplied by the chronological order – you can weave these threads into any pattern, bring one of them to the surface and then another. But with analysis of facts, the threads are hypotheses, to be tested in strength and consistency before you dare weave them into conclusions and illustrate them with facts. (1948, p. 47)

The worth of any particular explanatory ideas could not be told in advance. Some had to be thrown out after days of work as "absurdly insignificant" or "banal" (p. 47).

Over the course of their lives the Webbs took on the major social issues of the day – an enormous range of practical social problems up to no less a goal than the abolition of destitution. They examined institutions international, national and municipal, state, co-operative, and private industry. They examined the evolution of major institutions, tested them against current needs and moved to proposals for change. Their proposals for change ranged from massive centralization in some cases to the devolution of services and responsibilities to regions and municipalities in others. The example of the Webb research proves, yet again, that one need not choose between rigor and relevance.

JANE ADDAMS – SOCIOLOGY, PEACE, AND INTERNATIONALISM

The situation of Jane Addams (1860–1935) is somewhat different from that of the theorists just discussed. She did her most academic work while early in her career; *Hull-House Maps and Papers* was published in 1895. It seems she could have pursued a conventional academic career; Albion Small would have hired her in the Department of Sociology at the University of Chicago and she published occasionally in the *American Journal of Sociology*. But her applied interests took over and so she is known as a pioneer professional social worker, the founder of the American settlement house movement, a founder of the Women's International League for Peace and Freedom, a leading suffragist, Progressive, member of the Chicago School Board and fighter against municipal corruption. An excellent biography of her includes a 514-item bibliography of her publications (Farrell, 1967, pp. 221–41).

This is not to condone the exclusion of Addams's landmark *Hull-House Maps and Papers* from its rightful place in the history of sociology (Deegan, 1988). Nor does it excuse ignorance of her years of analysis of American society, mainly on what we would call urban sociology and ethnic relations. She astutely compared American society, with its emphasis on the private sector, market economy and individual enterprise, with European society and its comparatively greater emphasis on the public sector, state intervention in the economy and collective action (1932). Addams's contribution here was common garden variety institutional analysis, astutely done. She linked historical material on the different waves of immigrants to their political attitudes and social concerns. She included a paper on trade unions in *Hull-House Maps and Papers* and often returned to the subject later. A paper in the *American Journal of Sociology*

(1899), when it published much more on public policy than it does now, analyzed the wider role of trade unions in the development of public policy in the United States. Like Webb, Addams was at home with both quantitative and qualitative data and able at integrating the two components. *Hull-House Maps and Papers* shows this well.

Addams as the editor of *Hull-House Maps and Papers* could rely on considerable expertise, both on social problems and methodology, from among the residents of the settlement. She had founded it soon after a visit to England, which coincided with the first publication of results from the Booths' massive survey, *Life and Labour of the People in London*. The modest one-volume Hull House publication nonetheless contained more material on application than the entire seventeen volumes of *Life and Labour*. Methodologically the Hull House publication acknowledged similarity with the London work. The paper on methods even claimed "greater minuteness" and "photographic reproduction" of Chicago's poorest quarters (Holbrook, in Addams, [1895], 1970, p. 11).

Addams argued that the value of their observations stemmed from close connection with the neighborhood. The data collection took a year of painstaking work, with, as for the Booth study, visits to people's homes and independent corroboration of information. This component of the study was part of a major investigation into slum conditions by the United States government.

For both the London and the Chicago studies the investigators were middle to upper class and well educated. Yet Addams could claim, unlike the Booths, that all her writers were residents of the area. Charles Booth was only a visitor to East London, although he did participant observation to the extent of staying several weeks in working-class lodgings. Addams and her largely privileged colleagues were always aware of the class differences that separated them from their neighbors/participants in Hull House activities. When giving speeches on the settlement house, for example, Addams took the precaution of bringing a resident of the area, to make sure that she did not misrepresent it.

Dorothy Ross argues that Addams has been improperly left out of the literature on the development of interpretive sociology. Using early unpublished material she demonstrates that Addams had much to say about the problem of gendered knowledge. The "domestic discourse" she attributes to Addams refers to the connected discussion of home, women's nature, child rearing and education (Ross, 1996, p. 2). An essay from Addams's student years,

"Cassandra,"[6] recommended a synthesis of romantic interpretation and ordinary scientific method:

> Addams took with her this composite domestic/romantic epistemology into her early career, its feminine powers fortified by masculine ambitions. Likewise, sympathy, insight, and synthesis would remain the central terms in her understanding of her task, supplemented by scientific observations as their adjunct. (Ross, 1996, p. 6)

Note that Addams included scientific training as well as the broadened sympathies and intuitive skills, familiar points for anyone who has read de Staël, Macaulay, or Webb, but likely reached independently. Addams, no more than Max Weber rejected ordinary scientific work for an interpretive alternative.[7] The Addams *oeuvre* is much broader and more diverse than typically understood. And note how *early* she reached this conceptualization, 1881, *before* the methodological writing of Weber, Durkheim, and Webb.

Addams's writing on peace and negotiated conflict settlement is even more impressive with the benefit of hindsight. Many of the institutions and practices adopted eventually by the United Nations, *after World War II*, were actually proposed by Addams and her women colleagues *during World War I*. Addams was one of the founders of the Women's International League for Peace and Freedom, formed in World War I with the hope of bringing the war in Europe to an early end. She presided over the League's first meeting, held at The Hague in 1915 as the "International Congress of Women." The resolutions adopted at it are both a cogent statement of abhorrence of war, stressing women's particular vulnerability as victims of rape, and an argument for negotiated peace based on justice (Addams et al., [1915], 1972, pp. 150–9). The women advocated better measures for democracy, including the participation of women (when women had the vote only in such progressive countries as Norway and New Zealand). *Democratic*

---

[6]Nightingale's autobiographical essay of the same name, also from her youth, had not been published in 1881 when Addams wrote hers. Cassandra was the daughter of Priam, King of Troy. She used her gift of prophecy to foretell the fall of Troy but was not believed. She was taken by Agamemnon as his prize of war.

[7]Material to counter this all too frequent portrayal of Weber is provided in McDonald (1993, pp. 300–12). Interestingly, Marianne Weber's biography of her husband ([1926], 1975) stressed the integration of the objective/quantitative with the interpretive, giving full play to the former.

control of foreign policy was stressed, at a time when diplomacy was
an occupation restricted largely to male members of their country's
aristocracy. Woodrow Wilson's Fourteen Principles are believed to
have been influenced by the women's analysis.

The resolutions are noteworthy for offering practical proposals to
ensure that the peace, whenever achieved, would be lasting. A
permanent International Court of Justice was recommended, to be
developed from the Hague Court of Arbitration. A permanent
International Conference, including women, would promote cooperation among nation states. A permanent Council of Conciliation
and Investigation would be instituted to settle differences arising
from economic competition and population increase. The women
understood that new and unpredictable issues would arise for which
flexible international organizations had to be prepared. The League
opened headquarters in Geneva to serve as the base of its lobbying
activities, becoming the first non-governmental organization to
lobby regularly on peace issues. (Its full-time organizer, Emily Greene
Balch, was another neglected American woman theorist, an
economist/sociologist and, like Addams, winner of the Nobel Peace
Prize.)

The WILPF was the first organization, in 1919, to condemn the
harshness of the terms of the Treaty of Versailles which ended World
War I. It was critical of the treaty for condoning secret diplomacy
and its whole "spoils to the victor" approach. It correctly predicted
the creation of animosity which would lead to future war. It not only
condemned the economic blockade that caused serious hunger and
disease in the losing nations, but many of its members, notably
Addams, worked for food relief. Again this shows the integration of
theoretical and practical concerns typical of the women theorists. By
contrast Pitirim Sorokin is one of the very few male theorists to have
dealt with famine in his writing ([1922], 1975).

With the benefit of hindsight it could not be more obvious that
Addams and her colleagues were right on the failings of the peace
treaty:

> The International Congress of Women expresses its deep regret that
> the terms of peace proposed at Versailles should so seriously violate
> the principles upon which alone a just and lasting peace can be
> secured, and which the democracies of the world had come to accept.
>
> By guaranteeing the fruits of the secret treaties to the conquerors,
> the terms of peace tacitly sanction secret diplomacy, deny the
> principles of self-determination, recognize the rights of the victors to
> the spoils of war and create all over Europe discords and animosities
> which can only lead to future wars.

By the demand for the disarmament of one set of belligerents only, the principle of justice is violated and the rule of force is continued. By the financial and economic proposals a hundred million people of this generation in the heart of Europe are condemned to poverty, disease and despair, which must result in the spread of hatred and anarchy within each nation.

With a deep sense of responsibility, this Congress strongly urges the Allied and Associated Governments to accept such amendments of the terms as shall bring the peace into harmony with those principles first enumerated by President Wilson, upon the faithful carrying out of which the honour of the Allied peoples depends. (Bussey and Tims, 1965, p. 31)

Like so many activists in the peace movement today, Addams believed that women have a particular role to play because their roles as mothers make them highly sensitive to human life. Neither she nor other theorists asserted any innate *superiority* of women, but rather the closer involvement of women in the protection, nurture and conservation of human life. Soldiers were the sons of women who, more than anyone else, had cared for them and hoped that their lives would be fulfilled. Addams noted also practically that warring nations could not care adequately for either children or the aged when they were occupied with the death of their soldiers, even though the death toll might be five civilians for every soldier killed. She regretted that the war would prevent improvements in the standard of living that might otherwise have occurred. She predicted that Europe at the end of the war would be generations behind in its social and economic goals, which was indeed the case.

I do not assert that women are better than men – even in the heat of suffrage debates I have never maintained that – but we would all admit that there are things concerning which women are more sensitive than men and that one of these is the treasuring of life. I would ask you to consider with me five aspects concerning this sensitiveness, which war is rapidly destroying. (1915, 10)

Addams called these: the protection of life (or prevention of infant mortality), the nurture of life (war overthrows the work of mother, nurse, and teacher), the fulfilment of human life (but with war no one can expect anything but the soldier's death), the conservation of life (including public systems of child care and pensions) and the ascent of life (the hope that the next generation will advance further). Addams argued that women's heightened sensitivity for human life carried with it an obligation to act. She described how, historically, women had stopped the practice of child sacrifice and urged women to protest the war in the light of their consciences. Gender concerns were of enduring interest to Addams. Early in her career she published an article on domestic workers; her research interests changed over time to the international level but the concerns for application and sophistication in analysis were constant.

CONCLUSION

It is hoped that these brief examples will advance the case for inclusion of women in "the canon." I urge scholars to read these and other women theorists themselves, not just what they wrote on women's issues, important as they are, but on the full range of subjects from the philosophical foundations of the social sciences, research methods, theory on the social contract obligation, socialization, international relations, government and parliamentary institutions, stratification, imperialism, peace, war, militarism, justice, liberty, and equality. My collection, *Women Social and Political Theorists*, forthcoming, is intended to make much of this material more accessible. Women have been contributing ideas and examples from the seventeenth century on; the literature from the eighteenth and nineteenth centuries is substantial. Much of what appears to be new with the re-emergence of the women's movement in the 1960s and 1970s is simply the re-discovery of much older ideas unfortunately dropped from the history of ideas.

By all means let people study the contribution of women in courses formally labelled "women's studies," but let us not confine women there. Let us acknowledge that women are part of the history of the discipline of sociology, as other social science disciplines, and deserve to be included, on their merits, in the normal textbooks, histories, undergraduate and graduate courses, congresses, and colloquia. This should be obvious at any time. Today, with a greater sensitivity to gender and inclusivity, it is really time to give a well-deserved rest to that expression, "I'd be glad to include women theorists if only there were any."

REFERENCES

Abel-Smith, Brian 1964: *The Hospitals 1800–1948.* London: Heinemann.
Addams, Jane 1899: Trade unions and public duty. *American Journal of Sociology*, 4(4), 448–62.
—— 1915: Address given at the Organization Conference of the Women's Peace Party. Washington DC.
——1932: The process of social transformation. In Charles A. Beard (ed.), *A Century of Progress*, Freeport, NY: Books for Libraries, 234–52.

Addams, Jane (ed.) [1895], 1970: *Hull-House Maps and Papers*. New York: Arno reprint.

Addams, Jane and Balch, Emily Greene 1927: The hopes we inherit. In *Building International Goodwill*. New York: Macmillan.

Addams, Jane, Balch, Emily Greene, and Hamilton, Alice (eds) [1915], 1972: *Women at the Hague*. New York: Garland reprint.

Astell, Mary [1700], 1730: *Some Reflections upon Marriage*. London: Parker.

—— [1694–1720], 1986: *The First English Feminist*, ed. Bridget Hill. Aldershot: Gower.

Baly, Monica [1854–70], 1991: *As Miss Nightingale Said . . .* London: Scutari.

Bentham, Jeremy [1780–1820], 1962: *Works of Jeremy Bentham*, ed. John Bowring, 11 vols. New York: Russell & Russell.

Booth, Charles (ed.) 1902: *Life and Labour of the People in London*, 17 vols. London: Macmillan.

Bussey, Gertrude and Tims, Margaret 1965: *Women's International League for Peace and Freedom 1915–1964*. London: Allen & Unwin.

Cohen, I. Bernard 1984: Florence Nightingale. *Scientific American*, March, 246, 128–33, 136–7.

Deegan, Mary Jo 1988: *Jane Addams and the Men of the Chicago School*, New Brunswick, NJ: Transaction.

Diamond, Marion and Stone, Mervyn [1874], 1981: Nightingale on Quetelet. *Journal of the Royal Statistical Society*, (A), 144, 66–79, 176–213, 332–51.

Du Châtelet, Emilie [1735–7], 1947: Fable of the bees. In Ira O. Wade, *Studies on Voltaire with some Unpublished Papers of Mme du Châtelet*. Princeton: Princeton University Press.

Farrell, John C. 1967: *Beloved Lady: a history of Jane Addams' ideas on reform and peace*. Baltimore Md: Johns Hopkins University Press.

Gilligan, Carol 1982: *In a Different Voice*. Cambridge, Mass.: Harvard University Press.

Grouchy de Condorcet, Sophie 1798: *Théorie des sentiments moraux et huit lettres sur la sympathie*, 2 vols.

—— [1798], 1994. *Lettres sur la sympathie*, ed. Jean-Paul de Lagrave. Montreal: L'Etincelle.

Hill, Bridget 1992: *Republican Virago. The life and times of Catharine Macaulay, Historian*. Oxford: Clarendon.

Hobbes, Thomas [1651], 1968: *Leviathan*, ed. C. B. Macpherson. Harmondsworth: Penguin.

Hume, David [1751], 1920: *Enquiry concerning the Principles of Morals*, ed. Selby-Bigge. Oxford: Clarendon.

Macaulay, Catharine 1767: *Loose Remarks on Hobbes's Philosophical Rudiments*. London: Davies.

—— [1790], 1974: *Letters on Education*. New York: Garland reprint.

Martineau, Harriet [1832], 1834: *Illustrations of Political Economy*, 9 vols. London: Charles Fox.

—— 1836: Essays on the art of thinking. In *Miscellanies*, 2 vols. Boston: Hilliard, Gray.

—— [1838], 1989: *How to Observe Morals and Manners*, ed. Michael R. Hill. New Brunswick NJ: Transaction.

McDonald, Lynn 1993: *Early Origins of the Social Sciences*. Montreal: McGill–

Queen's University Press.

—— 1994: *Women Founders of the Social Sciences.* Ottawa: Carleton University Press.

—— (May) 1996: Women theorists on peace, war and militarism. Paper given to the International Sociological Association Research Group on the History of Sociology, Amsterdam.

—— forthcoming: *Women Social and Political Theorists.*

Nightingale, Florence 1871: *Introductory Notes on Lying-in Institutions.* London: Longmans, Green; and 1989 facsimile *Florence Nightingale on Hospital Reform*, ed. Charles E. Rosenberg. New York: Garland.

—— 1873: A sub-"note of interrogation." *Fraser's Magazine*, 8, 25–36.

—— [1849–1850], 1987: *A Journey on the Nile 1849–1850*, ed. Anthony Sattin. London: Barrie & Jenkins.

—— [1860], 1991: *Cassandra and Other Selections from Suggestions for Thought*, ed. Mary Poovey. London: Pickering & Chatto.

—— [1860–75], 1992: *Florence Nightingale's Notes on Nursing*, ed. Victor Skretkowicz. London: Scutari Press.

—— [1860], 1994: *Suggestions for Thought by Florence Nightingale*, ed. Michael D. Calabria and Janet A. Macrae. Philadelphia: University of Pennsylvania Press.

Pisan, Christine de [1410], 1984: Lament on the evils of the civil war. In *Epistle of the Prison of Human Life*, ed. Josette A. Wisman. New York: Garland.

Raison, Timothy (ed.) [1969], 1979: *Founding Fathers of Social Science.* Harmondsworth: Penguin; and rev. edn., ed. Paul Barker. London: Scolar.

Rawls, John 1971: *A Theory of Justice.* Cambridge, Mass.: Belknap.

Ross, Dorothy 1996: Domestic discourse, Jane Addams, and the possibilities of social science. In Helene Silverberg (ed.), *Gender and American Social Science: the Formative Years*, Princeton: Princeton University Press.

Smith, Adam [1759], 1976: *Theory of Moral Sentiments*, ed. D.D. Raphael and A.L. Macfie. Oxford: Clarendon.

Sorokin, Pitirim [1922], 1975: *Hunger as a Factor in Human Affairs.* Gainesville, Fla.: University of Florida Press.

Staël, Germaine de [1796], 1798: *The Influence of the Passions upon the Happiness of Individuals and of Nations.* London: Cawthorn.

—— 1818: *Considerations on the Principal Events of the French Revolution*, 3 vols. London: Baldwin, Craddock.

—— 1820–1: *Oeuvres complètes*, 17 vols. Paris: Treuttel & Würtz.

—— 1871: *Oeuvres complètes*, 2 vols. Paris: Firmin Didot.

—— 1918: Unpublished correspondence of Mme de Staël with Thomas Jefferson, tr. Marie G. Kimball. *North American Review*, 108 (752), 63–71.

—— [1798], 1979: *Des circonstances actuelles*, ed. Lucia Omacini. Geneva: Droz.

—— [1788], 1789: *Letters on the Works and Character of J. J. Rousseau* London: C. & J. Robinson.

Webb, Beatrice 1906: *Methods of Investigation.* London: Sociological Society.

—— [1926], 1938: *My Apprenticeship*, 2 vols. Harmondsworth: Penguin.

—— 1948: *Our Partnership*, ed. Barbara Drake and Margaret I. Cole. New York: Longmans.

—— [1880–1940]: Unpublished diary. In Passfield Papers, London: British

Library of Political and Economic Science.

—— [1897], 1902: *Industrial Democracy*. London: Longmans, Green.

Webb, Sidney and Webb, Beatrice [1932], 1975: *Methods of Social Study*. LSE/ Cambridge University Press.

Weber, Marianne [1926], 1975: *Max Weber: a biography*, tr. Harry Zohn. New York: Wiley.

Weber, Max [1903–20], 1947: *From Max Weber: essays in sociology*, ed. H. H. Gerth and C. Wright Mills. London: Kegan Paul.

—— [1903–17], 1949: *Methodology of the Social Sciences*, Edward Shils and Henry A. Finch. New York: Free Press of Glencoe.

Wollstonecraft, Mary [1787–97], 1989: *Works of Mary Wollstonecraft*, ed. Janet Todd and Marilyn Butler, 7 vols. New York: New York University Press.

5

The *Other* Durkheim: History and Theory in the Treatment of Classical Sociological Thought

Robert Alun Jones

INTRODUCTION

I was very grateful to receive Charles Camic's invitation to contribute to this volume, for at least two reasons. First, I think Camic has selected a theme that combines both interest and irony – i.e., the interest in the recent interpretive re-evaluation of past sociological thought, and the irony in its relative lack of diffusion within the consciousness of the larger discipline. Second, while I was trained to do intellectual history, I've spent all but two of my last twenty-six years in a sociology department, where I've tried to advance precisely this kind of historical revisionism, simultaneously being confounded and perplexed by the indifference and even hostility it has provoked. While my pretensions to being a sociologist are now behind me, the urge to contribute to a volume concerned with these issues has hardly abated. On the contrary, it has increased.

My chapter will fall into three parts. The first will provide an account of those ideas which have most decisively informed my own thinking on the theme of this volume. Having then arrived at Richard Rorty's distinction between the "rational" and "historical" reconstruction of past ideas, the second part will provide several examples from my research on Durkheim that I hope illustrate the potential benefits of the more historical – "revisionist" in the sense of Camic's introduction – approach. For one of the most frequent objections to the "historical" – by contrast with the "rational" –

reconstruction of past sociological ideas is that it holds no rewards for sociologists per se. If we are to be concerned with reasons for the lack of diffusion of revisionist historiography within the larger discipline, therefore, it is important to meet this objection head on, with substantive illustrations of at least potential, if not fully realized, rewards. My third section will combine these examples – as well as a more recent study of Durkheim's relationship to Rousseau – in the effort to articulate more fully what such a "historically reconstructed Durkheim" might look like, and also how this *other* Durkheim might be useful to us, serving sociological as well as historical interests and purposes.

1   ON THE "HISTORICAL" RECONSTRUCTION OF PAST IDEAS

More than fifty years ago, Herbert Butterfield used the phrase "Whig interpretation of history" to denote the tendency of historians to write on the side of Protestants and Whigs rather than Catholics and Tories, to praise revolutions once they have been successful, and to emphasize "progress" in the past and thus produce a story that implicitly ratifies if not glorifies the present (Butterfield, 1931). "Whiggish history" is thus a type of "presentism" – i.e., the effort to understand the past in terms of the present – and as such it contrasts sharply with "historicism" – i.e., the effort to understand the past, insofar as possible, in its own terms. The commitment to the latter in intellectual history is at least as old as Collingwood's *Autobiography* (1939); but until the 1960s, no history was more Whiggish than the history of science (Peel, 1971, p. 259). For however disillusioned we might be with the idea of progress in other areas, the development of science at least appeared to be a cumulative growth of ever-increasing rationality (Stocking, 1968, p. 6; Sarton, 1936, p. 5).

The shift away from such presentism began at least as early as the 1930s, among several writers attempting to show "what it was like to think scientifically in a period when the canons of scientific thought were different from those current today" (Kuhn, [1962], 1970, p. viii; see also Meyerson, 1930; Metzger, 1923, 1930; Maier, 1949; Fleck, 1935; and Koyré, 1939). But the most famous expression of this shift was of course Thomas Kuhn's *Structure of Scientific Revolutions* ([1962], 1970), with its elaborate and controversial discussion of paradigms, normal and extraordinary science, puzzle-solving, anomalies, scientific crises, incommensurability, revolutions and conversions. The particular relevance of Kuhn's work to the historiography of science (and subsequently, to that of social science) lay in his discussion of the manner in which scientific revolutions are rendered retrospectively "invisible." The image of scientific activity, Kuhn argued, is largely derived from scientific textbooks, which typically contain either an introductory chapter on the history of science or scattered references to the great heroes of an earlier day. The function of these chapters and references is to provide practitioners with a sense of participation in a long-standing historical tradition; but precisely because textbooks are primarily pedagogic vehicles for the perpetuation of "normal" scientific practice, the "historical tradition" to which they refer is one that never, in fact, existed. Textbooks thus refer only to that part of the work of past scientists that can be viewed as their "contribution" to the solution of the textbook's paradigmatic problems. Through such selection and distortion, past scientists are represented as having worked on "the same" set of fixed problems, and in accord with "the same" set of canons that the most recent changes in scientific theory and method have made to seem "scientific."

In sum, Kuhn's argument was not simply that scientists, like all human beings, are tempted to write their history in a Whiggish or presentist manner; rather, the force of his argument was that scientists are exceptionally vulnerable to such temptations, partly because the results of scientific research show no obvious dependence upon the historical conditions of the inquiry, and partly because the present position of the scientist is typically so secure. The greater emphasis given to the historical conditions of human idiosyncrasy, confusion, and error would thus seem only to elevate the status of precisely those factors that it is the purpose of science to transcend. For this reason, Kuhn concluded that "the depreciation of historical fact is deeply, and probably functionally, ingrained in the ideology of the scientific profession, the same profession that places the highest of all values upon factual details of other sorts" (Kuhn, [1962], 1970, p. 138).

For a graduate student in intellectual history in the late 1960s, these were intoxicating ideas indeed; for they suggested that the history of science – and, by implication, the history of the social sciences – was ripe for revision. This implication was drawn almost immediately by George Stocking, who argued that Kuhn's approach encourages us "to see a body of knowledge as a set of propositions 'together with the questions they were meant to answer,' to understand the 'reasonableness' of points of view now superseded, to see historical change as a complex process of emergence rather than a simple sequence – in short, to understand the science of a given period in its own terms" (Stocking, 1968, p. 8; Kuhn, [1962], 1970, pp. 4, 5, 13, 52). Unlike some later writers (Heeren, 1971; Hawthorn, 1976), Stocking argued convincingly that the "pre-paradigmatic" status of the social sciences rendered their historio-graphy still more vulnerable to presentism and anachronism than that of the natural sciences; and like Robert Merton (1947, 1957, 1967), he was convinced that the history of the social sciences could be useful to its current "systematics" only if the first was recognized as distinct from the second: "By suspending judgment as to present utility," Stocking argued, "we make that judgment ultimately possible" (1968, p. 12). Finally, and most importantly, Stocking provided a series of detailed, concrete studies of the history of anthropology, exemplifying his methodological precepts through substantive historical practice (Stocking, 1968).

At approximately the same time, a parallel but independent line of argument emerged in the history of political theory and moral philosophy. The leading figure here has been Quentin Skinner (1969, 1978; Tully, 1988), although similar ideas have appeared in the writings of Alasdair MacIntyre (1966, 1981), J. G. A. Pocock (1962, 1971, 1975), and John Dunn (1968, 1969). In what has become the most widely cited example of this approach, Skinner asked the question: What are the appropriate procedures to adopt in the attempt to arrive at an understanding of a "classic text" in political theory? The most traditional answer to this question, of course, is that the text itself is the sole – necessary and sufficient – key to its own meaning. This "textualist" approach, Skinner observed, is logically – and has been historically – bound to a particular justification for the study of such classic texts in the first place – i.e., that they contain certain themes, ideas, or truths of timeless relevance to the present (Lovejoy, 1936). This justification accepted, the appropriate method seems simply to concentrate on what the classic writer has said on each of the themes in question, reading the text "over and over again" if necessary, until the argument assumes some degree of coherence (Warrender, 1957; Plamenatz, 1963; Hood, 1964).

Skinner was not utterly disdainful of this approach, for there must be some similarity between the vocabulary of the classic text and our own, or we would be unable to recognize the text as an expression of "political theory" in the first place. *All* intellectual history is "presentist" in this sense, for we must understand the unfamiliar in terms of the familiar, and our descriptions of what past writers said or meant must thus, of necessity, include our own preconceptions (paradigmatic or otherwise) about what they must have been saying. The danger rather arises where these (unavoidable) preconceptions lead us into *anachronism* – i.e., the ascription to classic writers of actions and utterances that they would not (or even could not) have accepted as reasonable accounts of what they were doing or saying. The key here was Skinner's notion of *privileged access* – i.e., that historical agents are in some sense "privileged" with regard to the interpretation of their own actions and utterances. Where such claims are not respected, Skinner argued, the result is almost always a series of mythologies – e.g., of doctrines, coherence, and/or prolepsis – in which the distinction between past and present is ignored, and anachronism ensues.

The corrective to such anachronism, as both Kuhn and Stocking observed, was greater attention to the social and historical *context* of past ideas. But initially, Skinner was almost as skeptical about certain kinds of contextualism as he was about their textualist counterparts. Where antecedent or contemporary intellectual "influences" on a classic writer were alleged, for example, Skinner repeatedly questioned whether the minimal conditions of demonstrable similarity, awareness, and dependence required by such allegedly "causal explanations" were ever in fact met; and where the appeal was to a broader socio-economic context, Skinner questioned whether such transformations of complex intellectual performances into epiphenomenal effects were in fact sufficient to, or even consistent with, one of the primary tasks of intellectual history – i.e., the understanding of past ideas themselves.

For Skinner, much of the solution to *this* problem – i.e., of *understanding* past ideas – lay in the work of J. L. Austin (Collingwood, 1939; Austin, 1975). If speaking and writing are viewed pragmatically (i.e., as activities performed by speakers and writers), Austin suggested, they can be seen to comprise at least two kinds of action. First, the author is saying or writing something – that is, he or she is putting forward words, sentences, arguments, theories, etc., with a certain "locutionary" or "propositional" meaning (i.e., a certain sense and reference). Simultaneously, however, the author may also be said to be *doing something in* speaking or writing these words, sentences, and arguments – that is, his or her utterance has a certain intended point, which Austin called the "illocutionary force" of the linguistic act. To "understand" such a speaker or writer, Austin suggested, it can never be sufficient merely to grasp the first kind of action; in addition, it is essential to gain some sense of the second, "illocutionary force" of the author's utterance, an injunction which Skinner embraced as a part (though by no means the whole) of the historian's task.

How is one to achieve an understanding of this second type of action? And how does one proceed when the utterance in question is a "classic work" in the history of social and political theory? Skinner began with the hardly contentious claim that the text, as an extended act of communication, presupposed its author's intention to be understood. Otherwise it is difficult to see how there could be a text, and therefore anything to explain, in the first place. From this initial claim about the author, it was but a short step to a second, equally uncontentious, claim about the text. Specifically, this was that the text's content, if it was to be understood by its audience at all, must have been in some sense "conventional" – that is, it must have embodied a certain vocabulary, principles, assumptions, criteria for testing knowledge-claims, problems, conceptual distinctions, etc., with which its audience would have been familiar. From these two claims, it followed that at least an initial step to understanding the text, in the "illocutionary" sense specified above, would be to situate it in its linguistic or ideological context – that is, within the larger context of texts written or used in the same society and period, addressed to the same or similar issues, and sharing these same linguistic conventions. This ideological context (and the place of the text within it) firmly in hand, the historian is finally in a position to compare the text with the relevant features of the context; to answer questions about the extent to which the author is challenging, repudiating, accepting, endorsing, or even ignoring the prevailing conventions; and thus to make statements that count as descriptions of *actions*, as explanations of what an author was *doing in* saying what he or she said.

Quite aside from encouraging a different approach to the history of ideas, however, Skinner proposed a different reason for doing it altogether. As we have seen, the more traditional, textualist approach had been bound, both logically and historically, to a particular justification for the study of such classic texts in the first place – i.e., that the classic writers are in some sense our contemporaries, contributors to a debate over relatively timeless ideas, employing a more or less stable vocabulary of concepts of ongoing relevance to the present state of the discipline. By insisting that these writers must be understood within the ideological context of their own time, however, Skinner seemed to imply that these works lacked such timeless ideas altogether, and initially his approach thus seemed to purchase historical rigor at the cost of any justification for the activity itself.

Skinner's reply to this objection was that some of the greatest rewards to be derived from the study of such writers might, indeed, lie precisely in those places where they seem most distant – i.e., "in the fact that, instead of supplying us with our usual and carefully contrived pleasures of recognition, they enable us to stand back from our own beliefs and the concepts we use to express them, perhaps forcing us to reconsider, to recast or even . . . to abandon some of our current beliefs in the light of these wider perspectives" (Skinner, 1984, pp. 202, 197–8; Jones and Kibbee, 1993, p. 156 n. 12). To learn, from the detailed, contextual study of past ideas, that what we were previously disposed to accept as an utterance on some "timeless truth" was rather the merest contingency of a particular history, biography, language or social structure, is surely to learn a more general truth, not just about the past, but about ourselves. In short, there is a kind of self-knowledge born of the realization that there have been – and will continue to be – forms of intellectual life *different* from our own.

Skinner developed these arguments through a series of philosophically based methodological essays (esp. 1966b, 1969, 1970, 1972, 1974), as well as his substantive essays on Hobbes (1964, 1965, 1966a) and a two-volume history of early modern political thought (1978). The essays in particular aroused considerable opposition, including critical assessments of Skinner's contribution to Hobbes scholarship (Weiner, 1974), criticisms of his methodology (Tarlton, 1973; Parekh and Berki, 1973; Schochet, 1974) and its philosophical foundations (Mew, 1971), and a defense of the anachronistic reading of classic texts itself (Leslie, 1970). More recently, James Tully (1988) has brought together several of Skinner's more important essays, some additional substantive and methodological critiques, and an extensive reply by Skinner to these and other critics.

My enthusiasm for Skinner's intentionalism, with which I became familiar in the mid-1970s, rapidly surpassed that I had felt several years earlier for Kuhn and Stocking. For it seemed to me to cut through some of the more unfortunate, anachronistic practices in the current historiography of sociological theory, while simultaneously avoiding the more vulgar forms of their contextualist counterparts. On the model of Skinner's "Meaning and Understanding in the History of Ideas" (1969), I quickly fashioned my own polemical treatment of the secondary literature on Durkheim's *Les Formes élémentaires de la vie religieuse* (1912), and followed this with a review essay on Skinner and an intentionalist critique of Robert Merton's distinction between the "history" and "systematics" of sociological theory (Jones, 1977, 1981, 1982; Merton, 1947, 1957, 1967). I was soon gratified to receive critical attacks of my own (Johnson, 1978; Camic, 1979, 1981; Turner, 1982; Gerstein, 1982), to which I eagerly replied, thus belaboring ad nauseam arguments already carried on at a higher level of sophistication in the history of philosophy and political theory. But if there was thus nothing particularly original in my methodological arguments, they at least provided a new way of thinking and writing about Durkheim, as well as a reputable defense against what I then considered the excesses of certain kinds of literary criticism.

In 1984, Richard Rorty entered a qualified endorsement of Skinner's argument, agreeing that such "historical reconstructions" of what dead theorists might have said to one another – in their own terms rather than ours – help us to recognize that there have been forms of intellectual life different from our own. To learn in this way the distinction between what is necessary and what is merely contingent, what is past and what is present is "the key to self-awareness itself" (Rorty, 1984, pp. 50–1; Skinner, 1969, pp. 52–3). Such learning, Rorty observed, is not without relevance to our present sociological thinking. In his 1984 essay on the idea of negative liberty, for example, Skinner has argued persuasively that our modern notions of what might be said and done with that concept can be supplemented and corrected through the "historical reconstruction" of ideas long past. The relevance of such reconstructions, he argued, "may lie in the fact that, instead of supplying us with our usual and carefully contrived pleasures of recognition, they enable us to stand back from our own beliefs and the concepts we use to express them, perhaps forcing us to reconsider, to recast or even . . . to abandon some of our current beliefs in the light of these wider perspectives" (Skinner, 1984, pp. 202, 197–8).

But there are *other* kinds of conversations, Rorty argued, that we want to imagine between *ourselves* and our ancestors. In "rational reconstructions," for example, we are interested not in Skinner's real, historical agent, but rather in an ideally reasonable and educable agent – for example, the Durkheim who might be brought to describe himself as having overstated the "objectivity" of social facts the "normality" of crime, or the "pathology" of the forced division of labor. Having been brought to accept such a new description of what he meant or did, Rorty observes, this Durkheim has become

one of us: "He is our contemporary, or our fellow-citizen, or a
fellow-member of the same disciplinary matrix" (Rorty, 1984,
pp. 51–2). The goal of such reconstructions is not self-awareness,
but rather reassurance or self-justification, our quite natural desire
to see the history of sociological theory as "a long conversational
interchange" and thus to assure ourselves that "there has been
rational progress in the course of recorded history – that we differ
from our ancestors on grounds which our ancestors could be led to
accept" (Rorty, 1984, p. 51).

From the standpoint of historicists like Skinner, of course, such
an ideal, educable Durkheim will appear anachronistic; but as long as
such reconstructions are conducted in full knowledge of their
anachronism, Rorty insists, they are also unobjectionable. To the
same historicists, who seek consensus on the kinds of things
Durkheim might reasonably be said to have done, such an ideal agent
will also seem hopelessly controversial, yielding at least as many
"Durkheims" as there are schools of contemporary sociological
theory. But again, Rorty argues, as long as we are aware of the
relevant distinctions between historical and rational reconstructions, there is little to fear from the fact that the Marxist, the
Weberian, the symbolic interactionist, and the neo-functionalist will
each reeducate Durkheim in a different way before beginning to
converse with him (Rorty, 1984, p. 54).

Yet if a difference thus exists between the historical and the
rational reconstruction of Durkheim's texts, Rorty insists, it is not
a difference between what the text *really means* and what *significance*
it might later have acquired (Hirsch, 1976, pp. 2ff; Rorty, 1984, p. 55,
n. 2). The question of what a text "means" is never a question of the
text's essential nature, or what it is Really About; rather it is always
a question of how the text fits into some larger context of thought
and action. As a result the text will have as many meanings as there
are contexts in which it might be placed. If we want self-awareness,
like Skinner, we must avoid anachronism as much as possible, and
we will concentrate on what Durkheim was thinking, speaking, and
writing about when the text was written. Yet if, like most
sociologists, we seek reassurance and self-justification through
imaginary conversations with Durkheim about our current
problems, we are free to indulge ourselves – as long as we are
conscious of what we are doing. The question of what Durkheim's
text *means* is thus a question of the particular context to which we
grant some sort of privilege; and despite my 1977 argument, this will
always be a question of *our* interests and purposes – not
Durkheim's. In this sense, some of the more negative reactions to

my historicist proposals – although not articulated in this way – have been completely justified. In 1968, for example, John Dunn referred to "the weird tendency of much writing, in the history of political thought more especially, to be made up of what propositions in what great books remind the author of what propositions in what other great books" (1968, p. 87). The criticism was echoed in Skinner (1969, p. 26) and in Jones (1977, p. 294). In 1984, however, referring to the kinds of rational reconstructions just discussed, Rorty replied simply that "[t]his tendency . . . does not seem to me weird. It is the tendency both historians and philosophers indulge when they doff their robes and converse about what they have found useful in their favourite great books" (1984, p. 59 n. 5).

Rorty's insistence that textual interpretation is ultimately a matter of our own interests rather than Durkheim's introduces a second qualification to the kind of radical historicism advocated by Skinner. In his 1969 polemic, Skinner's argument relied heavily on the idea that every historical agent has a "privileged access" to his or her own intentions as a means to "close the context" of the historical meaning of a text (Skinner, 1969, pp. 28–9; Jones, 1977, p. 288). Skinner subsequently retreated from this early formulation, denying that it was essential to his argument and suggesting a variety of conditions under which it might be ignored (Skinner, 1972, 1974, p. 284; 1988, pp. 253–5). The issue is important, however, because it seems to raise one of the most fundamental principles of Diltheyan, "hermeneutic" social science – that is, that human beings (unlike rocks and trees) are self-conscious, intentional agents, that their actions are "meaningfully oriented," and that the accounts they might give of the reasons for their actions are thus, in some sense, epistemologically privileged. Writers like John Keane, for example, have attacked Skinner's program on the ground that it simply reintroduces the most widely discredited variety of nineteenth-century interpretive theory – i.e., the notion of "empathetically looking [historical agents] in the eye and stepping into their shoes" (Keane, 1988, p. 209).

Yet for Rorty, the suggestion that one must choose, once and for all, between an interpretive, hermeneutic position and some "scientific," behaviorist counterpart is as wrong-headed as the notion that one must make a similar choice between historical and rational reconstruction. Rorty, of course, has welcomed the interpretive protest against sociologists who are preoccupied with whether they are being "scientific"; but he also has objected to the extent that this protest has been coupled with a more principled, ontological distinction between human beings and nature, and between some "hermeneutic method" appropriate to the first and some "scientific method" more appropriate to the second. After all, in the early stages of paleontology, fossils in effect were "texts," and paleontologists followed "interpretive methods" in studying them – that is, they cast about for some vocabulary whereby one puzzling object could be related to another, more familiar object, and thus rendered intelligible. Once paleontology "became a science," its methods appeared less interpretive and less hermeneutic; but this development, Rorty argues, is simply to say – as Kuhn's notion of "normal science" implies – that the vocabulary has become stabilized, and that paleontologists no longer have many doubts about what kinds of questions to ask or what kinds of hypotheses to advance when presented with a puzzling fossil. Yet in Rorty's view, to say that there is a special "interpretive or hermeneutic method" uniquely appropriate for "getting at" the essential truths about human beings is simply a special case of the mistake made by Western philosophy since Descartes: the idea that the "scientific method" is a tool for "getting at" Nature's Own Language, the vocabulary that the universe uses to explain itself to itself (Rorty, 1979). Thus Durkheim's *own* account of what he was doing in writing certain passages of *De la Division de travail social* – say in his 1907 reply to Deploige's "accusation" that his ideas were "of German origin" (Durkheim, 1907, p. 606) – is not epistemologically privileged, nor is there any interpretive or hermeneutic method that would enable us to "discover" what that injunction meant. These works simply provide additional contexts into which Durkheim's demands can be placed, and thus rendered meaningful.

Why, then, in our efforts to understand Durkheim's texts, do we spend so much time examining his other texts, especially those where Durkheim seems to be explicating himself? One answer offered by Rorty is that it simply saves time – that is, if Durkheim himself can come up with a good vocabulary for describing and explaining his utterances, we are relieved of the burden of casting about for such a vocabulary ourselves (Rorty, 1982, p. 200). Rorty's second answer to this question is more interesting. Briefly, he suggests that even if someone's own account of their actions or assertions is not *epistemologically* privileged, it still might be said to be *morally* privileged. The anthropologist is obliged to listen to accounts of the Intichiuma offered by Australian aborigines, for example, not because they have privileged access to their own motives and intentions, and certainly not because these accounts will yield the Real Meaning of the ritual, but rather because the Australian aborigines are our fellow human beings, and also because (were the situation reversed) this is how we should like to be treated. Similarly, if we consider some of Durkheim's texts as privileged with regard to the interpretation of some of his other texts, it is not because the former will reveal to us what is Really Going On or what Durkheim Really Meant, but because, as sociologists and authors ourselves, we hope to be treated similarly. So, according to Rorty, what the interpretive social scientist treats as a special method, grounded in some fundamental distinction between human beings and natural objects, is nothing more – or less – than *civility*, the taking up of a certain moral attitude toward our fellow creatures. To take up such an attitude is simply to adopt another vocabulary, a language more useful for certain purposes, as it will be less so for others, but one that can never be more or less "objective" or "scientific." Such civility of course is not incompatible with a healthy dose of skepticism. Thus, as an anonymous referee has quite rightly suggested, Durkheim's responses to charges that his thought was German in origin are frequently disingenuous. "The reason why we invite the moronic psychopath to address the court before being sentenced," Rorty's more extreme example suggests, "is not that we hope for better explanations than expert psychiatric testimony has offered. We do so because he is, after all, one of us" (1982, p. 202). Again, however, civility is not a method – it is a virtue.

2   SOME HISTORICAL RECONSTRUCTIONS

By now the significance of my title should be clear. I agree with Rorty that any reading of a classic text involves a "real or imagined conversation" with its author. But theorists and philosophers typically seek to converse with a Durkheim who is in some sense their contemporary, who might assure us that we are on the right track, or from whom we might differ in ways of which he might, at least in principle, have approved. The goal, Rorty insists, is "self-assurance," or what Skinner calls "our usual and carefully contrived pleasures of recognition." Historians, by contrast, seek conversation with a more distant figure, a Durkheim who is not our contemporary, a Durkheim who is decidedly an "other"; and the point of such conversations is hardly self-assurance, but rather that kind of self-knowledge derived from the recognition that there have been forms of thought quite different from our own.

Although rarely at this level of self-consciousness, it is conversations of the latter kind that I have tried to reconstruct, and I think that this impulse underlies many of the revisionist efforts to which Camic has referred. This position, however, is far better advanced by substantive historical example than by theoretical argument. Without making any special claims for my own work on Durkheim, therefore, I'd like to provide three instances of reconstructions that are *historical* rather than *rational* in their orientation, and from which the alleged benefits are less *self-assurance* than *self-knowledge*.

My first example concerns what might well be the most familiar methodological injunction in all of Durkheim's writings – i.e., that we should consider social facts "as things" (*comme des choses*). Here Durkheim was emphasizing that society is not simply "similar to" nature, but is itself a *real, natural thing, a part of nature*, and subject to its laws. *Rational* reconstructions of Durkheim's thought take this utterance as epitomizing his "social realism," while focusing on the theoretical and methodological advantages and disadvantages that this position entails. By contrast, the *historical* reconstruction of Durkheim's thought raises quite different questions – e.g., What was Durkheim *doing*, for example, in saying what he said? To whom, and against whom, was this injunction addressed? What was the social context of thought and action within which it first became an intelligible, meaningful utterance at all?

Several years ago, together with a colleague of mine in the French department at the University of Illinois, I tried to answer some of these questions by conducting a fairly detailed examination of the way Durkheim used the word *chose*, not only in his four major sociological volumes, but also in his early essays on the social sciences in Germany and his writings on the history and philosophy of education (Jones and Kibbee, 1993). Our conclusion was that Durkheim's injunction to treat social facts "as things" reflected his frustration with the normative vocabulary of Cartesian rationalism, as well as his desire, through the educational reforms of the Third Republic, to replace this language with the more inductive, more experimental lexicon of German empiricism – i.e., a vocabulary that emphasized complexity over simplicity, the concrete over the abstract, induction over deduction, and so on. To some extent, this desire was motivated by the superiority – widely acknowledged among intellectuals of the Third Republic – of German science and German scientific education. But an additional motivation seems to have been Durkheim's belief that only a real, concrete entity – society as a "thing" – could provide an object worthy of the veneration of the "new man" of the Republic. Durkheim's insistence that social facts should be studied *comme des choses* thus reflects *political* as well as *sociological* interests, and holds *moral* as well as *methodological* force.

More recently (Jones, 1994), I've argued that reservations about Cartesian rationalism help to explain many aspects of Durkheim's treatment of Montesquieu, particularly as reflected in the Latin thesis – devoted to a study of Montesquieu's *De l'esprit des lois* – required for graduation from the Ecole Normale Supérieure. For as Isaiah Berlin (1980) has shown, Montesquieu was a most reluctant rationalist, an uneasy ally amidst the Enlightenment's celebration of reason, reform, and social progress, and an author whose greatest achievements derived precisely from those moments when, seduced by an insatiable curiosity and a fascination for the particular, the detailed, and the concrete, he digressed and thus deserted the rationalist credo of his milieu. In fact, it was precisely this reluctance and uneasiness, these digressions and this eventual apostasy, that excited Durkheim's interest. For Durkheim shared this ambivalence, sensed it in his predecessor, and thus used the Latin thesis as a vehicle for the "working out" of his own conception of the relative value of rationalism and empiricism.

Again, the point of this example is not to argue that this is what Durkheim's texts are "really about," or that the more "rational" reconstruction of these texts by Lukes is in any sense mistaken. Rather, in the manner endorsed by both Skinner and Rorty, it is to place these texts in the context of other texts in order to render them meaningful, to thus imagine various conversations that Durkheim might have had with his contemporaries. *Pace* Lukes, we have simply *used* these texts in a different way, "put them to work" for a different purpose. This purpose, I should add, is by no means the "reassurance" that follows so readily from "our usual and carefully contrived pleasures of recognition." On the contrary, the Durkheim whom we have historically reconstructed seems to have been concerned with interests that were his rather than ours, to have quite self-consciously used general methodological injunctions for moral and specific political purposes, and to have been constrained by a vocabulary that we no longer use. But to learn this about Durkheim – i.e., to learn, in a manner reminiscent of Foucault, how appeals to "universal" scientific principles disguise concrete political actions, and how "normative vocabularies" both impede and sustain social action – is surely to learn something about ourselves.

My second example (Jones, 1986) refers to one of the most oft-cited passages in discussions of Durkheim's sociology of religion. Briefly, in 1905–7, the Catholic philosophy journal *Revue néo-scolastique* published a series of articles by the Belgian priest Simon Deploige attacking Durkheim's elevation of "society" to a power superior to that of the individual. Durkheim responded in a series of letters to the editor, and it is from these that this now famous passage is taken:

> ... it was not until 1895 that I achieved a clear view of the essential role played by religion in social life. It was in that year that, for the first time, I found the means of tackling the study of religion sociologically. This was a revelation to me. That course of 1895 marked a dividing line in the development of my thought, to such an extent that all my previous researches had to be taken up afresh in order to be made to harmonize with these new insights ... [This reorientation] was entirely due to the studies of religious history which I had just undertaken, and notably to the reading of the works of Robertson Smith and his school. (1907, pp. 612–13)

Deploige's articles were subsequently published as *Le Conflit de la morale et de la sociologie* (1911). Durkheim's hostile review of that work in *l'Année sociologique* contains a similar reference to "all that we owe to Robertson Smith and to the works of the ethnographers of England and America" (1913, p. 326).

The difficulty for anyone trying to make sense of this rare, autobiographical passage in Durkheim's work is that there is almost no evidence, from the 1895 lecture course until "Sur le totémisme" (1902) that Robertson Smith had had any impact on Durkheim's thought whatsoever. The historical evidence rather suggests that Durkheim's religious thought went through at least three significant changes during this seven-year period: the first, cryptically referred to in the remark just cited, involved the extension of Durkheim's earlier interest in classical antiquity to the study of primitive peoples, as well as the parallel extension from the study of written legal documents to the study of primitive, and eventually Australian, ethnography; the second, which occurred approximately in 1897–8, involved Durkheim's increased interest in the psychology of the unconscious, possibly under the influence of the psychological experiments described in Pierre Janet's *L'Automatisme psychologique*, and his increased attraction for psychological metaphors to describe sociological phenomena; and the third, which took place only after 1899, was the development of Durkheim's increasingly "eudaemonic" conception of religious forces, in sharp contrast to his earlier view of religion in terms of externality and constraint.

This third shift took place immediately after the appearance of Baldwin Spencer and F. J. Gillen's *Native Tribes of Central Australia* (1899), a monumental ethnography containing detailed descriptions of the totemic beliefs and practices of Australian aborigines. This detailed, authoritative ethnography provoked a debate over the meaning of totemism – a debate in which the ethnographers themselves sided with the more rationalist interpretations of the British anthropologist Sir James Frazer, and in which Durkheim embraced and then forcefully manipulated the more "irrationalist" theories of Robertson Smith – a devout Calvinist minister – for the first time. Before this, Durkheim was far more interested in Frazer's notion of *taboo* than in Smith's eudaemonic (or, as Durkheim later styled it, "dynamogenic") conception of religious forces. Durkheim's attraction for the latter seems to have been provoked primarily by Frazer's offensively utilitarian interpretation of the Australian evidence – a putatively "crucial" experiment for the Victorian anthropological community – which challenged some of the most fundamental tenets of Durkheimian sociological theory.

Thus challenged, Durkheim seems to have used Smith's theories in a manner approximating what the sociologist of science Andrew Pickering has called the "articulation of exemplars" – i.e., whereby some new, "unsolved" aspect of a scientific field is organized and perceived analogically, as being "the same" as some already well-understood aspect of the field, and more sophisticated perspectives are then constructed at the research front by importation of conceptual resources ("exemplars") from the area with which the analogical connection has been made (Pickering, 1982, p. 126). In this particular case, the "unsolved" aspect of the scientific field was the meaning of the Arunta *Intichiuma*, a totemic ceremony performed at the end of the long Australian "dry" season, in anticipation of the rainy season with its regeneration of vegetation. It was the performance of this ceremony, Durkheim argued, which led to the socially-inspired "collective effervescence" productive of the religious life. Here Durkheim organized and perceived the *Intichiuma* analogically, as being "the same" as an already well-understood aspect of the field – i.e., the sacrificial rites of the ancient Semites described by Robertson Smith – importing a more sophisticated theoretical "exemplar" from an otherwise quite different context.

Historically reconstructed, therefore, the dispute between Durkheim and Frazer – i.e., over whether totemism was a religion born of the gathering of the clan, or magic designed to provide an adequate supply of food – seems less an argument over some fact of nature than over the right to speak about it one way rather than another. For here "nature" exhibited a charming indifference, even allowing Durkheim and Frazer to cite the same "fact" – i.e., the consubstantiality of clan member and totem – to two, precisely opposite, purposes, and with equal plausibility. The contest between

Durkheim and Frazer was thus not one over whose theories demonstrated a closer approximation to nature, but rather a quarrel over "concept application," over whose analogies would ultimately prove most compelling, and over whose exemplars would eventually serve to order and classify the chaos of primitive cultures for the post-Victorian anthropological community.

The point, therefore, is not that Durkheim finally "got it right." On the contrary, just fifty years after *Les Formes élémentaires*, Lévi-Strauss could insist that the entire late-Victorian obsession with totemism, from J. F. McLennan and Lewis Henry Morgan to Durkheim, Frazer, and Freud, was analogous to the almost simultaneous medical obsession with hysteria, whose symptoms vanished as soon as one sought to submit them to some unifying interpretation. Far from being an objective social institution, Lévi-Strauss observed, totemism was called into existence by intellectuals who sought an alien "natural kind" to protect the sovereignty of their own, distinctively rational moral universe (1963, p. 1). In this sense, Durkheim, Frazer, and Smith hardly appear to be our contemporaries; on the contrary, their intellectual world must seem as strange to us as that of the Australian aborigines seemed to them. But this "strangeness" is also edifying – i.e., it tells us something about ourselves, about the way social science responds to the social and cultural needs of its time, sometimes "constructing" and "objectifying" the phenomena it studies.

My final example concerns Durkheim's relationship with his philosophic mentor, the great French philosopher, Emile Boutroux (1845–1921). Durkheim scholars, of course, have long been aware of Boutroux, although usually in just one context – i.e., in 1907, responding to Simon Deploige's "accusation" that his distinction between psychology and sociology was German in origin, Durkheim insisted instead that: "I owe it to my master, Boutroux, who, at the Ecole normale supérieure, repeated frequently to us that each science must, as Aristotle says, explain [its own phenomena] by 'its own principles' – e.g., psychology by psychological principles, biology by biological principles. Most impressed by this idea, I applied it to sociology" (1907, pp. 612–13). But again, it is the *differences* between Durkheim and Boutroux that are the most interesting.

In the preface to the English translation of his *De la Contingence des lois de la nature* ([1874], 1916), Boutroux recalled the problem that led him to write his most famous book: "If [the laws of nature] were actually necessary," he reasoned, "[they] would signify the immutability and rigidity of death. If they are contingent, they dignify life and constitute points of support or bases which enable us constantly to rise towards a higher life" (1916, p. vii). In opposition to the rationalist conception of a single world comprised of logically deducible necessary relations, therefore, Boutroux insisted on "several worlds, forming, as it were, stages superposed on one another" ([1874], 1916, pp. 151–2). These include the world of pure necessity (i.e., of quantity without quality), the world of causes, the world of notions, the mathematical world, the physical world, the living world, and, at last, the thinking world. At first, Boutroux acknowledged, each of these worlds seems to depend on those beneath it, and to receive from them its existence and its laws; but again, the examination and comparison of these forms of being, as well as the sciences that study them, shows that it is impossible to connect the higher to the lower forms by any link of necessity. This means, in turn, that the universe is not made up of equal elements capable of being transformed into one another like algebraic quantities; on the contrary, each world contains something new, something more than the worlds below, so that within each world the amount of being and the degree of perfection is indeterminate ([1874], 1916, pp. 158–9). Each world, in short, is indeterminate and contingent – i.e., might *not* have existed, or might have existed *in some other form* – rather than logically or causally necessary.

It was to this argument that Durkheim referred when, in 1907, he defended himself against Deploige. But in fact, Durkheim never accepted Boutroux's doctrine of contingency, nor was he sympathetic to Boutroux's larger attack on determinism. On the contrary, Durkheim's dedication of *De la Division du travail social* to Boutroux is ironic in light of the latter's criticism, just two years later, of his effort to explain the division of labor as the "necessary consequence" of increasing density and volume of population. Despite his ambivalence over Cartesian rationalism and occasional empiricist gestures, Durkheim refused to sacrifice the notion of necessary laws, while Boutroux embraced a kind of empiricism heavily laced with spiritualism. As Durkheim began accumulating the evidence and argument that would become *Les Formes élémentaires*, Boutroux refused to acknowledge the generalizability of the Australian data, emphasizing instead how the historical evolution of religion led in the direction of an emphasis on belief rather than ritual, and on individual freedom rather than societal constraints. Unlike Durkheim, for whom "religion" and "science" were almost monolithic entities, the more historically minded Boutroux insisted that there were multiple, irreducible "religions" and "sciences" just as there were multiple, irreducible "levels of being." And while for Durkheim, society was always an externally observable, phenomenal object, for Boutroux it was a historical subject, acting in the pursuit of spiritual ideals.

By far the most interesting difference between Durkheim and Boutroux, however, is the one that erupted at a *séance* of the Société française de philosophie devoted to the discussion of Boutroux's *La Science et la religion dans la philosophie contemporaine* (1908). Boutroux's book attracted more than the usual philosophical attention, for it appeared at the height of the Catholic Modernist movement in France. For half a century, French Catholic theologians and philosophers – including Boutroux, Alfred Loisy, Lucien Laberthonnière, and Édouard Le Roy – had attempted to bring Catholic doctrine more in line with modern science, social theory, and Biblical criticism. This was a movement to which Pope Leo XIII was not unsympathetic; but with his death in 1903, and the accession of Pius X, five works by Loisy were instantly placed on the Index, followed by condemnations of works by Laberthonnière and Le Roy. By 1907, the Church had published a "catalog of errors," modeled on the *Syllabus Errorum*, titled *Lamentabili sane exitu*. The catalog condemned sixty-five Modernist "errors" concerning Scripture and Church doctrine, most extracted from the writings of Loisy, in effect calling "a halt to a genuinely historical study of the Scriptures and tradition." In the same year, the Pope published the encyclical *Pascendi dominici gregis*, which re-affirmed the teachings of the Church in opposition to the Modernist position, and enumerated the steps to be taken "to fight the growing contagion" (Livingston, 1971, pp. 291, 292). By 1908, Loisy had been ex-communicated.

Almost simultaneously, in a lecture course on the origins of religion at the Sorbonne (1906–7), Durkheim advanced a scientific explanation of religious belief as the consequence of a natural, externally observable, social process. Religious belief thus expresses and corresponds to something real, he explained, although the conception of this reality held by religious believers is "vulgar, irrational, and mysterious" – i.e., it stands outside of science. With the exception of those committed to a "determined confessional formula," however, Durkheim could not imagine why believers would refuse to see religion in these terms, for his own explanation demonstrated – at least to him – that religion is based upon and expresses real social facts. No science, Durkheim insisted, makes the phenomena it explains disappear; and it was in this sense, of course, that he argued that the vital, practical function of religion is eternal.

To this particular argument, the response of Boutroux and other

Catholic Modernists at the *séance* bordered on astonishment. Both Le Roy and Lachelier (Boutroux's philosophic mentor) went so far as to accuse Durkheim of "equivocation" in his insistence that his explanation of religion constituted no threat to the faith and that the Modernists, if not their more orthodox counterparts, should embrace it. Both Boutroux and Le Roy objected that science rather clearly *does* dissipate the things it explains, frequently replacing them with "facts and laws." But the more specific objection was most clearly stated by Le Roy four years later, when *Les Formes élémentaires* itself became the subject of a *séance* of the Société (Le Roy, 1913, pp. 45–7). Explaining religion, Le Roy (in effect) observed, is not the same as explaining the effects of gravitation or physio-chemical processes. For one of the *constitutive elements* of religious belief – indeed, the element that renders such a belief "religious" by contrast with other beliefs – is the conviction that it *cannot* be explained as the consequence of natural causes. Whatever takes place in other sciences, therefore, the sociological explanation of religious belief rather clearly *does* seem to dismember the phenomenon it attempts to explain. So, in the end, the conversation does seem to lapse into an almost classic confrontation between skeptic and believer.

What kind of "self-awareness" might we achieve through the historical reconstruction of this kind of conversation? An initial answer is that it invites us to think seriously about the criteria we use to evaluate past ideas. A knee-jerk response to the conflict between Durkheim and Boutroux, for example, is simply to resolve it through an appeal to one's own criteria of rationality. To the social scientist, many of Boutroux's beliefs will thus appear to be irrational and "unscientific," while to the Roman Catholic, Durkheim's attempt at a scientific explanation of religious belief will seem narrow, mechanical, and overly deterministic. The social scientist might respond – as Durkheim did – by insisting that the Roman Catholic thus places religion outside of science, and thus outside of reason, altogether; but this is to ignore the consistent effort of Boutroux and the other Modernists to distinguish themselves from those who would defend an entirely affective, non-cognitivist, "agapeistic" conception of religious experience. For *these* Roman Catholics, in any case, there is "a more general reason" which includes, but is not exhausted by, science. We might argue, of course, that these Roman Catholics were mistaken – i.e., that their "more general reason" is incoherent in the light of our own, allegedly superior rationality. But even if we were right and they were wrong, this would still not be the same as saying that they were irrational.

For the holding of beliefs that are *rational* is not equivalent to the holding of beliefs that we might later hold to be *true*, and vice versa.

What, then, does it mean to hold *rational* beliefs? Very briefly, I think it means only that the beliefs in question should be suitable beliefs for people to hold under the circumstances in which they find themselves. Beliefs that are "rational" would thus be those beliefs that people have achieved through some socially accredited process of reasoning. This process, in turn, would be one that, according to the prevailing norms of epistemic rationality, might be said to give people good reasons for assuming – by contrast with merely desiring or hoping – that the beliefs in question are true. The attitude of one holding these beliefs, therefore, should include some interest in the consistency of the beliefs, as well as some interest in their justification (Putnam, 1981, pp. 150–200; Skinner, 1988, pp. 239–40; Lewis, 1974, p. 336). These may seem to be minimal criteria, even to the point of depriving the concept of "rationality" of any content whatever (Skinner, 1988, p. 244; Rorty, 1979, p. 174). To go further, however, threatens to undermine the distinction between the holding of beliefs that are *rational* and the holding of beliefs that we might later hold to be *true*. By these criteria, it seems fairly obvious that the beliefs of both Durkheim and Boutroux were held rationally. Their disagreement rather derives from the fact that, in their respective vocabularies, important words like "reason," "religion," "science," etc. – are used in different ways, and thus seem to mean quite different things.

This brings me to the second potential benefit to be derived from the historical reconstruction of this particular conversation – i.e., it helps us to think seriously about the conditions requisite to an understanding of alien beliefs. When we speak of "alien" beliefs, of course, we normally think of the anthropologist confronting the beliefs held by the members of "primitive" societies. But the problem of understanding such beliefs is no less an obstacle for the intellectual historian seeking to comprehend "classic" texts or the religious skeptic (e.g., Durkheim) attempting to understand the devout believer (e.g., Boutroux). In each case, as Alasdair MacIntyre pointed out in his classic formulation of this problem (1964), the question is whether the anthropologist, the historian, and/or the skeptic may be said to share the concepts of the native, the classic writer, and/or the religious believer, and thus to "understand" him or her.

For our purposes, it is instructive that Macintyre's answer to this question depends heavily on an historical example. Until the seventeenth century, he observed, we should all have been believers;

indeed, there would have been no question of our having been anything else. Since the seventeenth century, even for those who still believe, the truth and intelligibility of their beliefs is not obvious in the same sense. What accounts for the difference? What explains the fact that nobody – not even Boutroux – could believe in God in the way that people in the Middle Ages believed implicitly? How is it that some of the alternatives to religious belief now seem as obvious to people like Durkheim as the belief in God did to the medieval Christian? In short, how is it that what appears intelligible in one social context can appear to make no sense in another? MacIntyre's answer was *secularization* – i.e., that process whereby sectors of society (e.g., the family, education, government, and the church itself) are gradually deprived of the support and/or domination of religious institutions and symbols. The apparent incoherence of Christian concepts, MacIntyre argued, was regarded as tolerable because the concepts were part of a larger vocabulary indispensable to contemporary social and intellectual life. As these institutions became secularized, the vocabulary changed, and the incoherence that had previously been merely "apparent" became the grounds for skepticism and disbelief (MacIntyre, 1970, p. 74).

MacIntyre's argument provides a new perspective from which to view the debate between Durkheim and Boutroux. However insensitive Durkheim might have appeared to Boutroux and the other Catholic Modernists, of course, there is no question that he was sincere in his effort to understand their beliefs. But there were at least two, formidable obstacles to his understanding. The first was – as MacIntyre has argued – that the social context of institutions and language within which beliefs like those of Boutroux might have been plausible to Durkheim had almost completely disappeared. This is why MacIntyre himself concluded that understanding Christianity is incompatible with believing in it – i.e., not because Christianity is so vulnerable to skeptical objections, but because its peculiar invulnerability belongs to it as a form of belief which has lost the social context within which it was once comprehensible.

The second obstacle, *pace* MacIntyre, suggests a sense in which the case of the skeptic and the believer is *not* analogous to that of the anthropologist approaching an alien culture, but in fact presents problems of understanding that are far greater. For, as we have seen, the anthropologist – *qua* anthropologist – is bound by the culture of his discipline to *assume* rationality on the part of the agents whom he seeks to understand. But the skeptic – *qua* skeptic – is bound by no such principle. On the contrary, it is at least a technique, if not a principle, of skepticism to strip away the supportive infrastructure of those ideas about which one is skeptical. By this criterion, of course, Durkheim was a particularly thorough and successful skeptic, not only in his *arguments* – i.e., which never acknowledged that it might be rational to hold beliefs similar to those held by Boutroux – but also in his *actions* – i.e., which were apparently consistent with those anticlerical policies of the Third Republic that stripped the Catholic Church of its influence on French education.

This is not to take a position on one side of this dispute or the other. On the contrary, as a historian – *qua* historian – I'm committed to assuming the rationality of the agents on *both* sides of the issue. But I think it is important to understand the nature of the dispute. It is not simply a disagreement over beliefs, for as MacIntyre has argued, that kind of disagreement presumes that the skeptic and the believer understand each other – i.e., that they agree on the application of crucial concepts like "reason," "science," and "religion." From what we have seen, however, it seems clear that the skeptic and the believer use these concepts in different ways, so that Durkheim "understands" Christianity only in a sense that Boutroux does not, and vice versa. So what at first appeared to be a disagreement over beliefs turns out, in the end, to be a misunderstanding over the criteria of intelligibility – quite literally, over what it means to "believe."

3   THE *OTHER* DURKHEIM

So who *was* this "other" Durkheim who emerges from more self-consciously *historical* reconstructions like the ones I have just described? To me he seems less the ideologue preoccupied with a kind of sociological metaphysic than a pragmatic and opportunistic *bricoleur*, casting about for tools that might be used to solve real social and political problems, and changing them frequently in response to changing circumstances. Jewish, secular, and socialist, his interests were inextricably bound to the success or failure of the Third French Republic, a regime that rose from the humiliation of the Franco-Prussian War, and whose severe political instabilities were constantly on his mind. Though a reformer rather than revolutionary, it is to Durkheim's profound and lasting credit that he understood how deep the roots of the problem were, and how fundamental a change would be necessary if the Third Republic were to survive. For Durkheim, the fundamental change was not a material but a linguistic revolution. His goal was to find and/or contrive a new moral vocabulary – i.e., a new way of thinking and speaking about society and ethics – and then do all that he could by means of political and educational reform to see that his fellow countrymen learned to think and speak in this way.

For Durkheim, there was never any question about this vocabulary being "scientific." The problem was that French science was largely Cartesian, emphasizing the rational and abstract rather than the concrete and empirical, individual genius rather than a Baconian division of scientific labor, deduction rather than induction, "clear and distinct ideas" rather than careful observation, comparison, and experiment, etc. With many of his contemporaries, Durkheim shared the view that it was this kind of science that had failed the French at Sedan, where they had confronted the superior force of German soldiers whose education was secular, Protestant, and empiricist. Returning from Germany in 1887, Durkheim's essays on "La Philosophie dans les universités allemandes" and "La Science positive de la morale en Allemagne" lavish praise on certain aspects of German science and education, and above all on their respect for things that are concrete rather than abstract, complex rather than simple – in short, for *things* rather than ideas. The Latin thesis on Montesquieu – who was himself an ambivalent Cartesian – was Durkheim's way of "working out" his ambivalence on these issues, weighing the benefits of French rationalism and German empiricism, and eventually settling on a formulation he would call the "new rationalism" of the Third Republic. This recognition that society was real, complex, and concrete was an essential requirement, not simply of the *science* of ethics Durkheim advanced in *De la Division du travail social* (1893), but of ethics *itself*. For if complex social wholes could be reduced to their constituent parts, then only the individual would be real, and society would be merely an idea; and an idea, Durkheim added, can never be the object of our moral allegiance ([1925], 1961, p. 257). As *L'Éducation morale* (1925) and *L'Évolution pédagogique en France* (1938) make clear, it is in this context that we should understand Durkheim's injunction to treat social facts *comme des choses*.

This moral allegiance of the citizens of the Third French Republic was thus the end for which social science was a means. But not all social scientists accepted Durkheim's "social realism" – i.e., the notion that social facts are real, concrete things, existing outside of individuals and exerting constraint upon them. Gabriel Tarde, in particular, attacked Durkheim's *De la Division du travail social* and then *Les Règles de la méthode sociologique* (1895), insisting that social phenomena could be explained as the consequence of the psychological tendency to imitation. These attacks led Durkheim back to Rousseau, whom he had previously treated critically as a subjective individualist, but whose *Du Contrat social* (1762) he now made the subject of a lecture course at Bordeaux (1897). This re-reading of Rousseau which was comprehensive, including not only *Du Contrat social*, the second *Discours* (1755), and *Émile* (1762), but a variety of Rousseau's other writings – was among the most important events in Durkheim's intellectual career. For Rousseau gave him the most important idea in *Le Suicide* (1897) – i.e., the notion that unregulated desires and aspirations lead to anomic suicide, and that for human beings, only society can provide the absolute, unequivocal kind of constraint that animals (and, for Rousseau, natural man) find in the state of nature (see Jones, 1996).

Regulation and external constraint thus played a major part in Durkheim's conception of religion until the end of the century. As we have seen, he was then confronted with Spencer and Gillen's *Native Tribes of Central Australia* (1899) and, more important, their utilitarian, Frazerian interpretation. Again, therefore, Durkheim was led back to a deeper, stronger reading of a writer – William Robertson Smith – with whom Durkheim had been familiar as early as 1895–6, when he taught a lecture course on religion at Bordeaux. And again, Durkheim found the tool he needed – i.e., Smith's communion theory of Semitic sacrifice – which he then applied analogically to explain the Arunta *Intichiuma* ceremony. Henceforth, Durkheim understood religion not only as a body of beliefs and practices imposed through external constraint, but also as comprising a "dynamogenic" quality capable of lifting the individual above himself, and thus of transcending his ordinary existence. Like society – which is what religion represents and expresses – religion thus constrains *and* inspires, regulates *and* liberates, in precisely the manner described in Rousseau's *Du Contrat social*.

By thus opposing Frazer and embracing Smith, of course, Durkheim reaffirmed his anti-reductionist view that social facts could only be explained by other social facts, and never by physical and/or psychological phenomena (e.g., Frazer's utilitarian notion that totemism was a form of rational – albeit primitive – ecology). But as we have seen, Durkheim's anti-reductionism was quite selective. In opposition to Boutroux (to whom Durkheim frequently appealed when confronted by psychological reductionists) Durkheim had no qualms about reducing religious phenomena to sociological causes, particularly in so far as this based religion on a "real" – by contrast with ideal – foundation. The reaction this provoked among the Catholic Modernists (which, as we have seen, was neither incomprehensible nor irrational) should remind us of

MacIntyre's observation – i.e., that the plausibility of arguments like Durkheim's (like the implausibility of arguments like Boutroux's) is itself the product of particular social and institutional arrangements, themselves subject to the contingencies of history.

Though hardly a complete stranger, this *historically* reconstructed Durkheim is less familiar to sociologists than those Durkheims found in sociology textbooks and treatises on classical social theory. For the point of these *rationally* reconstructed Durkheims, as I have said, is to provide *reassurance* – i.e., Rorty's "exercises in commensuration" or Skinner's "carefully contrived pleasures of recognition" – that we are on the right track, or part of a long and distinguished tradition. The Durkheim I have described above, of course, will serve no such purpose, for he was concerned, not with our society, but with his own; not with Marx, Weber, Simmel, and Mead, but with Wundt, Montesquieu, Frazer, Robertson Smith, Tarde, Rousseau, and Boutroux; and not with "timeless truths" of enduring relevance to all peoples, but with the quite different and quite specific issues of his own historical time and place. But to learn that Durkheim's project was to find and/or contrive a moral vocabulary more suitable to the needs of the Third French Republic; that he found useful resources for this purpose in Wundt's laboratory in Leipzig, Montesquieu's *De l'esprit des lois*, Smith's *Religion of the Semites*, and Rousseau's *Du Contrat social;* that he sometimes got lost, became confused, contradicted himself, and returned to writers he had attacked or dismissed to re-read them and appropriate them to his purposes; that his interests as a sociologist and methodologist were always subservient to his interests as a loyal, secular citizen of the Third French Republic; that he was at least as ill-equipped to understand Boutroux's Catholic Modernist beliefs as Boutroux was to understand his – to learn all these things is surely to learn something about ourselves as well.

CONCLUSION

In the three sections above, I have tried to identify what I consider the distinctively *historical reconstruction* of past sociological ideas, to provide some examples of benefits that such reconstructions might provide, and to tell a slightly different story about Durkheim than those that others have told. But Camic's question remains. Why, indeed, has the revisionist scholarship to which Camic draws our attention – i.e., the *historical* reconstruction of past sociological ideas – made such little headway in the discipline? Why has there been virtually no outward diffusion? Why do we see "a proliferation of books and articles that repeat again and again claims about the classics which the specialist scholarship has established to be serious misreadings and distorting cliches"? How, indeed, are we to "reclaim" the arguments of the sociological classics?

My first answer is to suggest that it is a mistake to conceive of the project of reading, thinking, and writing about the classics as one of the reclamation of arguments. On the contrary, I would like to suggest that it is always, in some sense, a project of finding a language, a vocabulary, a set of tools for the solution of the very practical kinds of concerns, interests, and purposes that we have in the present. This is certainly what Durkheim was doing in Germany, for example, or in his reading (and especially his re-reading) of Rousseau and then Robertson Smith. And as my examples suggest, these concerns, interests, and purposes not only vary from one scholar to another, but may also change with disconcerting frequency even in the lifetime of a single writer. In short, the reading of classical texts is a fundamentally pragmatic activity, and we should study it as such.

For some of us, this interest or purpose is in the kind of self-knowledge or self-awareness provided by detailed, contextualized accounts of past ideas. But for others, the goal is rather a kind of reassurance or self-justification provided by exercises in commensuration – the kind of conversation in which Durkheim is, anachronistically but unashamedly, our contemporary. Indeed, it is arguable that sociology, as an academic discipline, is still at that stage where self-assurance is far more frequently and eagerly sought than self-knowledge. It would be a grave error, however, to assume that historical reconstructions are irrelevant to the discipline. Self-knowledge – e.g., a sense that timeless and universal truths often prove to be contingent and arbitrary, that the forms of intellectual life are infinitely various, that history itself is deeply ironic and therefore occasionally quite humbling, etc. – is something sociologists can use.

REFERENCES

Austin, J. L. 1975: *How to Do Things with Words*. Cambridge: Harvard University Press.
Berlin, Isaiah 1980: Montesquieu. In Isaiah Berlin (ed.), *Against the Current: essays in the history of ideas*. New York: Viking, 130–61.

Boutroux, Émile, [1874], 1916: *The Contingency of the Laws of Nature*, tr. Fred Rothwell. Chicago and London: Open Court.

Butterfield, Herbert 1931: *The Whig Interpretation of History*. Harmondsworth: Penguin.

Camic, Charles 1979: The utilitarians revisited. *American Journal of Sociology*, 85, 516–50.

—— 1981: On the methodology of the history of sociology: a reply to Jones. *American Journal of Sociology*, 87(1), 139–44.

Collingwood, Robin George 1939: *An Autobiography*. Oxford: Oxford University Press.

Dunn, John 1968: The identity of the history of ideas. *Journal of the Royal Institute of Philosophy*, 43, 164, 85–104.

—— 1969: *The Political Thought of John Locke*. Cambridge: Cambridge University Press.

Durkheim, Émile 1898: Représentations individuelles et représentations collectives. *Revue de métaphysique et de morale*, 6, 273–302.

—— 1907: Lettres au Directeur de la *Revue néo-scolastique*. *Revue néo-scolastique*, 14, 606–7, 612–14.

—— 1913: Deploige, Simon. *Le Conflit de la morale et de la sociologie*. *Année sociologique*, 12, 326–8.

—— [1925], 1961: *Moral Education: a study in the theory and application of the sociology of education*, tr. Everett K. Wilson and Herman Schnurer. New York: Free Press of Glencoe.

Fleck, Ludwik 1935: *Enstehung und Entwicklung einer wissenschaftlichen Tatsache*. Basel: B. Schwabe.

Gerstein, Dean R. 1982. Durkheim's paradigm: reconstructing a social theory. In Randall Collins (ed.), *Sociological Theory*. San Francisco: Jossey-Bass, 234–58.

Hawthorn, Geoffrey 1976: *Enlightenment and Despair: a history of sociology*. Cambridge: Cambridge University Press.

Heeren, J.W. 1971: Review of R.W. Friedrich's *A Sociology of Sociology*. *Journal of the History of the Behavioral Sciences*, 7(2), 475–82.

Hirsch, E. D., Jr 1976: *The Aims of Interpretation*. Chicago: University of Chicago Press.

Hood, G. C. 1964: *The Divine Politics of Thomas Hobbes*. Oxford: Oxford University Press.

Janet, Pierre 1889: *L'Automatisme psychologique*. Paris: Alcan.

Johnson, Harry 1978: Comment on Jones' "Understanding a sociological classic." *American Journal of Sociology*, 84(1), 171–5.

Jones, Robert Alun 1977: On understanding a sociological classic. *American Journal of Sociology*, 83(2), 279–319.

—— 1981: On Quentin Skinner. *American Journal of Sociology*, 87, 435–67.

—— 1982: On Merton's "History" and "Systematics" of sociological theory. In L. Graham, W. Lepenies, and P. Weingart (eds), *Functions and Uses of Disciplinary Histories*. Dordrecht: D. Reidel, 121–42.

—— 1983: The new history of sociology. In *The Annual Review of Sociology*, San Francisco: Annual Reviews, Inc., 443–69.

—— 1986: Durkheim and the positive science of ethics in Germany. *History of Sociology: an international review*, 5–6, 177–91.

—— 1990: Religion and realism: some reflections on Durkheim's *L'Evolution*

Pédagogique en France. Archives de Sciences Sociales des Religions, 69, 69–89.
—— 1994: Ambivalent Cartesians: Durkheim, Montesquieu, and method. *American Journal of Sociology,* 100(1), 1–39.
—— 1997: Durkheim, realism, and Rousseau. *Journal of the History of the Behavioral Sciences* (forthcoming).
Jones, Robert Alun and Vogt, W. Paul 1984: Durkheim's defense of *Les Formes élémentaires de la vie religieuse.* In Henrika Kuklick and Elizabeth Long (eds), *Knowledge and Society: studies in the sociology of culture, past and present,* Greenwich: JAI Press, 45–62.
Jones, Robert Alun and Douglas A. Kibbee 1993: Durkheim, language and history: a pragmatist perspective. *Sociological Theory,* 11(2), 152–70.
Keane, John 1988: More theses on the philosophy of history. In James Tully (ed.), *Meaning and Context: Quentin Skinner and his critics.* Princeton, New Jersey: Princeton University Press, 204–17.
Koyré, A. 1939: *Études Galiléenes.* Paris: Hermann.
Kuhn, Thomas S. [1962], 1970: *The Structure of Scientific Revolutions,* 2nd edn. Chicago: University of Chicago Press.
Le Roy, Édouard 1913: Contribution to discussion of: Le Problème religieux et la dualité de la nature humaine. *Bulletin de la Société française de philosophie,* 13, 45–7.
Leslie, M. 1970: In defense of anachronism. *Political Studies,* 28, 433–7.
Lévi-Strauss, C. 1963: *Totemism.* Boston: Beacon.
Lewis, David 1974: Radical Interpretation. *Synthèse,* 27, 331–44.
Livingston, James C. 1971: *Modern Christian Thought: from the Enlightenment to Vatican II.* New York and London: Macmillan.
Lovejoy, Arthur O. 1936: *The Great Chain of Being.* Cambridge: Harvard University Press.
Lukes, Steven 1988: *Émile Durkheim: His Life and Work: a historical and critical study.* London: Penguin Books.
MacIntyre, Alasdair 1966: *A Short History of Ethics.* London: Macmillan.
—— 1970: Is understanding religion compatible with believing? In Bryan R. Wilson (ed.), *Rationality.* London: Basil Blackwell, 62–77.
—— 1981: *After Virtue: A study in moral theory.* Notre Dame: University of Notre Dame Press.
Maier, A. 1949: *Die Vorläufer Galileis im 14. Jahrhundert.* Rome: Edizioni de Storia e Letteratura.
Merton, Robert King 1947: Discussion of "The position of sociological theory," by Talcott Parsons. *American Sociological Review,* 13(2), 164–8.
—— 1957: *Social Theory and Social Structure.* New York: Free Press.
—— 1967: On the history and systematics of sociological theory. In Robert King Merton (ed.), *On Theoretical Sociology.* New York: Free Press, 1–37.
Metzger, Hélène 1923: *Les doctrines chimiques en France du début XVIIe à la fin du XVIIIe siècle.* Paris: Presses universitaires de france.
—— 1930: *Newton, Stahl, Boerhaave et la doctrine chimique.* Paris: Alcan.
Mew, P. 1971: Conventions on thin ice. *Philosophical Quarterly,* 21, 352–6.
Meyerson, E. 1930: *Identity and Reality.* New York: Macmillan.
Parekh, B. and Berki, R.N. 1973: The history of political ideas: a critique of Q. Skinner's methodology. *Journal of the History of Ideas,* 34, 163–84.
Peel, J.D.Y. 1971: *Herbert Spencer: the evolution of a sociologist.* New York: Basic Books.

Pickering, Andrew 1982: Interests and analogies. In Barry Barnes and David Edge (eds), *Science in Context: readings in the sociology of science.* Cambridge: MIT Press, 125–46.

—— 1984: *Constructing Quarks: a sociological history of particle physics.* Chicago: University of Chicago Press.

Plamenatz, J. 1963: *Man and Society.* London: Longmans.

Pocock, J. G. A. 1962: The history of political thought: a methodological inquiry. In Peter Laslett and W. G. Runciman (eds), *Philosophy, Politics and Society.* Oxford: Basil Blackwell, 183–202.

—— 1971: *Politics, Language and Time.* New York: Athenaeum.

—— 1975: *The Machiavellian Moment: Florentine political thought and the Atlantic republican tradition.* Princeton: Princeton University Press.

Putnam, Hilary 1981: *Reason, Truth and History.* Cambridge: Cambridge University Press.

Rorty, Richard 1979: *Philosophy and the Mirror of Nature.* Princeton, New Jersey: Princeton University Press.

—— 1982: Method, social science, and social hope. In Richard Rorty (ed.), *Consequences of Pragmatism (Essays: 1972–1980).* Minneapolis: University of Minnesota Press, 191–210.

—— 1984: The historiography of philosophy: four genres. In R. Rorty, J. Schneewind, and Q. Skinner (eds), *Philosophy in History.* Cambridge: Cambridge University Press, 49–75.

Sarton, George 1936: *The Study of the History of Science.* Cambridge: Harvard University Press.

Schochet, Gordon J. 1974: Quentin Skinner's method. *Political Theory,* 2(3), 261–76.

Skinner, Quentin 1964: Hobbes's *Leviathan. Historical Journal,* 7, 321–33.

—— 1965: Thomas Hobbes and his disciples in France and England. *Comparative Studies in Society and History,* 8, 153–67.

—— 1966a: The ideological context of Hobbes's political thought. *Historical Journal,* 9, 286–317.

—— 1966b: The limits of historical explanations. *Philosophy,* 41, 199–215.

—— 1969: Meaning and understanding in the history of ideas. *History and Theory,* 8, 3–53.

—— 1970: Conventions and the understanding of speech-acts. *Philosophical Quarterly,* 20, 118–38.

—— 1972: "Social meaning" and the explanation of social action. In P. Laslett, W. G. Runciman, and Quentin Skinner (eds), *Philosophy, Politics and Society,* Series 4. Oxford: Basil Blackwell, 106–26.

—— 1974: Some problems in the analysis of political thought and action. *Political Theory,* 2, 227–303.

—— 1978: *The Foundations of Modern Political Thought.* Vol.1: *The Renaissance;* Vol. 2: *The Reformation.* Cambridge: Cambridge University Press.

—— 1984: The idea of negative liberty: philosophical and historical perspectives. In Richard Rorty, J. B. Schneewind, and Quentin Skinner (eds), *Philosophy in History.* Cambridge: Cambridge University Press, 193–221.

—— 1988: A reply to my critics. In James Tully (ed.), *Meaning and Context: Quentin Skinner and his critics.* Princeton, New Jersey: Princeton University Press, 231–88.

Stocking, George W., Jr 1968: *Race, Culture, and Evolution: essays in the history of anthropology.* New York: Free Press.

Tarlton, Charles, D. 1973: Historicity, meaning and revisionism in the study of political thought. *History and Theory,* 12, 307–28.

Tully, James 1988: *Meaning and Context: Quentin Skinner and his critics.* Princeton, New Jersey: Princeton University Press.

Turner, Stephen 1982: "Contextualism" and the interpretation of the classical sociological texts. *Knowledge and Society,* 4, 273–91.

Warrender, H. 1957: *The Political Philosophy of Hobbes.* Oxford: Oxford University Press.

Weiner, J. M. 1974: Quentin Skinner's Hobbes. *Political Theory,* 2(3), 251–60.

6

Simmel Reappraised: Old Images, New Scholarship

Donald N. Levine

When I began my study of Simmel in the early 1950s, most philosophers seemed not to have heard of him, while not a few sociologists believed the discipline would best forget and move beyond him. For sociology, that spirit was captured in a memorandum circulated by W. F. Ogburn in 1952, urging sociologists to abstain from scholarship on earlier texts and likening instruction about the classics to teaching chemistry students about alchemy (Levine, 1995, p. 62). Regarding Simmel in particular, a common sentiment was that expressed by Sorokin in 1928: "To call sociologists back to Simmel . . . means to call them back to a pure speculation, metaphysics, and a lack of scientific method" (Sorokin, 1928, p. 506, n. 26). Even those who enjoyed reading Simmel typically viewed him as a talented essayist who possessed no coherent theoretical outlook nor any enduring significance for twentieth-century social thought.

Such responses bewildered me. I was experiencing a deep challenge in Simmel's writings. As I made my way laboriously through his many untranslated texts, I had the sense of being privileged to discover a treasure of unknown riches.[1] I could not

Thanks to Charles Camic, Nancy Chodorow, Thomas Powers, and Frédéric Vandenberghe for valuable suggestions that helped me in revising this chapter.
[1] It may be of anecdotal interest to recall how I came to discover these riches. During the year I spent as an exchange student at the University of Frankfurt in 1952–3, I lived in the home of a German family that had been active during the

suppress the suspicion that the intellectual world, far from having surpassed Simmel, had a way to go to catch up with him, nor could I avoid imagining an outlook embodied in his work that was coherent and significant.[2]

To my pleasant surprise, by the end of the 1950s a reversal of judgment was flickering. Some of this was sparked by the 1958 centennial of his birth, which occasioned a special issue of the *American Journal of Sociology*, a commemorative volume edited by Kurt Wolff, and a commemorative session at the ASA meetings where former antagonists spoke of him appreciatively (Levine et al. 1976a, p. 821). In Germany, a major spur to the renewed interest in Simmel appeared that year in the collection of materials published by Duncker & Humblot, *Buch des Dankes an Georg Simmel* (Gassen and Landmann, 1958; republished in 1993).

Even so, efforts to recover Simmel were eclipsed in the 1960s by the surge of interest in Marxian writings, which led to Marx's joining Durkheim and Weber to form a canonized trinity of sociological founders. Simmel's fate might have been sealed as a subject of serious investigation had it not been for the efforts of Michael Landmann, professor of philosophy at the Freie Universität Berlin. In addition to the landmark *Buch des Dankes* which he co-edited, Landmann encouraged the scholarly community to recover Simmel's oeuvre and explore his intellectual origins, impact, and contemporary significance. He organized a colloquium on Simmel in 1973 that resulted in a volume, *Aesthetik und Soziologie um die Jahrhundertwende*, which included fresh materials for Simmel scholars (Böhringer and Gründer, 1976).

Since that time, additional scholarship on Simmel has opened up

---

Nazi period in hiding Jews and helping them emigrate. One of their beneficiaries had left a crate of books in their basement. Since the family had lost track of him and believed him to be dead, they invited me to take my pick of the volumes in the crate, among which I discovered titles by Simmel that I had never heard of. Following that discovery, a search for additional titles in antiquarian bookstores gave me a small library of Simmeliana with which to embark on a search for treasures.

[2] As I then pursued a lonely quest to recover the Simmel I felt the sociological community was missing out on, three figures provided moral support: Everett Hughes, who kept alive the Chicago tradition of respect for Simmel, inherited from his mentors Albion Small and Robert Park; Kurt Wolff, who published the electrifying translations of Simmel for the anglophone community in 1950; and Lewis Coser, whose work on conflict I later described as "the most fruitful attempt to recover, modernize, and utilize Simmel's work as a basis for current sociological inquiry" (Levine et al, 1976, p. 1125).

new vistas of understanding of his life and work, much of it inspired by the effort to produce a critical edition of Simmel's writings – the 24-volume Suhrkamp *Georg Simmel Gesamtausgabe* (GSG) under the general editorship of Otthein Rammstedt, who succeeded Michael Landmann as a major booster of Simmel studies in Europe.[3] The work is hard and slow going; at least another decade may be needed before someone produces an intellectual biography of Simmel at the level of Steven Lukes's 1972 biography of Durkheim. That should not prevent us from taking stock at this point in order to correct the distorting or confused images that surround him.

Full appreciation of Simmel has been hampered by widespread clichés about his life and work that are misleading when not distorting. Many of those misleading notions have been purveyed by scholars who, for a time or in certain respects, sought to champion Simmel.[4] This exposition will sketch a few of those images and suggest how recent scholarly work can correct or fill in the gaps around them. These tenacious notions include the views that: (1) except for the influence of Kant, Simmel was a complete original; (2) his work developed in three sharply distinguished stages; (3) he

[3]One should mention, in particular, the renewed interest in Simmel stimulated in the anglophone community by David Frisby's heroic work in completing the English translation of *The Philosophy of Money* in 1978 and his numerous efforts to bring Simmel to a wider audience, including a three-volume collection of critical writings on Simmel (1994). A number of fresh translations of Simmel's works began to appear in Italy and France as well.

[4]To take a simple example that can stand for dozens if not hundreds, Peter Blau, whose work on exchange and power did much to popularize certain Simmelian notions, represents Simmel's analysis of triadic relations as indicating that power can be resisted by forming coalitions, and he cites Simmel's *tertius gaudens* as a case in point (1964, p. 32). For Simmel, however, the *tertius gaudens* designates the case when a third party exploits the tension between two others and, as Theodore Caplow correctly pointed out in his book on coalitions in triads: "It is noteworthy that Simmel never discussed coalitions directly. The impression that he did is difficult to dispel" (1968, p. 18). Numerous instances of such inaccurate readings of Simmel were recorded in my 1974 paper on the literature following Simmel's excursus on the stranger, and many more in the 1976 study, co-authored with Ellwood Carter and Eleanor Miller, "Simmel's influence on American sociology." My subsequent work on the ambivalent reception of Simmel by Durkheim, Weber, Lukács, Park, and Parsons included a brief discussion of the social psychology of reading informed by Simmel's assumption that human interactions necessarily draw on preformed notions about those we interact with, to which I now add that preset images of authors and texts often remain difficult to correct despite the availability of good evidence that contradicts them.

exerted no significant influence on twentieth-century thought; (4) he was socially unengaged – a parasite at best, a bourgeois ideologist at worst; (5) he should be construed as a utilitarian theorist; (6) he was essentially a (functionalist) conflict theorist; (7) he was a (Marxian) alienation theorist (manqué); and (8) there is no coherence or unity in Simmel's thought. I shall discuss these issues under two headings: those pertaining to Simmel's place in intellectual history and those pertaining to the substance of his theories.

BIOGRAPHICAL AND HISTORICAL ISSUES

1   Simmel's Virgin Birth

Simmel's failure to cite sources and references together with the innovative character of his productions has favored the perception that he came out of nowhere (except for Kant, whom he mentions in nearly all his publications[5]). This perception has been reinforced by the common view of him as a unique intellectual figure.[6]

Klaus-Christian Köhnke's magisterial work (1996) offers now a pioneering reconstruction of the genesis of Simmel's intellectual agenda. Köhnke locates its main source in the teachings of Moritz Lazarus, the preeminent figure in the field of folk-psychology (*Völkerpsychologie*). From Lazarus, young Simmel derived the conception that the social totality historically precedes the individual; that a major evolutionary trend involves the development (*Ausbildung*) of individuality; and that over time human cultural expressions get condensed (*verdichtet*) into forms of objective mind. Indeed, Köhnke shows that Simmel derived from Lazarus the idea for his first major project, published as *Einleitung in die Moralwissenschaft: Eine Kritik der ethischen Grundbegriffen*, the effort to develop a critique of fundamental ethical concepts based on an analysis of their psychohistorical roots.

Köhnke also throws light on the puzzling question of Simmel's indebtedness to Spencer. Although early Simmel has long been assumed to have been under the influence of Spencer, how and why this influence took place has not been understood. Köhnke

[5]The pervasive influence of Kant, and of Goethe, will be considered in the concluding section of this chapter.

[6]In the words of Dean Karl Hampe of Heidelberg, "One cannot categorize Simmel among the general intellectual currents of the time; he has always gone his own way" (Gassen and Landmann, 1958, p. 25).

demonstrates that Spencer's influence was more far-reaching than previously realized. The German edition of volume 2 of Spencer's *Principles of Sociology* appeared in 1887, and it was precisely within a few months of that time that Simmel undertook his first steps in sociological theory with attestable references to Spencerian points. Simmel also follows some of Spencer's formulations in his early philosophical statements.

What is more, Spencer was a major source Simmel used, in the original text of his doctoral dissertation, to refute Darwin's thesis about the origins of music. However, in preparing his dissertation for publication, Simmel deleted all references to Spencer and, indeed, refers to Spencer by name only once in his entire oeuvre. The motivation for his silence about so important an influence is not entirely clear. However, it is not irrelevant that Simmel's Spencerian dissertation on music was rejected by his examining committee in favor of an earlier prize essay on Kant, and that a member of that committee, Hermann von Helmholtz, supported the rejection with words that included a dismissive reference to Spencer. At any rate, Simmel was not the only German of his time who failed to acknowledge significant borrowings from Spencer.

Klaus Lichtblau (1984) has traced the impact of Nietzsche on Simmel's work, especially from 1890 onward. Simmel drew, in particular, on Nietzsche's interpretation of certain key features of modernity: the fragmentation of the unity of the soul, increased individual subjectivity, the instrumentality of modern life, the decline of a unified world view, the transformation of qualitative into quantitative values, and the modern antagonism to form. Nietzsche's identification of a tension between the leveling effects of modernity and its liberating consequences for individual subjectivity was a theme that Simmel continuously addressed. Nietzsche's discussion, in the first essay of *The Genealogy of Morals* and elsewhere, of the "pathos of distance" in the relations between the ancient noble and plebeian classes arguably influenced Simmel's own treatment of subordination and superordination. Albert Salomon has argued that the influence of Schopenhauer on Simmel was more extensive even than that of Nietzsche ([1963], 1995), although a close-grained study of that influence remains to be undertaken.

The Hegelian influence on Simmel's thought was illumined in a dissertation by Petra Christian (1978). Her evidence includes the fact that Simmel taught courses that covered Hegel, and that he was close to the two circles involved in the Hegel renaissance in the first two decades of this century, at Berlin and Heidelberg. Simmel's thought draws heavily on two core Hegelian concepts, *objectiver Geist* and dialectical process. The project of Hegel's early writings, to develop a concept of life based on the linkage between connection and non-connection, was recovered and developed in two of Simmel's foundational thoughts: his theory of self-consciousness as symbol or actual self-expression of life, and his conception of the intertwining of death and life. Christian links the appearance of Simmel's chief Hegelianizing productions, which appeared around 1910 – the *Hauptprobleme der Philosophie* and the *Logos* essays on Michelangelo, metaphysics of death, and the tragedy of culture – with the Hegel renaissance of that same period.

Unlike the aforementioned influences, the question of Dilthey's influence on Simmel has been fairly contested. Although earlier accounts of Simmel and Dilthey stressed the distance between them, writers like Horst Helle (1986), Uta Gerhardt (1992), and Victor Lidz (1993) have argued for a friendly relationship and a positive, determinative influence of Dilthey on the evolution of Simmel's sociology. Their argument goes as follows. As a vulnerable young scholar in a department where Dilthey's seniority gave him power, Simmel was naturally disposed to follow the former's cues in elaborating the principles of his sociology. Dilthey had railed against the sociologies of figures like Comte, Spencer, and Schäffle, and argued for an approach to the human sciences that focused on *Verstehen*, the interpretive understanding of the meanings of individual persons. Consequently, the argument goes, Simmel developed a sociology that eschewed social realism on behalf of individual realism and that rested on a methodology of *Verstehen*, which he elaborated in his *Probleme der Geschichtsphilosophie*.

Due to Köhnke's archival research and close textual analysis, this line of argument must be reappraised. Köhnke has securely established the fact of early and continuing antagonism between Simmel and Dilthey. Dilthey intermittently opposed Simmel's career opportunities at the University of Berlin, even if not so totally as Simmel believed he did. What is more, intellectual antagonism between the two prevailed for more than the two decades that they were together at Berlin. Dilthey was documentably dismissive of Simmel's work as late as 1904.

For Simmel's part, he attacked positions early on that Dilthey was famous for maintaining, albeit careful not to mention Dilthey by name when doing so. In his early writings he forthrightly attacked Dilthey's doctrines of the unity of the human soul and of methodological individualism, leaning instead on the ideas of his teacher Moritz Lazarus – a teacher under whom Dilthey also studied, but against whom Dilthey had come to feel uncompromising enmity. The problematics of *Verstehen* did not figure at all in the evolution of Simmel's conception of sociology, which he promulgated with his landmark 1894 paper, "Das Problem der Soziologie." Simmel's expressed interest in *Verstehen* developed only after 1900, and surfaced only in the second edition of *Probleme der Geschichtsphilosophie* – (1905) in other words, long after his programmatic formulations and first substantive work in sociology had been completed. Dilthey's late conciliatory statement about Simmel's sociology was published by their shared disciple, Bernhard Groethuysen – "the favorite student of these two philosophical antipodes" (Susman, 1964, p. 65) – only after both of them were dead.[7]

2   Periodization of Simmel's Intellectual Biography

The most common construction of Simmel's intellectual career divides it into three fairly distinct stages, a view that Michael Landmann himself has propounded (Gassen and Landmann, 1958; Landmann, 1968). This view holds that Simmel started as a positivistic Darwinist, became a neo-Kantian in mid-life, and was converted to a Bergsonian *Lebensphilosophie* during his last decade.[8] However, such a view flies in the face of the conspicuous fact that Simmel was deeply engaged with Kantian agendas all along. His teaching career began with lectures on Kant; the *Einleitung* includes sustained dialogues with Kant; and the early *Probleme der Geschichtsphilosophie* is nothing if not a neo-Kantian tract, as serious pre-war scholars were well aware (Gerson, 1932; Müller, 1935). What is more, Darwinian ideas of adaptation pervade Simmel's oeuvre, and in fact converge with the emphasis on life processes that informs his work later on. In short, one must affirm Frédéric Vandenberghe's judgment that Spencerian, neo-Kantian,

---

[7]The most that can be said for the Gerhardt line of argument is that in order to express his concealed critique of Dilthey safely, Simmel appeared to adopt Dilthey's position partially, namely, in affirming interaction (*Wechselwirkung*) as the key ingredient of societal phenomenon. However, it is likely that Simmel derived this central notion directly from Kant's first Critique, which makes several references to *Wechselwirkung*, and in fact includes a passage that defines community (*Gemeinschaft*) in terms of interaction (Liebersohn, 1988; Powers, 1996).

[8]This periodization was formulated initially by Max Frischeisen-Köhler in 1919. Since then, it has been repeated by numerous authors, including Nicholas Spykman (1925), Lewis Coser (1956), and Julien Freund (1981) as well as Landmann (1968).

and philosophy-of-life themes all recur throughout Simmel's oeuvre (1995, p. 6).[9]

For the record, the chief attested facts of Simmel's development as a sociologist are as follows. During 1876–7, he took three semesters of straight history courses at the Humboldt University in Berlin. He came to reject the field of history for not having deep enough psychological and epistemological foundations. The following year he shifted focus, taking psychology with Lazarus, ethnology with Bastian, logic and metaphysics with Harms, the history of German art and culture with Grimm, and the history of aesthetics with Lasson. He went on to take Droysen's course on the epistemology of historical studies (Köhnke, 1996, pp. 35–42).

In 1881, Simmel produced his first significant writings, an ethnopsychological dissertation on the origins of music, and two prize essays on Kant. Since the former was rejected by his doctoral examining committee, he accepted the advice to substitute a dissertation based on the Kant essays (Köhnke, 1996, pp. 42–77). This led to a teaching appointment in which he lectured on Kantian ethics from 1883 to 1886. His critical stance toward Kant reflected the teachings of Lazarus, who encouraged Simmel to undertake the project of a sustained critique of Kantian ethics. For Simmel as for Lazarus, Kant's ethics fail to deal with sociocultural realities, ignoring both the socially implanted sense of moral obligation and the socially structured conflicts of obligations that impose internal normative conflicts and the attendant evolution of individuality. Along the way, Simmel also expressed criticism of Dilthey's conception of the human sciences, both for its assumption that human selves are unified and for its failure to appreciate pre-individual social totalities and objectified culture (Köhnke, 1996, pp. 280–2, 390ff).

The project was sharpened after he read the German translation of the second volume of Spencer's *Principles of Sociology*, in 1887. Prior to that point, Simmel described his essays as "psychological" studies; after that, he began to gloss them as "sociological." The

[9]This is not to deny that Simmel's ideas developed substantially over the years and that a three-part periodization is not useful when handled with caution, even if the labels commonly used for those periods are not sufficiently descriptive. The superb, neglected dissertation of Hermann Gerson (1932) divides them into a sociological period, a period of ingestion (*Sammlung*), and a metaphysical period, with corresponding shifts in the view of moral values as socially instilled, relativistically grounded, and based on individual ontologies.

project issued in two major works of the early 1890s, his Spencerian treatise, *Über sociale Differenzierung* (*UsD; On Social Differentiation* [1890, GSG, vol. 2]) and the *Einleitung*, his sociocultural critique of Kantian ethics (1892–3, GSG, vols 3–4).

No sooner had Simmel completed the social evolution treatise than his continuing commitment to a Kantian epistemology induced him to undertake a searching inquiry into the cognitive presuppositions of historical understanding. This issued in *Die Probleme der Geschichtsphilosophie* in 1892, each of whose chapters advanced a critique of one of the main presuppositions of *UsD*. These critiques were that: (1) all reconstructions of historical developments rest on a priori assumptions; (2) general laws of history cannot plausibly be formulated; and (3) assumptions of progress in history cannot be justified.

Following that project, it was logical for Simmel to extend the epistemological concerns of the *Probleme* to questions about the epistemological foundations of the social sciences generally. Although Simmel had already broached such an investigation with the opening chapter of *UsD*, entitled, "Zur Erkenntnistheorie der Socialwissenschaft," he reworked its argument in 1893 by incorporating the Kantian distinction between forms and contents. This resulted in his seminal programmatic paper of 1894, "Das Problem der Soziologie." By making members of society creators of interactional forms, Simmel succeeded in the Kant-like project of affirming human dignity and autonomy by enabling human actors to be viewed as producers as well as products of society. At the same time, by restricting sociological investigation to the properties of those interactions and relegating the investigation of their contents to other disciplines, he defined a distinctive research program for the new discipline that had been having so much difficulty in establishing acceptable boundaries within the academic universe.

With the formulation of "Das Problem der Soziologie," Simmel believed he had solved the philosophical problem of how to ground the discipline of sociology. This led him to broach the project of realizing such a discipline by carrying out investigations in accord with that new conception. At this point, the evolution of Simmel's work depended as much on external responses as on internal development. Having formulated what he considered a compelling definition of sociology's mission, Simmel searched for colleagues to reinforce and collaborate on this program. The programmatic paper itself fared well; within a few years it had been published in France

(1894), United States (1895), Italy (1899), and Russia (1899). Even so, Simmel encountered unexpected difficulties in securing sociological collaborators. In Germany, academic hostility toward sociology in general and Simmel in particular prevented him from securing the kind of collegial response he badly needed. He was so demoralized about the matter that, toward the end of the decade, he wrote Rickert that he thought he should leave a field in which it would be irresponsible to train young scholars with no prospect of an academic future.

Discouraged by the dim prospects of collegial support in Germany, Simmel turned to France. As Christian Gülich (1992) has shown, at this time Simmel actively approached the available French sociological journals: the journal and the annual of the Institut International de Sociologie, and *L'année Sociologique*. Before long, however, Simmel broke with both of them, the former due to what he considered improper editorial behavior on the part of René Worms, the latter due to Durkheim's unconscionable deletion of certain passages of his article without Simmel's knowledge.[10]

With the French philosophical community Simmel established more enduring links. Thanks to Célestin Bouglé, he began a relationship with the newly founded *Revue de Métaphysique et de Morale* that flourished for years. One could speculate that Simmel might have turned all of his energies to philosophical work at this time, without ever completing the sociological investigations that culminated in his "great" *Soziologie*,[11] had it not been for the opportunity opened up by a journal established at the University of Chicago in 1896, the *American Journal of Sociology*. Its founding editor, Albion Small, knew German social science well from his days as a graduate student at the University of Berlin. Since Small visited Simmel during later trips to Germany and corresponded with him regularly, he kept abreast of Simmel's sociological productions from the outset. Small began to publish Simmel's writings in the *AJS* in 1897, a year after it was founded. With the *AJS* as a secure outlet, Simmel had the support he needed to continue the work of creating substantive sociological essays. Over the next fifteen years, Small published some fifteen pieces by Simmel in his journal, most of

---

[10]In "Comment les formes sociales se maintiennent," published in the first issue of *L'annee Sociologique* in 1896, Durkheim cut out all Simmel's references to the historical experiences of the Jewish people.

[11]Simmel scholars commonly refer to the *Soziologie* of 1908 as the *grosse Soziologie* to distinguish it from the "little" or *kleine Soziologie* of 1917, which Simmel titled *Grundfragen der Soziologie* (translated in Simmel, 1950).

which he translated himself. Some of these pieces thus appeared in English before they were published in German.

If the execution of the sociological project often seemed burdensome to Simmel, he threw heart and soul into the work he considered his jewel, the *Philosophie des Geldes*, first published in 1900. The preoccupation with the problem of value that nourished that work led him to reflect on his early writings and drew him closer to crystallize his own moral-philosophical position. This stressed the dimension of moral autonomy that had been in tension with his social determinism throughout the previous decade. From this point on he supplemented his Lazarussian perspective on the evolutionary emergence of individuality with a keener emphasis on the existential responsibility for personal decisions and judgment. His final set of sociological essays, including the magisterial "How is society possible?,"[12] went beyond the analysis of social forms into the phenomenology of personal experience.

The great *Soziologie* thus consists of three archaeological layers: the Spencerian chapters on group expansion and intersecting circles, the structural chapters on conflict and superordination, and the phenomenological chapters on interpersonal cognitions and attachments.[13] So disjointed a composition left Simmel with a feeling of marked discomfort when he finally released it for publication in 1908.

[12]Regarding that celebrated excursus, Don Martindale wrote: "This is undoubtedly as amazing a piece of pure theoretical brilliance as modern sociological theory displays" (Martindale, 1981 , p. 227).

[13](1) Chapters 6 and 10, "The intersection of social circles" (aka "The web of group-affiliations") and "Group expansion and the development of individuality," are Spencerian essays made up of revisions of chapters from the little treatise *On Social Differentiation* of 1892. (2) The bulk of the work, chapters 2 through 4 – on the quantitative determination of group properties, super- and subordination, and conflict – and chapters 8 and 9 – on the persistence of social groups, and the spatial ordering of society – consists of investigations of diverse social forms. These carry out the project set forth in the programmatic essay of 1894, "The problem of sociology," which appears revised here in the introductory chapter. Some were written in the mid-1890s, some between 1901 and 1903. (3) But some of the sections produced after 1905 seem to break with that project. Rammstedt (1992) has now argued that the essays produced after 1905 evince an attunement to the particularities of subjective experience more than a search for objective social structural regularities. These include the late essays that appear as chapter 5, on secrecy; chapter 7, on the poor; and as excursuses on topics such as faithfulness and gratitude, agreement, personal adornment, and letter-writing.

3   Simmel as Inconsequential

It is widely believed that although Simmel was a talented essayist, his work was without consequence, leaving no enduring influence on twentieth-century social thought. Now there is some truth to Erich Przywara's line that Simmel stands among those "great and forgotten" figures who "today are wells from which people secretly draw water, without running the danger that anyone else will discover these wells" (Gassen and Landmann, 1958, p. 224). Others have referred to Simmel as the man behind the curtain, the "prompter" (Christian, 1978, p. 11, n. 2). If someone did a citation study that measured the frequency with which authors were cited without attribution, Simmel would doubtless head the list. Nevertheless, Simmel's enormous influence on certain important streams of twentieth-century philosophy and sociology cannot be denied. This is hard for us to appreciate today since, as Jürgen Habermas has aptly remarked: "Following World War II, neither in Germany nor the United States did Simmel achieve an intellectual presence that would lead one to suspect the extent of the influence he exerted on his contemporaries" (Habermas, 1991, p. 157).[14] However, the past two decades have added much evidence to support the claim that, acknowledged or not, Simmel's influence on his contemporaries and beyond was profound and diverse.

Thus, recent scholarship reinforces the point that Martin Buber and Martin Heidegger, two of the most influential philosophers of the twentieth century, were led to some of their core insights through formulations by Simmel. Buber began his intellectual career as a Nietzschean enthusiast, one who celebrated the ecstatic experience of the individual in the form of what Paul Mendes-Flohr describes as *"Erlebnis* mysticism." Thanks to Simmel's lectures, Buber not only "learned how to think," as he later confessed to Simmel, but became acquainted with the notion of interhuman communication that would lead him to the road that made him famous (Mendes-Flohr, 1989).

Buber's early appreciation for Simmel was expressed by his effort to get the publishing house of Rütten & Loening to appoint Simmel as editor of a new series of monographs in sociology. When Simmel declined the invitation, Buber agreed to step in his place. In the statement with which Buber introduced the series, he presented

---

[14]Translation mine. This passage has been mistranslated in the English version published in *Critical Inquiry*, 22(3), 1996.

ideas about social interaction that read like verbatim transcripts of Simmel's teachings (Buber, 1992, pp. 93–6; also in Mendes-Flohr, 1989). This core ontological assumption, that human reality exists essentially in an interactive setting, became the foundational notion for Buber's philosophy of the dialogue. In addition the notion of religiosity that Buber developed replicates the cognate concept Simmel set forth in *Die Religion*. Above all, what Buber came to analyze as key features of the I–Thou relationship, intimacy and the threat of depersonalization, appear repeatedly in Simmel's analyses, as, for example, in his discussions of intimacy in dyads and, in the excursus on the stranger, of the thin line between closeness and estrangement in romantic couples.

As for Simmel's influence on Heidegger, already in 1934 Dolf Sternberger pointed out that the notion of authentic death developed by Simmel in his late "Metaphysik des Todes" made its appearance in Heidegger's philosophy of existence (1934, p. 113). Gadamer later recalled how taken Heidegger was by Simmel's late writings: Heidegger confessed to him that he had received important substantive stimulation from Simmel and was awed by Simmel's philosophical personality (Gadamer, 1975), even though Heidegger himself made only passing reference to this influence in *Sein und Zeit*. More recently, Michael Grossheim (1991) has traced the profound influence of Simmel on the gestation of Heidegger's existential philosophy. For example, in a 1919 lecture Heidegger embraced Simmel's notion that philosophy is not a foundational discipline (*Urwissenschaft*), but a mental attitude, and went on to incorporate Simmel's notion that life is not *in* time but life *is* time: life experiences its own continuity as it stretches between past and future.[15]

One of the most significant cultural developments of the past generation has been the transformation of feminist ideology from an appeal simply for rights and status equal to men toward defining qualitatively distinctive female contributions and uncovering ways in which presumptively universal cultural norms can represent specifically male points of view, a "phallocentric" bias. Psychoanalytic discourse has supplied a major medium for this shift, both because of apparent male-centered biases of Freud and other founding analysts and because of internal challenges to those biases by psychoanalytic feminists.

[15]Future scholarship may be expected to divulge comparable influences on other major European thinkers, such as Norbert Elias, Max Scheler, and José Ortega y Gasset.

Simmel's essays on femininity (1984) not only prefigured that transformation but played a notable role in its actual evolution. As Nancy Chodorow (1989) and others have stressed, Karen Horney was the key originary figure in the creation of psychoanalytic feminism.[16] Horney received her psychoanalytic training in Berlin when Simmel's fame was at its height, and in the seminal paper which initiated her revisionist current of thought, "The flight from womanhood" (1926), Horney claimed it was Simmel's essays that inspired her to question Freudian assumptions about female psychosexual development:

> The new point of view of which I wish to speak came to me by way of philosophy, in some essays by Georg Simmel [who writes]: Our whole civilization is a masculine civilization ... Simmel by no means deduces from these facts, as is commonly done by other writers, an inferiority in women, but [argues that] the very standards by which mankind has estimated the values of male and female nature are "not neutral, arising out of the differences of the sexes, but in themselves essentially male." ([1926] 1967, pp. 55–6)

Here and elsewhere, Horney draws crucially on Simmel's essays from *Philosophische Kultur* to develop her points about the hegemony of male standards and the distinctive qualities of the genders, including the (unacknowledged) Simmelian formulation that woman "performs her part by merely *being*, without any *doing*– a fact that has always filled men with admiration and resentment. The man on the other hand has to *do* something in order to fulfill himself" (1967, p. 145; cf. Simmel, 1984, p. 107).

Simmel's extensive influence on twentieth-century cultural criticism has been more evident, especially through his direct impact on Lukács, Bloch, Kracauer, Benjamin, and Adorno. Summing up this tradition, David Gross wrote: "Today a rigorous *Kulturkritik* is virtually unthinkable without a methodological grounding in the entire German tradition [beginning with] Simmel's work in the 1890s" (Gross, 1982, p. 98).

I have already written at length about Simmel's impact on such key figures of twentieth-century sociology as Weber, Lukács, Park,

---

[16]"Psychoanalytic feminism has a rather complex and sometimes underground history ... I locate its political and theoretical origins with Karen Horney [whose] theories form the basis, acknowledged or unacknowledged, for most of the recent revisions of psychoanalytic understandings of gender and for most psychoanalytic dissidence on the question of gender in the early period as well" (Chodorow, 1989, p. 3).

Moreno, Parsons, Merton, and Goffman (Levine, 1971; 1985, ch. 5; Levine et al., 1976a, 1976b). Suffice it here to repeat the claim which my colleagues and I made two decades ago: "Georg Simmel stands in the unusual position of being the only European scholar who has had a palpable influence in sociology in the United States throughout the course of the 20th century" (Levine et al., 1976a, p. 813).

4   Simmel as Socially Unengaged

Some of the negativity toward Simmel has derived from an image of him as a detached, privileged, aestheticized intellectual. I refer to comments such as those by George Lukács, depicting Simmel as a self-complacent cynic who unwittingly served as an ideologist of imperialist *rentier* parasitism ([1954] (1962); Theodore Adorno, who spoke of Simmel's asocial, aristocratically tainted irrationalism (Christian, 1978, p. 12n.); the earlier writings of Sibylle Hübner-Funk, who worried that Simmel's sociology would "end up in the dangerous waters of aestheticism" (1976, p. 58), and David Frisby, who rebuked Simmel for indulging in an "inward retreat" (1981, p. 156); and Randall Collins, who has linked Simmel's family connections to "the luxury side of business" and his "never [having] had to enter the grubby world of work" with an alleged pandering to "the drawing room culture of his day" filled with "sexual gossip," resulting in a frivolous sort of sociology ([1985], 1994, pp. 116–17).[17]

This is the slightest critique of Simmel and can be dealt with quickly. The aestheticist charge itself seems silly. "People have often

---

[17]There is a triple irony in the contrasts that Collins draws to favor Weber over Simmel. It was Simmel, not Weber, who had to spend every year of his adult life in the grubby business of teaching, and who depended on student fees for his livelihood. Moreover, although Collins chides Simmel for his supposed antisocialist utterances, it was Weber who wrote the devastating critique of socialism, whereas Simmel maintained an even-handed critical stance toward liberalism and socialism, and in fact contributed a number of articles, often anonymously, to socialist publications in the 1890s. In addition, to hold that Weber took his value neutrality more seriously than Simmel would seem to fly in the face of what scholarship on Weber has revealed about his bigoted utterances in public academic settings, not to mention his famous tirades against alleged repressive forces of modern economic systems, capitalist and socialist. As a final gloss on Simmel's supposedly luxurious and frivolous lifestyle, one might mention, beyond the grief that Simmel suffered for not securing a professorial chair, and spending his last four years at Strasburg in what he experienced as exile, his terminal months enduring cancer without any medication so that his mind might be clear to complete his testamentary *Lebensanschauung*.

attacked Simmel on grounds of aestheticism," quips Vandenberghe, "as if scientificity is measured by the degree of boredom and dullness that it arouses" (1995, p. 3). For the record, however, recent scholarship has unearthed much evidence regarding areas of Simmel's social engagement that previously were little known. Beginning with his early years, when Simmel expressed himself cautiously and anonymously, and expanding in the 1890s when he figured as a public lecturer and social critic, Simmel was involved in a number of the social movements of his day, including the movements for women's rights, workers' rights, penal reform, public hygiene, and poverty relief (Köhnke, 1996). Throughout his career Simmel wrote on issues regarding the status of women, work that issued in a radical critique of male cultural hegemony. In the face of contemporaries who denounced repression of all kinds without thinking about the status of women in male-dominated societies, he uttered a new emancipatory word by identifying the subjection of women to "universal" norms that were in fact male in character as well as origin (Coser, 1977; Simmel, 1984; Vromen, 1987).

Simmel also came to exert himself actively to minister to what he came to diagnose as a cultural crisis: an era of increasingly objectified and dehumanized cultural production. As Rüdiger Kramme has now shown, Simmel's enormous activism on behalf of the journal *Logos* during the years after 1909 – just after he published the first of several essays addressing what he came to call the crisis of modern culture – stemmed from his conviction about the need to counteract the dehumanizing effects of modern objectified culture and to protect the individual's capacity for self-development and cultivation (Kramme, 1993). His strong advocacy of this cause was also manifest in his daring ideas for the reform of pedagogy (Simmel, 1922; Levine, 1991b). Simmel's affinity with the socialist movement, dating from the 1890s, was retained in his repeatedly voiced concern about the blows to human self-esteem caused by rank subordination (a problem for which he did not think socialization of the economy was necessarily the best solution). One should also remember, albeit painfully, how very active Simmel was in his enthusiasm for the national cause at the outbreak of World War I; but also, how eloquently he defended the ideal of pan-Europeanism soon after (Simmel, 1917).

Finally, just for the record, Simmel's luxurious life circumstances have been exaggerated. It appears that Simmel was not so well off as he has previously been thought to be. His failure to be granted a professorial appointment at the University of Berlin was a severe hardship, financial as well as psychological. Although he received financial support from his uncle following his father's untimely death, this source proved limited, and part of Simmel's bitterness about his marginal status at Berlin was because it was hard for him to make ends meet.

Substantive Issues

5   Simmel as a Utilitarian

Insofar as Simmel's ideas have entered mainstream theorizing, he has often been represented as propounding a utilitarian theory of action. Such a theory, as schematized by Parsons, rests on the assumptions of methodological individualism and of the instrumental rationality of all action, and manifests itself in current approaches variously labeled as rational choice theory and exchange theory.

One possible reason that Simmel has come to be viewed as a utilitarian theorist is the prominence given to the selection on exchange that introduced the unit on forms of association in the collection of Simmel's writings I assembled in 1971. In foregrounding the selection in that manner, I did not, a quarter century ago, have any wish to suggest that a rational exchange model was central to Simmel's sociological thinking. Rather, my intention was to exhibit the irony of the fact that George Homans, in his seminal paper, "Social Behavior as Exchange," showed no awareness that Simmel had published six decades earlier an argument that in some ways resembled his own, even though the 1959 *AJS* issue in which it appeared was organized to commemorate Simmel!

Even so, what was perhaps the most creative and widely hailed extension of Homans's approach, Peter Blau's *Exchange and Power in Social Life* (1964), drew explicitly on Simmel in formulating a theory that would account for power imbalances and social norms in terms of the exchange of rewards and deprivations in social transactions. From this it was a short step to formalizing the notion of Simmel as a utilitarian action theorist. Thus, throughout his writings, Raymond Boudon (1984, pp. 10–17) has drawn on Simmel to justify his version of utilitarian theory. Jonathan Turner's treatise on social interaction (1988) hailed Simmel as the dominant utilitarian of early sociology, one who "employed utilitarian ideas in a sophisticated exchange model of structuring processes [and] viewed interaction as an exchange of valued resources, with actors being differentiated in terms of the respective value of the resources they hold" (p. 128). While Turner faults Parsons for failing to appreciate the scope of Simmel's achievement as an early utilitarian action theorist, Alexander's most recent interpretation of Parsons (1993) contends that Parsons was quite conscious of Simmel as a utilitarian action theorist. Indeed, Alexander claims that that was the reason Parsons decided to exclude Simmel from the group of authors he celebrated as participants in the grand convergence.[18]

Nevertheless, Alexander was right to raise the question of whether Simmel should be considered as a utilitarian thinker. That view of him can be substantiated only by reference exclusively to the section on economic value theory in *The Philosophy of Money*, as Turner has done. Here, as so often with the interpretation of classic authors, it is dangerous to represent their entire thought by referring to a small slice of their total output, taken out of context. In so much else of what Simmel wrote, including other portions of *The Philosophy of Money*, he illuminated the effect of norms and moral sentiment on the structuring of human action as well as being a consistent critic of methodological individualism.

As I noted above, the point of departure for Simmel's first major philosophical publication, *Einleitung in die Moralwissenschaft*, was a conviction about the efficacy of social conventions in implanting a deep and barely conscious sense of normative obligation. The *Einleitung* includes a devastating critique of egoism as an explanatory as well as a general normative principle, in arguments that later critics of utilitarianism have yet to recover. *Soziologie* contains many passages that continue this emphasis on social normation, including the discussion of conscience in the chapter on super- and sub-ordination, and the discussion of morality, honor, and law in the chapter on the persistence of social groups. What is more, Simmel's sociology emphasizes non-utilitarian sentiment in his discussion of the overlay of fidelity that attaches to so many human relationships as well as in his concern about the erosion of sentiment due to the hypertrophy of rationalization in modern society (Levine, 1985, ch. 9).[19]

Simmel's strictures against methodological individualism take two forms. From the outset he argued that no perspective on humans can be privileged as more real or fundamental; rather, the

---

[18]Other reasons for Parsons's omission of Simmel in *The Structure of Social Action* seem far more plausible to me, as I have argued in a number of publications ([1957], 1980, 1985, 1991a, 1993, 1997.)

[19]For a provocative discussion of ways in which Simmel's views of exchange differ from more recent rational exchange theories, see Hayakawa (1993).

epistemic interest of investigators determines what level of interactions should be examined (Simmel, 1890, ch. 1). Beyond that, in his doctrine of social forms Simmel consistently argued that interactional structures have sui generis properties. While individuals interact to satisfy urges and interests, Simmel insists that their interactions produce "forms of association by which a mere sum of separate individuals are made into a 'society' " which he describes as a "a higher unity" (*höhere Einheit*) (Simmel, 1971, p. 127ff). As Rousseau and Durkheim appealed to the difference between chemical elements and compounds to make the point about emergent properties, Simmel took as his self-evident example the kiss, which designates a phenomenon different from two individuals' pressing their lips to one another.

It was because of this perceived kindred interest in identifying supraindividual parameters that Durkheim embraced Simmel initially and included his essay on the persistence of social groups in the first issue of *l'Année sociologique* (Levine, 1985, p. 90). That essay includes formulations like: "when we consider the development . . . of language, morals, church, law, political and social organization," the conception of society as "a structure of independent reality, which leads its life after peculiar laws and by virtue of peculiar forces . . . seems inevitable" (Simmel, 1897, p. 666). When Simmel then goes on to say that closer analysis would resolve the apparently super-individual character of those structures into more minute phenomena, the resolution he calls for is to analyze them, not into individual acts, but into structures of reciprocity – a position that Vandenberghe aptly labels "methodological interactionism" (1995, p. 21).

To find telling critiques of the exclusive utilitarian focus on instrumentally rational orientations, Parsons turned to Pareto and Weber; to find a decisive critique of their methodological individualism, he turned to Durkheim. Unbeknownst to Parsons, both strands of the critique had been woven already by Simmel.[20] Indeed, when Simmel insists in *The Philosophy of Money* that the operation of markets involves social and cultural institutions that are preconditions of extensive exchange, he in effect conjoins an implicit critique of both strands of the utilitarian position ([1907], 1978, pp. 98–100).

---

[20]This argument is developed further in Levine (1997).

6   Simmel as a (Functionalist) Conflict Theorist

Simmel's ideas on social conflict have probably enjoyed the most active afterlife of any of his sociological productions. In some compendia of sociological theory he is classified simply as a conflict theorist.

Lewis Coser (1956) and Randall Collins (1988, pp. 119–24; [1985, pp. 110–16], 1994, pp. 112–18) have been the most vocal proponents of this interpretation. Coser created an inventory of propositions through critically scrutinizing Simmel's chapter on conflict in *Soziologie*. He divides them into propositions concerning different forms of conflict; conditions and consequences of conflict within groups; and the effects of conflicts with external groups. Collins then assimilates Coser to Simmel, offering two sets of "Simmel–Coser" theories about conflict (1988, pp. 119–24). The first set consists of propositions on conflict as a source of social integration: conflict sharpens group boundaries, heightens group identity, centralizes group structure, and stimulates a search for allies. The other set concerns the self-limitation of conflict: combatants seek to protect objects over which they fight, establish norms to regulate the conditions of battle, and often maintain their enemies as unified parties; and, in what Collins attributes to Coser as a "pluralist" theory of conflict, conflict is also self-limiting when group members have cross-cutting affiliations such that conflict on one dimension reduces conflict on others.[21]

Both Coser and Collins have made substantial contributions to understanding the forms and consequences of conflict as well as important revisions of some of Simmel's arguments. Even so, a

---

[21]In his other book on general theory, Collins differentiates the two on ideological grounds, calling Simmel an "anti-socialist" and Coser a supporter of left-wing movements for social change (1994, p. 117). However, it is misleading to represent Simmel's stance toward socialism as simply antagonistic (see note 17). Moreover, Coser did not originate the theorem about cross-cutting conflicts— that was the work of E. A. Ross, as Coser notes. Nor does Coser refer to that proposition as a "pluralist" theory, as Collins avers. And, to correct a couple of other minor errors, Bendix was not a co-translator of the essay on conflict, which incidentally appeared in English in the *AJS* in translations by Small long before Wolff's translation of the chapter from *Soziologie*, and Simmel's excursus "How is society possible?" (written around 1907) is not where he placed his argument for viewing sociology as the study of forms, which appeared rather in the programmatic essays of the early 1890s. Some other errors that appeared in the 1985 edition were removed in the 1994 revision.

number of their glosses on Simmel have to be questioned. It is questionable to classify Simmel as a conflict theorist *tout court*, since his analysis of social conflict was but one of dozens of essays he composed on a wide variety of social formations. It is surely questionable to assert, as Collins does, that Simmel originated the modern sociology of conflict and that his ideas on conflict arose in polemical opposition to Marx. At the time Simmel was writing, most of the leading sociologists of the day – Bagehot, Gumplowicz, Oppenheimer, Ratzenhofer, Ross, Small, Spencer, Sumner, Max Weber – emphasized the role of conflict in social life.[22] And few if any of them devised their theories in polemical opposition to Marx. They simply understood conflict of all sorts to constitute a fundamental process in all social life, as did Simmel. If anyone might be considered the key inspiration for Simmel's view of social conflict, it should probably be Kant, especially in his discussion of "unsocial sociability." Simmel's late discussion of the history of cultural conflicts actually contains an appreciative allusion to Marx's dialectical historiography (Simmel, 1971, p. 376).

Perhaps most misleading are the notions that Simmel viewed conflict as always socially functional (Coser) and as an essentially conservative force in society (Collins). The former view was long since criticized by Beals and Siegel (1966), who argued that since conflicts have dysfunctional as well as functional aspects, nothing was to be gained by debating whether or not conflict in the abstract is functional.[23] In contrast to Durkheim, who emphasized functional as well as efficient causal analysis, Simmel emphasized the structural properties of social forms more than their functions. He examined the conditions under which conflict was more or less intense, more or less personal, engaged in instrumentally or for its sheer intrinsic pleasure. And when he did consider the effects of conflict, he was quite ready to identify patterns in which conflicts led to harmful outcomes: the "wholly disproportionate violence" which normally

---

[22]Coser even begins his book by noting that social conflict formed the main topic of one of the first meetings of the newly organized American Sociological Society in 1907 (1956, p. 15). Martindale (1981) provides a useful summary of their ideas.

[23]In Coser's defense, it should be noted that his book aimed explicitly to correct an imbalance in the current conception of social conflict, not to present a comprehensive treatment of the subject. He also identified conditions in which external conflict produced the dysfunctional effect of group disintegration (Propositions 7 and 9). However, Beals and Siegel correctly fault Coser for saying that Simmel holds that genuine, "realistic" conflict typically arises over scarce goods. See Levine et al. (1976b, p. 1,124).

well-controlled people can inflict on intimates, producing "tragic
results"; the "degeneration" of a difference in convictions into
hatred and fight; the eruption of a "tragic breach" even among close
associates; the cases where conflict eventuates in irreconcilability,
which "must be compared with a lost limb, not with a scar"
(Simmel, 1971, pp. 92–5; Simmel, 1955, pp. 45–8; 120–1).

For these and other reasons, including Coser's own caveat
that he was only using Simmel to correct an imbalance in the social
theorizing of his day, Coser's book should not be read uncritically as
a faithful exposition of Simmel's writings on conflict (Levine et al.,
1976b, pp. 1124–5). But Collins goes on to amplify these problematic readings by extending the questionable pan-functionalist
interpretations of Simmel and Coser – "Simmel and Coser tend to
go to the extreme of asserting nothing but functional interpretations
of conflict" (Collins, 1988, p. 120n.) – into a view of conflict as an
inherently conservative process: "for Simmel, conflict does not
produce social change" ([1985], 1994, p. 117). Collins is surely right
to emphasize the Simmelian proposition, overlooked too often, that
social conflict is crucially *constitutive* of social order. But
other parts of Simmel's work do attend to the role of conflict in
promoting change. Thus, he notes the "indisputable" fact that
conflict produces all manner of changes in the organization of
groups and that, indeed, conflict is essential for "change and
development" (1971, pp. 70, 72). In Simmel's general view of
life, there is a continuous struggle between the forms that life
has produced and the ongoing contents of life which find themselves
in opposition to objectified forms. In "The conflict in modern
culture," Simmel applies this metaphysical framework to the
whole span of culture history, which he depicts as a panorama
of transformations produced by the inexorable conflicts between
ongoing life processes and established forms (1971, ch. 24).

7   Simmel as (Marxian) Alienation Theorist (Manqué)

Quite the opposite view of Simmel has been taken by those who
have tried to make Simmel, not a polemicist against Marx, but a
halting ally of the Marxian tradition. Insofar as Simmel's ideas have
entered neo-Marxist theorizing, they have been represented as tracts
about alienation under capitalism which, from a Marxian perspective, means faulting him for regarding alienation as a metaphysical
tragedy rather than as something historically contingent that can be
combated. This interpretation has been advanced by a number of
commentators including Brinkman (1974), Frisby (1981), Cavalli

(1984), and Pohlmann (1987). An early proponent of this interpretation was Andrew Arato, who wrote that "Simmel rediscovered major moments of Marx's theory of alienation that most interpreters (except Lukács in 1923) associated with Marx only after the discovery of the 1844 Paris Manuscripts" (Arato, 1974, p. 153). The notion has been widely spread that Simmel was praiseworthy for having articulated a quasi-Marxian theory of alienation, but blameworthy for failing to contextualize alienation in a capitalist system of production and thereby indicate a way to transform society so as to eliminate it.

For some time I have felt that such an interpretation of Simmel was misleading. It is true that Simmel talks about the enslavement of workers in capitalist society to a production process that channels energies "as if cut off from the core of the personality" (Simmel, 1978, p. 454). He also talks about the enslavement of consumers to an inventory of industrial products that interpose "an insuperable barrier of media, technical inventions, abilities, and enjoyments . . . between [humans and their] most distinctive and essential being" (p. 484). Above all, he analyzes the oppression of moderns by a world of cultural objects that are relevant to personal cultivation but have become too numerous to assimilate – his major theme, and one that does not exist in the Marxian conception.

Nevertheless, Simmel devotes even more attention to the resources that modern society has created for the cultivation of authentic selfhood. He argues, for example, that specialized labor affords a medium for individuation, that money provides access to a wide range of resources for self-realization, and that rationalization and urbanization diminish customary constraints which inhibit authentic individual expression. Indeed, Simmel explicitly contests the view that makes the separation of workers from their means of production the focal point of social misery, suggesting that such separation may rather be viewed "as a salvation." This is because such separation frees workers from bondage to their tools and thereby liberates them as human subjects from the objectified technical apparatus of productivity (p. 337).

Above all, as I have argued repeatedly (Levine, 1981, 1991b, 1995), the hallmark of Simmel's interpretation of modernity is not a one-sided focus on the dynamics of alienation, but an emphasis on the amplification of opposed tendencies in modern society. In this vein, Birgitta Nedelmann (1993) has added a fresh challenge to the depiction of Simmel as an alienation theorist by insisting on a closer reading of Simmel's argument in the famous sixth chapter of *The Philosophy of Money*. Simmel designated this chapter, she reminds

us, not as an essay on alienation but as a portrait of the modern style
of life. He analyzes the modern style of life with respect to the three
dimensions of distance, rhythm, and tempo. By reducing his
complex argument to a marxisant tract on alienation, one loses the
full texture of Simmel's subtle analysis. Above all, she confirms, for
Simmel the modern style of life is characterized by an intensification
of opposite directions – of emancipation as well as unfreedom,
greater closeness as well as greater distance, greater meaning as well
as greater meaninglessness.

As for the notion that Simmel's metaphysical view of the tragedy
of culture inclined him to acquiesce passively in the suffocation of
individuality in the modern era, nothing could be further from the
truth. As noted above, his activism on behalf of *Logos* sprang
precisely from an expressed commitment to promote the cultivation
of human subjects, and his then radical ideas for educational reform
offered a climactic expression of that agenda.

8   Simmel as Unsystematic

Perhaps the most common view of Simmel is that for all his
intuitive genius and pedagogical talent, he functioned as a
dilettante and failed to offer a systematically developed intellectual
outlook. This image has a long lineage, from von Wiese, who
found Simmel's an "aesthete sociology [suited] for the literary
salon" (1910, p. 300) and Kracauer, who complained that Simmel's
essays contain no "central idea" and "indicate no course in
which our life should flow" (cited Frisby, 1981, pp. 8, 79) to
appellations by Parsons ("talented essayist," not a *"theorist"*, 1968,
p. xiv), Frisby (*"flâneur"* [1981]), and Collins ("salon entertainment"
[1985], 1994, p. 117).[24] The image persists tenaciously, in spite of the
fact that numerous scholarly investigations have revealed a striking
degree of coherence in Simmel's thought. Indeed, at one point it
occurred to me that because Simmel's substantive sociological
productions proceeded from his programmatic formulation of the
early 1890s, one could even say that Simmel's sociology evinced a
greater degree of coherence than those of his illustrious contemporaries![25]

---

[24]For longer catalogues and commentary regarding such judgments, see Frisby
(1981, ch. 1); Levine (1985, 133ff); and Green (1988, 83ff).

[25]The view that Simmel's sociological writings embody no coherent theoretical
outlook, I said then, "can be sustained only by a studiously superficial reading.
On five different occasions spanning his whole scholarly career (1890, 1894,
1896, 1908, 1917) Simmel took pains to articulate a carefully argued conception

Much of the difference among these synthesizing interpretations reflects a focus on varying aspects of Simmel's complex thought. Thus, some attend to his theory of culture (Weingartner, 1960; Levine, 1971; Oakes, 1980), some to the unity of his method (Steinhoff, 1925; Levine, [1957], 1980; Backhaus, 1996), some to his ethics (Gerson, 1932), some to his view of modernity (Frisby, 1981, 1991; Levine, 1981, 1991b; Pohlmann, 1987; Maffésoli, 1992), in addition to a number on his general sociology (Spykman, 1925; Coser, 1956; Blau, 1964; Becher, 1971; Schnabel, 1974; Levine et al., 1976a, 1976b; Levine, 1981, 1991a; Dahme, 1981) or to the connections between his social thought and his epistemology (Levine, 1971; Helle, 1988; Vandenberghe, 1995). Bevers (1985) has attempted to identify linkages among Simmel's epistemology, static sociology, evolutionary theory, and philosophy of life.

Although a critical synthesis of all these interpretive efforts has yet to be undertaken, certain general themes and points seem fairly well established. A number of them were proposed in my writings of the late 1950s, and subsequent scholarship has deepened our understanding of them. These include the centrality of the notion of *interaction* (*Wechselwirkung*) and the different ways in which it grounds Simmel's thinking (Levine, [1957], 1980, 1959, 1971; Mahlmann, 1983; Bevers, 1985; Liebersohn, 1988, p. 127ff); the emergence of protoforms, *forms*, and objectified forms through such interaction, and their chronic tension with ongoing life processes (Weingartner, 1960; Levine, 1971; Oakes, 1980); the pervasive use of *dualistic constructs* – both as heuristic antinomies that represent what are actually encompassing unities, and as constitutive opposed elements – static or dynamic, constructive or tragically conflictual (Levine, 1959, 1971; Bevers, 1985; Nedelmann, 1992; Sellerberg, 1994; Vandenberghe, 1995); the characterization of modernity as an amplification of dualisms (Levine, 1981, 1991b, 1995; Nedelmann, 1993); the thematic centrality of the subject–object dualism, including the historic processes of subjective emancipation and *individuation* as well as the conflict between

---

of the field of sociology. He even posted a warning at the entrance to his magnum opus *Soziologie* advising the reader to *keep that conception in mind* while reading the book 'or else,' he wrote, 'these pages might appear as a heap of disconnected facts and reflections' (1908, p. 1). Paradoxically, despite his reputation for being so unsystematic Simmel may well have produced the most unified conception of any of the classic sociologists, since his sociology is not only internally unified by a single guiding conception but it is also consistently linked with the meticulously elaborated ideas of his metaphysics and epistemological thinking" (Levine, 1981, p. 65).

Table 1 A neo-Simmelian schema of social forms

Relation	Process	Role	Collectivity	Dynamic pattern	Variable
Super/subordination	Domination	Superior	Ruling elite	Imposition of rule	Inequality
Enmity	Conflict	Enemy	Army	Escalation	Antagonism
Host-stranger relation	Sojourning	Stranger	Stranger collectivity	Estrangement	Assimilation
Secrecy	Concealment	Secret-holder	Secret society	Declassification	Publicity
Dissimilarity	Social differentiation	Individualized member	Heterogeneous group	Group expansion and individuation	Individuation
Triad	Triad formation	Tertius gaudens	Triple entente	Triangulation	Group size

objectified forms and life process (Levine, 1971, 1981, 1991b; Bevers, 1985; Pohlmann, 1987); the appeal to the dimension of *distance* as a means for analyzing those forms (Levine, [1957] 1980, 1971, 1991a; Nedelmann, 1993); and the reliance on a methodology that proceeds by intuiting the essences of forms (Steinhoff, 1925; Levine, [1957] 1980; Backhaus, 1996).

The application of these ideas to the domain of sociology involves the analysis of forms of interaction in terms of the dimensions of size, distance, position, valence, self-involvement, and symmetry (Levine, 1981). Simmel's own analyses can be represented by construing the great variety of forms that he treats in terms of relations, processes, roles, collectivities, dynamic patterns, or structural variables, as schematized in Table 1 (Levine, 1991a, p. 1107)[26].

It has been clear for some time now that the piecemeal appropriation of Simmel's work by earlier sociologists – involving as it did the neglect of his writings on epistemology, culture theory, metaphysics, aesthetics, and modernity theory – made it nearly impossible to grasp the unity even of his sociological thought. As these other parts of his oeuvre have become better known, it has become increasingly apparent that all parts of his work embody the

---

[26]Table 1, slightly modified from Levine, 1991a, represents a systematic extrapolation of what Simmel implicitly treats as legitimate sociological topics. The topics Simmel treated are indicated by italics there. Thus, *super/subordination*(Simmel, 1971, ch. 7) is a relational form, considered with respect to the kind of connection that links a number of statuses; *conflict*(1971, ch. 6) designates a kind of process – an activity that goes on among the incumbents of a set of statuses; the *stranger* (1971, ch. 10) represents a particular status-role, the set of features of one party to a relationship; the *secret society*(Simmel, 1950, pp. 345–76) represents a status-role when it takes the form of a collectivity; *group expansion and the development of individuality* (1971, ch. 18) represents a developmental pattern – some identifiable regularity in formal changes exhibited by groups over time; and *group size* (1950, part 2) represents a structural variable, some dimension of organization whose changes are accompanied by changes in other aspects of organization. From this analysis one can derive a paradigm that offers the basis for a systematic research program in Simmelian sociology, a set of questions to pose for a complete investigation of any form of association. In the case of conflict, for example, one would ask: (1) What properties are associated with relationships based on opposition among statuses, such as enmity or mutual hatred? (2) What characterizes various types of conflictual interactions? (3) What are the properties of a status-role in such a relationship, e.g., being an enemy? (4) What characterizes collectivities engaged in such relationships, like armies or political parties? (5) What characteristic transformational patterns do conflicts exhibit, such as escalation or reconciliation? (6) What effects do differing degrees of antagonism have on other relationship forms? (Levine, 1981, pp. 67–8).

distinctive constellation of ideas and methods I have outlined above. It has also become increasingly apparent how that unity arose from a lifelong engagement with the figures of Kant and Goethe (Gerson, 1932, pp. 31ff) and the streams of idealism and vitalism which they inspired (Bevers, 1985; Köhnke, 1991, 1996; Levine, 1995). Kant was clearly the main protagonist with whom Simmel wrestled throughout his life. To some extent, this strenuous engagement meant extending Kantian ideas into new terrains – the critique of historical realism, the notion of regulative ideas, the promise of a formal principle of ethics, the protection of human autonomy, the guiding concept of interaction, the form–content distinction, the use of antinomies, and the notion of unsocial sociability. To a considerable extent, however, it involved an unceasing effort to combat some central Kantian notions: the assumptions about ahistoric ethics, universalized ethics, and fixed a prioris. Goethe provided the inspiration for Simmel's addiction to the modern principle of "life," as well as the model for his culminating ethical formulation, *das individuelle Gesetz*.

> The manifold and deeply rooted influences of Goethe on Simmel appear above all in the example of Goethe's own life: the harmonious unity of that life, nourished in every moment out of its own root and at the same time resulting in works that satisfy some objective ideal standards . . . the exemplary breadth, the continuous change in the life course which, far from destroying the person, enables it to emerge completely. The life process is here never directed by an external goal, however ideal, but grows continuously out of its own root. (Gerson, 1932, p. 33)

Scholars like Bevers and Köhnke have deepened our understanding of how that double engagement took shape in the hothouse intellectual milieu of Simmel's time, wherein vitalistic ideas proceeding from Schopenhauer, Darwin, Nietzsche, Lazarus, and, finally, Bergson formed a context in which the ideas and categories of neo-Kantians could be reconfigured.

It would seem, therefore, that we have reached a point where no informed reader can deny a substantial amount of coherence in Simmel's thought. We even seem to have reached some consensus regarding the key features of Simmel's ideas and their interconnections, although divergent emphases continue to produce fresh insights. And yet, in spite of these achievements of Simmelian scholarship, there remains for the reader *the undeniable experience of Simmel as an unsystematic writer.* Indeed, although many have found his work powerfully stimulating, virtually no one knows how to practice as a full-blown proponent of Simmelian social science, as have followers of Marx or Durkheim, Weber or Mead, Parsons or Merton, Bourdieu or Luhmann. How can this enigma be understood?

Perhaps a new way of approaching the question may be helpful. I find it apt to consider what Arthur Melzer said of Rousseau: that "Rousseau's *thought* is indeed exceptionally systematic – but his *writings* are exceptionally unsystematic" (1990, p. 7). This seems to hold a fortiori for Simmel. This is because some of what is systematic in Simmel's thought *disposes him to produce a corpus of writings that are unsystematic.* I believe this is true in several senses.

The most conspicuous reason for the unsystematic appearance of Simmel's writings lies in his consistent commitment to a distinctive sort of *method*, one that seeks to *intuit the essence of forms.* This fact has been largely overlooked in the literature, despite the fact that Simmel warns the reader of his great *Soziologie* at the outset that it will exhibit no systematic unity of content, only a unified methodological approach; and despite the fact that features of this method were identified and discussed in critical articles already in the early 1920s by Siegfried Kracauer and Maria Steinhoff. As suggested in the introduction to my collection of Simmel pieces published in 1971, it is this search for form – whether of the personality, of social interaction, or cultural domain – that is the hallmark of Simmel's intellectual work. More recently, Gary Backhaus (1996) has brought new light to the understanding of this method by showing that Simmel's method in fact amounts to a quest for "eidetic essences" as advocated by Husserl. Inherent in such a method is the resistance of its analyses to being subsumed under broader systems, either comprehensive deductive theoretical systems or the grand dialectical systems of macroscopic history.

Simmel offers another reason for the unsystematic character of his productions: he remarks that the only kind of closure he can properly claim is in extending his inquiry as far as he himself possibly can. Guy Oakes has embellished this point by noting that Simmel "repeatedly emphasizes the importance of the process of the investigation over the significance of its results or findings. There is a sense in which the definitive purpose of the investigation does not lie in the conclusions it reaches, but rather in the activity or process of the inquiry itself" (1980, p. 86). In other words, if there is to be any kind of completion, it is to be based on the needs and abilities of the human subject, not on the systematic coherence of an objectified subject-matter.

This theme in turn links with Bryan Green's suggestion that while Simmel's method of writing may be maddening, there is method in his way of causing madness. When Green examines Simmel's writing, he looks directly at the effect it has on the reader. The effect is the same as has been reported about Simmel's style of lecturing: that he continually jolted listeners by showing them some feature of an object, then turning it abruptly so as to exhibit another facet. Similarly, Simmel's writing style forces the reader to deal with one feature after another of some topic; in Green's felicitous phrase, Simmel's style is "writing that refuses settlement" (Green, 1988, p. 103).

Whether or not Simmel employed such a style deliberately as an educational device – and it is not unreasonable to suppose that he did – the tenets of Simmel's world view would have led him to produce seemingly fragmentary and disjointed writings in any case. Simmel's theory of culture held that humans produce a great multi-plicity of symbolic forms in worlds that are not intertranslatable. In turn, each of these worlds possesses internally a multiplicity of incommensurable forms. Moreover, what is a form in one perspec-tive may be a content in another. Consequently, as Simmel shifted from the domain of value to the domain of art to that of science to that of religion, his particular statements would expectably be disjointed if not incommensurable. Moreover, the involvement of individuals in networks of social relations inevitably subjected them to a plurality of crosscutting attachments. Finally, each individual must be seen to possess a unique individuality that stands as a regulative ideal for personal growth. In sum, "human experience is defined and molded by a plurality of forms of life that are independent and irreducibly different from one another" (Oakes, 1984, p. 36).

Considerations of this sort may help to reconcile the experience of coherence in Simmel's thought with the undeniable experience of disjointedness in his written work, and with his apparent espousal of contradictory positions in different places. Without grasping the diverse domains of culture, social interaction, and individuated personality in Simmel's larger philosophical framework, one can never do justice to the complexity and challenge of his thought. For Simmel scholars, it remains now to develop this intuition more fully and then to locate Simmel's diverse contributions within his developmental history as well as within his own architectonic. For sociologists generally, the way is open to reconsider Simmel's sociological writings not merely as occasional sources of catchy hypotheses but as the matrix of one of the most sophisticated perspectives on social interaction that we possess.

REFERENCES

Alexander, Jeffrey 1993: "Formal sociology" is not multidimensional: breaking the "code" in Parsons' fragment on Simmel. *Teoria Sociologica*, 1(1), 101–14.

Arato, Andrew 1974: The neo-idealist defense of subectivity. *Telos*, 21, 108–61.

Backhaus, Gary 1996: Georg Simmel as an eidetic social scientist. Paper presented at Conference on Georg Simmel's Actual and Potential Impact on Contemporary Sociology. University of Colorado, Boulder: April 11–13.

Bevers, Antonius M. 1985: *Dynamik der Formen bei Georg Simmel: Eine Studie über die methodische und theoretische Einheit eines Gesamtwerkes.* Berlin: Duncker & Humblot.

Blau, Peter 1964: *Exchange and Power in Social Life.* New York: Wiley.

Böhringer, Hannes and Gründer, Karlfried, 1976: *Ästhetik und Soziologie um die Jahrhundertwende: Georg Simmel.* Frankfurt am Main: Vittorio Klostermann.

Boudon, Raymond 1984: Introduction to Simmel, *Philosophie de l'histoire.* Paris: Presses universitaires de France.

Brinkman, Heinrich 1974: *Methode und Geschichte: Die Analyse der Entfremdung in Georg Simmels* "Philosophie des Geldes." Giessen.

Buber, Martin 1992: *On Intersubjectivity and Cultural Creativity.* S. N. Eisenstadt (ed.), Chicago: University of Chicago Press.

Caplow, Theodore 1968: *Two Against One: coalitions in triads.* Englewood Cliffs, NJ: Prentice-Hall.

Cavalli Allessandro 1984: Introduzione. In *Filosofia del Denaro*, tr. A. Cavalli and L. Perucchi. Turin.

Chodorow, Nancy J. 1989: *Feminism and Psychoanalytic Theory.* New Haven: Yale University Press; Cambridge: Polity Press.

Christian, Petra 1978: *Einheit und Zwiespalt: Zum hegelianisierenden Denken in der Philosophie und Soziologie Georg Simmels.* Berlin: Duncker & Humblot.

Collins, Randall 1988: *Theoretical Sociology.* New York: Harcourt Brace Jovanovich.

—— [1985], 1994: *Four Sociological Traditions.* New York: Oxford University Press.

Coser, Lewis 1956: *The Functions of Social Conflict.* Glencoe: The Free Press.

—— 1977: Georg Simmel's neglected contributions to the sociology of women. *Signs*, 2, 869–76.

Dahme, Heinz-Jürgen 1981: *Soziologie als exakte Wissenschaft: Georg Simmels Ansatz und seine Bedeutung in der gegenwärtigen Soziologie,* 2 vols. Stuttgart: Ferdinand Enke Verlag.

Freund, Julien 1981: Introduction to Simmel, G. *Schriften zur Soziologie. Eine auswahl.* Paris: PUF.

Frisby, David 1981: *Sociological Impressionism: a reassessment of Georg Simmel's social theory.* London: Heinemann.

—— (ed.) 1994: *Georg Simmel: critical assessments*, 3 vols. London: Routledge.

Frischeisen-Köhler, Max 1919: Georg Simmel. *Kantstudien*, 24, 1–51.

Gadamer, Hans-Georg 1975: *Truth and Method,* New York: Seabury Press.

Gassen, Kurt and Landmann, Michael 1958: *Buch des Dankes an Georg Simmel: Briefe, Erinnerungen, Bibliographie.* Berlin: Duncker & Humblot.

Gerhardt, Uta 1992: Die Konzeption des Verstehens und der Begriff der Gesellschaft bei Georg Simmel im Verhältnis zu Wilhelm Dilthey. *Annali di Sociologia/Soziologisches Jahrbuch*, 8, 245–74.

Gerson, Hermann 1932: *Die Entwicklung der ethischen Anschauungen bei Georg Simmel.* Berlin: Friedrich-Wilhelms-Universität.

Green, Bryan S. 1988; *Literary Methods and Sociological Theory: case studies of Simmel and Weber.* Chicago: University of Chicago Press.

Gross, David L. 1982: *Kultur* and its discontents: the origins of a "critique of everyday life" in Germany, 1880–1925. In Gary D. Stark and Bede Karl Lackner (eds), *Essays on Culture and Society in Modern Germany*, College Station: Texas A&M University Press, 70–97.

Grossheim, Michael 1991: *Von Georg Simmel zu Martin Heidegger. Philosophie zwischen Leben und Existenz.* Bonn: Bouvier.

Gülich, Christian 1992: Georg Simmel und seine französische Korrespondenz. Historische Rekonstruktion eines wissenschaftlichen Netzwerkes um die Jahrhundertwende. *Critique and Humanism International*, special issue, 7–29.

Habermas, Jürgen 1991: Georg Simmel über Philosophie und Kultur. *Texte und Contexte.* Frankfurt: Suhrkamp. Translated as Georg Simmel on Philosophy and Culture: Postscript to a Collection of Essays. *Critical Inquiry*, 22 (3), 1996.

Hayakawa, Hiroyuki 1993: The significance of Georg Simmel's exchange theory. *Simmel Newsletter*, 3 (1), 16–22.

Helle, Horst Jürgen 1986: *Dilthey, Simmel und Verstehen: Vorlesungen zur Geschichte der Soziologie.* Frankfurt am Main: Verlag Peter Lang.

—— 1988: *Soziologie und Erkenntnistheorie bei Georg Simmel.* Darmstadt: Wissenschaftliche Buchgesellschaft.

Homans, George C. 1959: Social behavior as exchange. *American Journal of Sociology*, 63 (May), 597–606.

Horney, Karen 1926: The flight from womanhood: the masculinity-complex in women, as viewed by men and by women. *International Journal of Psychoanalysis*, 7, 324–39. Reprinted in Horney, 1967.

—— 1967. *Feminine Psychology.* Edited and with an introduction by Harold Kelman. New York: W. W. Norton.

Hübner-Funk, Sibylle 1976: Ästhetismus und Soziologie bei Georg Simmel. In Hannes Böhringer and Karlfried Gründer (eds), *Ästhetik und Soziologie um die Jahrhundertwende: Georg Simmel*, Frankfurt: Vittorio Klostermann, 44–71.

Köhnke, Klaus-Christian 1991: Der junge Simmel zwischen Positivismus und Neukantianismus. *Simmel Newsletter*, 1, 123–37.

—— 1996: *Der junge Simmel in Theoriebeziehungen und sozialen Bewegungen.* Frankfurt am Main: Suhrkamp Verlag.

Kracauer, Siegfried 1920–21: Georg Simmel. *Logos*, 9, 307–38.

Kramme, Rüdiger 1993: Brücke und Trost? Zu Georg Simmels Engagement für den "Logos," *Simmel Newsletter*, 3 (1), 64–73.

Landmann, Michael 1968: Introduction to *Das Individuelle Gesetz: Philosophische Exkurse.* Frankfurt: Suhrkamp.

Levine, Donald N. 1959: The structure of Simmel's social thought. In Kurt H. Wolff (ed.) *Georg Simmel 1858–1958.* Columbus: Ohio State University Press, 9–32.

—— 1971: *Georg Simmel: on individuality and social forms.* Chicago: University of Chicago Press.

—— [1957], 1980: Simmel and Parsons: two approaches to the study of society. New York: Arno Press.

—— 1981: Sociology's quest for the classics: the case of Simmel. In Buford Rhea (ed.), *The Future of the Sociological Classics*, London: Allen & Unwin.

—— (ed.) 1985: *The Flight from Ambiguity: essays in social and cultural theory.* Chicago: University of Chicago Press.

—— 1989: Simmel as a resource for sociological metatheory. *Sociological Theory*, 7 (2), 61–74.

—— 1991a: Simmel and Parsons reconsidered. *American Journal of Sociology*, 96 (5), 1,097–116.

—— 1991b: Simmel as educator: on individuality and modern culture. *Theory, Culture and Society*, 8, 99–117.

—— 1991c: Review of Mendes-Flohr 1989. *Contemporary Sociology*, 20 (5), 807– 8.

—— 1993: Further comments regarding Parsons's chapter on Simmel and Tönnies. *Teoria Sociologia*, 1 (2), 360–74.

—— 1995: *Visions of the Sociological Tradition.* Chicago: University of Chicago Press.

—— 1997: On the critique of economistic thinking: newly identified convergences among Simmel, Weber, and Parsons. For International Conference on Talcott Parsons's *Structure of Social Action after Sixty Years*, Heidelberg, June 26–7.

Levine, Donald N., Carter, E.B. and Gorman, Eleanor Miller 1976a, Simmel's influence on American sociology, I. *American Journal of Sociology*, 81, 813– 45.

—— 1976b, Simmel's influence on American sociology, II. *American Journal of Sociology*, 81, 1,112–32.

Lichtblau, Klaus 1984: Das "Pathos der Distanz." Präliminarien zur Nietzsche-Rezeption bei Georg Simmel." In Heinz-Jürgen Dahme and Otthein Rammstedt (eds), *Georg Simmel und die Moderne: neue Interpretationen und Materialien,* Frankfurt: Suhrkamp, 231–81.

Lidz, Victor 1993: Parsons and Simmel: convergence, difference, and missed opportunity. *Teoria Sociologia*, 1 (1), 130–42.

Liebersohn, Harry 1988: Fate and utopia in German sociology, 1870–1923. Cambridge, Mass.: MIT Press.

Lukács, Georg [1923], 1968, 1971: *History and Class Consciousness: studies in Marxist dialectics*, tr. Rodney Livingstone. Cambridge, Mass.: MIT Press.

—— [1954], 1962: *Die Zerstörung der Vernuft.* Neuwied and Berlin: Luchterhand.

Lukes, Stephen 1972: *Emile Durkheim: his life and work.* New York: Harper & Row.

Maffésoli, M. 1992: G. Simmel: modernité et post-modernité. In Otthein Rammstedt and Patrick Watier (eds), *G. Simmel et les sciences humaines.* Paris: Klincksieck, 151–60.

Mahlmann, Regina 1983: *Homo duplex: die Zweiheit des Menschen bei Georg Simmel.* Würzburg: Königshausen & Neumann.

Martindale, Don 1981: *The Nature and Types of Sociological Theory*, 2nd edn. Prospect Heights, Ill.: Waveland Press.

Melzer, Arthur M. 1990: *The Natural Goodness of Man: on the system of Rousseau's thought.* Chicago: University of Chicago Press.

Mendes-Flohr, Paul 1989: *From Mysticism to Dialogue: Martin Buber's transformation of German social thought.* Detroit: Wayne State University Press.

Müller, Herwig 1935: *Georg Simmel als Deuter und Fortbildner Kants.* Dresden: Dittert.

Nedelmann, Birgitta 1992: L'ambivalenza come principio di socializzazione. *Rassegna Italiana di Sociologia,* 33 (2), 233–55.

—— 1993: Geld und Lebensstil: Georg Simmel – ein Entfremdungstheoretiker. In Jeff Kintzelé and Peter Schneider (eds), *Georg Simmels Philosophie des Geldes,* Frankfurt: Anton Hain, 398–418.

Oakes, Guy 1980: Introduction to *Essays on Interpretation in Social Science,* Totowa, NJ: Rowman and Littlefield, 3–94.

—— 1984: Introduction to Simmel, pp. 3–62.

Parsons, Talcott [1937], 1968: *The Structure of Social Action.* New York: The Free Press.

Pohlmann, Fredrich 1987: *Individualität, Geld, und Rationalität. Georg Simmel zwischen Karl Marx und Max Weber.* Stuttgart: F. Enke.

Powers, Thomas 1996: Simmel as a neo-Kantian. Paper presented at Conference on Georg Simmel's Actual and Potential Impact on Contemporary Sociology, University of Colorado, Boulder, April 11–13.

Rammstedt, Otthein 1992: Programm und Voraussetzungen der *Soziologie* Simmels. *Simmel Newsletter,* 2 (1), 3–21.

Salomon, Albert [1963], 1995: Georg Simmel Reconsidered. *International Journal of Politics, Culture, and Society,* 8 (3), 361–78.

Schnabel, P. E. 1974: *Die soziologische Gesamptkonzeption Georg Simmels.* Stuttgart: G. Fischer.

Sellerberg, Ann-Mari 1994: *A Blend of Contradictions: Georg Simmel in theory and practice.* New Brunswick and London: Transaction Publishers.

Simmel, Georg 1980: Über sociale Differenzierung. In *Georg Simmel Gesamtausgabe,* 2. Frankfurt: Suhrkamp.

—— 1892–3: Einleitung in die Moralwissenschaft. In *Georg Simmel Gesamtausgabe,* 3–4. Frankfurt: Suhrkamp.

—— 1894: Das Problem der Soziologie. *Jahrbuch für Gesetzebung, Verwaltung und Volkwirtschaft,* 18, 257–65. In *Georg Simmel Gesamtausgabe,* 5, 52–61. Frankfurt: Suhrkamp.

—— 1896: Zur Methodik der Sozialwissenschaft. *Jahrbuch für Gesetsgebung, Verwaltung und Volkswirtschaft,* 20, 227–37.

—— 1898: The persistence of social groups, I, tr. Albion Small. *American Journal of Sociology,* 3, 662–98.

—— 1908: *Soziologie.* Leipzig: Duncker & Humblot.

—— 1917: *Der Krieg und die geistigen Entcheidungen: Reden und Aufsätze.* Munich and Leipzig: Duncker & Humblot.

—— 1922: *Schulpädagogik.* Osterwieck/Harz: A.W. Zickfledt.

—— 1950: *The Sociology of Georg Simmel,* tr. Kurt H. Wolff. Glencoe, Ill.: The Free Press.

—— [1908], 1955: *Conflict and the Web of Group-Affiliations,* tr. Kurt Wolff and Reinhard Bendix. Glencoe, Ill.: The Free Press.

—— 1971: *On Individuality and Social Forms,* ed. Donald N. Levine. Chicago: University of Chicago Press.

—— [1907], 1978: *The Philosophy of Money,* tr. T. Bottomore and D. Frisby.

London: Routledge & Kegan Paul.

—— 1984: *Georg Simmel: on women, sexuality and love*, tr. Guy Oakes. New Haven, Conn.: Yale University Press.

Sorokin, Pitrim A. 1928: *Contemporary Sociological Theories*. New York: Harper & Brothers.

Spykman, Nicholas J. 1925: *The Social Theory of Georg Simmel*. New York: Atherton.

Steinhoff, Maria 1925: Die Form als soziologische Grundkategorie bei Georg Simmel. *Kölner Vierteljahrshefte für Soziologie*, 4, 215–59.

Sternberger, Dolf 1934: *Der verstandene Tod: Eine Untersuchung zu Martin Heideggers Existenzial-Ontologie*. Leipzig.

Susman, Margaret 1964: *Ich habe viele Leben gelebt: Erinnerung*. Stuttgart.

Turner, Jonathan 1988: *A Theory of Social Interaction*. Stanford: Stanford University Press.

Vandenberghe, Frédéric 1995: Georg Simmel: entre Marx et Weber. Dialectiques de la modernité. *Métacritique de la réification*, Vol. 1. Thèse de doctorat, Ecole des Hautes Etudes en Sciences Sociales, Sociologie, Paris, ch. 3.

Vromen, Suzanne 1987: Georg Simmel and the cultural dilemma of women. *History of European Ideas*, 8, 563–79.

Weingartner, Rudolph, H. 1960: *Experience and Culture: the philosophy of Georg Simmel*. Middletown, Conn.: Wesleyan University Press.

Wiese, Leopold von 1910: Neuere soziologische Literatur-Kritische Literaturübersichten. *Kölner Zeitschrift zur Soziologie*, 11, 11–20.

7

Max Weber's Sociology: Research Strategies and Modes of Analysis

Stephen Kalberg

The reception of Max Weber in the United States charts a twisting and turning path that ranges across an unusually wide horizon. Exceedingly rich and provocative, Weber's texts appeared to offer sustenance to a broad variety of competing American schools. However, while frequently cited, his works were only sporadically the subject of in-depth analysis and were often viewed through the lens of a national tradition mainly indebted to French and English structural-functionalism. Fundamentally incompatible with this tradition and standing firmly within a German discourse, Weber's sociology for decades was either utilized as intellectual capital by participants in American debates or mined alone for its precise definitions. Its underlying tenets remained misunderstood or neglected even as sociologists in the United States continuously discussed his pathbreaking essays on charisma, power, rulership (*Herrschaft*), bureaucratic organizations, status groups, and the rise of modern capitalism (see Zaret, 1980, 1994; Kalberg, 1996).

Only very recently have the outlines of a distinct, rigorous, and broad-ranging *Weberian sociology* become apparent. To examine its basic research strategies and modes of analysis in succinct form constitutes the major task of this chapter. A brief overview of the Weber reception in the United States first locates his approach in

I would like to thank Charles Camic, Lewis A. Coser, and Sylvia Dominguez for very helpful comments.

reference to familiar aspects of the American landscape and, as well, introduces a number of the major dimensions of his sociology.

THE WEBER RECEPTION IN THE UNITED STATES

Weber's most famous book, *The Protestant Ethic and the Spirit of Capitalism*, was translated in 1930 by Talcott Parsons. Although not the only early translation (see also Weber, [1923], 1927, 1946a, 1947, [1922], 1949), this acclaimed and controversial investigation of a cultural force putatively at the origin of modern capitalism – a "modern economic ethic" – set the tone for the understanding of Weber's sociology until the 1960s. Despite Weber's vigorous disclaimers (see [1920], 1930, pp. 183/205–6),[1] *The Protestant Ethic* cast him as a proponent of the "power of ideas"; by the 1950s, his works became understood as constituting a worthy alternative to the Marxian focus upon classes, interests, ideology, and the economy as the "engine of history."

This reading of Weber's sociology became strongly confirmed as attention turned in the 1950s and 1960s to his seminal essays on topics such as "objectivity" and "ethical neutrality" in the social sciences, the importance of charismatic leadership for an understanding of social change, the capacity of bureaucracies to prevent social change, the centrality of rulership, and the manner in which status groups oriented to social honor often oppose classes. To this day, almost every *Introduction to Sociology* textbook examines this "Weber–Marx contrast" in its opening chapter. Other interpreters in the 1950s and 1960s praised – and debated widely – Weber's precise formulation of a variety of concepts and his typologies of "ideal types." In this commentary, Weber emerged as an ahistorical theorist and talented classifier who formulated a lexicon for sociology and sought conceptual exactness for its own sake.

Both of these interpretations – Weber as an "idealist" in opposition to Marx's "materialism" and as a taxonomist skilled in the formulation of concepts and typologies for understanding modern industrial societies – restricted the capacity of American commentators to comprehend the full theoretical and empirical range of Weber's sociology. In the 1960s and 1970s, Reinhard Bendix (1962, 1965, 1968, 1970, 1977; Bendix and Roth, 1971) and his

---

[1] All references to Weber's texts cite the original German in square brackets, then the English translation, followed by the page numbers in the original German.

students (Bendix and Roth, 1971; Roth, 1968; Collins, 1968, 1975) took a large step away from these readings. In turning from *The Protestant Ethic* and addressing mainly Weber's analytic treatise *Economy and Society (E&S)*, they presented a very different Weber: his deep concern with power, inequality, conflict, and rulership now came prominently to the fore. Moreover, rather than simply an array of disconnected and static concepts, Weber's sociology became viewed as a coherent body of theorizing that articulated an internally consistent, non-Marxist conflict theory. In addition, Bendix, Roth, and Collins further opposed the earlier reception by insisting that Weber offered an empirically based *historical* sociology focused upon the causal explanation of particular cases. Thus, Weber now stood in strict opposition to all attempts to define sociology, following the English, French, and American traditions, as an ahistorical and positivist science engaged in a quest for the "general laws" of society.

Yet this interpretation was found wanting in the 1970s and 1980s. Bendix, it was argued, had overreacted to the search among American sociologists for a conflict theory to stand against Parsonsian and Mertonian structural-functionalism; hence, he exaggerated Weber's emphasis upon conflict, inequality, power, and rulership at the expense of the more "cultural Weber" of *The Protestant Ethic.*[2] Weber's focus in the later work, as well as in the *Economic Ethics of the World Religions* (see [1920], 1946b, [1920], 1946c, [1920], 1951, [1920], 1952, [1920], 1958) and in the "Sociology of Religion" chapter in *E&S*, on religion, values, and "ideas" was perceived as downplayed. Benjamin Nelson (1973, 1974), Friedrich Tenbruck (1977, 1980), and Wolfgang Schluchter (1979, 1981, 1983, 1984, 1989), in particular, called attention to the centrality of the massive comparative studies on the "world religions" in Weber's works.

These commentators, as well as several others (see Münch, 1982; Hennis, 1983, 1987a, 1987b; Habermas, 1984; Brubaker, 1984; Levine, 1985; Whimster and Lash, 1987; Kalberg, 1980) in the 1980s,

---

[2]Thus, while structural-functionalism found Weber to be both a systems-builder (see Zaret, 1980) and a strong opponent of Marxism, Bendix and his students discovered in Weber a forceful critic of structural-functionalism, who stood opposed to its ahistorical theorizing and orientation to social order. While structural-functionalism pronounced Weber a theorist of culture, Bendix and his students trumpeted him as a theorist of conflict. That Weber's works could be perceived in these ways itself testifies to their unusual breadth and complexity. (Whether it could have been otherwise, given the debates and parameters of American sociology, must be left open. See Zaret, 1994; Kalberg, 1996.)

faulted Bendix and his students in another manner: their interpretations (not to mention the earlier Weber–Marx and concepts-oriented receptions) failed to note adequately how major themes played a pivotal role throughout Weber's sociology, both uniting its exceedingly heterogeneous components and adding a stronger theoretical aspect to his sociology than recognized by Bendix's orientation to Weber as a historical sociologist. In particular, Weber's focus upon "Western rationalization" – the uniqueness of the modern West and its causal origins – here advanced to the forefront. Weber's works, it was asserted, could finally be understood as unified, indeed even around a theme of immense importance today.

However, in the 1980s this interpretation in turn came under attack. While calling attention to the centrality of the overarching "rationalization theme" in Weber's sociology, Nelson, Tenbruck, and Schluchter all overemphasized, it was argued, the "idealism" component. Tenbruck in particular insisted that Weber understood the rise of the modern West mainly by reference to an "inner logic" of religious ideas rooted in the problem of theodicy; in turn, these ideas eventually gave birth to a Calvinist work ethic of extreme intensity, leading directly to modern capitalism (see Tenbruck, 1980, pp. 334–7, 341–2; Riesebrodt, 1980; Winckelmann, 1980; Kalberg, 1979). Schluchter as well tended to focus, in his highly schematic analysis in *The Rise of Western Rationalism*, upon the role played by Calvinism at the expense of various economic and political factors (see 1981, pp. 139–74). Thus, having identified the "Western rationalism" theme, none of these commentators offered a reconstruction of Weber's analysis that would allow adequate understanding of his convoluted argument concerning "ideas and interests." On the contrary, too often he was presented as a diffuse, global, and even evolutionary thinker (Hennis, 1983; 1987a, 1987b), far distant from his empirically based and comparative research strategies (Kalberg, 1983, 1985, 1989).[3]

The unifying effect of the "Western rationalism" discussion upon the Weber reception began to wane by the mid-1980s and investigations on a variety of delineated themes quickly appeared. Studies explored Weber as a historian (Kocka, 1986), legal thinker (Kronman, 1983; Turner and Factor, 1994), and sociologist of culture (Schroeder, 1992) and of modernity (Glassman and Murvar,

---

[3]Perhaps for this reason, this commentary focused upon the rationalization theme, which, unlike the earlier receptions, had very little impact upon American sociology generally.

1983; Scaff, 1989). Others examined his influence upon his contemporaries (Mommsen and Osterhammel, 1987), and his view of history (Nelson, 1981; Mommsen, 1987), politics (Mommsen, 1985, 1989), and the "irrational" (Sica, 1988). Weber's writings on capitalism in antiquity (Love, 1991), war, the Russian empire, and technology (Collins, 1986), "personality" (Goldman, 1988), women and love (Bologh, 1990), and Islam (Turner, 1992, 1996; Schluchter, 1996) have also been explored, as has his biography (Käsler, 1988; Roth, 1993) and the intellectual background of his sociology (Seidman, 1983). Finally, Weber's "Protestant ethic thesis" has continued to be the subject of an intense debate (Lehmann and Roth, 1987; Marshall, 1982; Poggi, 1983; Oakes, 1988–9; Kalberg, 1996). As with work on the rationalization theme, this massive literature investigated Weber's writings largely on their own terms and, compared to the earlier receptions, far less in reference to intellectual debates in sociology. It dramatically broadened the understanding of his sociology among specialists on Weber, as did studies of the rationalization theme.

While all of these interpretive trends have been of relatively short-term duration, two particular issues have captured the attention of Weber scholars for nearly sixty years. Since these issues focus almost exclusively on exegetical questions, they have been only marginally noted by mainstream American sociology. They concern: (1) explorations of Weber's social science methodology, seen as rooted in interpretive understanding (*Verstehen*), subjective meaning, and his four "types of social action" (see Parsons [1937], 1949; von Schelting, 1922, 1934; Salomon, 1934; Tenbruck, 1959; Rex, 1971; Bruun, 1972; Truzzi, 1974; Outhwaite, 1975; Burger, 1976; Oakes, 1977, 1989; Albrow, 1990; Drysdale, 1996); and (2) investigations of the modes of analysis and research strategies that characterize Weber's comparative-historical texts (see Salomon, 1935; Gerth, 1946; Eisenstadt, 1968; Roth, 1971a, 1971b, 1971c, 1976; Warner, 1970, 1972, 1973; Bendix, 1977; Fulbrook, 1978; Alexander, 1983; Smelser, 1976; Collins, 1981; Molloy, 1980).

This chapter takes this latter theme as its focus and seeks to build upon this literature. In so doing, it hopes not only to address a number of inaccurate perceptions of Weber's works still widespread in American sociology, but also to clarify the manner in which these modes of analysis and research strategies contribute even today to sociology's intellectual capital. The central argument is that Weber created a distinctly *Weberian* comparative-historical sociology in *E&S* and *The Economic Ethics of the World Religions* – a sociology scarcely visible from the extensive commentary on his view of modernity, his politics, or his participation in the debates of his time. Neither can it be comprehended by reference to the "ideas" and "material interests" dichotomy, nor to major Weberian concepts (bureaucracy, status groups, or charisma), conflict theory, or the overarching rationalization theme. Rather, only an investigation of Weber's *practiced* sociology captures his distinctive approach.

Five central dimensions of Weber's mode of analysis and research strategies serve to organize this study: (1) a level of analysis that is *both* empirically based *and* vigorously theoretical; (2) an intimate interweaving of history and the present, to such an extent that past and present cannot be separated in Weber's sociology; (3) a broad multicausality that endows the rulership, law, economy, religion, status groups, and family and clan "societal orders," as well as historical events, "social carriers," ideas, and power, with independent causal effectiveness; (4) a *verstehende* methodology that seeks to *interpretively understand* the social – or meaningful – action of persons in groupings; and (5) an emphasis upon the ineluctable embeddedness of social action in contexts of social action, to such an extent that in Weber's sociology all causal analysis must attend primarily to *constellations* of social action. These major components of Weber's comparative-historical sociology will be explored here in brief, overview fashion.[4]

His fundamental level of analysis understood as rooted in ideal types and societal domains[5] stands at the center of this exploration. These theoretical constructs offer the means of orientation (*Orientierunsmittel*) for research which endow Weber's texts *both* with a distinct analytic dimension and with a deep rooting in empirical reality. Moreover, they offer a "vision of society" that directly opposes all schools of societal organicism and all approaches that utilize global dichotomies – such as *Gemeinschaft* and *Gesellschaft*, tradition and modernity, particularism and universalism – to depict a putatively evolutionary course of history. Finally, Weber's ideal types and societal domains comprise the core building blocks for his broadly multicausal and contextual mode of analysis, and offer the conceptual foundation for a *verstehende* sociology that strongly interweaves past and present.

However, these heuristic constructs never stand alone in anchoring these basic features of Weber's practiced sociology; they

---

[4] A great deal must be, for reasons of space, omitted. See my *Max Weber's Comparative-Historical Sociology* (1994). Various sections of this chapter draw from this study.

[5] I am using the terms "societal orders" and "societal domains" synonymously.

are also rooted in a number of demarcated causal forces which are central throughout his works: historical events, power, social carriers, and ideas. As will become apparent, when combined with ideal types and societal domains, these forces both broaden Weber's multicausality and further embed social action within contexts of social action. For example, cultural forces ubiquitously penetrate into economic and rulership forces, while economic and rulership forces penetrate ubiquitously into cultural forces. Furthermore, contexts of social action vary in terms of internal cohesion: sometimes they may consist mainly of traditional action; at other times they may best be characterized as more "open" and in flux, constituted mainly from means–end rational action.

The highly contextual character of Weber's sociology, as well as the central role played in it by interpretive understanding, will be discussed in the concluding section of the chapter. Weber's "methodological individualism" stresses the ways persons attribute subjective meaning to certain actions and the capacity of the sociologist to understand the meaningfulness of this action. On the other hand, his works also emphasize that, when persons gather into delineated groupings, *patterns and regularities* of social action *do* exist – and these too can be understood by the sociologist.

Before turning to these prominent features of Weber's comparative-historical texts, two basic points must first be discussed: the aim of Weber's sociology, and the nature and use of the ideal type. A brief delineation of his aim will enable us to distinguish his approach from the Durkheimian and Parsonsian organicist traditions and to set the stage for the subsequent discussion. Examination of Weber's central heuristic construct – the ideal type – will convey the fundamental level of analysis used in his sociology.

THE GOAL OF WEBER'S SOCIOLOGY[6]

Discussions of Weber have often failed to note that he orients his research to discrete problems and to the causal analysis of specific cases and developments – or, in his terms, of the specific "historical individual." He proposes that the causal explanation of the unique case and development should serve as sociology's primary aim:

[6]For a more detailed discussion, see Kalberg, 1994, pp. 81–4.

The type of social science . . . *we* wish to put forth is an *empirical science* of concrete *reality* (*Wirklichkeitswissenschaft*). We wish to understand the reality that surrounds our lives, in which we are placed, *in its characteristic uniqueness.* We wish to understand on the one hand its context (*Zusammenhang*) and the cultural *significance* of its particular manifestations in their contemporary form, and on the other the causes of it becoming historically so and not otherwise [1922], 1949, pp. 72/170, transl. altered, emph. orig.; see also [1924], 1976a, pp. 385/288; [1921], 1968, pp. 10/5).

Weber inquires repeatedly into the *uniqueness* of a case or development, seeking to identify the causal determinants of this uniqueness.

Hence, he opposed strongly the numerous positivist schools of thought in his day which sought to define general laws of history and social change and then to explain all specific developments by deduction from these laws. Forcefully rejecting the position that the social sciences should aim "to construct a closed system of concepts which can encompass and classify reality in some definitive manner and from which it can be deduced again" ([1922], 1949, pp. 64/184; see also pp. 56–7/171–4, 80–1/179–81; [1921], 1968, pp. 263–4/154), he expressed his clear opposition to the view that laws themselves comprise causal explanations. Because concrete realities and individual cases cannot be deduced from them, laws are incapable of providing the knowledge of reality that would offer causal explanations. Due to their abstract and general character, laws possess no explanatory value – even if a "closed" and "complete" system of laws could be formulated (a theoretical possibility that Weber denies). Only a lexicon would result from such a system. Indeed, the more abstract and general the laws, the less are they capable of providing explanations of individual cases. The latter can be explained causally, in Weber's sociology, only by "other equally individual configurations" ([1922], 1949, pp. 75–6/174–5; see also pp. 78–80/178–80; [1903–6], 1975, pp. 63–6/12–15; [1922], 1949, 113–88/ 215–90).

Similarly, Weber's focus upon the "historical individual" led him to oppose with particular vehemence the use of analogies (see [1924], 1976a, pp. 39/4, 341/257, 385/288). Parallels, historical constants, universal stages of development, as well as analogies and laws, fail to offer explanations of distinctiveness. Although these "abstract uniformities" fulfill an instrumental purpose on the route toward establishing causal relationships, they are only *means* to elucidate and facilitate comparisons which reveal where similarities between two social phenomena end and differences begin (see [1922], 1949,

p. 135/237; [1924], 1988, p. 517/524). Moreover, abstract concepts can be utilized as heuristic instruments only if anchored closely to history: "The existence of a connection between two historical occurrences cannot be captured abstractly, but only by presenting an internally consistent view of the way in which it was concretely formed" (Weber, [1891], 1966, p. 2). This level of concrete causality pervades Weber's history-saturated sociology.

Nonetheless, he avoids historical narrative and largely retains, throughout his substantive texts, an *ideal-typical* level of analysis. Indeed, he understands the ideal type as best suited to his purpose of defining "individual concrete patterns" and uniqueness (see [1922], 1949, pp. 72/170–1, 99–101/201). How is this the case? What is the indispensable role of the ideal type in Weber's sociology?

The Ideal Type[7]

Many interpreters of Weber have noted that ideal types anchor his sociology in empirical reality rather than in a theoretical scheme; however, few have understood that these heuristic constructs aim to conceptualize *patterned orientations of social action*. Moreover, Weber's ideal types aim neither to provide an exhaustive description of empirical reality nor to formulate the "laws" of society.

His *verstehende* sociology selects the social action of individuals as its unit of analysis and attempts to comprehend the subjective meaning that persons attribute to their action. Nonetheless, Weber never views social life as an "endless drift" of solitary and unconnected action-orientations. The diverse ways that persons act *in concert* in groupings, rather than the social action of the isolated individual, capture his attention. He argues that patterns of action-orientations and definitions of "meaning" that are held in common by persons surface, frequently and regularly, in all societies throughout history. Indeed, Weber defines the sociological enterprise as focused on action by persons in delimited groups and as concerned with the identification of *regularities of action*: "There can be observed, within the realm of social action, actual empirical regularities; that is, courses of action that are repeated by the actor or (possibly also: simultaneously) occur among numerous actors because the subjective *meaning* is typically meant to be the same. Sociological investigation is concerned with these *typical* modes of action" ([1921], 1968, p. 29/14, emph. orig., transl. altered; see also

[7]For a more detailed discussion, see Kalberg, 1994, pp. 81–142.

pp. 19–21/9–10, 311/181; [1922], 1949, p. 67/165). Moreover, regular action in Weber's sociology results not only from an orientation to values, but also from affectual, traditional, and even means–end rational action. The manner in which action is *uprooted* from its random flow and transformed into *meaning*-based regularities anchored in these *four types of social action*[8] constitutes one of the most central and basic themes of his sociology, especially in *E&S*.[9]

Ideal types "document" these regularities of meaningful action. This remains the case even though these types often appear static or even reified in Weber's substantive work, to such an extent that his attention to the interpretive understanding of action seems scarcely visible at times. However, far from supplanting his methodological individualism and emphasis upon the four types of social action, Weber's ideal types – e.g., the family, the capitalist economy, the ascetic path of salvation, and bureaucratic rulership – always chart the patterned and meaningful action-orientations of individuals in groupings – and nothing more. Thus, Weber's ideal type, "the Calvinist," identifies orientations of action toward methodical work and an ascetic style of life; "the civil servant" identifies orientations toward reliability, punctuality, a chain of command, and the performance of specialized tasks; and "the charismatic leader" identifies orientations toward heroism and a rejection of everyday routine.

Because each ideal type implies regular action-orientations with a degree of endurance and firmness, each indicates both a continuity of meaningful action and a clear resistance against both random and competing action-orientations. Thus, apparent with respect to each ideal type is the likelihood of the persistence of certain uniform actions and the exclusion of others. The patterned action-orientations demarcated by ideal types imply the possibility that an indigenous causal thrust and staying power – or, in Weber's terms, an *autonomous (eigengesetzliche)* aspect – exists empirically.

In capturing meaningfully patterned action through ideal types, Weber's sociology steers away from a focus upon isolated action-orientations, on the one hand, and an organicist level of analysis – directed to societal evolution, social differentiation, and the question of social order – on the other hand. His attention centers

---

[8]On Weber's four types – affectual, traditional, means–end rational, and value-rational – of social action, see *E&S*, pp. 24–6/12–13.

[9]This major theme running throughout *E&S* – the appearance on a regular basis of social, or *meaningful*, action – is scarcely noted in the secondary literature.

on the multifarious sources of empirical uniformities of action and, in addition, on the attempt to understand the particular content of such regular action, not on a global shift from "traditional" to "modern" societies or the *Gemeinschaft* to the *Gesellschaft*. Least of all are Weber's ideal types capable of introducing general laws or theories. They preclude the construction of universal uniformities, as well as all general theorizing in the manner of Marx, Parsons, or Wallerstein.

By no means should the ideal type be understood as an "average type." It is not a simple encapsulation of elements common to empirical phenomena, nor merely a classification of events. Instead, although constructed in reference to empirical reality, the ideal type is formulated, on the one hand, through a conscious exaggeration of those *essential* features of action-orientations significant for the research task at hand and, on the other hand, through a synthesis of these orientations into an internally unified and logically rigorous concept. While inductive procedures from empirical observations are followed in the formation of the ideal type, deductive procedures guide the logical ordering of its separate action patterns into a unified and precise construct. At the same time, the empirical anchoring of ideal types, their historically relative nature, and their capacity to be reformulated and improved upon in respect to empirical reality, all preclude interpreting them as "abstract" or "reified" concepts ([1922], 1949, pp. 92–107/193–209). Above all, concepts serve, for Weber, *to assist* research, not to capture reality accurately – an impossible task, he emphasizes. Selection and arrangement occur inevitably in the process of ideal type construction. Rather than possessing the capability to "replicate" the external world or to define a particular phenomenon, ideal types are constructed "utopias" whose sole aim is to facilitate empirical, cause-oriented inquiry. Thus, Weber's conceptualization of "the civil servant" or "the Calvinist" accurately portrays the action-orientations of neither a particular Calvinist or a particular civil servant, nor all civil servants or Calvinists ([1921], 1968, pp. 19–22/9–11). As Weber notes: "Concepts are primarily analytical instruments for the intellectual mastery of empirical data and can be only that" ([1922], 1949, pp. 106/208). This level of analysis, rather than historical narrative or the diffuse concepts of societal organicist schools, prevails throughout Weber's comparative-historical texts.

What is his most fundamental usage of ideal types? Once formed as clear concepts that capture regular action-orientations, ideal types anchor Weber's sociology in a fundamental fashion: they enable the precise definition of empirical cases. Utilized as "yardsticks," ideal types serve to define discrete empirical cases. Each ideal type can be employed as an orientational instrument that provides a clear "standard" against which given patterns of action can be "measured." By assessing their deviation from the standard, these empirical cases can be defined clearly (see [1922], 1949, pp. 93/194, 97/198–9, 43/535; [1903–6], 1975, pp. 189/130; [1921], 1968, pp. 263–4/154; [1920], 1946c, pp. 323–4/536–7).

Instead of "capturing reality," the ideal type thus establishes points of reference and orientational guidelines against which a given slice of empirical reality can be compared and measured. An examination of the ways in which the action-orientations that are under investigation approximate or diverge from the ideal type discloses the characteristic features of the empirical case and defines its boundaries. Weber states this general mode of procedure explicitly: "[We] proceed from the most rational forms reality *can* assume [and we] attempt to find out how far certain rational conclusions, which can be established theoretically, have been drawn in reality" ([1920], 1946c, pp. 324/537–8, emph. orig.).

Ideal types provide constructs indispensable for grasping "infinite and multifarious historical life" ([1920], 1946b, p. 300/273). Without these conceptual instruments as standards, it is not possible to conduct comparative "mental experiments" (*Gedankenbild*) that seek to isolate significant causal patterns of action. Thus, although ideal types exist in Weber's comparative-historical sociology exclusively as heuristic means rather than as ends, without them all causal attribution remains impossible (see [1922], 1949, pp. 101–2/202–4).

In sum, for Weber, ideal types: (1) facilitate the grasping of diffuse empirical reality; (2) assist the ordering and clear conceptualizing of the particular empirical problem that is under scientific investigation; and (3) enable identification of significant causal action-orientations. They stand in opposition to both historical narrative and all societal organicist approaches.

WEBER'S FUNDAMENTAL LEVEL OF ANALYSIS AND VISION OF SOCIETY: IDEAL TYPES AND SOCIETAL ORDERS

Only a very few commentators on Weber have observed that, in addition to ideal types, societal orders stand at the very core of his sociology.[10] Throughout his comparative-historical texts, both conceptualizing mechanisms capture the intimate interweaving of past and present; they also provide the analytical foundation for Weber's radical multicausality, his contextual embedding of social action, and his *verstehende* methodology which seeks interpretively to understand the social action of persons in groupings.

Ideal Types

Weber's ideal types imply a vision in which society is constructed from the innumerable action patterns of persons in delimited groupings. This fundamental aspect of his sociology stands against all interpretations that have sought to define this classical theorist as assigning causal priority to single factors, whether religious ideas, bureaucratic organizations, or the like. Moreover, his radically multicausal position forcefully asserts an intimate intertwining of past and present. How is this the case?

Grounded in ideal types, Weber's practiced sociology takes cognizance of both stagnant, all-encompassing tradition and continuous movement and flux. As heuristic constructs that document regularities of social action, ideal types perpetually jostle against one another, at times coalescing into alliances and at other times standing in relationships of antagonism and shifting conflict. His level of analysis rooted in ideal types assumes *all* possibilities. For Weber it is a subject exclusively for empirical investigation whether what takes shape are multiple alliances and coalitions marked by "traditionalism" and overarching "societal unity," or whether the social action of persons in demarcated groupings flows in the opposite direction toward societal fragmentation and the development of enduring antagonisms not amenable to negotiation and compromise. No assumptions regarding an empirical "drift toward" coalitions, social harmony, or "traditionalism" underlie his sociology. Whether normative integration, "adaptive upgrading," and "value-generalization" (see Parsons, 1966, 1971) take place is not an issue that constitutes, in his view, a central theoretical theme for the sociology of development; rather, these processes must be investigated on a case-by-case basis. Likewise, it is always an

---

[10]Weber uses the terms *gesellschaftliche Ordnungen, Lebensordnungen, Lebensbereiche, Lebensmächte,* and *Lebenssphären.* The title of Weber's analytic treatise, *Wirtschaft und Gesellschaft,* was given by Marianne Weber. His title for its Part 2, *Die Wirtschaft und die gesellschaftlichen Ordnungen und Mächte,* would more likely have been his own title choice for the entire treatise.

empirical question whether disintegration or internal unity will reign in any particular time and place.

According to Weber's "open" procedures, all "general axiom" schools – whether they postulate "inevitable conflict" or "social order and equilibrium" – must be rejected. Moreover, anchored in ideal types, his broadly multicausal sociology acknowledges an intimate interweaving of past and present. Patterns of social action in some groupings can be recognized as living on, and even developing "autonomously" in terms of their indigenous problematics, while other patterns prove fleeting. The vision of society that flows from Weber's ideal type-based sociology always takes cognizance too of the "survival" of regularities of action from the past, regardless of whether groupings tightly coalesce or stand in relations of antagonism.

Societal Orders

Although tension and conflict are ubiquitous, social action is never random according to Weber. Rather, patterns of social action are apparent in all societies. However, conceptualization of these patterns is not only the task of ideal types, as commentators have often claimed; the societal orders that undergird Weber's comparative-historical texts serve this purpose as well. Although constructed from ideal types, these domains constitute an independent analytic dimension. Amidst the "infinite multiplicity of successively and coexistently emerging and disappearing events, both 'within' and 'outside' ourselves" ([1922], 1949, p. 72/171), the societal orders assist research (as do ideal types) by offering guidelines for the identification and conceptualization of a wide array of causally significant forces. Moreover, like ideal types, they comprise a central analytic mechanism that connects past and present, embeds social action in contexts of social action, and assists the interpretive understanding of the social action of persons in groupings. Ideal types *and* a variety of societal orders together stand at the foundation of Weber's comparative-historical texts – not a global concept such as "society"[11] or the atomistic individual, nor simply the economic, political, or religious domain alone.

Societal domains are most evident in *E&S*.[12] This three-volume work discovers and charts the patterned social action of persons in

---

[11] Let alone some general question such as the origin of social order or the evolution of society.

[12] Though also forcefully in *The Economic Ethics of the World Religions*.

diverse groupings, as captured by ideal types. In turn, these action
patterns are conceptualized as taking place within demarcated
societal orders, each of which is conceived, vis-a-vis other domains,
as a clearly bounded realm: viz., the status group, universal organizations, religion, law, rulership, and economy societal orders. An
array of ideal types is analytically associated with each domain: these
types include the paths to religious salvation (through a savior, an
institution, ritual, good works, mysticism, and asceticism); the types
of law (primitive, traditional, natural, and logical formal); the stages
of development in the economy (the agricultural and industrial
organization of work; the natural, money, planned, market, and
capitalist types of economies); the types of rulership (charismatic,
patriarchal, feudal, patrimonial, and bureaucratic); the types of
universal organizations (the family and clan); and major status
groups (such as intellectuals, civil servants, and feudal nobles).

From the vantage point of his comparisons across civilizations
ranging from Antiquity to the present and from East to West,
Weber concluded that patterned social action significantly occurs in
reference to these domains and their respective ideal types. No
ontological assumptions play a part in this idea; Weber attends alone
to patterns of social action that have repeatedly been important
empirically. Given the "meaningless infinity of the world process,"
he does not seek to capture *all* regular action; Weber's societal
orders do not aim to be "exhaustive," "complete," or eternally
valid[13] (see [1922], 1949, pp. 72–3/170–2, 81/180–1).[14] Hence, any
particular civilization or epoch may be characterized by the
prominence of a societal domain or ideal type not included among
those offered in *E&S* as sociologically most significant.

According to Weber, the societal domains and domain-specific
ideal types provide a survey of sociologically significant social
action – and nothing more. They must be understood solely as a
useful *means* for orientation designed to assist researchers, on the
one hand to isolate and define causally important empirical action-
orientations and, on the other, to conceptualize clearly otherwise
random and diffuse social action, thus allowing research questions
to be formulated regarding causality.

Thus, the societal orders never posit an evolutionary theory nor
any empirically rooted linkages across their associated ideal types.
To Weber the stages of any "developmental model" constructed

---

[13]Weber's principle of value-relevance (*Wertbeziehung*) prohibits such an
attempt. See [1922], 1949, pp. 50–112/146–214.
[14]On Weber's criteria for selecting societal domains, see Kalberg, 1994, p. 104, n.
20.

from these ideal types can never be viewed as capturing the course of history, as constituting "effective forces," or as depicting a "lawful" and universal tendency of history to pass through a succession of invariable stages ([1922], 1949, pp. 102–3/203–5).[15] The concern of Weber's work is not to trace some linear historical expansion of means–end rational and value-rational action, nor to depict a process of general societal evolution that involves the substitution of "particularistic" by "universalistic" values.[16] Rather, ideal types, societal orders, and developmental models stand at the core of his comparative-historical sociology. Whether the history of a particular epoch or civilization followed the analytic path of development indicated by a particular model, or deviated from it, always remains an issue for detailed empirical investigation by specialists, especially historians ([1922], 1949, p. 103/205).

What does this societal domains analytic imply about multi-causality and the influence of the past upon the present? It affirms, again, Weber's principled and broad multicausality. The very core of this analytic – its recognition of the *pluralistic* sources of social action – encourages sociologists to consider a variety of patterned action-orientations in their empirical investigations rather than to focus simply on religious ideas, the economy, the state, etc. Weber's comparative-historical sociology opposes in principle the elevation of a particular domain or ideal type to a position of general causal priority. At the analytic level, it postulates no "superiority" for the action-orientations indigenous to any particular ideal type or societal domain.[17]

As in the case of his ideal types, Weber's domains-based

---

[15]For example, when viewed from the perspective of a change from "substantive" to "formal" rationality, the *types of legitimate rulership* can be arranged in a *developmental model (Entwicklungsform)* (see Kalberg, 1994, pp. 117–42) that moves from charismatic and traditional to rational-legal rulership; however, this mode of conceptualization should not lead to the conclusion that such a transformation actually occurred empirically. See, e.g., [1924], 1988, pp. 517, 524; [1922], 1949, pp. 101–3/203–6.

[16]Of course, Weber sees *specific* empirical developments toward universalistic values (e.g., in the Greek polis, the medieval cities, the examination system in China, and the modern bureaucracy). However, no progressive, continuous and lawful evolutionary continuum from an ancient era of particularism to a modern epoch of universalism can be drawn from his sociological investigations, as Parsons, Tenbruck, and Hennis imply.

[17]For example, the orientation of social action to the sib group implies, analytically, a causal weight equal to that of the modern capitalist economy. Similarly, the orientation of action to laws must be viewed, according to Weber,

sociology provides a conceptual foundation built to capture a close interwovenness of past and present. On the basis of empirical investigations, Weber asserts two points: that each societal order is potentially endowed with empirical causal viability – an independent, or "autonomous," developmental capacity rooted in indigenous questions and problems;[18] and that the societal orders unfold at varying rates and in a non-parallel manner.[19] Moreover, like ideal types, the various "autonomous" orders jostle continuously against one another. The result is a vision of society in which certain patterns of social action in some societal orders may endure, and even penetrate deeply into subsequent epochs (in scarcely visible, even clandestine ways), while other patterns prove fleeting and without significant causal impact. Although recognizing the uniqueness of every "present" and the efforts of charismatic rulers to break all linkages to the past, Weber's societal orders conceptualize past and present as firmly interconnected. In his view, even the abrupt appearance of "the new" – indeed, even the "supernatural" power of charisma – never fully ruptures ties to the past (see, e.g., [1921], 1968, p. 577/349; [1920], 1946b, p. 273/245). To him: "That which has been handed down from the past becomes everywhere the immediate precursor of that taken in the present as valid" ([1921], 1968, p. 29/15, transl. altered).[20]

These considerations raise a fundamental question: *on what basis* do the patterned action-orientations, as conceptualized by the ideal types associated with a particular societal order, acquire such prominence that they actually influence social action, indeed even

---

at the analytic level as the equal of the orientation of action to the economy. Law is particularly strong empirically when it is strengthened by religion: "The dominance of law that has been stereotyped by religion constitutes one of the most significant limitations on the rationalization of the legal order and hence also on the rationalization of the economy" ([1921], 1968, p. 577/349).

[18]For example, questions of unjust suffering in the domain of religion (see below), of the legitimacy of commands in the rulership order, of social honor in the status groups domain, etc.

[19]Weber had rejected the "parallel development," evolutionary position even as early as *The Protestant Ethic*. In this classic work, he contested Werner Sombart's view that the development of the fundamental feature of the modern economy, "economic rationalism," could be explained by appeal to a *general* historical advance of rationality that encompassed all societal domains in an overarching manner. See [1920], 1930, pp. 75–8/60–2; Kalberg, 1996, p. 51.

[20]Two distinct "modes of diachronic interaction" – legacies and antecedent conditions – prominent in Weber's comparative-historical texts capture this firm interconnection of past and present (see Kalberg, 1994, pp. 158–68).

across epochs? *Why* do some patterns of social action endure across the ages? Given Weber's broad multicausality, reference to charismatic rulership alone fails to offer a full response to these questions. Nor is it adequate simply to refer to the domains and domain-specific ideal types as "autonomous." Instead, Weber's own answers to these questions turn away from ideal types and societal domains and toward various demarcated causal forces that push historical development. And here too his analysis evidences a broad multicausality, a tight linking of past and present, a contextual mode of analysis, and a *verstehende* methodology that seeks to understand the social action of persons in groupings.

DEMARCATED CAUSAL FORCES: HISTORICAL EVENTS, SOCIAL CARRIERS, POWER, AND IDEAS

Weber's texts are characterized not only by ideal types and societal orders, but also by an array of demarcated action-orientations, only a few of which have generally been noted in the secondary literature. In particular, historical events, social carriers, power, and ideas comprise – along with charismatic rulership and the societal domains and domain-specific ideal types – pivotal causal forces which firmly intertwine past and present. Given his vision of society as constituted from patterned action-orientations indigenous to the clan and family, to status groups, and to the domains of religion, economy, rulership, and law, it is not surprising that Weber stressed the causal importance of these delimited forces rather than social differentiation in general or global evolutionary developments. A few examples must suffice to demonstrate their centrality in his comparative-historical sociology.[21]

Historical Events

Weber attended closely to the causal significance of delimited historical events and even historical "accident." His appreciation of the unpredictability of history convinced him that the imponderable and the unexpected appear on a regular basis and have the capacity to cast their influence far into the future.

For example, the defeat of the Persians by the Greeks at the Battle of Marathon proved pivotal for the development of Hellenic culture and thus for the entire course of Western history ([1922], 1949,

---

[21]Again, a more detailed discussion can be found in Kalberg, 1994, pp. 68–71.

pp. 171–4/273–7, 184–5/286–7). The eucharist at Antioch was likewise of "tremendous importance." By cutting across all ritual barriers of exclusion, the commensalism of the Lord's Supper demonstrated the universalism of the Pauline mission. In doing so, it provided the "hour of conception" for the Occidental notion of citizenship ([1920], 1958, pp. 37–8/39–40). This mission also brought about the adoption of the Old Testament by Christianity. Had this not occurred, no Christian church or ethic could have been formulated and the Christian congregation would have remained simply one among many Jewish pariah sects ([1920], 1952, pp. 4–5/6–8). Weber pointed to the importance of historical events in Asia as well. The conversion in India of King Ashoka during the third century AD to Buddhism, for example, led to a pacifistic welfare state and gave the first impetus to the development of Buddhism as a world religion (see [1920], 1958, pp. 238–42/256–62). Similarly, had the Tai-Ping rebellion (1850–64) been successful, it might well have set the history of East Asia on an entirely different track (see [1920], 1951, pp. 294–5, n. 52/505, n. 3).

Weber awards great significance to a certain type of historical event: technical change. He frequently discusses its great influence upon military organization in *The Agrarian Sociology of Ancient Civilizations* (1976a). In Antiquity, for example, the introduction of the horse was instrumental in creating the Near Eastern conquest state and the knightly society of the Mediterranean; and in China this same innovation proved pivotal in introducing a "Homeric" age of heroic combat. In addition, the utilization of iron in weapons in Antiquity played a crucial role in calling forth mass armies and, ultimately, in creating the ancient "citizen polis" ([1924], 1976a, pp. 352–3/266–7; [1920], 1951, pp. 24/302). Technological innovation in agriculture – better tools for threshing, ploughing, and harvesting – was particularly significant in the Ancient Near East in increasing the productivity of labor ([1924], 1976a, pp. 354/268–9). Many further examples could be noted.

Social Carriers

Cohesive bearers of social action are always necessary, according to Weber, if patterned action-orientations are to become sociologically significant. In every society, only certain traditional, affectual, value-rational, and means–end rational regularities of action acquire sufficiently strong proponents to become prominent in the social fabric and cast an influence across decades and centuries. As Weber notes: "Unless the concept 'autonomy' is to lack all precision, its definition presupposes the existence of a bounded group of persons which, though membership may fluctuate, is determinable" ([1921], 1968, p. 699/419; transl. altered). Status groups, classes, and organizations (*Verbände*) serve as the most significant social carriers throughout Weber's texts.[22]

In some civilizations, according to Weber, a great continuity of social carriers across epochs has been typical. The patrimonial bureaucracy and the stratum of Chinese literati, for example, remained the central carriers of Confucianism for more than two thousand years. In India, the Brahmins carried Hinduism for more than a millennium. In Japan, "the greatest weight in social affairs was carried by a stratum of professional warriors . . . Practical life situations were governed by a code of chivalry and education for knighthood" ([1920], 1958, p. 275/300).

But such continuity is not the only possibility. Weber's treatment of neo-Calvinism – the major carrier of the Protestant ethic in the United States – illustrates how patterned social action may change its carrier status group or organization, thus surviving into a subsequent epoch and even influencing it. Weber observes in *The Protestant Ethic* how ethical values of religious origin "migrated" from their original carriers – ascetic Protestant churches and sects – to another carrier organization: Protestant families. Consequently, even as some secularization occurred, these values remained central in childhood socialization. Families taught children to esteem upward mobility, heroic individual achievement, self-reliance, honesty and fair play in business transactions, the just price, ascetic personal habits, methodical work, and hard competition. Children were socialized as well to oppose worldly authority, to avoid all ostentatious display, and to distrust the state (see [1920], 1930, pp. 155–83/163–206). Even as such values gradually lost their explicitly religious roots, they became firmly anchored in the family, where they were taught through intimate, personal relationships to children. In other words, these values were further cultivated – or *carried* – as binding ethical principles by this organization, through which they continued to influence social action. In this way, action-orientations toward values originally cultivated in ascetic Protestant sects and churches endured in a later epoch, long after the weakening of these organizations themselves (see Kalberg, 1992, 1993a, 1996).

Power

One force is linked with particular closeness to Weber's emphasis on social carriers, multicausality, and the impact of the past upon

---

[22]I have discussed social carriers in detail in Kalberg, 1994, pp. 58–62.

the present: this force is power, or the capacity to carry out one's will. In his classic formulation on the subject, Weber defines power thus: "Within a social relationship, power implies the probability that an actor is able to carry through his own will despite resistance, regardless of the basis on which this probability exists" ([1921], 1968, p. 53/28; transl. altered). A certain minimum of power always exists as a prerequisite for success against opposing carriers of regular action. Weber sees power as ubiquitous in social life, and believes that it may prove critical in respect to the long-range endurance of patterns of social action. A few examples will illustrate its pervasiveness throughout his comparative-historical texts.

Officials in patrimonial (monarchical) and bureaucratic forms of rulership, particularly as a result of struggles against rulers, often develop their own vested interests and domains of power. They seek to monopolize the prerogatives of their positions and to appropriate privileges and power, to such an extent that the wishes of rulers may be regularly obstructed. Whether rulers succeed in overcoming this resistance depends largely upon power, especially military power ([1921], 1968, pp. 232–5/134–6, 1040/604, 1042/605, 1028/596). Similar tendencies appear elsewhere. Even priests seek to secure power when, for example, they adjust religious doctrines to the emotional needs of the laity ([1921], 1968, p. 457/279), support a traditional economic ethic and patriarchal authority against forces seeking to rationalize the economy ([1921], 1968, pp. 584–5/353), and coalesce with the petty-bourgeoisie either to confront great capitalist families, as in Antiquity and the Middle Ages ([1921], 1968, pp. 1,180–1/704), or to pacify the masses ([1921], 1968, pp. 1,161–2/ 690–1; [1920], 1958, p. 236/254). Members of the aristocracy have also acted in accord with power interests, as when they embraced established religions as instruments to control the masses, or when local French notables opposed the rise of organized political parties which encompassed the entire country and threatened their in- fluence ([1921], 1968, pp. 516/314, 984/568).

Power and its long-term consequences are also central when Weber explores related issues: whether compromises between political and hierocratic organizations produce caesaropapist or hierocratic forms of rulership; whether feudal princes succeed in limiting or forbidding subinfeudation; and whether the routin- ization and transformation of charismatic education lead to the formation of an ecclesiastic institution. Similarly, the development of law from primitive to patrimonial law often depends on the relative power of rulers against other social carriers: sib organizations, status groups, and the church hierocracy (on these examples, see [1921], 1968, pp. 1015/586, 1021–2/591, 1027–8/595–6, 1174/700, 1144/677, 258/150, 883/505; [1920], 1946b, pp. 298/271).

Rulers are particularly adept, according to Weber, at forming alliances with the sole purpose of maintaining and aggrandizing power. As a matter of course, they seek to balance classes, status groups, and organizations off against one another. It was thus that kings and princes sought out priests and religious intellectuals, for if controlled, the latter groups were capable of leveling and pacifying the masses (see, e.g., [1920], 1952, pp. 348–9/364). On the other hand, if power is lacking and alliances fail to form, new action-orientations frequently fade or undergo suppression by opposing coalitions. Buddhism in India comes to mind here, as does the suppression of the Old Confederacy's patriarchalism by Solomon's patrimonial monarchy in ancient Israel. Weber's texts offer many further examples of the manner in which sheer power influenced the long-term course of history (see Kalberg, 1994, pp. 71–4).

Ideas

Finally, in his comparative-historical sociology, ideas are also endowed with causal efficacy and seen as strongly linking past and present. For Weber, *religious* ideas in particular illustrate the ways in which ideas may endure across millennia and cast their influence far and wide. In his view, a burning question stood at the beginning of "religious development," and the search for answers to it gave religious development a long-range thrust and continuity. This was the question of human suffering: why did it occur so frequently and randomly? Why did it endure? (see [1921], 1968, pp. 399–439/245–67, 518–29/314–21; [1920], 1946b, pp. 271–7/241–8).

Weber asserts that the wish to offer reasons for suffering *itself* contributed to the development of "relations to the transcendent realm":[23] ideas that explained misery and hardship pushed religious development across epochs, from religions rooted in magic and ritual all the way to salvation religions with elaborate conceptions of an "other-world." To him, the realm of religion is thus characterized not only by distinct boundaries, but also by an indigenous developmental dynamic (see e.g., [1920], 1946b, pp. 269–70/240, 275/247, 281/253, 286/258–9; [1921], 1968, pp. 577–8/349, 1179/703–4; Kalberg, 1990). In Weber's terms, the religion domain follows its own laws: it develops to a significant extent in relation to ideas regarding human suffering, not solely in relation to practical

---

[23]This is the single definition of religion Weber offers. See [1921], 1968, pp. 399/245, 403/247, 424/259.

interests (see e.g., [1920], 1946b, p. 275/247; [1921], 1968, p. 519/315). Historically, prophets, priests, monks, and theologians addressed a specifically religious dilemma: the stubborn persistence of suffering and misfortune. In doing so, they sought to clarify the relation of believers to transcendent beings and to define specific actions as capable of alleviating believers' distress. Rather than simply a response to "the social conditions of existence" or to economic forces, this religious   development exhibited an "imperative of consistency" that endowed it with a long-term continuity, especially once intellectuals came to be influenced by religion and emerged as a cohesive status group (see [1920], 1946c, p. 324/537; [1920], 1946b, pp. 286/258–9). By expressing "the metaphysical needs of the human mind as it is driven to reflect on ethical and religious questions not by material need but by a particular inner compulsion (*Notigung*) to understand the world as a *meaningful* cosmos and to take up a position toward it" ([1921], 1968, p. 499/304; transl. altered; emph. orig.; see also pp. 506/307–8, 568/343; [1920], 1946c, pp. 324/537, 352/565; [1920],   1946b, pp. 281/253, 286/258–9), religious intellectuals were driven to systematize ideas, values, and traditions into internally consistent salvation doctrines. As unified views of the cosmos and the place of believers within it, such doctrines sought to offer exhaustive explanations for suffering and to designate actions to banish it ([1920], 1946b, pp. 280–1/252–3; [1921], 1968, pp. 577–9/ 349–50; see Kalberg, 1990, pp. 64–7; 1996; forthcoming).[24]

But not only is Weber convinced that the problem of suffering played a pivotal role for centuries and in most civilizations;[25]

---

[24]Weber always understands religious development as occurring *also* in direct reference to an economic and political context. The problem of suffering can be understood as possessing the capacity to call forth new "relations to the transcendent realm," other-worldly salvation religions, and altered social action among believers only if this dilemma is itself examined at each stage in terms of its "worldly" context. He emphasizes that "religion nowhere creates economic conditions unless there are present in the existing relationships and constellations of interests certain possibilities of, or even powerful drives toward, such an economic transformation" ([1921], 1968, p. 577/349; see also [1920], 1946b, pp. 268/238–9, 287/259; [1920], 1930, pp. 277–8n./192n.). For a detailed discussion of this "ideas and interests" theme, see Kalberg, forthcoming.

[25]The "modern person," he argues, accustomed to understand social realities by reference to secular questions and dilemmas rooted in sheer means–end rational action and "all the interests of life in this world" ([1920], 1930, pp. 110/103), is "scarcely in a position, even with the best of will, to imagine the significance which religious consciousness actually had upon the conduct of life, culture generally, and group character" (*Volkscharakter*) ([1920], 1930, p. 183/205; transl. altered; see also pp. 109–10/102–3, 155/163–4, 233n./113n.; [1910], 1972, p. 33).

religious development is seen as crucial in a further, long range sense. He repeatedly argues that religious belief was of great importance for the rise of the "fateful force" today: modern capitalism. Standing firmly in opposition to all Marxian, technology-based, and "great man" theories of historical change, Weber holds that a "modern economic ethos" – viz., the spirit of capitalism as rooted in the "Protestant ethic" – constituted a significant causal force in the rise of modern capitalism. However, had the ascetic Protestant idea of other-worldly salvation not come at the end of a long development, the type of action uniquely capable of shattering the "traditional economic ethos" – i.e., value-rational action based in the Protestant ethic and oriented to "world mastery" (*Weltbeherrschung*)[26] – would never have appeared. Thus, Weber's treatment of the major theme of all his work – the rise of modern Western capitalism and, more generally, of a singular "Western rationalism" – accords centrality to the ideas and values that emerged from new explanations for perpetual suffering. In this way, ethical values, which originated in ancient ideas about the supernatural realm, significantly influenced the rise of the modern world.

These brief examples must suffice to demonstrate that the broad multicausality and close interweaving of past and present that are at the core of he comparative-historical sociology are anchored not only in his ideal types and the societal domains analytic of *E&S*. Rather, he also attributes causal efficacy, and the capacity to link past and present, to historical events, social carriers, power, and ideas – forces he is careful never to view in isolation. Yet, instead of defining their significance in terms of global, evolutionary trends, Weber always sees these forces as deeply embedded in constellations of regular action-orientations, many of which can be identified using the societal orders analytic. As noted, even those charismatic leaders who have moved history by the sheer force of their personalities have done so, in his sociology, within *contexts* of patterned social action. Even mighty missionary prophets were normally dependent for their development on a "certain minimum of intellectual culture" ([1921], 1968, p. 486/296). Indeed, Weber's works, in advocating – via its emphasis on ideal types, societal orders, historical events, social carriers, power, and ideas – a broad

[26]Weber is convinced that means–end rational action – which has existed universally in the sheer pursuit of profit and wealth as well as in business activity in general – was not sufficiently methodical to shatter the traditional ethos. See [1920], 1930, pp. 57/42–3, 51/33, 74–8/59–62, 117–28/114–28, 155–83/163–206; Kalberg, 1996, pp. 57–64.

multicausality and tight interlocking of past and present, also articulate a sociology that captures the embeddedness of social action in contexts of social action. Analysis of these contexts also promotes the sociologist's interpretive understanding of the social action of persons in groupings.

Conclusion: Weber's *Verstehende* Sociology and the Embeddedness of Social Action in Contexts of Social Action

This analysis of Weber's comparative-historical sociology calls into question the common characterization of his "view of history" as an alternation between charismatic rulership and the rigid forces of tradition. This analysis rejects as well all interpretations of Weber's sociology that assign causal priority to a particular factor, whether "ideas" or "interests." What stands at the foundation of Weber's practiced sociology, instead, is a broad array of independent causal forces: (1) the societal orders of rulership, law, religion, economy, status groups, and family and clan, as understood in terms of their respective ideal types; and (2) historical events, power, social carriers, and ideas. Partly as a consequence of this emphasis upon a multiplicity of causal forces, Weber's sociology unequivocally affirms an interwovenness of past and present.

Moreover, Weber's research strategies and modes of analysis suggest that, if the causal origins of individual cases are to be adequately explored, formulation of theoretical concepts *and* close attention to historical particularity are both indispensable. In every causal analysis, societal orders and order-specific ideal types belong as heuristic means of orientation; but equally central is attention to historical events, social carriers, power configurations, and ideas specific to the case under investigation. Weberian causal analysis includes both the historically particular and the conceptual generalization. Indeed, to accomplish his goal of offering causal explanations of the "historical individual," Weber advocates a *continuous back and forth* movement between conceptualization and the detailed investigation of the unique case. Hence, although powerfully theoretical, his sociology abjures any attempt to construct ahistorical "laws" of social life or to discover overarching evolutionary developments. Even his analytic constructs remain rooted in complex empirical realities and aim simply to offer hypotheses that assist the in-depth, causal exploration of a particular empirical case.

Weber's research strategies and modes of analysis also capture the *varying degree to which* the past influences the present in different settings. Examining the extent to which tradition-oriented action acquires prominence in a variety of societal orders, Weber's sociology holds that, wherever this type of social action is widespread, there occurs an encompassing penetration of the past into the present which constricts even the influence of charismatic personalities, as well as the capacity of historical events, power, ideas, and new carrier strata to become significant causal forces.[27] On the other hand, wherever means–end rational action reigns across a variety of domains, any tight interweaving of past and present is lessened. Weber does not impute this, however, simply to a general "weakening of tradition," for means–end rational action is itself quite capable of introducing firm patterns of action (see [1921], 1968, pp. 30–1/15–16). Instead, he argues that the dominance of means–end rational action implies greater "autonomy" for the different societal orders: a stronger capacity to develop in reference to their own distinctive problems and questions. When this occurs, a further weakening of traditional action follows, if only due to the competition and tension (*Spannung*) that becomes typical of cross-domain interaction (see [1920], 1946c, pp. 328–40/541–54; [1921], 1968, pp. 576–610/348–66). In this way, Weber's comparative-historical sociology, even as it argues for the inexorable interweaving of past and present, conceptualizes variation in the extent to which the past actually influences the present. His mode of analysis thus challenges contemporary sociologists not only to acknowledge in principle the importance of the past for the present, but also to assess the relative importance of that relationship.

As a consequence of its multicausality, its linking of past and present, and its back-and-forth movement between theoretical abstraction and historical particularity, Weber's practiced sociology continually attends to the *contexts* of social action. To him, whether patterns of action-orientations prove causally significant depends not simply upon the firmness of their boundaries, their power, or the weight of a carrier stratum or organization; also pivotal is the manner in which *constellations* of action-orientations *interact*. Each milieu of regular action places a particular imprint upon patterned action, thereby shaping its impact as well as its substance. Weber thus focuses not on the action-orientations themselves or the simple

---

[27]Weber's examples in this regard are often ancient Egypt and China. He speaks of an "Egyptianization" and a "Chinese ossification (*Versteinerung*) of intellectual life" (see, e.g., [1922], 1949, p. 84/184; [1921], 1968, p. 1402/332).

fact of their appearance, but on the social settings in which they occur; the latter, he insists, are decisive in the process whereby new patterned action expands and attains sociological significance. In undertaking causal analyses of specific cases, Weber always seeks, therefore, to integrate "the 'particular fact' . . . as a real causal factor into a real, hence concrete context" ([1922], 1949, pp. 135/237).[28]

His pivotal notion of interpretive understanding (*Verstehen*) also serves to define his sociology as attentive to the contexts in which social action appears. For Weber, sociologists must never seek, in a unilinear fashion, to understand motives for action. Instead, he argues that the understanding of subjective meaning requires its location within a context of action. Again, his societal orders and order-specific ideal types serve as heuristic means of orientation that assist the contextual location of action, if only because they reveal an immense spectrum of subjectively meaningful action, thereby facilitating efforts to understand particular actions as plausible and meaningful. Weber's distinctive synthesis of the method of interpretive understanding with his societal orders analytic assists sociologists in recognizing actions otherwise perceived as "irrational" as, in fact, "rational" when located contextually. Even the neo-Calvinist's extremely methodical, even obsessive, orientation toward work – so irrational from the standpoint of an eudaemonistic attitude toward life – can be understood as meaningful once the neo-Calvinist search for "signs" of salvation is comprehended (see [1920], 1930, pp. 53/36, 78/62; Kalberg, 1996, pp. 58–64). Appreciation of Weber's concerns here – to contextualize a specific course of social action so as to identify it as subjectively meaningful to social actors and as thus "understandable" to the sociologist – belies any depiction of his work as merely a different variety of structuralist analysis.

Yet Weber's notion of *Verstehen* emphasizes the contextual embedding of action in a further way. Even as they stress the deep penetration of the past into the modern West, his modes of analysis and research strategies assist, even challenge, sociologists to become cognizant of this era's uniqueness. To be sure, Weber also laments the widespread tendency for social scientists to define the present epoch as unchained from a sacred and feudal past: to him, insofar as this tendency occurs, a greater likelihood exists that interpretations of the past will be governed by the radically different assumptions of

---

[28]Unfortunately, the complex contextuality of Weber's sociology and his conjunctural causal methodology cannot be explored further here. See Kalberg, 1994, pp. 39–46, 98–102, 168–77.

the present. Again and again asserting that "we moderns" can barely comprehend the actual character of major questions and dilemmas that suffused past epochs, Weber fears that present-day assumptions will be unknowingly imposed upon the past. For example, only with great difficulty can those in the secular world of today imagine the extent to which the overriding religious conundrum in the sixteenth century – "am I among the saved?" – stood as the most urgent concern in the lives of the devout (see, n. 25 above). The burning significance of this question to believers – its subjective meaningfulness – can be comprehended, Weber insists, only if sixteenth-century believers are located, via the herculean labors of the sociologist, within their own time.

Only if "we moderns" are prepared to comprehend decidedly different epochs and civilizations contextually and, through interpretive understanding, "from within" can the full promise of Weber's comparative-historical sociology be realized: an extension across history and civilizations of the sociologist's capacity to understand social action as meaningful will then take place. If this extension occurs, researchers will become, Weber believes, more aware of the great diversity of subjectively meaningful actions. By calling attention to action that otherwise might be belittled or dismissed, Weber's own broad societal orders analytic expands – even encourages – the capacity of sociologists *to understand* action as subjectively meaningful, even action in civilizations radically different from their own. Determined to comprehend the human species as a "meaning-seeking creature" (see Salomon, 1962, p. 393) and to understand how persons in various epochs and civilizations endowed their actions with meaning, Weber wished the notion of *Verstehen* and his other heuristic constructs to be utilized in this "universal-historical" manner. If this happened, the sociologist's horizon and cross-cultural understanding would be enlarged. As well, through comparison, the unique features and parameters of epochs, civilizations, and distinct groupings would be isolated. Such achievements were central for Weber simply because they offer important insight. In addition, he emphasized that they constitute the indispensable first step toward a definition of what is sociologically possible in respect to social change.

REFERENCES

Albrow, Martin 1990: *Max Weber's Construction of Social Theory.* New York: St Martin's Press.

Alexander, Jeffrey 1983: *The Classical Attempt at Theoretical Synthesis: Max Weber.* Berkeley: University of California Press.

Bendix, Reinhard 1962: *Max Weber: an intellectual portrait.* New York: Doubleday Anchor.
—— 1965: Max Weber's sociology today. *International Social Science Journal,* 17 (1), 9–22.
—— 1968: Introduction. In Reinhard Bendix (ed.), *State and Society,* Berkeley: University of California Press, 2–13.
—— 1970: Concepts and generalizations in comparative sociological studies. In *Embattled Reason,* New York: Oxford University Press, 175–87.
—— 1977: Tradition and modernity reconsidered. In *Nation-Building and Citizenship,* enlarged edn. Berkeley: University of California Press, 361–433.
Bendix, Reinhard and Roth, Guenther 1971: *Scholarship and Partisanship.* Berkeley: University of California Press.
Bologh, Roslyn W. 1990: *Love or Greatness: Max Weber and masculine thinking – a feminist inquiry.* London: Unwin Hyman.
Brubaker, Rogers 1984: *The Limits of Rationality.* London: Allen & Unwin.
Brunn, H. H. 1972: *Science, Values and Politics in Max Weber's Methodology.* Copenhagen: Munksgaard.
Burger, Thomas 1976: *Max Weber's Theory of Concept Formation.* Durham, NC: Duke University Press.
Collins, Randall 1968: A comparative approach to political sociology. In Reinhard Bendix (ed.), *State and Society.* Berkeley: University of California Press, 42–68.
—— 1975: *Conflict Sociology.* New York: Academic Press.
—— 1981: Weber's last theory of capitalism: a systematization. *American Sociological Review,* 45 (6), 925–42.
—— 1986: *Weberian Sociological Theory.* London: Cambridge University Press.
Drysdale, John 1996: How are social-scientific concepts formed? A reconstruction of Max Weber's theory of concept formation. *Sociological Theory,* 14, 71–88.
Eisenstadt, S. N. 1968: Introduction. In S. N. Eisenstadt (ed.), *Max Weber on Charisma and Institution Building.* Chicago: University of Chicago Press.
Fulbrook, Mary 1978: Max Weber's "Interpretive sociology": a comparison of conception and practice. *British Journal of Sociology,* 29 (1), 71–82.
Gerth, H. H. 1946: Introduction. In H. H. Gerth and C. Wright Mills (eds), *From Max Weber.* New York: Oxford.
Glassman, Ronald and Murvar, Vatro (eds) 1983: *Max Weber's Political Sociology: a pessimistic vision of a rationalized world.* Westport, Conn.: Greenwood Press.
Goldman, Harvey 1988: *Max Weber and Thomas Mann.* Berkeley: University of California Press.
Habermas, Jürgen 1984: *The Theory of Communicative Action,* Vol. 1, tr. Thomas McCarthy. Boston: Beacon Press.
Hennis, Wilhelm 1983: Max Weber's "central question." *Economy and Society,* 12 (2), 136–80.
—— 1987a: *Max Weber: essays in reconstruction.* London: Allen & Unwin.
—— 1987b: Personality and life orders: Max Weber's theme. In Sam Whimster and Scott Lash (eds), *Max Weber, Rationality and Modernity.* London: Allen & Unwin, 52–74.
Kalberg, Stephen 1979: The search for thematic orientations in a fragmented

oeuvre: the discussion of Max Weber in recent German sociological literature. *Sociology*, 13 (1), 127–39.

—— 1980: Max Weber's types of rationality: cornerstones for the analysis of rationalization processes in history. *American Journal of Sociology*, 85 (3), 1145–79.

—— 1983: Max Weber's universal-historical architectonic of economically-oriented action: a preliminary reconstruction. In Scott G. McNall (ed.), *Current Perspectives in Social Theory*, Greenwich, Conn.: JAI Press, 253–88.

—— 1985: The role of ideal interests in Max Weber's comparative historical sociology. In Robert J. Antonio and Ronald M. Glassman (eds). *A Weber–Marx Dialogue*. Lawrence, Kansas: University Press of Kansas, 46–67.

—— 1989: Max Webers historisch-vergleichende Untersuchungen und das "Webersche Bild der Neuzeit": eine Gegenüberstellung. In Johannes Weiss (ed.), *Max Weber heute*. Frankfurt: Suhrkamp, 425–44.

—— 1990: The rationalization of action in Max Weber's sociology of religion. *Sociological Theory*, 8 (1), 58–84.

—— 1992: Culture and the locus of work in contemporary western Germany: a Weberian configurational analysis. In Richard Münch and Neil J. Smelsed (eds), *Theory of Culture*, Berkeley: University of California Press.

—— 1993a: Cultural foundations of modern citizenship. In Bryan S. Turner (ed.), *Citizenship and Social Theory*. London: Sage.

—— 1993b: Salomon's interpretation of Weber. *Int. J. of Politics, Culture and Society*, 6 (4), 585–94.

—— 1994: *Max Weber's Comparative-Historical Sociology*. Chicago: University of Chicago Press.

—— 1996: On the neglect of Weber's *Protestant Ethic* as a theoretical treatise: demarcating the parameters of postwar American sociological theory. *Sociological Theory*, 14 (1), 49–70.

—— Forthcoming. Ideas *and* interests: Max Weber on the origin of other-worldly salvation religions.

Käsler, Dirk 1988: *Max Weber: an introduction to his life and work.* Chicago: University of Chicago Press.

Kocka, Jürgen (ed.) 1986: *Max Weber, der Historiker*. Göttingen: Vandenhoeck & Ruprecht.

Kronman, Anthony 1983: *Max Weber's Sociology of Law*. Stanford: Stanford University Press.

Lehmann, Hartmut and Roth, Guenther (eds) 1987: *Weber's Protestant Ethic: origins, evidence, contexts.* Cambridge: Cambridge University Press.

Levine, Donald N. [1981], 1985: Rationality and freedom. In *The Flight from Ambiguity*. Chicago: University of Chicago Press, 142–78.

Love, John 1991: *Antiquity and Capitalism: Max Weber and the sociological foundations of Roman civilization.* London: Routledge.

Marshall, Gordon 1982: *In Search of the Spirit of Capitalism*. London: Hutchinson.

Molloy, Stephen 1980: Max Weber and the religions of China. *British Journal of Sociology*, 31 (3), 377–400.

Mommsen, Wolfgang J. 1985: *Max Weber and German Politics, 1890–1920.* Chicago: University of Chicago Press.

—— 1987: Personal conduct and societal change. In Sam Whimster and Scott Lash (eds), *Max Weber, Rationality and Modernity*. London: Allen & Unwin.

——— 1989: *The Political and Social Theory of Max Weber.* Chicago: University of Chicago Press.

Mommsen, Wolfgang J. and Jürgen Osterhammel (eds) 1987: *Max Weber and his Contemporaries.* Boston: Unwin Hyman.

Münch, Richard 1982: *Theorie des Handelns.* Frankfurt: Suhrkamp.

Murvar, Vatro 1983: *Max Weber Today: selected bibliography.* Brookfield, Wis.: Max Weber Colloquia at the University of Wisconsin-Madison.

Nelson, Benjamin 1973: Weber's Protestant Ethic: its origins, wanderings, and foreseeable futures. In Charles Y. Glock and Phillip E. Hammond (eds), *Beyond the Classics?* New York: Harper and Row, 71–130.

——— 1974: Max Weber's "Author's introduction" (1920): a master clue to his main aims. *Sociological Inquiry,* 44, 269–78.

——— 1981: *On the Roads to Modernity,* ed. Toby E. Huff. Totowa, NJ: Rowman and Littlefield.

Oakes, Guy 1977: The Verstehen thesis and the foundations of Max Weber's methodology. *History and Theory,* 16 (1), 11–29.

——— 1988–9: Farewell to *The Protestant Ethic? Telos,* 78, 81–94.

——— 1989: *Weber and Rickert.* Cambridge, Mass.: MIT Press.

Outhwaite, William 1975: *Understanding Social Life: the method called Verstehen.* London: Allen & Unwin.

Parsons, Talcott [1937], 1949: *The Structure of Social Action.* New York: Free Press.

——— 1966: *Societies: evolutionary and comparative perspectives* Englewood Cliffs, NJ: Prentice-Hall.

——— 1971: *The Evolution of Societies.* Edited and with an Introduction by Jackson Toby. Englewood Cliffs, NJ: Prentice-Hall.

Poggi, Gianfranco 1983: *Calvinism and the Capitalist Spirit: Max Weber's Protestant Ethic.* Amherst: University of Massachusetts Press.

Rex, John 1971: Typology and objectivity: a comment on Weber's four sociological methods. In Arun Sahay (ed.), *Max Weber and Modern Sociology.* London: Routledge.

Riesebrodt, Martin 1980: Ideen, interessen, rationalisierung. *Kölner Zeitschrift für Soziologie und Sozialpsychologie,* 32 (1), 111–29.

Roth, Guenther 1968: Introduction. In Max Weber, *Economy and Society.* Edited and translated by Guenther Roth and Claus Wittich. New York: Bedminster Press, xxvii–ciii.

——— 1971a: The genesis of the typological approach. In Reinhard Bendix and Guenther Roth, *Scholarship and Partisanship.* Berkeley: University of California, 253–65.

——— 1971b: Sociological typology and historical explanation. In Reinhard Bendix and Guenther Roth, *Scholarship and Partisanship.* Berkeley: University of California Press, 109–28.

——— 1971c: Max Weber's comparative approach and historical typology. In Ivan Vallier (ed.), *Comparative Methods in Sociology.* Berkeley: University of California Press, 75–93.

——— 1976: History and sociology in the work of Max Weber. *British Journal of Sociology,* 27 (3), 306–18.

———1993: Between cosmopolitanism and ethnocentrism. *Telos,* 96, 148–62.

Salomon, Albert 1934: Max Weber's methodology. *Social Research,* I (May), 147–68.

—— 1935: Max Weber's sociology. *Social Research*, II (Feb.), 60–73.

—— 1962: *In Praise of Enlightenment.* Cleveland: World Publishing Co.

Scaff, Lawrence 1989: *Fleeing the Iron Cage: culture, politics and modernity in the thought of Max Weber.* Berkeley: University of California Press.

Schelting, Alexander von 1922: Die logische Theorie der historischen Kulturwissenschaft von Max Weber und im besonderen sein Begriff des Idealtypus. *Archiv für Sozialwissenschaft und Sozialpolitik*, 49, 623–752.

—— 1934: *Max Webers Wissenschaftslehre.* Tübingen: Mohr.

Schluchter, Wolfgang 1979: The paradox of rationalization: on the relation of ethics and world. In Guenther Roth and Schluchter, *Max Weber's Vision of History.* Berkeley: University of California Press, 11–64.

—— 1981: *The Rise of Western Rationalism.* Berkeley: University of California Press.

—— (ed.) 1983: *Max Webers Studie über Konfuzianismus und Taoismus.* Frankfurt: Suhrkamp.

—— (ed.) 1984: *Max Webers Studie über Hinduismus und Buddhismus.* Frankfurt: Suhrkamp.

—— 1989: *Rationalism, Religion, and Domination: a Weberian perspective.* Berkeley: University of California Press.

—— 1996: *Paradoxes of Modernity.* Berkeley: University of California Press.

Schroeder, Ralph 1992: *Max Weber and the Sociology of Culture.* London: Sage.

Seidman, Steven 1983: *Liberalism and the Origins of European Social Theory.* Berkeley: University of California Press.

Seyfarth, Constans and Schmidt, Gert 1982: *Max Weber Bibliographie: Eine Dokumentation der Sekundärliteratur.* Stuttgart: Enke Verlag.

Sica, Allen 1988: *Weber, Irrationality, and Social Order.* Berkeley: University of California Press.

Smelser, Neil J. 1976: *Comparative Methods in the Social Sciences.* Englewood Cliffs, NJ: Prentice-Hall.

Tenbruck, Friedrich 1959: Die Genesis der Methodologie Max Webers. *Kölner Zeitschrift für Soziologie und Sozialpsychologie*, 11, 573–630.

—— 1977: Abschied von "Wirtschaft und Gesellschaft." *Zeitschrift für die gesamte Staatswissenschaft*, 133, 703-36.

—— [1975], 1980: The problem of thematic unity in the works of Max Weber. *The British Journal of Sociology*, 31 (3), 316–51. Originally published in *Kölner Zeitschrift für Soziologie und Sozialpsychologie*, 27, 663–702.

Truzzi, Marcello 1974: *Verstehen: subjective understanding in the social sciences.* Reading, Mass.: Addison-Wesley.

Turner, Bryan 1992: *Max Weber: from history to modernity.* London: Routledge.

—— 1996: *Weber and Islam*, 2nd edn. London: Sage.

Turner, Stephen P. and Factor, Regis 1994: *Max Weber: the lawyer as social thinker.* London: Routledge.

Warner, R. Stephen 1970: The role of religious ideas and the use of models in Max Weber's comparative studies of non-capitalist societies. *Journal of Economic History*, 30, 74–99.

—— 1972: The methodology of Max Weber's comparative studies. Unpublished dissertation: University of California at Berkeley.

—— 1973: Weber's sociology of nonwestern religions. In Robert W. Green (ed.),

Protestantism, Capitalism, and Social Science: the Weber thesis controversy,
Lexington, Mass.: D. C. Heath and Co, 32–52.
Weber, Max [1923], 1927: *General Economic History,* tr. Frank H. Knight.
Glencoe, Ill.: Free Press. Originally: [1923]. *Wirtschaftsgeschichte,* ed. S.
Hellman and M. Palyi. Munich: Duncker & Humblot.
—— [1920], 1930: *The Protestant Ethic and the Spirit of Capitalism,* tr. Talcott
Parsons. New York: Scribner's. Originally: [1920], 1972. In *Gesammelte
Aufsätze zur Religionssoziologie* (hereafter *GARS*), Vol. 1. Tübingen: Mohr,
1–206.
—— 1946a: *From Max Weber,* tr. and ed. H. H. Gerth and C. Wright Mills. New
York: Oxford.
—— [1920], 1946b. Introduction [The social psychology of the world religions].
In *From Max Weber*, 267–301. Originally: [1920], 1972. Einleitung. In *GARS*,
Vol. 1, 237–68.
—— [1920], 1946c: Religious rejections of the world. In *From Max Weber: essays
in sociology,* ed. and tr. H. H. Gerth and C. Wright Mills. New York: Oxford,
323–59. Originally: [1920], 1972. Zwischenbetrachtung. In *GARS*, Vol. 1, 537–
73.
—— 1947: *Max Weber: the theory of social and economic organization,* tr. Talcott
Parsons. New York: The Free Press.
—— [1922], 1949: *The Methodology of the Social Sciences,* ed. and tr. Edward A.
Shils and Henry A. Finch. New York: Free Press. Originally: [1922], 1973. In
Gesammelte Aufsätze zur Wissenschaftslehre, ed. Johannes Winckelmann.
Tübingen: Mohr, 489–540, 146–214, 215–90.
—— [1920], 1951: *Confucianism and Taoism* (tr. as *The Religion of China*), ed.
and tr. Hans H. Gerth. New York: The Free Press. Originally: [1920], 1972.
Konfuzianismus und Taoismus. In *GARS*, Vol. 1, 276–536.
—— [1920], 1952: *Ancient Judaism,* ed. and tr. Hans H. Gerth and Don
Martindale. New York: Free Press. Originally: [1920], 1971. *Das antike
Judentum.* In *GARS*, Vol. 3.
—— [1920], 1958: *The Religion of India.* ed. and tr. Hans H. Gerth and Don
Martindale. New York: The Free Press. Originally: [1920], 1972. *Hinduismus
und Buddhismus.* In *GARS*, Vol. 2.
—— [1891], 1966: *Die Römische Agrargeschichte.* Amsterdam: Schippers.
—— [1921], 1968: *Economy and Society,* ed. Guenther Roth and Claus Wittich.
New York: Bedminster Press.
—— [1889], 1970: *Zur Geschichte der Handelsgesellschaften im Mittelalter.*
Amsterdam: E. J. Bonset.
—— [1910], 1972: *Max Weber: Die protestantische Ethik II, Kritiken und
Antikritiken,* ed. Johannes Winckelmann. Hamburg: Siebenstern Verlag.
—— [1903–6], 1975: *Roscher and Knies: the logical problems of historical
economics.* New York: Free Press. Originally: [1903–6], 1975. In *Gesammelte
Aufsätze zur Wissenschaftslehre,* ed. Johannes Winckelmann. Tübingen:
Mohr, 1–145.
—— [1924], 1976a: *The Agrarian Sociology of Ancient Civilizations,* tr. R. I.
Frank, London; NLB. Originally: [1924], 1988. In *Gesammelte Aufsätze zur
Sozial- und Wirtschaftsgeschichte.* Tübingen: Mohr/UTB, 1–288.
—— [1921], 1976b: *Wirtschaft und Gesellschaft,* ed. Johannes Winckelmann.
Tübingen: Mohr.

—— [1924], 1988: Der Streit um den Charakter der altgermanischen Sozialverfassung in der deutschen Literatur des letzten Jahrzehnts. In *Gesammelte Aufsätze zur Sozial- und Wirtschaftsgeschichte*. Tübingen: Mohr/UTB, 508–56.

Whimster, Sam and Lash, Scott (eds) 1987: *Max Weber, Rationality and Modernity*. London: Allen & Unwin.

Winckelmann, Johannes 1980: Die Herkunft von Max Webers "Entzauberungs-Konzeption." *Kölner Zeitschrift für Soziologie und Sozialpsychologie*, 32 (1), 12–53.

Zaret, David 1980: From Weber to Parsons and Schutz: the eclipse of history in modern social theory. *American Journal of Sociology*, 85 (3), 1,180–1,201.

—— 1994: Max Weber und die Entwicklung der theoretischen Soziologie in den USA. In Gerhard Wagner and Heinz Zipprian (eds), *Max Webers Wissenschaftslehre*. Frankfurt: Suhrkamp, 332–66.

8

W. I. Thomas and Robert E. Park: Conceptualizing, Theorizing, and Investigating Social Processes

Martin Bulmer

INTRODUCTION

Some eighty years ago, looking back in 1916 to the previous fifty years of sociology in the United States, Albion Small, head of department at the University of Chicago, lamented that his subject had become established in the United States without a distinctive intellectual content, a distinctive method, or even a point of view (Small, 1916). Twenty years later in 1936, or thirty years later in 1946, no one could have argued for such a view, and the picture was very different.

Two of the most influential figures in the process of making American sociology different were William Isaac Thomas and Robert Ezra Park. They were by no means the only figures making the discipline different. In another chapter in this volume, the influence of George Herbert Mead, a philosopher, is discussed, and one could make a convincing case for adding as sociologists requiring major reassessment for the period up to 1940 Ernest Burgess, George Lundberg, Robert Lynd, W. F. Ogburn, Pitrim Sorokin, Samuel Stouffer, Florian Znaniecki, and possibly others. The work of the younger Parsons has received increasing attention (see Camic, 1991). Mead, Parsons, and Sorokin apart, the contribution made by these others was not primarily theoretical, whereas what Thomas and Park contributed was in significant respects theoretical.

This, however, is not the conventional view, which has been to see these two figures as primarily empirical sociologists who opened up new research agendas, but are not part of the highest reaches of the sociological pantheon inhabited by theorists. The argument of this chapter is that Thomas and Park are significant and neglected sociological theorists. Arguments such as that "the history of sociology in America of the 1920s is indeed the history of institutional rather than intellectual success" (Hawthorn, 1987, p. 209), or that the students of Park and Burgess "went through a transformation away from 'do-gooderism' to something akin to intellectual voyeurism" (Turner and Turner, 1990, p. 48), miss the significance of the changes that took place in American sociology between about 1915 and 1935, and the point that what Thomas and Park injected was a way of seeing the world theoretically.

W. I. Thomas is most often remembered as the co-author of one of the first notable empirical monographs in American sociology, *The Polish Peasant in Europe and America* (written with Florian Znaniecki) (1918–20), while R. E. Park is remembered for the group of studies carried out by his students in and on the city of Chicago. Why should they appear alongside Marx, Comte, Spencer and Durkheim in this volume? I want to argue both for their historical significance in the development of sociology, and for their contemporary relevance as theorists. Both turned sociology in the United States in a more empirical direction, but that does not mean that they were empiricists. Both had finely tuned theoretical antennae. Their conception of theory may have been rather different from that of Comte or Spencer, but they are in many respects closer to the use of theory in contemporary sociology than Comte and Spencer are, notwithstanding the rise of neo-evolutionism in recent years. Sociology today is what it is in part as a result of the influence of Thomas and Park. For this and other reasons they are therefore worth attending to.

BACKGROUND AND CONTEXT

The first third of the twentieth century was a defining period for American sociology, in which the more speculative works of the first generation, by Ward, Sumner, Ross, Giddings, and Small, were succeeded by a more empirical turn (see Shils, 1980, pp. 95–133). Thomas and Park were both instrumental in making that turn, while at the same time infusing the sociology of the period with some theoretical muscle. The latter is the subject of this paper. But the significance of the empirical turn needs emphasizing, even though it is not peculiar to sociology.

American sociology today, and indeed much of sociology world-
wide, is characterized by an empirical orientation based on the use of
powerful methods, some of them not available to other disciplines
such as economics or history, for the empirical investigation of the
social world. Although individual social investigators made important studies during the nineteenth century, and the early
twentieth-century works of Durkheim, Max Weber, Charles Booth,
and W. E. B. DuBois are still landmarks of empirical inquiry, such
studies were fragmentary. Indeed, in 1900, one could hardly refer to
a discipline of sociology with a substantial empirical base, although
departments of that name had begun to be established in American
universities. W. I. Thomas and Robert Park were key figures in the
development of the discipline in an empirical direction, and part of a
wider movement in the social sciences – evident also in economics,
psychology, political science, and social anthropology – towards a
more concentrated focus upon the investigation of contemporary
American society (see Ross, 1991, pp. 390–470). Sociology became
established more solidly from 1900 onwards for many reasons, but
partly because its subject matter – which included the study of urban
problems, race and ethnic relations, crime and deviance, and gender
– addressed subjects that no other discipline regarded as central.
Possessing a distinctive subject matter, and doing so in the context
of a general societal predisposition toward empirical inquiry, the
stage for sociology's growth was set, although in the period before
1945 the actual growth was rather modest (Halliday and Janowitz,
1992). This historical legacy, moreover, has tended to become the
conventional wisdom: viz., that Chicago sociology, as represented by
its leading spokesmen Thomas and Park, turned American sociology
away from armchair theorizing to empirical inquiry, perhaps even
reducing the impact of grand theory in the period when the two
figures had maximum influence.

There is an element of caricature of the sociological enterprise in
this way of characterizing empirical sociology. Sociology is nothing if
it is not a generalizing discipline, and all sociology worth its salt
aspires to produce results of general significance. Not only did
Thomas and Park aspire to make generalizations, they also sought to
develop theoretical formulations that adequately captured some of
the more general processes at work. So to view them as preoccupied
with documenting the problems faced by migrant Poles in Chicago,
or with describing the micro-sociology of the juvenile gang or the
hobo or the ghetto, was, and is, a misunderstanding of their general
significance of considerable proportions.

Thomas and Park are often linked together; Thomas was born in

1863, Park in 1864; Park died in 1944, Thomas in 1947. They were of the same generation. Inseparably linked in the sociological canon with the University of Chicago, they only taught briefly there together between Park's arrival at Chicago in 1913 and Thomas's dismissal in 1918, although remaining in touch after Thomas moved to New York. Thomas was a Chicago faculty member of the Sociology Department from 1895 to 1918; Park from 1914 to 1934, initially part time. While Park only turned to academic sociology at the age of 50, Thomas was forcibly ejected from his academic position at the age of 55, though he thereafter actively pursued his sociological interests as an independent scholar (Coser, 1977, pp. 366–83, 530–6). The two men first met in 1912 when Thomas attended a conference which Park organized at Tuskegee, and they struck up an immediate rapport. Thomas then became instrumental in bringing Park back into academic life, initially via a part-time appointment. Immediately after the conference, Thomas wrote to Park: "I am amazed to find how ignorant I was before I met you, and how wise I seem to be now. Truly it was a great experience to meet you"; Park reported that "I found in Thomas, almost for the first time, a man who seemed to speak the same language as myself" (Bulmer, 1984, pp. 61–2).

However one defines the influence of the "Chicago School," and whether one treats it in terms of individuals and their subsequent influence, or in terms of the institutionalization of the discipline and its partial hegemony for the period 1915 to 1935, Thomas and Park are at the center of its claim to be taken seriously. They were both keenly interested in understanding the ways in which the world works. Thomas was perhaps the more adventurous theorist, Park the more perspicacious formulator of theoretical propositions, but they complemented each other, while sharing a focus upon phenomena which helped to give American sociology a distinctive character. What do I mean by this?

GENDER AND "RACE"

There is in the present much interest in gender and "race" as key sociological phenomena and central theoretical issues. In the UK today, at least, they stand alongside social stratification as a triptych of central theoretical and empirical concern. It is my impression that gender and "race" are at least as central if not more so to theoretical interpretations of American society today. W. I. Thomas in his work focused particularly upon gender and ethnicity, Robert Park and his students upon "race" and ethnicity. For this reason alone, we should pay fresh attention to the contribution of Thomas and Park, whose impact may be taken much too much for granted.

This impact was exerted on several fronts: the substantive concerns of sociology; the methodological orientation of sociology; the classification of social phenomena; and the development in embryo of a theory of social process. All these areas changed distinctively as a result of the influence of Thomas and Park. In some respects, contemporary sociology still follows maxims or directions which they established. For example, there has been a recent revival of interest in Thomas's early work on gender, which is less well known than his and Park's work on ethnicity and race. Described by Deegan (1988, p. 202) as "a major theorist in the sociology of women," his ideas and writings on the subject went through a series of transitions.

Thomas's Ph.D. dissertation of 1897 on the origins of the sexual division of labor in society posited separate spheres for men and women on the basis of distinct metabolic types of 'katabolic' and 'anabolic' energy (Rosenberg, 1982, pp. 122–3). By 1907, when he published a reader *Sex and Society*, Thomas was moving toward a functionalist view, influenced by some of his colleagues in psychology, who put more emphasis on woman as a purposive agent adapting to an ever-changing environment. The transition is evident if one compares his 1899 article "The psychology of modesty and clothing" (Thomas, 1899), which argued that modesty was a habit rather than an instinct, a practical aid to psychological equilibrium, with that of 1906 (Thomas, 1906), on "The adventitious character of women," focusing on the female criminal. Here Thomas argued that female criminality resulted from the failure of the group in which a woman lived to satisfy the basic desires for activity and response that motivated all people, men and women alike – thus prefiguring his theory of the four wishes. These themes were pursued two decades later in Thomas's *The Unadjusted Girl* (Thomas, 1923; see also Platt, 1992). His work in the field of gender would make an excellent topic for further research, for his pioneering role as a man sympathetic to women's aspirations, and having large numbers of women students, has been unduly neglected.

The interest of W. I. Thomas in ethnicity and of Robert Park in ethnicity and race is better known and more extensively documented. Thomas and Znaniecki's study of *The Polish Peasant* sought to understand the dynamics of Polish–American migration and problems of adaptation and integration of the new migrants into urban America. The work of Park and his students, focused around urban structure, examined a variety of aspects of race and ethnicity. Charles S. Johnson studied the Negro in Chicago, Emory Bogardus social distance, Everett Stonequist the marginal man, E. T. Thompson the plantation, Pauline Young the pilgrims of Russian Town in Los Angeles. Park himself ruminated about social relations between the races, undertook a survey of race relations in the Pacific, traveled in China, and formulated as theory a cycle of race relations in which interracial contact was followed by conflict, competition, accommodation, and ultimately assimilation. These concerns were distinctive and helped to establish sociology as an autonomous discipline. Together with gender, they are also modern concerns.

THE SUBSTANTIVE CONCERNS OF SOCIOLOGY

Thomas and Park pushed sociologists in the direction of particular substantive concerns, and these concerns interacted with their theoretical interests. Both were intrigued by the social circumstances of the society in which they lived. In addition to gender and ethnicity, Thomas sought to understand phenomena such as deviance, and to formulate social psychological theories of the foundations of behavior, such as the four wishes and the definition of the situation. *The Polish Peasant* included an extended "Methodological note," (to which Znaniecki also contributed a good deal) setting out the scientific principles on which the study was based. Robert Park's interests were if anything broader, centered around urban structure and process, but extending through the work of his students, to include deviance and outsiders such as the hobo, political phenomena such as strikes and revolution, and institutions such as hotels and real estate. One of Park's principal interests, reflecting his background as a reporter, was in the news and public opinion, and more generally in the phenomena of social movements and collective behavior. He and Thomas collaborated in a study of the immigrant press and its control.

But what above all characterized Thomas and Park, and distinguished them from several of the other sociologists discussed in this volume, was their commitment to empirical social inquiry informed by, and carried out in close conjunction with, more general sociological concepts, ideas, and theoretical formulations. Research and theory reinforced and complemented each other. Neither sociologist was content to remain in the library. Famously, Park enjoined his students to seek out the real world:

You have been told to go grubbing in the library, thereby accumulating a mass of notes and a liberal coating of grime. You have been told to choose problems wherever you can find musty stacks of routine records based on trivial schedules prepared by tired bureaucrats and filled out by reluctant applicants for aid or fussy do-gooders or indifferent clerks. This is called "getting your hands dirty with real research." Those who counsel you are wise and honorable; the reasons they offer are of great value. But one more thing is needful: first hand observation. Go and sit in the lounges of the luxury hotels and on the doorsteps of the flophouses; sit on the Gold Coast settees and on the slum shakedowns; sit in the Orchestra Hall and in the Star and Garter Burlesk. In short, gentlemen, go get the seat of your pants dirty in *real* research. (quoted in Lofland, 1971, p. 2)

This orientation could be traced back to Park's earlier career as a journalist, which he pursued first in Minneapolis and then in New York, Detroit and Chicago between 1889 and 1898. As a reporter on a city beat, Park fulfilled the role of the informal and intuitive sociologist,

acting as eyes, ears and moral censor for the audience removed by size and distance from the direct exercise of these traditional communal roles. As the specialized crystallization of what had been a generalized means of social control, the reporter gave his readers information not only about singular happenings – murders, elections, stuffed ballot boxes – but also about the slower changes in environment which underlay these colorful events – the growth of new urban neighborhood and institutions, the appearance of novel personality types, ways of making and spending money, modes of entertainment. (Matthews, 1977, p. 10)

One of the characteristics of the reporter was detachment from the urban life being studied, viewing it with natural curiosity rather than through the moralistic spectacles so characteristic of the Protestant middle class of the time. Though they did not know each other at the time, Thomas shared a similar orientation to Park, inquiring into the social circumstances of the new urban dwellers in Chicago, mixing with immigrants and slum-dwellers, venturing where most middle-class academics would not dream of going. "I remember that [Chicago] Professor [Charles] Henderson, of sainted memory, once requested me to get him a bit of information from the saloons. He said that he had never himself entered a saloon or tasted beer" (Thomas, [1928], 1973, p. 248). Park at one point in New York had sampled opium while trying to investigate a gambling ring.

This was not, however, pure social description on the part of either Park or Thomas. As he peregrinated the city, Park ruminated upon the nature of city life as he experienced and observed it. "I expect that I have actually covered more ground, tramping about in cities in different parts of the world, than any other living man. Out of all this [he later recalled], I gained among other things, a conception of the city, the community and the region, not as a geographical phenomenon merely but as a kind of social organism" (Park, [1944], 1950, p. viii). At around the same time, Thomas was grappling with ideas about the basis of social difference and using observations, made by himself but principally by others, to develop his ideas about the basis of gender differences in society.

Thomas was interested in and read widely in anthropology, both nineteenth-century evolutionist ethnology and physical anthropology (see Stocking, 1968, pp. 247–69). But he also read extensively in contemporary ethnology, and in this he found evidence for the reinterpretations of sex and race that he developed between the late 1890s and 1910. At this point, he abandoned the evolutionary theory with which he had begun, along with its assumptions that characteristics of sex and race were fixed and immutable, and realized that the evidence about primitive societies pointed to great instability in the definition of these properties. The work of Franz Boas made a particular impact upon him, as did Gabriel Tarde's idea that mental development takes place not via the evolution of the brain, but through the imitation that occurs when one group comes into contact with another.

These developments in Thomas's thought in the first few years of the century were profoundly shaped by his observations in the immigrant neighborhoods in Chicago, where he spent much time. The massive changes in behavior and ways of life among immigrants newly arrived in the city could not be explained by the old evolutionary theory. The individuals he observed were not instinctual beings directed by fixed patterns of behavior, but purposive agents adjusting to an ever-changing environment. His analysis of the position of women, evident in his 1906 article on "The adventitious character of women," drew from his experience teaching women students who departed from the current stereotypes of femininity and passivity, as well as from his interaction with women in public positions such as Jane Addams and Florence Kelley. When Thomas published *Sex and Society* in 1909 he wrote to Addams:

I think I shall appreciate your noticing my book more than anything
that could happen to it. At the same time, I want you to know that I
hope you will not be sparing of your criticism and that anything of this
sort will interest me almost more than anything good you may be able
to say. (Deegan, 1988, p. 129)

In his work first on sex and gender, and then on *The Polish Peasant*,
Thomas laid the foundations on which Park and Ernest Burgess
were able to build after Thomas's departure from the University of
Chicago in 1918. Park's students filled out the picture of urban
structure for which Park had provided the overall view. But this was
a view grounded in the intimate acquaintance with actual human
behavior in its urban manifestations.

METHODOLOGICAL ORIENTATION

Thomas and Park adumbrated an approach to sociological
understanding and explanation that was distinctive – an approach
through which sociology as we now know it was established in the
United States. Their methodological orientations, though by no
means identical, emphasized the autonomy of the social in
explanation, a focus upon the individual as the unit of study, and an
action orientation that recognized the subjectively meaningful
character of human action. That all of these ideas are today taken for
granted owes a good deal to Thomas and Park.

W. I. Thomas's intellectual development would repay more study
than it has so far received. His critical contribution to the
conceptualization of "attitude" is well known. In the
"Methodological note" introducing *The Polish Peasant*, he
adumbrated a wholly sociological definition (or, more strictly, a
definition from the standpoint of sociological social psychology)
that excised biology from the determination of mental states and
orientations to human action (see Fleming, 1967). What, however,
had been the route by which Thomas reached this conclusion? In his
studies of the differences between the sexes in the first decade of the
century, how did he come to move away from a biologically based
view of sex differences to one that was almost entirely environmentally oriented? The influence of German "folk-psychology" and
of Franz Boas were both very important. Part of the task of studying
the history of sociology involves recovering some of the interdisciplinary influences at work on the field – and to these Thomas

was more open than most of his contemporaries. The extent to which he drew on folk psychology, ethnology, anthropology, and psychiatry was significant for the development of sociology as a discipline. Living in New York later in life, Thomas was still in active collaboration with the social psychiatrist Harry Stack Sullivan and the anthropologist Edward Sapir exploring some of the interdisciplinary frontiers of the social sciences (see Perry, 1982).

For Robert Park, influences from elsewhere were also important, particularly from the philosopher and psychologist William James. The influence of James's paper "On a certain blindness in human beings," combined with the urge to understand the social world from the point of view of the social actor – an urge reinforced, as Lyman (1992) has shown, by the years Park had spent working in the Congo Reform Association and at Tuskegee with Booker T. Washington – provided the basis for an orientation to sociological analysis in terms of subjectively meaningful social action. Park did not encapsulate this approach in a phrase such as Thomas's "definition of the situation," nor elaborate it in the manner that Florian Znaniecki formulated his theory of action (1936). But through the research of his students, Park's view was very influential in linking a particular sociological perspective up with concrete empirical research – and in recasting the discipline's primary methodological orientation. Many historical accounts of "symbolic interactionism," insofar as they relate to Thomas or Park rather than to Mead, seem to be a post factum reinterpretation at odds with the actual history of the approach. These accounts do, nevertheless, contain a kernel of truth. At the University of Chicago, under the influence initially of Thomas and Park, there developed an orientation to the interpretation of subjectively meaningful action that is now widely taken for granted, but was a novel innovation in their time.

CLASSIFICATION, CATEGORIZATION, AND REPORTAGE

The activity known as sociology, as W. G. Runciman (1983) has emphasized, may be distinguished in terms of four activities: description, classification, theoretical understanding, and reportage. Both Thomas and Park made singularly important contributions to the process of classification in sociology. Classificatory work was not in itself new, but it acquired novelty when Thomas and Park brought it into relation to empirical social research. In their eyes, classification was both a means of putting forward more general statements – nomothetic rather than ideographic in form, thus according with a sine qua non of sociology – and as a means of making sense of empirical materials that the sociologist has assembled either at first- or second-hand. Thomas and Park used materials of both kinds. Thomas collected extensive secondary materials on gender difference for his early researches and first-hand materials in the form of letters, diaries, and the life history for *The Polish Peasant*. Park drew on his first-hand acquaintance with urban life as a journalist, on his experiences in Congo Reform, and on the knowledge of the south and race relations he acquired at Tuskegee to inform his essays. Even more importantly, he encouraged his students to collect first-hand data to inform the analyses that they produced. In this respect, Thomas and Park more resembled social anthropologists such as Bronislaw Malinowski and A. R. Radcliffe-Brown than they did some of their predecessors in the first American generation of sociologists, such as E. A. Ross or William Graham Sumner.

Thomas's contribution was made through formative conceptualizations that have had an enduring influence upon the development of sociological social psychology (the definition of the situation, the four wishes, and so on) and revolved around the notion of types – as illustrated in *The Unadjusted Girl*. In Park's case, this interest in the typological analysis of empirical materials was even more marked and penetrating. Park sought to frame classificatory questions as a means to achieve the empirical understanding of the contemporary American city. Thus, in his famous essay on "The city" (Park 1915, p. 39), he posed the questions:

> What is news?
> What are the methods and motivations of the newspaper man?
> Are they those of an artist? an historian? or merely a merchant?
> To what extent does the newspaper control, and to what extent is it controlled by, public sentiment? . . .
> What is the difference between advertising and news?

Here one has a series of penetrating theoretical questions, lightly wearing their theoretical apparatus, but theory-laden nevertheless. For Park's sociological imagination was one that sought answers to general questions through the study of particulars. His student Norman Hayner, for example, reported an intensive discussion with Park on the question "what is a hotel"? and on the associated logical problems of the definition of this phenomenon. Given the patterns of American urban hotel residence at the time, the answer was not as simple as one might think, as Hayner's monograph on *Hotel Life* (Hayner, 1936) demonstrated. As Park himself put it:

> When a student proposed a topic for a thesis, I invariably found myself asking the question: what is this thing you want to study? what is a gang? what is a public? what is a nationality? What is a race in the sociological sense? What is graft? etc. I did not see how we could have anything like scientific research unless we had a system of classification and a frame of reference into which we could sort out and describe in general terms the things we were attempting to investigate. (Park quoted in Odum, 1951, p. 132)

Reportage, which played so important a role in Park's conception of sociology, was thus theoretically informed and part of an active process of making sense of the world. Lindner (1996) characterizes this approach in terms of "nosing around" and seeing with one's own eyes. " 'Go into the district,' 'get the feeling,' 'become acquainted with people' " – these were Park's injunctions to his students, urging them to get out in the field and experience society for themselves. Lindner suggests that Park's conception of himself as a captain of inquiry drew on an analogy between the professor directing students' research and the city editor directing a team of journalists. The difference was that Park had not only a sociological eye but a sociological cast of mind; he could thus locate the observations he and others made within a wider theoretically informed matrix.

EMBRYO THEORIES OF SOCIAL PROCESS

Thomas and Park are not usually thought of as general theorists in sociology; and they are certainly not in the sense in which someone like Talcott Parsons is a general theorist developing a general theoretical system. Both, however, were concerned to provide general theoretical orientations to, and explanations of, social processes, in the course of making sense of the changing social worlds that they observed. And both were quite insistent that doing so was a scientific task, distinct from the examination and treatment of social problems so characteristic of many of their contemporaries.

Thomas's *Source Book for Social Origins* (1909) offered a very important statement of his theory of social change. In this work, he identified three factors that together accounted for observable patterns of change: control, attention, and crisis. The stability of institutions depended on the observance of habit, the satisfaction of conditioned expectations, the maintenance of tradition, and the concentration of individual attention on traditional objects. In Thomas's scheme, "control" replaced Tarde's "imitation" and Gumplowicz's "conflict" as the central conception, and it was a conception inherently more sociological in its formulation. Thomas's analysis of "crisis," moreover, provided the basis of the theory of social disorganization that he developed. In his account, stability and change are explained in terms of the consistency and vigor of the attitudes and values that cultures provide for their members, and in terms of the ability of these values to satisfy the personal desires of individuals and give meaningful outlets for action within the established rules of conduct. Although social psychological in orientation, Thomas here implicitly provided a way of bridging micro-sociology and macro-sociology *and* a means of gaining concrete understanding of how social change impacted, for example, on the Poles as an ethnic group in migration and in the United States.

Robert Park developed these ideas further and gave them a deeper sociological cast. Although Park was historically oriented – his whole approach involving a focus on *process* rather than *structure* – he sought to frame generalizations whereby society could be understood. His theoretical contributions were several, and they have had a lasting impact, though more within subdisciplines than upon the field of general sociology. These contributions include:

1 *Ecological theory* (Park, [1921], 1952): an analysis of the development and growth of the city, drawing upon theoretical ideas originating in biology and then concretely applied to the study of the city of Chicago. This work exercised a powerful influence in Park's time and even up to the present on urban sociology and human geography.

2 *A theory of the "natural history" of social processes* (Park, [1921], 1955). This can be seen, for example, in Park's famous race relations cycle, which posited successive phases of contact, competition, conflict, accommodation, and eventual assimilation. Embodied in this formulation was an evolutionary view of social change, conceptualized in terms of a sequence of developmental stages in which one stage triggered the next (Park, [1926], 1950, pp. 149–51). Although this approach to generalization later proved difficult to substantiate and fell into disrepute, the concept of natural history still survives both in symbolic interactionism and in studies of occupations in the tradition of Park's student, Everett Hughes.

3 *A theory of social control* (Park, [1921], 1955). This aspect of Park's work focuses on the processes by which the individual is integrated into society. It addresses the question: "How does a mere collection of individuals succeed in acting in a corporate and consistent way?"

(Turner, 1967, p. xii). An empirical example of this interest was the research programme and analysis in the report on *The Negro in Chicago*, which was carried out, under Park's influence, by his friend Charles S. Johnson (see Chicago Commission on Race Relations, 1922). "Social control" was also the conceptual basis for the contribution Park believed that sociology could make to public policy (see Janowitz, 1975).

4 *A theory of collective behavior* (Park, [1921], 1955). Park named the field of collective behavior and identified the major elements involved in its study – thus reflecting his interest in Tarde and his own Berlin Ph.D., published as *The Crowd and the Public* (1904). Defining society as the traditional and established patterns of cooperation, Park viewed the central problem in the study of collective behavior as that of identifying the processes by which society is formed and reformed. He paid detailed attention to the sect, to news, and to morale as empirical instances of the processes by which the individual components of society were integrated. Public opinion and mores are collective responses to changing situations. To Park, collective behavior referred to the process, social control to the mechanism, whereby the larger problem of human collaboration in societies is accomplished.

Park and his students also introduced a significant number of sociological concepts of some lasting significance, including the marginal man, social distance, the zone of transition, and the public.

CONCLUSION: THE INTEGRATION OF THEORY AND RESEARCH

The significance of W. I. Thomas and Robert Park for a volume of essays on sociological theory lies in the extent to which the two thinkers offered the possibility of integrating sociological theory with the study of real world issues. Thomas and Park's theoretical contributions were not mainly as "stepping stones to the middle distance" or as "theories of the middle range," but as orientations to the collection of sociological data and to the integration of theory and research. This integration is something nowadays taken for granted, but in the early decades of the century it was a comparative novelty. It was this feature that distinguished the writings of Thomas and Park from those of progressive "do-gooders" (whom Park so much despised) and from the early social investigators who documented the social conditions of the slums in largely empiricist terms. One exception to this pattern was W. E. B. DuBois's study of the Philadelphia Negro (Bulmer, 1991); but at the time of this work DuBois was almost entirely ignored by white sociologists, who later defined him as a race activist, rather than fellow social scientist, after he joined *The Crisis* in 1910 (for a fuller account, see Lewis, 1993).

Scholars who portray Thomas and Park, and early Chicago sociology more generally, merely as part of the *institutional* establishment of American sociology miss the point. Hawthorn's (1987) condescending critique is particularly off target, mistakenly based as it is either on an antipathy to empirical inquiry or on the conviction that American sociologists are simply not on a par with their European coevals. The *hauteur* of the grand theorist is of course a fairly general phenomenon, as is the belief that thinkers of great thoughts are somehow on a higher plane than men and women who conduct mere empirical inquiries. What those who espouse this belief are guilty of is not only unrealistic condescension, but a failure to appreciate the central sociological challenge of bringing theoretical ideas and empirical data *together* in conjunction and confrontation with one another. Only when more general ideas inform research, and when the results of research are confronted with more general formulations, will sociology as a discipline advance. Thomas and Park perhaps did not achieve a perfect blending of the activities, but they went a very long way to bringing theory and evidence into relation with each other.

In their institutional analysis of twentieth-century American sociology, Turner and Turner (1990) assert that the students of Park (and Burgess) were responsible for "a transformation away from "do-gooderism" to something akin to intellectual voyeurism" (p. 48) – a change that entirely overlooks the extent to which Thomas and Park offered a way of seeing the world theoretically. In focusing upon the institutional context in which sociology was practiced, Turner and Turner minimize the content of the field and the intellectual frame within which it was set (see Bulmer, 1994). In Park's case, this frame was not a grand overarching Parsonsian schema, which some scholars credit with establishing, at Harvard in the 1930s, the presence of sociological theory on the American scene. It was a more subtle but nevertheless theoretically informed orientation – an orientation that has greater affinities with sub-sequent developments in sociology than the work of many of the so-called great figures of sociological theory. Rather than the contrast that is often implicitly drawn between Thomas and Park and such theorists and system builders in economics as Alfred Marshall or Maynard Keynes, a far more fruitful comparison may be that between the Chicagoons' use of theory and the incorporation of theory into the discipline of social anthropology by scholars such as Malinowski, Radcliffe-Brown, and Nadel (Kuper, 1983).

More serious than these misleading critiques is the criticism that, under the influence of Thomas and Park, Chicago sociologists came to embody pragmatist philosophy working without the benefit of a formal theory. "In the absence of an integrated sociological theory, the discipline was organized around practice. In Chicago that practice was inspired by the driving enthusiasm of Robert Park" (Smith, 1988, p. 132). "Park taught sociology by example and eschewed both formal statements of methodology and theory. Thus, the model was not readily transmitted as either theoretical or methodological doctrine; at Chicago, it was taught through immersion and osmosis" (Turner and Turner, 1990, p. 49). This was indeed a key characteristic of the Chicago approach. As we have seen, however, this does not mean that the Chicago approach was atheoretical. Even if it did not involve elaborating a formal theoretical scheme, this approach *did* involve integrating empirical inquiry with more general insights. And the extent to which particular subfields of the discipline – the sociology of "race" and ethnicity, the sociology of deviance, urban sociology, the sociology of social problems, the study of collective behavior, for example – can trace their antecedents to studies carried out by Chicago sociologists is evidence of the enduring value and strength of this approach. It certainly involved a conception of the role of theory in sociology rather different from that found in the work of other theorists, but my argument is that this distinctive conception was precisely a strength that contributed to Thomas and Park's lasting influence.

Indeed, their work has left a considerably greater residue than did the writings of the first generation of American sociologists, Ward, Ross, Sumner, Small, and Giddings. Thomas and Park addressed modern issues, twentieth-century issues, issues that are still with us. To be sure, the specific terms in which Thomas addressed issues of gender and ethnicity, or Park issues of "race" and ethnicity, are not those used today, and they have been rightly criticized with the benefit of hindsight. But to stop with this observation is to neglect the fruitfulness of Thomas and Park's unique combination of methodological orientation (emphasizing the autonomy of the social, etc.), substantive puzzlement about the concrete transformations taking place in particular aspects of American society (sex roles, "race" and ethnicity, the city, deviant behavior, etc.), and their attempt to categorize social phenomena and to then frame explanations of social behavior.

FURTHER RESEARCH

Despite the burgeoning of research about the Chicago School of Sociology in recent years (see Faris, 1967; Carey, 1975; Bulmer, 1984; Kurtz, 1984; Harvey, 1987; Smith, 1988; Lindner, 1996), many issues remain to be studied further. Partly due to the lack of archival material, W. I. Thomas remains relatively neglected as a subject of research, and a biography is still not available. Central aspects of Thomas's work, including his research on gender and his peasant studies, still merit careful investigation. Thomas's evolutionary ideas have occasionally been touched on, but also deserve fuller treatment, as do his ideas on the relationship between sociology and social action. There is, in any event, much about Thomas's work that makes him now more our own contemporary than simply a founding father in the history of the discipline.

Park has, since the 1970s, been the subject of two biographies (Matthews, 1977; Raushenbush, 1979) and a monograph (Lindner, 1996); but, as the latter shows, there is still much material to be garnered and more to be written about him. One useful task would be the systematic examination of Park's influence in terms both of empirical research and sociological ideas, particularly in subfields such as collective behavior, race and ethnicity, urbanism, deviance, and the study of the news. Much of Park's work in these areas is now neglected, but investigation of it could throw important light on his larger sociological contribution. Both Thomas and Park could likewise provide valuable case studies relevant to the ongoing debate about the relationship between external funding, on the one hand, and the development of sociology as a body of ideas and a set of institutional practices, on the other (see Platt, 1996, pp. 142–99 for an overview of this debate). Thomas and Park's connection with this debate, which has rumbled on for many years since, provides a further reminder that both thinkers were acutely interested in the relationship between sociology and the wider society in which sociological research was conducted.

REFERENCES

Bulmer, Martin 1984: *The Chicago School of Sociology: institutionalization, diversity, and the rise of sociological research*. Chicago: University of Chicago Press.

—— 1991: W. E. B. DuBois as a social investigator: *The Philadelphia Negro*, 1899. In Martin Bulmer, Kevin Bales and Kathryn Kish Sklar (eds), *The Social Survey in Historical Perspective, 1880–1940*, Cambridge: Cambridge University Press, 170–188.

—— 1994: The institutionalization of an academic discipline, *Social Epistemology*, 8 (1), 3–8 (part of a symposium on Turner and Turner, 1990, including replies from the authors).

Camic, Charles (ed.) 1991: *Talcott Parsons: the early essays*. Chicago: University of Chicago Press.

Carey, James T. 1975: *Sociology and Public Affairs: the Chicago School*, Beverly Hills, Calif.: Sage.

Chicago Commission on Race Relations 1922: *The Negro In Chicago*. Chicago: University of Chicago Press.

Coser, Lewis 1977: *Masters of Sociological Thought: ideas in historical and social context*, 2nd edn. New York: Harcourt Brace Jovanovich.

Deegan, Mary Jo 1988: *Jane Addams and the Men of the Chicago School, 1892–1918*. New Brunswick, NJ: Transaction Books.

DuBois, W. E. B. [1899], 1967: *The Philadelphia Negro: a social study*. Philadelphia, Pa.: University of Pennsylvania. Reprinted by New York: Shocken Books.

Faris, Robert E. L. 1967: *Chicago Sociology, 1920–1932*. Chicago: University of Chicago Press.

Fleming, Donald 1967: Attitude: The history of the concept in America. *Perspectives in American History* 1, 287–365.

Halliday, Terence C. and Janowitz, Morris (eds) 1992: *Sociology and Its Publics: the forms and fates of disciplinary organization*. Chicago: University of Chicago Press.

Harvey, Lee 1987: *Myths of the Chicago School of Sociology*. Aldershot: Avebury.

Hawthorn, Geoffrey [1976], 1987: *Enlightenment and Despair*. Cambridge: Cambridge University Press.

Hayner, Norman 1936: *Hotel Life*. Chapel Hill, NC: University of North Carolina Press.

Janowitz, Morris 1975: Sociological theory and social control. *American Journal of Sociology*, 81, 82–108.

Kuper, Adam [1973], 1983: *Anthropology and Anthropologists: the Modern British School*. London: Routledge.

Kurtz, Lester 1984: *Evaluating Chicago Sociology*. Chicago: University of Chicago Press.

Lewis, David Levering 1993: *W. E. B. DuBois: biography of a race, 1868–1919*. New York: Henry Holt.

Lindner, Rolf [1990], 1996: *The Reportage of Urban Culture: Robert Park and the Chicago School*. Cambridge: Cambridge University Press (first published in German).

Lofland, John 1971: *Analyzing Social Settings*. Belmont, Calif.: Wadsworth.

Lyman, Stanford M. (ed.) 1992: *Militarism, Imperialism and Racial Accommodation: an analysis and interpretation of the early writings of Robert E. Park*. Fayetteville, Ark.: University of Arkansas Press.

Matthews, Fred H. 1977: *Quest for an American Sociology: Robert E. Park and the Chicago School*. Montreal: McGill-Queens University Press.

Odum, Howard 1951: *American Sociology: the story of sociology in the United States through 1950.* Westport, Conn.: Greenwood Press.

Park, Robert Ezra 1915: The city: suggestions for the investigation of human behavior in an urban environment. *American Journal of Sociology*, 20 (March), 577–612.

—— [1944], 1950: An autobiographical note. In Park, 1950, pp. v–ix.

—— [1926], 1950: *Race and Culture: the collected papers of Robert Ezra Park*, Vol. 1, ed. E. C. Hughes, J. Masuoka, R. Redfield, and L. Wirth. Glencoe, Ill.: Free Press.

—— [1921], 1952: *Human Communities: the city and human ecology: collected papers*, Vol. 2. Glencoe, Ill.: Free Press.

—— [1921], 1955: *Society: collective behavior, news and opinion, sociology and modern society: collected papers*, Vol. 3. Glencoe, Ill.: Free Press.

—— [1904], 1967: *Masse und Publikum*. Berne: Lack and Grunan. Published in English as *The Crowd and the Public.* Chicago: University of Chicago Press.

Park, Robert Ezra and Burgess, Ernest W. 1921: *Introduction to the Science of Sociology*. Chicago: University of Chicago Press.

Perry, Helen S. 1982: *Psychiatrist of America: the life of Harry Stack Sullivan.* Cambridge, Mass.: Belknap Press.

Platt, Jennifer 1992: Acting as a switchboard: Mrs Ethel Sturgess Dummer's role in sociology. *The American Sociologist*, 23 (3), 23–36.

—— 1996: *A History of Sociological Research Methods in America, 1920–1960.* Cambridge: Cambridge University Press.

Raushenbush, Winifred 1979: *Robert E. Park: biography of a sociologist.* Durham, NC: Duke University Press.

Rosenberg, Rosalind 1982: *Beyond Separate Spheres: intellectual roots of modern feminism*, New Haven, Conn.: Yale University Press.

Ross, Dorothy 1991: *The Origins of American Social Science*, Cambridge: Cambridge University Press.

Runciman, W. G. 1983: *A Treatise on Social Theory*, Vol. 1: *The Methodology of Social Theory*, Cambridge: Cambridge University Press.

Shils, Edward 1980: *The Calling of Sociology and Other Essays on the Pursuit of Learning.* Chicago: University of Chicago Press.

Small, Albion 1916: Fifty years of sociology in the United States. *American Journal of Sociology*, May, 1–56.

Smith, Dennis 1988: *The Chicago School: a liberal critique of capitalism.* Basingstoke: Macmillan.

Stocking, George W. Jr 1968: *Race, Culture and Evolution: essays in the history of anthropology.* New York: Free Press.

Thomas, William Isaac 1897: On a difference in the metabolism of the sexes. Ph.D. dissertation submitted to the University of Chicago.

—— 1899: The psychology of modesty and clothing. *American Journal of Sociology*, 5 (September), 246–62.

—— 1906: The adventitious character of woman. *American Journal of Sociology*, 12 (July), 32–44.

—— 1923: *The Unadjusted Girl: with cases and standpoint for behavior analysis.* Boston: Little Brown and Co.

—— [1928], 1973: Life history. *American Journal of Sociology*, 79, 248.

Thomas, William Isaac (ed.) 1907: *Sex and Society: studies in the social psychology of sex*. Chicago: University of Chicago Press.

—— (ed.) 1909: *Source Book for Social Origins: ethnological materials, psychological standpoint, classified and annotated bibliographies for the interpretation of savage society*. Chicago: University of Chicago Press and Boston: Richard Badger.

Thomas, William Isaac and Znaniecki, Florian [1918–20], 1927: *The Polish Peasant in Europe and America*. Boston: Richard G. Badger, 5 vols. Reprint edition 2 vols. by Alfred A. Knopf, New York.

Turner, Ralph H. (ed.) 1967: *Robert E. Park on Social Control and Collective Behavior*. Chicago: University of Chicago Press.

Turner, Stephen P. and Turner, Jonathan 1990: *The Impossible Science: an institutional analysis of sociology*. Newbury Park, Calif.: Sage.

Znaniecki, Florian 1936: *Social Actions*. New York: Farrar and Rinehart.

9

George Herbert Mead and the Renaissance of American Pragmatism in Social Theory

Hans Joas

There can be no doubt that American pragmatism has experienced, since approximately 1979, a genuine renaissance in intellectual life in America and, to some extent, the world over. I use this date, which may appear arbitrary, because 1979 witnessed the publication of Richard Rorty's highly influential study, *Philosophy and the Mirror of Nature*. In the introduction to this work, Rorty mentioned John Dewey in a way which has since become almost proverbial: namely, as standing, alongside Heidegger and Wittgenstein, as the most important philosopher of the twentieth century. There was irony in this. For in being classified by Rorty as belonging together both with the prototype of Continental philosophy and with the inaugurator of analytic philosophy, Dewey – who had never before been taken seriously as a philosopher in Europe and who had long been regarded as obsolete by powerful schools of American thought – suddenly rose in reputation in America. In this way, dialogue with Dewey's ideas became not the continuation of an uninterrupted cultural tradition, but the rediscovery of a neglected and underestimated heritage.

Yet, at almost the same time as this beginning of the recent revival of pragmatism, an American intellectual historian described the quiet disappearance of pragmatism from the discourse of American self-understanding as if it were an indisputable fact. "In

I would like to express my gratitude to Charles Camic for his help in improving the English style of this contribution and to Gary Allan Cook for his comments.

1980," wrote David Hollinger, " 'pragmatism' is a concept most American historians have proved they can get along without. Some nonhistorians may continue to believe that pragmatism is a distinctive contribution of America to modern civilization and somehow emblematic of America, but few scholarly energies are devoted to the exploration or even the assertion of this belief. The space devoted to pragmatism in textbooks has diminished markedly . . . The concept of pragmatism has not entirely disappeared from monographic and synthetic writing about American history and culture, but the decline in its popularity has been abrupt, has issued from no concerted attack upon it, and has gone virtually without comment" (1980, p. 88). While certainly accurate when it appeared, this description demonstrates how modest is our ability to predict cultural and intellectual developments.

This chapter is not the place for an extensive account of this renaissance of pragmatism, nor for an interpretation of its origins and causes. Suffice it to say that this development was an unexpected and dramatic phenomenon. If we follow Bernstein (1992a, 1992b) and consider anti-foundationalism, the fallible nature of truth, the social nature of the self, the importance of inquiry, and pluralism as the elements of the intellectual constellation we call "pragmatism," it becomes immediately clear that these elements are all right at the center of contemporary debates. For me it has always been striking how incredibly modern the problems with which the pragmatists dealt are (see Joas 1993, pp. 1–13). To write about pragmatism and to relate one's own thinking to historical pragmatism has become an almost fashionable activity among contemporary American philosophers. The renaissance of pragmatism is clearly an interdisciplinary phenomenon, exceeding in its sweep even the large range of topics present in the original pragmatists' writings. Indeed, the whole history of twentieth-century American thought has been redescribed in the light of this revival of pragmatism (Bernstein, 1992b; Kloppenberg, 1996).

Instead of attempting to analyze here all aspects of this development, I will restrict myself to the following three points. First, I will give a brief retrospective account of the state of research on George Herbert Mead at the time when I began my own work in this field. Second, I will attempt to summarize the present state of the art in the field of Mead research. Lastly, I will consider the relationship between the rediscovery of the ideas of pragmatists and recent developments in sociological theory.

264 Hans Joas

1

In the 1970s, the image of George Herbert Mead's work was rather disparate. There was not much connection between the reception of his writings in the social sciences, on the one hand, and in philosophy, on the other.[1]

The most important school of sociological theorizing and research that claimed to continue Mead's work was, of course, symbolic interactionism. And, indeed, Herbert Blumer, Anselm Strauss, and many other proponents of this approach deserve praise for creatively appropriating Mead's ideas and transforming them into imaginative projects of empirical sociological research. Symbolic interactionists never really attempted, however, to produce a comprehensive treatment of Mead's work. Their reception of his ideas was utterly fragmentary and – perhaps for this reason – somewhat one-sided. Neither the corporeal basis of human action, nor the large-scale and political aspects of societal life, received in symbolic interactionist work the same attention they had in Mead's own thinking (cf. Blumer, 1966).

A second social-scientific tradition of interpretation took advantage of Mead's self-characterization as a "behaviorist." Although Mead had made absolutely clear that his own brand of behaviorism was completely different from the anti-mentalistic reductionism of John Watson's psychology, during the time of behaviorist hegemony in psychology, several authors tried to include Mead in the behaviorist camp.[2] The fact that symbolic interactionists and behaviorists could each claim the same thinker for its own side produced considerable confusion, particularly given the opposition between the two groups on most theoretical and methodological points.

In philosophy, other views of George Herbert Mead took hold. In some quarters, his work became assimilated with "phenomenology" – via a process not unlike what happened when sociologists later intermingled symbolic interactionism, ethnomethodology, and ethnographic approaches into a unitary "interpretive approach." Maurice Natanson's *The Social Dynamics of George Herbert Mead* (1956) proved influential in this respect. Though Natanson himself

[1]For my own interpretation of Mead's work, see Joas, 1985a (original German edition [1980]), 1993, pp. 238–61. These sources offer more extensive discussion than is contained above of the older literature on Mead.
[2]This behaviorist interpretation has continued more recently in the hotly debated work of Lewis and Smith (1980) and Baldwin (1986).

showed some awareness of differences between Mead and phenomenologists like Alfred Schutz, in the reception of Natanson's work the
two thinkers emerged as the twin progenitors of the interpretative
strain of modern social thought.

Unrelated to this tendency among philosophers, certain specialists
in the history of American philosophy developed or continued an
interest in Mead that was inspired either directly by his teachings or
by the influence of his immediate disciples. Here analytical
philosophy and Whitehead's metaphysics became the main reference
points for the interpretation of Mead's thought. This was true in the
important work of David Miller (1973) and also in the writings of
Andrew Reck (1963) and Harold Lee (1963). The difficulty with the
Whiteheadian strain of this work, however, was that Mead's interest
in Whitehead was actually strong and important only during the last
ten years of Mead's life. The literature's emphasis on his late
"metaphysics of sociality" did not, for this reason, facilitate
understanding Mead's intellectual development in general, nor the
roots of those innovations that later established his fame among
symbolic interactionists and others. (Examining Mead's late work
would only serve these goals if we were to assume, a priori, that
Mead's development was without ruptures and that his later writings
thus articulate what was only implicit in his earlier works.) And the
relationship between Mead and analytic philosophy as an intellectual
tradition was certainly no closer than his relationship to
phenomenology.

Taken together, the secondary literature on Mead in the 1970s thus
increased confusion more often than it shed light on his writings. To
be sure, there were occasional suggestions of developing an interpretation of Mead's work in terms of its *pragmatist* origins – notably, in
the writings of sociologists Blumer and Strauss, as well as in the
research of philosophers Miller and Reck. But the connections
between these various interpretations were by no means fully clear.
Nor was there an attempt to describe the way in which Mead's work
had evolved: the heavy German influence on Mead was, for example,
almost completely ignored. In most cases, even the available
philological basis for a serious interpretation of Mead was neglected.
But some work at least tended in this direction, particularly that by
younger scholars like Gary Allan Cook (1972) and Sandra Rosenthal
(1969), who later became major voices in Mead research.

My own study of Mead (Joas, 1985a) tried to avoid these pitfalls
and to fill the obvious gaps in the literature. Making use of a large
number of bibliographical discoveries, particularly of Mead's early
publications, my goal was to provide an account of the development

of Mead's thinking and to demonstrate its basis in American *and* European philosophical traditions. Attention to Mead's political biography and role in public life had also been long overdue. The study gave particular emphasis to Mead's attempt to transform his philosophical views into a scientific approach to psychology; from this perspective, it also examined the gradual development of his theory of human communication in terms of symbolically mediated interaction. This analysis made it possible also to interpret lesser-known and previously-ignored aspects of Mead's work, including his ethics, his theory of temporality and historicity, and his integration of the developmental psychologies of cognitive and communicative abilities. At the time, it was my conviction that only through a comprehensive reconstruction and reexamination of his work could Mead's standing as one of the classical authors of philosophical pragmatism, social psychology, and sociology be ensured. This, moreover, was the standing claimed for Mead both by John Dewey and Alfred North Whitehead in their obituaries of him – and then by the symbolic interactionists in post-World War II sociology.

2

This chapter concentrates on George Herbert Mead because it is Mead's work that has formed the bridge between pragmatism and sociology. In the case of the other pragmatists this linkage has been more tenuous. Charles Peirce remained quite aloof from the questions of political theory and social science; and despite occasional efforts to emphasize his importance for sociology (see Rochberg-Halton, 1986), his work has been peripheral to sociology. William James and John Dewey were clearly influential upon the early generations of Chicago School sociology. But both thinkers later remained relatively marginal even in the symbolic interactionist tradition which claimed to continue the earlier Chicago School.

Despite his considerable interest in the social sciences, Mead never dreamed of becoming a sociologist. As he was elevated since his death into a classical figure in the discipline of sociology, he paid for this unrequested honor by the fragmentary sociological – and philosophical – reception of his work recounted in the previous section. Today, this situation has clearly changed. Students of Mead's work are no longer asked – as I was some fifteen years ago –whether this man was Margaret Mead's husband and whether a study of her husband is really worthwhile. Nevertheless, research about Mead is still in no sense the hot topic that research on Dewey and the pragmatists is; nor do debates about Mead play a comparable role in American self-understanding and public philosophy.

In any case, the sad history of Mead reception continues – and for reasons partly inherent in the subject. Mead was not the author of a single exemplary book that could produce its effects completely detached from its author. His publications and numerous unpublished manuscripts formed a large tissue that remained incomplete in every part and left many fringes. Wherever one starts with Mead's work, one gains the impression of a highly original approach which Mead lacked the vitality to elaborate comprehensively – perhaps because the time was not ripe. The remark by the German poet Heinrich Heine about the French composer Hector Berlioz often comes to mind when pondering Mead: He did not have enough talent for his genius.

Any attempt to assess the present state of the art in Mead research also immediately encounters the difficulty that, in contrast to the situation with other classic sociological thinkers, there is still no coordinated scholarly research on Mead at all. As a result, even the editorial situation of Mead's writings continues to be a disaster. There exists no edition of Mead's writings comparable to the editions of Dewey, James, and Peirce in philosophy, or the editions of Marx, Weber, and Simmel in sociology. The editors of Mead's posthumously published works in the 1930s never explained their selections from Mead's papers; they abridged and dismembered texts and combined them in new forms with new headings. Particularly in the case of texts based on students' notes (see Mead, 1934, 1936, 1938), while we should be grateful to scholars like Charles Morris for editing these works at all, their editions took such liberties in supplementing and amending the originals that one can never be sure whether a sentence is really Mead's or Morris's. This uncertainty extends even to passages crucial for characterizing Mead's approach and to some of the most famous quotations from *Mind, Self, and Society* (1934). And neither Miller's (1982) edition of other versions of Mead's social psychology class, nor Reck's (1964) selection and abridgement of some of Mead's essays, have subsequently improved the situation. From time to time, I hear of plans to edit Mead's correspondence, though I sometimes fear that premature publication of part of this will only increase the existing confusion. A serious critical edition of Mead's collected writings is urgently needed.

For all these difficulties, however, the bibliographical and historical study of Mead's work has made considerable progress in recent years. Gary Allan Cook's (1993) study of the life and work of Mead brings together his masterful earlier studies of Mead's intellectual developments and complements these with the most detailed available examination of Mead's earlier phase and the controversies at the University of Chicago that led to his retirement (and presumably to his death) in 1931. In addition, Dmitri Shalin (1988) has contributed to a better understanding of Mead's political activities and his role in progressive politics in Chicago during the Progressive Era.[3] Several authors have also examined Mead's importance for the sociology of women and feminism (Deegan, 1988; Aboulafia, 1993).

Also relevant are two more widely focused studies of the history of the American social sciences. The first of these is Andrew Feffer's *The Chicago Pragmatists and American Progressivism* (1993; see also Feffer, 1990), which covers terrain similar to Rucker's earlier *The Chicago Pragmatists* (1969). Feffer's is not simply a study of Mead's role as a democratic citizen, but of the whole cultural and political atmosphere in which the activities and scholarly efforts of Mead (and Dewey) took place. Feffer emphasizes two aspects underestimated in Joas (1985a). First, is the role, in late nineteenth-century America, of what he calls "producer republicanism": "an artisanal ethic celebrating the dignity of productive labor as the source of civic virtue and the foundation of just government" (1993, p. 11). Second, is the complicated conflict (which Feffer analyzes by drawing on the history of Protestant theology in America) between Christianity and Darwinism; as Feffer shows, this conflict had many more outcomes than has usually been assumed in reconstructions of the pragmatists' intellectual development. Feffer's important insights on these points are somewhat diluted, however, by his general interpretative framework in which he criticizes the Chicago pragmatists for their extreme naivete toward the reality of class conflict and for playing a mostly negative role in the transformation of America into a social order dominated by new capitalist elites.

Something similar must, unfortunately, be said about a second important work – the most ambitious study to date of the history of the American social sciences from the eighteenth century to 1929, namely, Dorothy Ross's *The Origins of American Social Science* (1991). Dedicating the whole third part of this study to the social sciences in the "Progressive Era," Ross examines the fundamental innovations within liberalism that were initiated throughout the social sciences by pragmatism, especially Dewey's pragmatism and

[3]It would also be a great favor to the scientific community if Harold Orbach, who knows more important details about Mead's life than anyone, would bring this information together in a full-fledged biography of Mead.

the functionalist psychology that resulted. For Ross, though, Dewey's writings (and very modern reaction to the historical changes of his time) are merely the exception that proves the rule: i.e., that the ideology of American exceptionalism – the alleged ideological core of the American tradition – remained in place despite all renovations. In taking this position, Ross exhibits a sympathy for socialist positions, which is unobjectionable in itself; but it is problematical that she simply dismisses Dewey and Mead's attempts to find a middle way as "centristic" and "opportunistic" without really justifying socialist interpretations of America and the political program aligned with them. To Ross, liberal and social democratic positions necessarily smack of a disheartened accommodation to capitalism. This perspective colors her extensive reconstruction of the concept of "social control" and its uses in research. Ross argues that this concept – which played so important a role for Mead – offered the ideal means for professionalized social science to claim leadership and dominance over urban and rural lower classes and over capitalists as well. But this interpretation is a clear misreading, backed not even by the author's own quotations. The pragmatist notion of social control did not posit a relation of control between society and individuals; instead, what the pragmatists took as their decisive conceptual starting point was collective *self-control* in groups of socialized individuals (for a more extensive treatment of Ross, see Joas, 1992).

Another important field of scholarship concerns the mutual intellectual influences between Mead and his American con-temporaries. Here there are still considerable voids, even about the relationship between Mead and John Dewey. When working on my own study of Mead (Joas, 1985a), my knowledge of Dewey was still very limited – as those such as Cook (1986) and Shalin (1986) rightly pointed out. But the scholarly situation has scarcely improved in recent years, for nobody has yet clarified the exact relationship between Dewey's early Hegelianism and Mead's concentration on problems of intersubjectivity; nor between Dewey's later work and Mead's further elaborations of his insights; nor between Dewey's metaphysics and Mead's metaphysical writings.

A study of the exact relationship between William James's writings and those of Mead would also be fruitful. One of my own students, Hans-Joachim Schubert, has recently completed a long-needed study of Charles Horton Cooley, which defends Cooley against Mead's criticisms (and against general sociological folklore) and demonstrates his important role in the development of the concept of the self (see

Schubert, 1995). But a study of the relationship between William
Isaac Thomas and Mead is still missing.[4]

The situation is much better in another area, namely the
comparison of Mead's work with comparable schools of thought.
Here the most fruitful recent research has centered on Mead and
phenomenology. As indicated above (see section 1), with American
scholarship before the 1970s, there was a misleading tendency to
lump phenomenology together with Meadian pragmatism or
symbolic interactionism. In this context, clarification of the exact
relationship between Mead's ideas and those of phenomenological
philosophers, psychologists, and sociologists became a serious
business. My own work (Joas 1985a) addressed this only in part. By
concentrating on the *differences* between Mead and Edmund
Husserl, the founder of the phenomenological movement, it
disguised the ways in which later so-called social-phenomenological
approaches actually came quite close to Mead's pragmatism in the
process of the immanent improvement and transformation of
Husserl's phenomenology. More than a decade ago, Bergmann and
Hoffmann (1985) already compensated for this lacuna in my work by
comparing Mead with Alfred Schutz, Aron Gurwitsch, Martin
Heidegger, Jean-Paul Sartre, and Maurice Merleau-Ponty. They did
all this in one essay, however, and it is fortunate that other scholars
have subsequently written much longer studies of the relationship of
Mead and various individual phenomenologists.

Rosenthal and Bourgeois (1991), for example, have carefully
analyzed Mead's similarities and dissimilarities with that most
brilliant of social-phenomenologists, Merleau-Ponty. Their study
sees Mead and Merleau-Ponty as united "in a shared rejection of
substance philosophy as well as the spectator theory of knowledge in
favor of a focus on the ultimacy of temporal process and the
constitutive function of social praxis. They both attempt to integrate
the characteristics of consciousness that emerges from its natural
empirical conditions with the idea of consciousness as the tissue of
significations," and for both Mead and Merleau-Ponty "this
intentional link is rooted . . . in the total corporeal dimension of
existence" (1991, p. 3). The relationship between Mead and Sartre has
been clarified by Aboulafia (1986), who focuses on the notion of the
self and the idea of self-determination. The German sociologist
Heuberger (1992) has analyzed Mead in relation to Schutz and

[4]On the parallels between Mead's ideas and those of Veblen, see Fontana et al.,
1992. For a comprehensive study of the importance of American Populism for
the early history of the social sciences in America, see Schimmer, 1996.

developed an ambitious program to synthesize the phenomeno-logical understanding of "experience" with the pragmatist logic of discovery; for him, phenomenology helps to transfer experience gained in "passive synthesis" into the abductive logics of creative hypothesis-formation (see my review of this work, Joas, 1995). Tugendhat, perhaps the leading German-language analytical philosopher, has compared Mead and Heidegger in *Self-Consciousness and Self Determination* (1986), a work full of in-teresting ideas, though resting on relatively shaky philological grounds. Jung (1995) has usefully situated Mead in relation both to Heidegger and to Wilhelm Dilthey. And Rehberg (1985) has examined Mead and the early proponents of German "philosophical anthropology," such as Max Scheler and Helmuth Plessner, who were also deeply influenced by phenomenology.

In an important study (completely neglected by sociologists), the philosopher Karen Hanson (1986) has placed Mead's theory of the self in relation to the ideas of Jean-Paul Sartre, Gilbert Ryle, and Ludwig Wittgenstein. Hanson takes issue with Mead over the question of whether the emergence of the self can be explained by the perception of one's own vocal gestures. In doing so, she possibly overestimates Mead's insistence on vocal gestures as the unavoidable "vehicle of transformation" (in my view, Mead was here making an empirical claim with respect to phylogeny not ontogeny), but the direction in which Hanson is heading is sound and innovative. She emphasizes the role of imagination in human communication, self-perception, and the emergence of the self; and this emphasis enables her not only to present a penetrating analysis of phenomena like self-deception and egocentricity, but also to provide a new interpretation of major parts of the Meadian heritage, notably the analysis of play and games.

This rich literature on Mead and phenomenology contrasts sharply with the paucity of work on the relationship between Mead and structuralism. The only contribution in this field I am aware of is a (German-language) study by Wagner (1993), which unfortunately deals mostly with an idiosyncratic form of structuralism proposed by Ulrich Oevermann. Wagner makes abundantly clear, however, that a comparison between Mead and structuralism heavily depends on an adequate understanding of Freud and Piaget. Poststructuralism has also aroused some interest among symbolic interactionists like Norman Denzin, although it has yet to inspire much new interpretative or "deconstructive" work. A very creative analysis that may be subsumed under this heading, though, is a study by Leys (1994) that examines Mead's theory of the genesis of the self with a view to the theory of imitation proposed by Gabriel Tarde and explicitly rejected by Mead. While I disagree with many details of Leys's analysis, her idea of identifying traits of the de-centered self in late nineteenth-century psychological writings on imitation, suggestion, hypnosis, and telepathy and of then relating Mead to these types of thinking is quite stimulating.

For East European intellectuals the way to Mead often goes via the most important Russian psychologist, L. S. Vygotsky. Indeed, it is astonishing how close the two thinkers were in some respects – and this despite their extremely different cultural and political backgrounds. Several authors, notably the Polish philosopher Koczanowicz (1994), have contributed to the understanding of the Mead–Vygotsky relationship. But more remains to be done, and other Russian thinkers, perhaps especially Mikhail Bakhtin, merit similar comparison with Mead. To make this relationship clearer, research on the Russian reception of pragmatism and early empirical psychology is also needed.

A final comparison noted in the recent scholarly literature relates Mead to functionalist theorists, especially Talcott Parsons. This may sound like a less interesting subject of investigation because Parsons was of a later generation of sociological theorists and thus actually had a chance – which he missed – to integrate Mead's thinking with his own approach. But Wenzel, who has written both on Parsons and on Mead (see Wenzel, 1985, 1990, 1991), relates the two via their common dialogue with Alfred North Whitehead. Wenzel emphasizes the importance of Whitehead's philosophy of "realism" for Parsons's early theory; in so doing, he criticizes the common interpretation of Parsons as a Kantian for its neglect of Parsons's antidualistic ambitions. However, Wenzel considers Mead's appropriation of Whitehead to be superior to Parsons's own. Moreover, he interprets Parsons's less critical attitude toward Whitehead as the source of a remaining dualism in Parsons that is analogous to Whitehead's dualism between "events" and "eternal objects." According to Wenzel, it is this remaining dualism that leads Parsons to assign a transcendental role in society to culture. Aside from Wenzel's research, Bender (1989) has made an attempt to compare Mead's work with the functionalist systems theory of Niklas Luhmann.

3

Consideration of the relationship between Mead and theorists like Parsons raises a final question: To what extent has contemporary sociological theory built upon the recent rediscovery of pragmatism? The question admits of no simple answer.

In some of the most ambitious contemporary syntheses, Mead and the other pragmatists are still completely absent. James Coleman's *Foundations of Social Theory* (1990), for example, mentions Mead only once and the other pragmatists not at all; and the one reference to Mead is a passing, awkward presentation of his concept of the self.

In other theoretical works, Mead is more in evidence but scarcely better understood. Here one may include the writings of Randall Collins. Collins (1989), the main proponent of a conflict approach in contemporary sociology, has ventured a synthesis of Mead's theory of mind and his own theory of "interaction ritual chains" – attempting to establish a kind of "neo-Meadian" sociology of mind. He combines this attempt with an effort to explain Mead's own intellectual development in a strictly nomological manner. In this way, Mead himself becomes a case study for the application of Collins's sociology of mind. But the responses thus far to Collins's attempt have been highly critical on the part of Mead scholars and symbolic interactionists alike (see, e.g., Joas, 1989).

Still another possibility is illustrated by the theoretical work of Anthony Giddens. Giddens's "theory of structuration" comes very close to Mead's thinking in some respects, e.g., in Giddens's notion of intentionality as the capacity for self-reflective control of ongoing behavior, his distinction between discursive and practical consciousness, and his interest in temporality and historicity. Yet, while he has offered long interpretations of other sociological classics and written extensively on interpretive schools of sociological research, Giddens has given little attention to the interpretation of the ideas of Mead and the other pragmatists. His theory has been influenced more clearly by Erving Goffman, ethnomethodological sociology, and Heideggerian philosophy than by Mead or pragmatism in general (see, e.g., Giddens, 1976). Inattention to the latter sources weakens the anthropological grounding of crucial assumptions in Giddens's theory.[5]

An even more complex case in this context is that of Jeffrey Alexander. In the four volumes of his ambitious *Theoretical Logic in Sociology* (1982–3), Alexander dealt extensively with Emile Durkheim, Karl Marx, Max Weber, and Talcott Parsons, but had

[5]For a more extensive discussion, see Joas, 1993, pp. 172–87. I should like to gratefully acknowledge, however, that it was Anthony Giddens who took the initiative to have my book on Mead translated into English (Joas, 1985a), thus making it available to other scholars interested in Mead.

literally nothing to say about Mead or pragmatism. He thus
continued the strange silence toward the pragmatists that Parsons
himself had kept in *The Structure of Social Action* (1937).
Alexander's attitude changed to some extent in *Twenty Lectures*
(1987), an analysis of American sociological theory after 1945 which
acknowledged the great importance of the pragmatist tradition and
provided a serious overview of the major sociological aspects of
Mead's work. Here Alexander even observed "that Mead's early
theory of interaction had the potential to make a considerable
contribution to theoretical debate in the post-Parsons period" (1987,
p. 214). "Unfortunately," he then continued, "this is not what has
happened at all" because symbolic interactionism moved away from
Mead's legacy (1987, p. 214). For Alexander, the divergence of
Blumer and Goffman from Mead remains more important than their
similarities; Blumer, for example, is interpreted as an
"individualistic" thinker who neglected the institutional and collective thrust of Mead's work. Yet, while there is certainly some truth in
this judgment, Alexander encounters difficulties when he places
Blumer and (a fortiori) Mead within his own framework of
metatheoretical alternatives. But this was not Alexander's last word
on the subject. For he has subsequently become more constructive
and less critical toward Mead and symbolic interactionism.
Following Eisenstadt's revisions of differentiation theory, Alexander
has, for example, proposed a theory of societal change focused on
"temporal development and the capacity of individuals and groups to
define and redefine their situation" as the macro-sociological
complement to symbolic interactionist micro-sociologies (Alexander,
1988, pp. 193–221, quoting p. 218). In other respects, too,
Alexander's theorizing has grown more synthetic – more open to
incorporating Mead's achievements as important elements of an
analytical frame of reference for sociological theory (see 1988, pp.
301–33). In his most recent work, moreover, Alexander's interest in
normative questions has become stronger; this development has
brought him closer to Dewey, Habermas, and other contemporary
authors influenced by them. As a result, Alexander now stands on the
verge of breaking with his previous "neo-functionalism" and moving
toward schools of thought inspired by pragmatism (see Alexander,
1996).

But the best-known exception to sociological theorists' neglect of
Mead remains the work of Jürgen Habermas. His *Theory of
Communicative Action* (1987) treats Mead – along with Weber,
Marx, and Durkheim – as one of the classics worthy of extensive
interpretation and considers Mead – alongside Wittgenstein and the

later Durkheim – as a crucial source for a fundamental paradigm shift: the shift Habermas himself proposes "from purposive to communicative action." Habermas's emphasis on Mead has also enormously spurred the recent reception of Mead in Germany, paralleling Rorty's praise of Dewey in the US. Yet, for all this, even Habermas fails to put Mead on a par with other classical sociologists: significantly, his chapter on Mead wants the lively portrait of the development of the theorist's ideas found, for example, in Habermas's companion chapter on Max Weber. What he presents, instead, is a highly selective conceptual reconstruction of certain parts of Mead's theory through the lens of analytical philosophy.

This is not to deny the value of this conceptual reconstruction. And it should be recognized that Habermas's later work, *Post-metaphysical Thinking* (1992), offers a much richer interpretation of Mead's theory of self-formation. But his reconstructions in *The Theory of Communicative Action* and resulting criticisms of Mead nonetheless suffer very much from superficial hermeneutical groundings. Several points of Habermas's interpretation are completely misleading and can be understood only if one allows a very selective reading of Mead. Habermas reduces Mead to a theoretician concerned with immediate interpersonal relationships on a relatively primitive level, accusing Mead of totally neglecting social spheres that cannot be regulated by communicative action. However, while it is true that Mead's work does not increase our understanding of economic or military processes, the key question is whether this can properly be attributed – as Habermas suggests – to deficiencies in Mead's theory of human communication and notion of democracy. As I have tried to demonstrate (see Joas, 1985b, 1993, pp. 125–53), this is not the case: Habermas concludes otherwise because he misunderstands Mead's (and Dewey's) ideas about democratic politics. Furthermore, contra Habermas, Mead's theory of symbolically mediated interaction is not restricted to the most primitive level of communication. Habermas's analysis of this subject misconstrues Mead's interest in the *origins* of human communication as an approach confined to these origins. It should also be emphasized that when Habermas faults Mead for failing to explain the genesis of norms, his formulation of the issue is at variance with Mead's own. For Habermas, the genesis of norms raises the problem of the differentiation of the normative dimension out of the original undifferentiated unity of the normative, expressive, and descriptive dimensions contained in primitive signs; in contrast, Mead located the normative with this original unity and then explored the genesis of this unity itself. Lastly, it is quite questionable that Mead's work can be claimed for Habermas's paradigm shift from instrumental to communicative action, since Mead's achievement was to change our understanding of action *as such*; he elaborated a new theory of human communication to accomplish this objective, not simply to identify another *type* of action.

Despite its limitations, Habermas's interpretation of Mead has not generally been scrutinized very thoroughly by Mead scholars in America (but cf. Aboulafia, 1995). Instead, they have tended to greet Habermas's views fairly uncritically, seeing in his engagement with Mead (and Dewey and Peirce) the hope that the American tradition of symbolic interactionism might itself develop a macro-sociological approach once again and resuscitate the "critical" impulse of pragmatism's founding fathers (see, e.g., Hinkle, 1992). And there has doubtless been some justification in the feeling that symbolic interactionism has indeed "created a space for itself within American sociology, [as its proponents have] avoided the errors of biological, cultural, and structural determinism, debunked behaviorism, side-stepped cognitive social psychologies, and refused to engage psychoanalysis" (Denzin, 1994, p. 458).

But recent authors have begun to move beyond an uncritical acceptance of Habermas's interpretation. Antonio (1989; see also Antonio and Kellner, 1992) and Shalin (1992), for example, have attempted to initiate a dialogue between Habermas and the pragmatist heritage – a dialogue that goes beyond one-sided admiration for Habermas to emphasize what "critical theorists" can learn from the pragmatist treatment of "embodied experience and objective uncertainty."[6] And Honneth (1995), in an important effort to overcome the formalism of Habermas's "discourse ethics" and integrate his emphasis on intersubjectivity into a more conflict-centered approach, has made penetrating use of Mead's work.

The focus of all these observations has been work in contemporary sociological theory, but many of the same points apply when one turns to contemporary social theory more generally. Some of the major figures who declare themselves pragmatists do not even mention Mead, while others who are close to pragmatism do not discern this closeness. Chief among those in the former group is Richard Rorty (1979), who lavishes praise on Dewey but is simply silent on Mead (as is Hilary Putnam, Rorty's major opponent). The writings of many "communitarians" illustrate the other possibility: they develop arguments very similar to Mead's without mentioning

[6]On the superiority of pragmatism in relation to the older critical theory, see Joas, 1993 (pp. 79–93).

him. This statement applies to the works of both Michael Sandel and Amitai Etzioni. And Charles Taylor – "for the most part a Deweyan without knowing it," according to Alan Ryan (1995, p. 361) – refers to Mead only superficially and misleadingly even in his wide-ranging *Sources of the Self* (1989). For Taylor, "Mead is too close to behaviorism and not aware of the constitutive role of language in the definition of self and relations" (1989, p. 525, n. 12) – an odd characterization, to say the least, of the figure who is considered the inaugurator of the symbolic-interactionist tradition.[7]

Among leading communitarian theorists, the major departure from the pattern here is Philip Selznick, whose recent work (Selznick, 1992) on the moral implications of social theory makes clear that his own thinking is based firmly on the works of John Dewey *and* George Herbert Mead. Selznick's interest in the normative aspects of modernity leads him "to a fairly close inspection of what it means to be both genuinely other-regarding and constructively self-regarding. This difficult union may be thought of as the creation of a *responsible self*, which is manifested in three main ways: character-defining choice, self-affirming participation, and personal statesmanship" (1992, p. 227). To work out this conception of the "responsible self," Mead's ideas on the connection between the development of the self and moral consciousness prove crucial for Selznick. But his work is clearly an exception.

Taken together, these considerations suggest that the strange history of the reception of pragmatism in general and of Mead in particular infects even some of the most advanced present-day undertakings in social and sociological theory. I do not claim that Mead and Dewey (or James and Peirce) had the correct answer to everything, nor that all problems of contemporary theorizing could be solved if their writings were taken seriously. To the contrary, I am convinced that the pragmatists tended to neglect those important forms of political and sociological analysis that lie between abstractly universal statements about the origins of human communication, on the one hand, and overly concrete comments about the social conflicts of the day, on the other.

What I do claim, however, is that pragmatist ideas about human action and experience potentially provide a serious competitor to other synthetic approaches in social theory today. In my recent work

---

[7]I have discussed the relationship between Taylor and American pragmatism, as well as some of the strange omissions and distortions in Taylor's (1989) superb work, in Joas, 1996b.

(Joas, 1996a), I have systematically examined what a contemporary pragmatist action theory would look like, what this theory would presuppose or preclude in terms of macro-sociological theory, and what would distinguish such a theory from other sociological approaches.[8] While this analysis cannot be presented here, it is clear that the renaissance of pragmatism in contemporary intellectual life can bear fruit for sociology only if there is an opening up in the structure of existing theoretical schools. Then might pragmatism emerge as an unexpected but welcome voice in sociological discourse: an old voice made new again.

[8]On the consequences of such a pragmatist theory for understanding norms and values, see Joas, 1997.

REFERENCES

Aboulafia, Mitchell 1986: *The Mediating Self: Mead, Sartre, and self-determination.* New Haven, Conn.: Yale University Press.
—— 1993: Was George Herbert Mead a feminist? *Hypatia*, 8, 145–58.
—— 1995: Habermas and Mead: on universality and individuality. *Constellations*, 2, 93–113..
Alexander, Jeffrey 1982–3: *Theoretical Logic in Sociology*, 4 vols. Berkeley: University of California Press.
—— 1987: *Twenty Lectures: sociological theory after 1945.* New York: Columbia University Press.
—— 1988: *Action and Its Environments: toward a new synthesis.* New York: Columbia University Press.
—— 1996: Theorizing the good society: ethical, normative and empirical discourses. Unpublished paper.
Antonio, Robert J. 1989: The normative foundations of emancipatory theory: evolutionary versus pragmatic perspectives. *American Journal of Sociology*, 94, 721–48.
Antonio, Robert J. and Kellner, Douglas, 1992: Communication, modernity, and democracy in Habermas and Dewey. *Symbolic Interaction*, 15, 277–98.
Baldwin, John D. 1986: *G. H. Mead: a unifying theory for sociology.* Beverly Hills: Sage.
Bender, Christiane 1989: *Identität und Selbstreflexion. Zur reflexiven Konstruktion der Wirklichkeit in der Systemtheorie und im Symbolischen Interaktionismus von G. H. Mead.* Frankfurt/Main: Peter Lang.
Bergmann, Werner, and Hoffmann, Gisbert, 1985: Mead und die Tradition der Phänomenologie. In Hans Joas (ed.), *Das Problem der Intersubjektivität. Neuere Beiträge zum Werk G. H. Meads.* Frankfurt/Main: Suhrkamp, 93–130.
Bernstein, Richard 1992a: *The New Constellation.* Cambridge, Mass.: MIT Press.
—— 1992b: The resurgence of pragmatism, *Social Research*, 59, 813–40.
Blumer, Herbert [1966], 1969: Sociological implications of the thought of G. H.

Mead. In Herbert Blumer, *Symbolic Interactionism*. Englewood Cliffs, NJ. Prentice-Hall, 61–77.

Coleman, James S. 1990: *Foundations of Social Theory*. Cambridge: Mass.: Harvard University Press.

Collins, Randall 1989: Toward a neo-Meadian sociology of mind. *Symbolic Interaction*, 12, 1–32.

Cook, Gary Allan 1972: The development of G. H. Mead's social psychology. *Transactions of the Charles Sanders Peirce Society*, 8, 167–86.

—— 1986: Review of Hans Joas, *George Herbert Mead: a contemporary reexamination of his thought*. *Transactions of the Charles Sanders Peirce Society*, 22, 338–43.

—— 1993: *G. H. Mead: the making of a social pragmatist*. Urbana, Ill.: University of Illinois Press.

Deegan, Mary Jo 1988: *Jane Addams and the Men of the Chicago School*. New Brunswick, New Jersey: Transaction Books.

Denzin, Norman 1994: Postpragmatism: beyond Dewey and Mead: a review of Anselm Strauss, *Continual Permutations of Action*. *Symbolic Interaction*, 17, 453–63.

Feffer, Andrew 1990: Sociability and social conflict in G. H. Mead's interactionism, 1900–1919. *Journal of the History of Ideas*, 51, 233–54.

—— 1993: *The Chicago Pragmatists and American Progressivism* Ithaca, New York: Cornell University Press.

Fontana, Andrew, Tilman, Rick and Roe, Linda, 1992: Theoretical parallels in G. H. Mead and Thorstein Veblen. *The Social Science Journal*, 29, 241–57.

Giddens, Anthony 1976: *New Rules of Sociological Method*. New York: Basic.

Habermas, Jürgen 1987: *The Theory of Communicative Action*. Vol. 2. Boston: Basic.

—— 1992: *Postmetaphysical Thinking*. Cambridge, Mass.: MIT Press.

Hanson, Karen 1986: *The Self Imagined: philosophical reflections on the social character of psyche*. New York: Routledge & Kegan Paul.

Heuberger, Frank 1992: *Problemlösendes Handeln: Zur Handlungs- und Erkenntnistheorie von George Herbert Mead, Alfred Schutz und Charles Sanders Peirce*. Frankfurt/Main: Campus.

Hinkle, Gisela 1992: Habermas, Mead, and rationality. *Symbolic Interaction*, 15, 315–32.

Hollinger, David 1980: The problem of pragmatism in American history. *Journal of American History*, 67, 88–107.

Honneth, Axel 1995: *The Struggle for Recognition*. Cambridge: Polity Press.

Joas, Hans 1985a: *George Herbert Mead: a contemporary reexamination of his thought*. Cambridge, Mass.: MIT Press.

—— 1985b: Introduction. In Hans Joas (ed.), *Das Problem der Intersubjektivität, Neuere Beiträge zum Werk G. H. Meads*, Frankfurt/Main: Suhrkamp, 7–25.

—— 1989: How to explain what Collins thinks. *Symbolic Interaction*, 12, 63–4.

—— 1992: Review of Dorothy Ross, *The Origins of American Social Science*. *Acta Sociologica*, 35, 247–50.

—— 1993: *Pragmatism and Social Theory*. Chicago: University of Chicago Press.

—— 1995: Review of Frank Heuberger, *Problemlösendes Handeln: Zur Handlungs- und Erkenntnistheorie von George Herbert Mead, Alfred Schutz und Charles Sanders Peirce. Soziologische Revue*, 18, 233–4.

—— 1996a: *The Creativity of Action*. Cambridge: Polity Press.

—— 1996b: Ein Pragmatist wider Willen. *Deutsche Zeitschrift for Philosophie*, 44, 661–70.

—— 1997: *Die Entstehung der Werte*. Frankfurt/Main: Suhrkamp.

Jung, Matthias 1995: From Dilthey to Mead and Heidegger: systematic and historical relations. *Journal of the History of Philosophy*, 33, 661–77.

Kloppenberg, James 1996: Pragmatism: an old name for some new ways of thinking? *Journal of American History*, 83, 110–38.

Koczanowicz, Leszek 1994: G. H. Mead and L. S. Vygotsky on meaning and the self. *Journal of Speculative Philosophy*, 8, 262–75.

Lee, Harold N. 1963: Mead's doctrine of the past. *Tulane Studies in Philosophy*, 12, 52–75.

Lewis, J. D. and Smith, R. L. 1980: *American Sociology and Pragmatism: Mead, Chicago sociology, and symbolic interaction*. Chicago: University of Chicago Press.

Leys, Ruth 1994: Mead's voices: imitations as foundation, or the struggle against mimesis. In Dorothy Ross (ed.), *Modernist Impulses in the Human Sciences 1870–1930*. Baltimore, Md.: John Hopkins University Press, 210–35.

Mead, George Herbert 1932: *The Philosophy of the Present*. La Salle, Ill.: Open Court.

—— 1934: *Mind, Self, and Society*. ed Charles Morris. Chicago: University of Chicago Press.

—— 1936: *Movements of Thought in the Nineteenth Century*. Chicago: University of Chicago Press.

—— 1938: *The Philosophy of the Act*. Chicago: University of Chicago Press.

Miller, David L. 1973: *G. H. Mead: self, language and the world*. Austin, Texas: University of Texas Press.

—— 1982: *The Individual and the Social Self: unpublished work of G. H. Mead*. Chicago: University of Chicago Press.

Natanson, Maurice 1956: *The Social Dynamics of G. H. Mead*. Washington: Public Affairs Press.

Parsons, Talcott 1937: *The Structure of Social Action*. New York: McGraw-Hill.

Reck, Andrew 1963: The philosophy of G. H. Mead. *Tulane Studies in Philosophy*, 12, 5–51.

Reck, Andrew (ed.) 1964: *G. H. Mead: Selected Writings*. Indianapolis: Bobbs-Merrill.

Rehberg, Karl-Siegbert 1985: Die Theorie der Intersubjektivität als eine Lehre vom Menschen. George Herbert Mead und die deutsche Tradition der Philosophischen Anthropologie. In Hans Joas (ed.), *Das Problem der Intersubjektivität, Neuere Beiträge zum Werk G. H. Meads*, Frankfurt/Main: Suhrkamp, 60–92.

Rochberg-Halton, Eugene 1986: *Meaning and Modernity: social theory in the pragmatic attitude*. Chicago: University of Chicago Press.

Rorty, Richard 1979: *Philosophy and the Mirror of Nature*. Princeton: Princeton University Press.

Rosenthal, Sandra 1969: Peirce, Mead, and the logic of concepts. *Transactions of the Charles Sanders Peirce Society*, 5, 173–87.

Rosenthal, Sandra, and L. Bourgeois, Patrick 1991: *Mead and Merleau-Ponty: toward a common vision*. Albany, NY: SUNY Press.

Ross, Dorothy 1991: *The Origins of American Social Science*. Cambridge: Cambridge University Press.

Rucker, Darnell 1969: *The Chicago Pragmatists.* Minneapolis: University of Minnesota Press.

Ryan, Alan 1995: *John Dewey and the High Tide of American Liberalism* New York: Norton.

Schimmer, Ralf 1997: *Populismus und Sozialwissenschaften im Amerika der Jahrhundertwende.* Frankfurt/Main: Campus.

Schubert, Hans-Joachim 1995: *Demokratische Identität. Der soziologische Pragmatismus Charles Horton Cooleys.* Frankfurt/Main: Suhrkamp.

Selznick, Philip 1992: *The Moral Commonwealth: social theory and the promise of community.* Berkeley: University of California Press.

Shalin, Dmitri 1986: Review of Hans Joas, *G. H. Mead: a contemporary re-examination of his thought. Symbolic Interaction,* 9, 273–6.

—— 1988: G. H. Mead, socialism, and the progressive agenda. *American Journal of Sociology,* 93, 913–51.

—— 1992: Critical theory and the pragmatist challenge. *American Journal of Sociology,* 98, 237–9.

Taylor, Charles 1989: *Sources of the Self.* Cambridge, Mass.: Harvard University Press.

Tugendhat, Ernst 1986: *Self-Consciousness and Self-Determination.* Cambridge, Mass.: MIT Press.

Wagner, Hans-Josef 1993: *Strukturen des Subjekts: Eine Studie im Anschluss an George Herbert Mead.* Opladen: Westdeutscher Verlag.

Wenzel, Harald 1985: Mead und Parsons. Die emergente Ordnung des sozialen Handelns. In Hans Joas (ed.), *Das Problem der Intersubjektivität, Neuere Beiträge zum Werk G.H. Meads,* 26–39.

—— 1990: *G. H. Mead zur Einführung.* Hamburg: Junius.

—— 1991: *Die Ordnung des Handelns. Talcott Parsons' Theorie des allgemeinen Handlungssystems.* Frankfurt/Main: Suhrkamp.

10

Acclaiming the Reclaimers: The Trials of Writing Sociology's History

Alan Sica

Considering what my colleagues have written in the preceding chapters, and thinking again about Camic's strong introduction in light of the novel positions they took, certain anomalies peculiar to this scholarly orbit subtly begin to arrange themselves into meaningful patterns. In doing so, they define in oblique terms what has become over the last several decades a heterodox approach to our knowledge of the past, one which is more complex than the easy counterpoising of "presentist" to "historicist" poles would suggest. The singularities of viewpoint and judgment that identify this posture repeatedly surface among all the chapters, no matter how unalike they may be on other grounds. These very characteristics and the world view they emblematize explain in part the enduring divide between historians of sociology, notably deviant within the discipline's dominant subculture, and other practitioners less formally concerned with the past.

One recalls that some fifty years ago Merton established a correlative distinction when he separated "history" from "systematics" in the development of theory (Merton, [1949], 1968, pp. 1–38). By means of this defining essay, more often cited than studied, he unintentionally gave his less learned colleagues a sturdy excuse to sidestep history entirely in favor of what they imagined Merton meant by "systematics," and their desired roles in elaborating same. They took comfort in a pseudo-Mertonian position which has slowly effaced the sterling quality of the *actual* argument, subtle and demanding as it is when studied closely (which in some ways is the culmination of Merton's thoughts about such matters during the preceding 15 years). The airy call to "do" science rather than merely "venerating" the past fit too well with the times and the prevailing American temperament, and a flimsy reading of Merton's essay seems to have propelled many sociologists down this ill-lit path.

Thus, the ordinary practitioner has found it ever more "rational," during graduate school and after, to remain unconcerned about the field's heritage, or perhaps merely bemused by whatever quaint fragments of it happen to be noted, particularly those most closely associated with "pure" ideas. It is less taxing, for example, to dismiss Spencer than to read him, despite his contemporaries' widely voiced belief that he was the modern successor to Aristotle, or, as the leading historian of philosophy has put it, "one of the major prophets of an era" (Copleston, 1966, p. 142). The very words – "heritage," "founders," "lineage," "development" – upon which that scholarship best suited to repair faulty historical reconstructions depends and enlarges, now play a strictly cosmetic role within the rhetorical lexicon of conventional sociology, if mentioned at all. (By "conventional" I mean, of course, "scientific" articles in journals, plus those limited-circulation monographs, made up of stitched together research reports, that would have retained their more modest form were it not for authors' egos and publishers' seasonal need for "product").

Noted sociologists will admit, after fleeting hesitation, that they do little more with the "top" journals than skim the tables of contents. And 80 percent of the competitors for space in these outlets are novices in search of tenure, who themselves read only those selections which might impinge on their own efforts to succeed. Nevertheless, this no-person's land of arid, formulaic artifice – resolutely free of historical materials – has for the last several decades pretended to the title of "The Mainstream." Administrators, especially those whose institutions are loudly "on the make," become notoriously obsessed with identifying the kill zone for each field, then demanding that their younger charges be seen within it or face dismissal. It is this peculiarly deadened site of earnest and hopeful labors which one seasoned New York book editor called "painting by the numbers," when comparing works which speak to an audience that lies outside the citadel of standardization to those articles that guarantee early job security (or did until recently).

With several notable exceptions – so exceptional in fact that they become by definition notable – most historians of sociology cannot expect to see their work very often in the journals that are used to define the field qua Big Science. It is these few outlets which ignite the imaginations of deans and their administrative collaborators, in addition to funding agencies, influential colleagues, and those scholars who believe their work is truly "advancing the field." Unfortunately, there is nothing less ingratiating for academic characters such as these than to learn from the dust-covered historian that ideas currently being touted as "the next advance in sociological thought" were adumbrated years, decades, even centuries before by writers or political actors about whom current movers and shakers know nothing. Naturally, it is professionally convenient to remain in a condition of comfortable ignorance.

Nobody wants to hear, least of all from an unproven colleague, that there is nothing new under the intellectuals' sun, for careers are often at stake, or, just as disturbing, they appear to be. The polarizing psychological mechanism at work in this situation seems similar to that set of uncomfortable sensations which goes through an adult when a savvy child points out a patent contradiction in a parent's version of past events; or posits reminders of forgotten promises that stemmed from a less vigilant mental condition. For reasons that are too obvious yet in some ways too elusive to explain here satisfactorily, everyone who is paid to "be creative" retains a vested interest in propagating the illusion that tremendous growth and progress lie just around the corner. Consider, to take a painful example, a professor of music composition at one of the world's leading conservatories who must write a grant proposal in support of a new symphonic work (if any such money exists today). Can this poor victim of history, who happens to be living now rather than in 1790 Vienna, argue that "there is anything left to say" in the aftermath of symphonic writing between Haydn and Mahler? (Similar observations hold regarding rock music between 1950 and 1970 compared with the years that have elapsed since, except for the fact that rock musicians know better than to apply for grants.)

All these observations are more interrelated than they may first appear. As such, they lead inexorably, it seems to me, to that reservoir of intellectual inspiration from which the historian Mary Pickering drew when she produced her extraordinary biography of Comte in 1993. Surely someone at Harvard had pointed out to the student Pickering that writing multi-volume biographies of "minor" (male) social theorists from previous centuries would not *now* win her a stellar faculty position (perhaps in contrast to an earlier time when, for example, Keith Baker's lifework on Condorcet seemed to serve him well enough). Nevertheless, she took the trouble to learn scholarly French, to visit foreign archives and work under what were probably the cramped and penurious conditions common to such endeavors, and then fashioned this great mass of work into a large volume which a worthy publisher was somehow persuaded to publish – if only in an expensive cloth edition that few scholars will own. (Smaller academic libraries may even question its fit with their "acquisitions mission.") Why, then, did she bother, surely knowing long before the project was concluded, that the probable ratio of return between her investment of time and soul, and the likely professional rewards she might eventually receive would be much smaller than her less sociologically minded, more "rationally" motivated, colleagues would tolerate.

To find answers to these puzzles, her chapter might be searched for clues. Pickering punctures five widely held and substantially mistaken notions that surround the persona of Comte, not only among the great Ignoranti, but even theory "specialists" who do not have access to her biography or to her unrivaled knowledge of our "founder." It is quite likely an impossible task for Americans today to understand Comte in the *verstehende* sense that Dilthey applied in his biographical attempts to encircle Goethe and Schleiermacher. And one could argue on technical or existential grounds that even Pickering's ventriloquist rendering of Comte's voice does not capture "the real Comte," that is, the "God's-eye view" which surpasses human understanding. Nevertheless, the poignancy emanating from Pickering's chapter resembles what one hears in the tales told by an explorer who has seen a land everyone believes they know from pictures or folk tales, but which "in fact" is quite distinct from common perceptions, and that the adventurer *alone* knows to be illusory. Yet the explorer is viewed, particularly by those with the most to lose in terms of their previous "learning," as having become slightly deranged owing, perhaps, to the unique thrill of the adventures which gave rise to the discordant tale in the first place.

Pickering has spent more imaginative time in Comte's head and with his friends than anyone currently alive and willing to talk about it. She understands him, therefore, as more interesting than textbook treatments make him out to be, less simple-minded in his theory of history, and more psychologically absorbing than one might otherwise imagine. Consider, as just one example, Pickering's redemption of Comte's indispensable helpmate and wife, Caroline Massin. To follow Pickering's explanation of her real place in Comte's life, her job as a highly literate attendant in a Bourbon reading room rather than as a "sexual service worker" on the Paris streets and then to think for the first time about Comte's willful distortion of the record in his "Secret Addition" to his *Testament*, is to move much closer to Comte's theorizing than one could before Pickering did her spadework. Such micro-knowledge may or may not alter the overall view taken today of Comte's theoretical accomplishment. But any hope of appreciating his work with the sort of precision now applied, by contrast, to Marx, Durkheim, or Weber must rely precisely on the quality of historiography that Pickering's chapter exemplifies.

Sad to say, though, by making the discoveries and performing the rereadings she has done, she becomes virtually a woman without a scholarly country. And her railing against others in the historical vineyard must be taken either as a sign that she has lost her mind, like Comte himself, or that everybody else is wrong and her new view must over time become the conventional wisdom. While it is hardly impossible that this transformation of the common landscape could occur, the nature of innovation as a human (or scholarly) process suggests, first, that wholesale acceptance of her viewpoint will not occur unless she hammers away for many years, and second, that a proper understanding of Comte, complexly laid out as Pickering would wish, overtaxes whatever constituency there might be for such work; and that he will therefore be left aside entirely for another in the pantheon who is more easily reshaped to suit current interests. Or – the same thing – who has not yet found his Mary Pickering.

Moishe Postone's valiant attempt to help save Marxist social thought from the strange turns of current world history reminds me of a recent article by another leftist from an even older generation, Norman Birnbaum, now 70. With the appearance of *The Crisis of Industrial Society* (1968) and *Towards a Critical Sociology* (1970), and owing to audiences for his work in Germany, France, Britain, and Italy, this American theorist represented a type of urbane "real-world" leftism which was serious about its sources and its "founders," yet never allowed itself to become closeted in academic hideaways. During the late 1960s or early 1970s, Birnbaum was as likely to publish in *Die Zeit* or Italian communist periodicals as in *The Nation* or *Partisan Review*. As for the "mainstream" journals in sociology, the lack of interest between himself and them was mutual and complete. Like his friends, Alain Touraine and Habermas, he viewed his principal audience as being outside, yet attentive to, the academy. In "Socialism reconsidered" (*World Policy Journal*, Fall, 1996), Birnbaum once again writes a sharply chiseled requiem for a mode of political action and thought which he knows has had its day, but from which he hopes a residue of worthwhile motives and inspiration can still be preserved. These may be able to counter the forces of unrestrained global capitalism which have deposed an equally obnoxious, if ethically similar, Stalinism. Yet the references to Gramsci, Marx, Habermas, Henri Lefebvre, Touraine, even Weber, which informed his earlier works as a political analyst and social theorist, have disappeared, and in their place are comments for and about political actors who may know very little about these iconic leftists.

Postone is a member in good standing of what Birnbaum some-times calls "the sixty-eighters," by which he means of course "the events of May, 1968," now entirely forgotten by official sociology and almost everyone else who was not a participant. These were the students who during the 1960s embraced almost uncritically the works of certain "activist" scholars – nearly all male, European, and with elite educational credentials – the same names that fill Postone's copious bibliography some thirty years later. Surely readers under 35 cannot now imagine the sustained "rush" that came from spending long evenings reading and discussing the works of Adorno, Althusser, Perry Anderson, Aron, Avineri, Tom Bottomore, Harry Braverman, Castoriadis, G. A. Cohen, Lucio Colletti – and I have moved sequentially through only the first fifth of Postone's reference list! If it was, as somebody who was there later put it, "very heaven" to have been in one's twenties during the 1920s, then for apprentice Marxists, it was equally magical to be learning one's Gorz, Gouldner, Gramsci, or Habermas, just as the works rolled off the presses, in print runs the sizes of which serious publishers can now remember only with the deepest nostalgia. In those days Lukács was venerated almost beyond criticism, Lichtheim was looked to as the friendly guide through Hegel or Feuerbach, David McLellan's biography of Marx became bedside reading, and Marcuse's books flew off bookstore shelves and into "revolutionary" garrets in a volume that has not occurred since for any "product" of scholarly creation that is remotely comparable in terms of intellectual depth or political daring.

Yet what is new and what is left from the New Left? Recall Quixote. One admires the imagined knight for his fearlessness, resolution in the face of poor odds for success, dignity, honor, and lack of compunction when everyone around him pointed out that by "tilting at windmills," he was not going to further his "career" of hunting or overseeing his lands. Nevertheless, Quixote refuses to die as a world-class literary character. Not only did he sell arable land "in order to buy and read the books that he loved," but in so doing, he stood for something which is always estimable: the refusal to give up a vision that is personally meaningful because of its morally upright origins – no matter how unfashionable at the moment. Quixote "was in the

habit of reading books . . . with such pleasure and devotion" that he
foreswore the everyday and took refuge in a more noble and worthy
past (Putnam translation, chapter 1).

Postone's chapter is, indeed, a Quixotic enterprise, particularly if
today's headlines are any indication of "reality," indicating that
Marxism is as dead as the social philosophies of Max Stirner or
Moses Hess, which Marx himself consigned to oblivion. His scholarship is careful, his reference to the canonical texts of the left,
beginning with fiercely attentive study of Marx/Engels, is exacting,
and his theoretical points well taken. The putative goal of the chapter
is to prove that reference to Marxist ideas should remain a vital part
of how the postmodern, postcommunist social world is to be
measured and improved. Detailed "reconstruction" of, for example,
Marx's value theory, or a refreshed appraisal of how capitalism's
latest forms corrupt social relations and jeopardize "democratic self-
determination," can indeed make for exemplary scholarship, along
with grist for what is left of the Marxology mill. Whether such labors
reach beyond the cloister, though, is something Postone's elder
leftist, Birnbaum, has been wondering aloud for many years. And as
reasonable hope for "emancipated" social relations recedes, ever
further from the grasp of ageing leftists, worries like Birnbaum's
become ever more pressing, due perhaps to that same sort of sober
realism Weber recommended to the socialist students in his bitter
audiences following World War I.

Put another, and more Marxist way: When does Marxology
become theology? How far away must the world move from a species
of social interaction of which Marxists could honestly approve
before it collapses into quasi-theological debates of the sort that
scholars today imagine filled the hours of Aquinas and his lesser
colleagues? The sheer level of intellectualism at work in writing like
this is often remarkably high. But the ultimate payoff, either as social
theory or as implementable notions transferred to lived politics, may
prove quite otherwise. It is this nagging worry that lies behind both
Postone's and Birnbaum's current writings, and causes one to wonder
where exactly the emancipatory impulse will come to rest if the left
rides off the stage, with Quixote, and becomes little more than good
intentions gone awry.

Valerie Haines, picking up the lance recently carried by J. D. Y.
Peel and Jonathan Turner, has her work cut out for her. She means to
prove that contemporary readers, even her most informed and
sympathetic predecessors, do not understand Spencer's achievement,
nor his errors, and that given increasing interest in evolutionary
theory, he deserves another, more careful reading. And since Darwin

has prompted no fewer than three full-scale biographies in the last few years, including one that promises to be multi-volume (Bowlby, 1990; Browne, 1995; Desmond and Moore, 1992) – not to mention the paperback reissue in 1995 of his son's biography of him – it is at least plausible that Darwin's occasional correspondent might be worth another look. Of course, one may eventually agree with Darwin who famously wrote in his *Autobiography*, "Herbert Spencer's conversation seemed to me very interesting, but I did not like him particularly, and did not feel that I could easily have become intimate with him. I think that he was extremely egotistical" (Darwin [1887], 1958, p. 108.) But (as Haines also points out) Darwin was ever the empiricist, and judged Spencer on the basis of his work: "After reading any of his books, I generally feel enthusiastic admiration for his transcendent talents, and have often wondered whether in the distant future he would rank with such great men as Descartes, Leibnitz, etc., about whom, however, I know very little" ([1887], 1958, pp. 108–9). He had earned the right to disregard the younger man on legitimate intellectual grounds: "Nevertheless I am not conscious of having profited in my own work by Spencer's writings. His deductive manner of treating every subject is wholly opposed to my frame of mind ... His fundamental generalisations ... have not been of any use to me" ([1887], 1958, p. 109). Still, there is little question that Darwin respected Spencer's fantastic energy and ingenuity in his effort to forge a universal synthesis of natural and social science knowledge. Whether even Darwin understood it entirely is another question.

But aside from Darwin's familiar critique of Spencer, there is another, even more potent dismissal, probably the single best known in the history of modern social theory, to which Haines must respond if she is to revive Spencer's reputation. I mean, of course, the opening line to Parsons's most enduring book, *The Structure of Social Action* (1937), the only one that still deserves study by theory specialists. Haines is savvy enough to open her paper with the quotation itself (as have innumerable others wanting to show how distant we are from the antiquated ideas of the preceding century, or how quickly reputations disappear, or how keenly they enjoy a good joke): "Who now reads Spencer?" Haines quotes another three lines, but, like almost every other writer whose reference to this inflammatory passage I have seen, she allows the reader to think this sharp castigation is Parsons's own. But as theory experts know too well, Parsons never wrote this well in his life (even in this book, with his father's helpful editing [1937, p. xxiii]), and he properly credits his colleague at Harvard, Crane Brinton, as the author.

Brinton published a number of "good reads" in his time (e.g., *The Anatomy of Revolution*), and his estimate of Spencer is no exception. As a special and unusual treat, let us watch without interruption Brinton's entire demolition of a reputation, in the same way that Parsons would have delighted in it when it was first published, four years before his own book appeared (with Parsons's quoted material in italics):

> *Who now reads Spencer? It is difficult for us to realize how great a stir he made in the world.* The *Synthetic Philosophy* penetrated to many a bookshelf which held nothing else quite so heavy. It lay beside the works of Buckle and Mill on the shelf of every Englishman of a radical turn of mind. It was read, discussed, fought over. And now it is a drug [sic] on the second-hand market and hardly stirs the interest of the German or American aspirant to the doctorate in philosophy. We are more indifferent to this modern *summa* than to the *summa* of Thomas Aquinas. The completeness of Spencer's downfall is almost sufficient to disarm the critic, and it certainly should predispose him to mercy. But Spencer himself was never merciful, not merciful intellectually at least. He seems never to have harboured any kind of doubt. In a century surely not predisposed to skepticism, few thinkers surpass him in cock-sureness and intolerance. *He was the intimate confidant of a strange and rather unsatisfactory God, whom he called the principle of Evolution. His God has betrayed him. We have evolved beyond Spencer.* (Brinton [1933], 1962, pp. 226–7)

Haines follows convention by incorrectly crediting Parsons with wit that was mostly Brinton's. But she then fails to separate the former's knife thrusts into the *corpus delicti* as incorporated in the remains of Parsons's first paragraph: "Professor Brinton's verdict may be paraphrased as that of the coroner, 'Dead by suicide or at the hands of person or persons unknown.' We must agree with this verdict. Spencer is dead. [Parsons's footnote: 'Not, of course, that nothing in his thought will last. It is his social theory as a total structure that is dead.'] But who killed him and how? This is the problem" (Parsons, 1968, p. 3). Parsons may have been inspired here by early Raymond Chandler or Agatha Christie.

One could, in turn, easily joke about Parsons's own resurrecting of Spencer thirty years later, about his own attempt to paint a global theoretical portrait of the social world. But for the moment it is more important to consider Haines's substantive argument because her complaints against Spencer's detractors, who now seem to be as much in the majority as they were nonexistent a hundred years ago, could be applied equally well to those many misreaders of other classical figures. She responds with spirit to the Brinton/Parsons barbs: "If

Spencer is dead, then, he is dead because the developmental reconstruction misrepresents his assumptions about the nature of social change." She will answer his critics by "setting out as clearly as possible *what Spencer actually said* about the mechanisms of organic and social evolution in his published work and letters." I have emphasized the controlling phrase. Establishing, thinking through, and reappropriating in a thorough fashion "what Somebody Smart but Long Ago actually said" is never a task suited to the fainthearted. In this case, Haines's complex argument – which is constructed around a subtle and complete understanding of nineteenth-century debates regarding development *as distinguished from* evolution – must be followed as it would have unfolded at the time, with all the reservations and nuances that today's synonymous use of "development" and "evolution" fails to capture.

Haines's accusation, then, is fairly simple: If one takes the time to understand the differences and similarities between Darwin and Spencer (e.g., "use inheritance" as modified by natural selection theory), then the latter does not turn out to be the boneheaded Lamarckian his unread critics imagine him to be, for the entire debate was carried on at a level far higher and more careful than we now allow ourselves, smugly enough, to believe. Is it perhaps still too painful to realize what our 99 percent DNA identity with chimps might mean for the "development" of social theory? Or is the entire evolutionary program too embarrassing to tolerate given world history's unrelieved barbarism since the sunny days of the fin de siècle departed with Nietzsche's death in 1900?

There must be something profoundly disconcerting about facing the past with eyes and mind completely open. Otherwise, why would Haines, in her effort to do just that, have felt it necessary to invoke a set of phrases which all point in the same direction: "misrepresents his assumptions," "this one-sided approach," "to bring out as clearly as possible what Spencer actually said," "contextualizing Spencer's evolutionary theorizing also highlights where modern critics went wrong," or "the developmental model of evolution may belong to the 19th century, but it does not belong to Spencer." She is battling a uniform enemy, not necessarily "Whiggish presentism," nor "priggish historicism," but simply Amnesia by Convenience. If "we" all agree that Spencer accepted a version of Lamarckianism (finally disproved only in the 1940s); if we also agree that his teleological urges pushed him toward seeing Progress as inevitable (as Brinton claimed, and Parsons believed), then we can set aside with palpable relief his gilt-edged, leather-bound collected works that adorned Victorian parlors – all twenty-one shelf inches of them, so he reported – and "get on with the business of science."

But what if we are not as smart as he, not as hard-working, more easily distracted from the job of collecting "data" and analyzing it systematically (in the literal sense of making a system out of it), less humorlessly tenacious in our beliefs about what is true and what is very likely only wish fulfillment – how then do we dispense with Mr Spencer? Could this explain why Parsons in the late 1960s revived his former nemesis and hailed him as a guiding light into systemic functionalism? Is this why Haines, Peel, Turner, and a few others continue to blow Spencer's horn? If Haines's chapter fails to convince an informed readership – one that has come to terms, say, with Richards's detailed studies of the period's achievements (1987, 1992), with Mayr's history of biological thought (1982), and with Bowler's study of evolution as a long-term intellectual project (1989) – at least Spencer's subsequent removal from the pantheon will be done for reasons other than the wish to avoid what takes effort to learn.

Very much the same could be said regarding Simmel as portrayed by Donald Levine. Single-handedly at times, Levine has been practicing "in your face" Simmel work for forty years, and must now take a vindicated pleasure in attending conferences held to determine "Georg Simmel's Actual and Potential Impact on Contemporary Sociology." Yet his chapter, which might be taken as a small summa of his Simmel labors ever since discovering "these riches" by accident in Germany some forty-five years ago, amplifies just the sort of objections to conventional opinion that were enunciated earlier by Pickering, Postone, and Haines after they had absorbed the "actual words" of classical theorists, and then compared them with the ersatz notions normally attributed to them. Levine is not shy of naming names, and to learn that some very distinguished experts have propagated characterizations of Simmel, the person and the theorist, which are seriously at odds with Levine's reporting of "the facts," gives pause even to the most optimistic student of social theory as produced over the last two centuries.

Levine's new purchase on Simmel's intellectual property need not be repeated here, since his eight points are very clearly, even entertainingly, laid out. An obvious general response to his con- trarian position might be put this way: "Why have so many reasonably smart theorists misunderstood Simmel in the eight ways so identified?" Perhaps bad or incomplete hermeneutics is at work, based on simple misinformation, e.g., either Simmel was well off and taught "for fun" in a dilettantish manner, or he seriously needed a job and suffered cruelly by being refused one. Levine's claim for the second set of facts contradicts almost everything currently in print about Simmel's finances. But beyond questions of simple fact that can fairly easily be resolved given enough data, even attentive and skilled readers often disagree in their estimate of complex, multivalent, intentionally ambiguous texts (Plato and Hegel being obvious cases of current interest). But after all that is taken into account, there still remain characteristics of Simmel's person and work that seem always to excite similar responses in certain categories of readers, all of which Levine sees as denigrative of Simmel's proper stature. And yet contemporary accounts of his lecturing style and presentation of self often fixed on a detectable aloofness, both from everyday awareness and from conventional modes of social science expression that infuriated his stuffier colleagues, even while mesmerizing a long list of distinguished students. Levine acknowledges that certain conundrums have long been attached to Simmel when, for instance, he writes, "And yet . . . there remains *the undeniable experience of Simmel as an unsystematic writer*" (his emphases), even after patiently explaining the systemic character of the work available to eyes trained to see it.

When Levine writes that "preset images of authors and texts often remain difficult to correct despite the availability of good evidence that contradicts them," he knows of what he speaks. Correcting what he regards as deficient understandings of Simmel's goals and achievements has required considerable effort on his part, particularly during the last twenty-five years or so, as Simmel's star began to rise again in league with theories of postmodernism. Yet "the good evidence" to which he refers must be taken in, digested, and then allowed to reconfigure the "preset images" that live on in textbooks and other standard sites of image-creation. And given the energy committed to learning original images which new evidence calls into question, one can easily enough imagine why ordinary practitioners want "their" Simmel to retain the familiar, ossified form they learned as novices. Levine's chapter is loaded with surprises, for example: Spencer's profound but hidden influence on the young Simmel; likewise Hegel's role in Simmel's thought as opposed to his obvious Kantianism; the inscrutable position of Dilthey in Simmel's ideas; Durkheim's bowdlerization of Simmel's prose; Heidegger as a spiritual student of Simmel; Karen Horney's blunt admission of her debt to him as well; Simmel's participation in the public sphere of social reform, far removed from the overheated salons to which he's usually consigned; and his genuine need for money. Yet to what extent these "new" bits of historical data will be allowed to rearrange "our" conception of Simmel, the one common to textbooks and the underground stream of "knowledge" they feed, is not easily knowable.

As Levine observed, with wry understatement given all that has come before in his chapter, "as so often with the interpretation of classic authors, great danger lies in representing their entire thought by making reference to a small slice of their total output, taken out of context." Yet even well-read theorists today are more than likely to draw their Simmel knowledge either from Levine's own selection (1971) or from the venerable anthology of Kurt Wolff (1950). The chance that a hermeneutically competent rendering of Simmel will glide into the canon (in the way, for instance, that Weber and Durkheim are now being "rewritten" to accommodate a host of intellectual currents) is small, it seems to me, until Levine or a similarly knowledgeable expert displaces the earlier definitive texts with new ones more reflective of the "complete" Simmel that begins to emerge from Levine's characterization. If we are to avoid what Levine charmingly calls "a studiously superficial reading," then Simmel must be reconsidered along broader lines. (A return to Gerson's realization in 1932 of Goethe's fundamental role in Simmel's *Weltanschauung* would be one good starting point for an entire revaluation of Simmel, now known as the great postmodernist *avant de lettre*.)

From an entirely different angle of attack, Robert Alun Jones enters the fray over how to appropriate the past, first by acknowledging the utility of such a goal, then registering a number of reservations about its likely success. As a battered veteran of the presentist–historicist wars, and also one who, it seems, has given up trying to convince sociologists that they "ought" to pay attention to proper historical reconstruction, he now moves on ground familiar to followers of Quentin Skinner and Richard Rorty. Rather than accepting at face value the idea that sympathetic readings might be able to bring back to life sets of textualized ideas born in alien lands, he proposes other motivations for such labors, none of them very consoling to scholars who think they are "setting the record straight" by paying close attention to the facts of each case. Believing that "history itself is deeply ironic," he extends Rorty's "commensuration" idea and Skinner's "contrived pleasures" with the acute observation that "the point of these *rationally-reconstructed* [theories] . . . is to provide *reassurance*." That is, "we" go about relearning the past with as much skill as we can muster *not* in order to communicate with voices trapped in mausoleums, nor to see what they "actually said," but instead because we want badly to "feel better" about a given cause, political position, epistemological scheme, or some other such pre-scholarly accoutrement.

For some of the writers in this book and the few other hearties who work what Ivan Illich calls "the vineyard of the text," such a viewpoint might be regarded either as high cynicism, adolescent sulking, or deepest wisdom, depending on the quality of their research and the "data" they have at their disposal. One wonders, for instance, which contemporary axe Mary Pickering might be grinding as she marches through Comte's papers and those of his intellectual environment. Does she hope to revive positivism of a special type, or is she francophilic, and wants to ingratiate an important but neglected Parisian to the anglophone world? It is certainly easy to see that Lynn McDonald's identification of women who were important to the development of social science, and have thus far been slighted, bears the unmistakable imprint of contemporary feminism in its more serious form. And Stephen Kalberg's approach to Weber (especially in his recent book) seems to carry one overarching message, that comparative-historical research of the last several decades cannot match Weber's in scope or acuity; that the estimable works, for example, of Charles Tilly, Theda Skocpol, and Reinhard Bendix do not add up to, nor properly extend, Weber's own achievement in the same general bailiwick.

And what of Joas's portrait of Mead, emphasizing as it has for some time the impact of Dilthey and other German thinkers on Mead's development in his early years. Is this an attempt to co-opt Mead's "American" achievement in the pragmatic stream by re-assigning ownership to the German *Lebensphilosophie* he so admired when young? Camic's own redefinition of the young Parsons, fantastically more interesting and worth study than the desiccated functionalist of the 1950s and 1960s now seems to be – could this be Camic's unvoiced pitch for displacing Parsons's dictated later works by the carefully written, historically anchored political economy of his youth? While any of these rhetorical questions might be answered in reasoned tones, their purpose is to show how quickly one risks falling into reductio ad absurdum unless an author's expressed motivations are given the benefit of the doubt, when they are very likely more in control of the "data" than anyone else in the academy.

Jones has forcefully brought forward an important and thus far skirted component toward a fuller understanding of Durkheim. From this new vantage point, we will look to Durkheim's ideas only at our peril if we believe he was trying to offer timeless truths. His paramount concern lay instead with the fate of France, not with global social science or the survival of bourgeois morality across the West. Perhaps because he was a patriot, while a Jew, he wanted most of all to speak immediately to a range of political problems and risks that he and the other dedicated Republicans needed to address, if repressive forces were to be kept at bay in the French political setting *of his time.* In this he was very much like Weber – and Pareto, Comte, Spencer, Marx, et al. – since sociology for nearly all classical theorists owed its creation and appeal to the promise of solving pressing difficulties that were not being suitably handled by other available disciplines, or by the resources common to nonacademic political culture.

Nevertheless, Rorty's ideas seem more appealing today, given the somewhat narcissistic impulse that feeds a fair percentage of intellectual and quasi-intellectual work. If studying classical writing provides "a key to self-awareness itself" and a way of therefore understanding our own predicaments better, this should be a strong selling point to unbelievers who would rather bury the classics permanently beneath their naturally acquired dust, or, at most, to "mine" them for usable bits of lore which happen to suit con-temporary projects. The very effort that goes into "historical reconstructions" of the sort which seem most successful to our suspicious eyes – Skinner's recent magnum opus on Hobbes's rhetoric is the obvious example – makes this mode of inquiry risky for the most able scholars, foolhardy for many others.

And if Jones's fluid approach to the question of historical truth is accepted, then the risks become even greater: "The question of what a text 'means' is never a question of the text's essential nature, or what it is Really About; rather, it is always a question of how the text fits into some larger context of thought and action. As a result the text will have as many meanings as there are contexts in which it might be placed." These remarks are the sort that send the more scientistic sociologist into a rage of righteous indignation or, if he/she begins to believe they might be "true," then into the slough of despond. They question the purpose of social "science" at its deepest level, and seem to take sustenance in this critique from the very Sacred Books of Europe from which modern sociology draws its legitimacy.

There is no doubt that Jones's chapter is as intriguing as it is frustrating, depending on one's position along that continuum of scholarly faith that extends from Dilthey's *Verstehen* on one end to Homans's propositional inventory on the other. In some ways it seems to reflect a postmodern mindset in ways that none of the other chapters do, although its author never makes this claim explicitly.

If there is anything truly common, though, to all the chapters it is the authors' passionate belief in the intrinsic importance of reclaiming the past masters (and now mistresses), to recapture their collective intelligence, their courage in the face of almost always triumphalist opposition, and to see what it takes to do something creative in the field of social theory or social analysis. As a leading American sociologist of Russian history recently put it after reading Weber's *The Russian Revolutions* (written in 1905, 1906, and 1917), "Weber's incisive analysis has acquired even greater richness with the passage of time" (Bonnell, 1996, p. 823). Virtuosic study of other classical texts would likely reveal similar treasures. But the work of digging them out is hard, and the results never guaranteed. Who can blame the "routineers," consumed as they usually are with more topical research, if they choose to leave the past unattended? Only the reclaimers can know the value of what they seek.

REFERENCES

Baker, Keith Michael 1975: *Condorcet: from natural philosophy to social mathematics.* Chicago: University of Chicago Press.

Birnbaum, Norman 1968: *The Crisis of Industrial Society.* New York: Oxford University Press.

—— 1970: *Toward a Critical Sociology.* New York: Oxford University Press.

—— 1996: Socialism reconsidered – yet again. *World Policy Review*, 13 (3), 40–51.

Bonnell, Victoria 1996: Review of Max Weber, *The Russian Revolutions. Contemporary Sociology*, 25 (6), 821–3.

Bowlby, John 1990: *Charles Darwin: a new life.* New York: Norton.

Bowler, Peter J. 1989: *Evolution: the history of an idea*, rev. edn. Berkeley: University of California Press.

Brinton, Crane [1938], 1965: *The Anatomy of Revolution*, rev. and expanded edn. New York: Vintage Books.

—— [1933], 1962: *English Political Thought in the 19th Century.* New York: Harper & Row.

Browne, Janet 1995: *Charles Darwin: Voyaging. Volume 1 of a Biography.* New York: Alfred Knopf.

Copleston, Frederick, S. J. 1966: *A History of Philosophy*, Vol. 8: *Modern Philosophy: Bentham to Russell*, Part 1: *British Empiricism and the Idealist Movement in Britain.* Garden City, NJ: Image Books.

Darwin, Charles [1887], 1958: *The Autobiography of Charles Darwin, 1809–1882*, ed. Nora Barlow. New York: Norton.

Desmond, Adrian and Moore, James 1992: *Darwin: the life of a tormented evolutionist.* New York: Warner Books.

Gerson, Hermann 1932: Die Entwicklung der ethischen Anschauungen bei Georg Simmel. Unpublished doctoral dissertation, University of Berlin, 81 leaves.

Kalberg, Stephen 1994: *Max Weber's Comparative-Historical Sociology.* Cambridge: Polity Press.

Levine, Donald (ed.) 1971: *Georg Simmel: on individuality and social forms.* Chicago: University of Chicago Press.

Mayr, Ernst 1982: *The Growth of Biological Thought: diversity, evolution, and inheritance.* Cambridge: Harvard University Press.

Merton, Robert K. [1949], 1968: *Social Theory and Social Structure*, enlarged edn. New York: Free Press.

Parsons, Talcott [1937], 1968: *The Structure of Social Action*. New York: McGraw Hill. References to paperback edition, Free Press, Glencoe, Ill.

Pickering, Mary 1993: *Auguste Comte: An intellectual biography*. Cambridge: Cambridge University Press.

Richards, Robert 1987: *Darwin and the Emergence of Evolutionary Theories of Mind and Behavior*. Chicago: University of Chicago Press.

—— 1992: *The Meaning of Evolution*. Chicago: University of Chicago Press.

Weber, Max [1906, 1917], 1995: *The Russian Revolutions*, tr. and ed. Gordon Wells and Peter Baehr. Cambridge: Polity Press.

Wolff, Kurt (ed.) 1950: *The Sociology of Georg Simmel*. Glencoe, Ill.: Free Press.

Index

Aboulafia, M., 270
Addams, Jane, 112, 113, 114, 115, 134, 135, 249; and institutional analysis, 133–5; on peace and conflict settlement, 135–8; as pioneer professional social worker, 133; *see also* gender issues; Macaulay, Catherine; Nightingale, Florence; Staël, Germaine de; Webb, Beatrice; women
Adorno, T., 47, 186, 187, 287
Alexander, J., 190, 273–4
alienation, 27, 48, 62, 194–6
Anderson, P., 287
anomie, 27
Arato, A., 195
Aristotle, 158, 283
Astell, M., 112, 113, 114
attitude, 250
Austin, J.L., 146–7

Backhaus, G., 201
Baer, K.E. von, 88, 89, 94, 95, 103–4
Bagehot, W., 193
Baker, K., 284
Bakhtin, M., 272
Bastian, A., 180
Beccaria, C., 121
behavior, 247, 264, 277
Bell, D., 46, 55–6
Bender, C., 272
Bendix, R., 192n, 209, 212, 295; and Roth, G., 209–10
Bentham, J., 113, 122
Bergmann, W. and Hoffmann, G., 270

Berlin, I., 155
Berlioz, H., 267
Birnbaum, N., 286–7, 288
Bismarck, Count von, 128
Blau, P., 175n, 189, 197
Bloch, E., 186
Boas, F., 249, 250
Bogardus, E., 247
Booth, C., 129, 244
Booth, M., 129
Boudon, R., 189
Bouglé, C., 182
Bourdieu, P., 63n, 70, 201
Boutroux, É., 158–64, 166, 167
Bowler, P.J., 88
Braverman, H., 50n, 287
Brinton, C., 289–90, 291
Buber, M., 184–5
Burgess, E., 242, 250, 256
Butler, J., 127
Butterfield, H., 143

capitalism: critical theory of, 52–6, 70–2; historical dynamic, 49–50, 55–6, 57–67, 70–2; labor in, 58–63, 71; post-liberal, 53–5, 71; production in, 61, 65–6; as quasi-objective social system, 61, 63, 64, 67, 71–2; social theory of, 46–52; structural contradiction of, 49-50 *and notes*, 54–5, 67
Caplow, T., 175n
Carpenter, W.J., 89
causal explanation, 81–2, 93–105
Chadwick, E., 125
Chambers, R., 89, 94